Professional Twitter® Development
With Examples in .NET 3.5

Professional
Twitter® Development
With Examples in .NET 3.5

Professional
Twitter® Development
With Examples in .NET 3.5

Daniel Crenna

WILEY

Wiley Publishing, Inc.

Professional Twitter® Development With Examples in .NET 3.5

Published by
Wiley Publishing, Inc.
10475 Crosspoint Boulevard
Indianapolis, IN 46256

www.wiley.com

Copyright © 2009 by Wiley Publishing, Inc., Indianapolis, Indiana

ISBN: 978-0-470-53132-7

Manufactured in the United States of America

10 9 8 7 6 5 4 3 2 1

For general information on our other products and services please contact our Customer Care Department within the United States at (877) 762-2974, outside the United States at (317) 572-3993 or fax (317) 572-4002.

Wiley also publishes its books in a variety of electronic formats. Some content that appears in print may not be available in electronic books.

Library of Congress Control Number: 2009931751

Dedicated to my family:

Those we recently lost who remain, those who will join with us soon, and those yet to be.
There is so much love here, and if we seldom speak of our feelings
it is only because it is difficult to express the irreplaceable.

About the Author

Daniel Crenna is a Microsoft MVP and the creator of TweetSharp, an open-source .NET Twitter API development library. He runs www.dimebrain.com, a blog and software company in Canada. His Twitter client project, currently in development in partnership with Jason Diller, was a Top 5 Finalist in the Microsoft BlueSky Innovation Excellence Awards in 2009. Daniel was a contributor to the Microsoft AJAX Control Toolkit, and is a Microsoft Certified Professional Developer.

Credits

Acquisitions Editor
Paul Reese

Project Editor
Ed Connor

Technical Editor
Jason Diller

Production Editor
Rebecca Anderson

Copy Editor
Tricia Liebig

Editorial Director
Robyn B. Siesky

Editorial Manager
Mary Beth Wakefield

Production Manager
Tim Tate

Vice President and Executive Group Publisher
Richard Swadley

Vice President and Executive Publisher
Barry Pruett

Associate Publisher
Jim Minatel

Project Coordinator, Cover
Lynsey Stanford

Proofreader
Nate Pritts, Word One

Indexer
J&J Indexing

Acknowledgments

Writing a book is never a solo effort. This particular one would not exist without the efforts of Ed Connor at Wiley keeping me on track and focused on the next milestone, and Jason Diller for a matchless technical review and development assistance, and keeping the lights on our community efforts while I was consumed by this project. Ingrid Alongi at Gnip was an immediate source of encouragement and advice, and I was fortunate to have Doug Williams and Alex Payne at Twitter on tap for any questions I had throughout the evolutions that occurred with the Twitter API. Above all my wife Beth, who single-handedly moved us across the country and tolerated my mental and physical absence during the writing of this book, is as much a part of this project as I am.

Contents

Contents

Contents

Introduction

Since Twitter launched in March 2006, it has grown steadily into one of the simplest, most popular, and most powerful social networking platforms. Perhaps more compelling than Twitter itself is the growing community of developers building applications for the service and taking it far beyond its roots as a simple messaging service. This book will teach you how to get the best out of Twitter to build your own applications for this exciting new technology, as well as provide some guidance on using some of the latest developer evolutions in the .NET Framework, like Silverlight and Windows Azure.

After spending a great deal of time building TweetSharp, an open source Twitter library, as well as a prototype for a commercial Twitter client application, it was clear that many developers would find a single resource on consuming RESTful services, and Twitter's RESTful API in particular, a valuable addition to their capacity to build applications on this new and exciting service. With Twitter's growth exploding and already enjoying major mainstream adoption, application developers need a timely resource to prepare to build applications for this new and lively audience. Twitter has many millions of users and this book can help you support that growth in the developer community.

Who This Book Is For

The primary readers for this book are web or Windows developers who are pursuing Twitter application or client development, or are developing part of a system that integrates core Twitter functionality, such as a web-based widget. The early chapters of the book deal with establishing a foundation for web programming using HTTP and RESTful service concepts. If you have lots of experience working with social APIs in multiple data formats using REST, you might want to advance to Chapter 2 and Chapter 4 right away to start learning the particulars of Twitter's API, otherwise beginning at the beginning will help you understand Twitter, but also any social web API that employs REST concepts.

What This Book Covers

The book will focus on C# and .NET with supporting examples using a broad range of .NET technologies, such as Windows Forms, ASP.NET, Silverlight 3, WCF, LINQ, and Windows Azure. At the time of writing, Silverlight 3 is in Beta 1, and Windows Azure is in Community Technology Preview (CTP) status. Most of the examples of the book are designed to run in .NET 3.5, though you may reasonably adapt the code and understanding to function in previous versions of .NET, by rewriting any LINQ expressions to programmatically achieve similar results, and replacing extension methods with classic static methods. You will get the most benefit out of this book by using .NET 3.5, however, which supports development for Silverlight and Azure, which, combined with Twitter, will allow you to build next generation applications that will appeal to the broadest base of users.

How This Book Is Structured

Chapters 1 through 6 focus on RESTful services, the backbone of Twitter and many social data APIs are covered in sufficient depth for the developer to know how to structure their queries, handle asynchronous operations, utilize headers and post binary data. Continuing from an understanding of RESTful web communication, you will learn how to request and retrieve responses from Twitter's API, with forays into data processing with XML and JSON (for REST API data), and RSS and Atom (for Search API data). Core topics conclude with coverage for application authentication and security, including Twitter's upcoming OAuth security model at the forefront; you will learn how to authenticate with the OAuth specification for web and Windows applications.

Following from authentication and security are performance and feature considerations. In Chapters 7 through 10 you are introduced to a variety of important topics for developing custom applications; caching, third party application interoperability, push vs. pull data scenarios, and Twitter's anatomy and constraints are explored in detail to paint a bigger picture of how a Twitter application is best designed. Next, you will get an in-depth look of TweetSharp, a .NET library for developing Twitter applications that will speed up your development and time to market for your own application ideas. Finally, you will bring many new concepts together using Windows Azure to go through the steps needed to build a Twitter application in the cloud.

Armed with a solid understanding of Twitter's API, and the ability to fetch and process web data, you can now tackle the specific challenges of Twitter application development. You'll learn how to design and build responsive applications that consider caching, multi-threading, and real time data binding to ensure your ideas convert smoothly to compelling experiences for Twitter users.

What You Need to Use This Book

This book focuses on building Twitter applications on the .NET Framework 3.5 SP1, including some emerging technologies like Silverlight 3 Beta 1 and the Windows Azure CTP. To ensure your environment is ready to work with the concepts and code provided in the book and its accompanying source, you can follow along with this introductory chapter. While some nascent technologies are showcased, using them is not necessary to benefit from the fundamentals of web programming and Twitter development and design concepts that you'll learn and employ.

Setting Up Your Development Environment

The following steps outline the required server components, frameworks, and tools necessary for the various examples provided in the book. To help streamline the process, you will use a new Microsoft installation experience designed specifically for web application development; the Microsoft Web Platform Installer. With it, you can easily locate, download, install, and configure your web environment, saving time locating and setting up separate libraries around the web.

Using the Microsoft Web Platform Installer

Microsoft's new Web Platform Installer, available at http://www.microsoft.com/Web/, provides a unified experience for installing and configuring most Microsoft web infrastructure components as well as popular open source software from a simple interface. After downloading and running the application, you are presented with an interface similar to Figure I-1, which shows the Web Platform Installer 2.0 Beta in action.

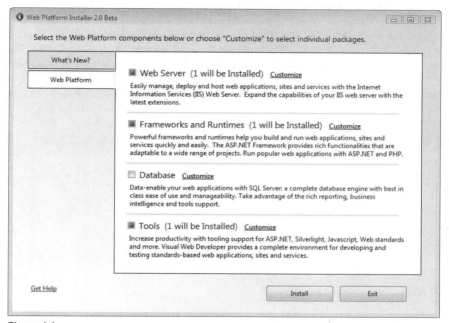

Figure I-1

IIS 7.0 with ASP.NET Components

Windows Azure's SDK relies on Internet Information Services (IIS) 7, which means your development operating system must be Windows Vista or above to work with those features. You can find the required ASP.NET support through the Web Server section of this installer. Selecting ASP.NET from the menu will install several dependencies to enable .NET extensions in IIS 7.

ASP.NET MVC 1.0

While the book doesn't cover the particulars of ASP.NET MVC, most of the code examples apply to any .NET environment. If you are planning to build your Twitter application on the ASP.NET MVC framework, now is a great time to install the bits. You can find this download under Frameworks and Runtimes.

Microsoft® Silverlight™ 3 Tools Beta 1 for Visual Studio 2008 SP1

To take advantage of the latest advancements in rich client technology, including running Silverlight applications out of the browser, you can download this dependency from the Tools section of the platform installer. You can also elect to download Silverlight 2, instead, if your projects don't require or are not ready for out of browser support.

Introduction

SQL Server 2008 Express

While not specifically required, SQL Server 2008 is installed as part of the Web Platform Installer components, and is used by Windows Azure to run a simulated cloud service environment locally, so you are able to test your applications before deploying them.

Visual Studio Web Developer Express and Above

Both the Windows Azure CTP and Silverlight 3 Tools for Visual Studio Beta 1 support Visual Studio Web Developer Express, so it is possible to run the examples in this book without a full-fledged professional development environment. You will also need to ensure you have installed the .NET Framework 3.5 SP1 from either Windows Update or the web before installing supporting libraries and SDKs. Figure I-2 demonstrates Visual Studio Web Developer Express with the code examples loaded and ready for testing.

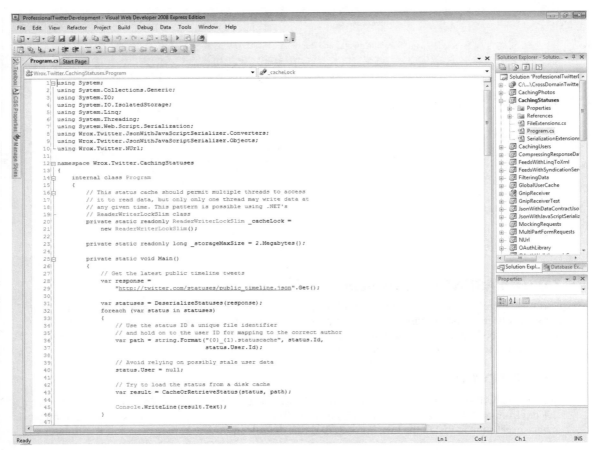

Figure I-2

There are a few Windows Forms-based examples in the book as well, which you can run as executables, or use Visual C# Express available at http://www.microsoft.com/express/vcsharp/ to compile and edit those examples.

SDKs and Libraries

Beyond the Web Platform Installer are an SDK and a third-party library you will use to build cloud-based web applications. The SDK provides utility code for communicating with core Azure services, and the library helps you to work effectively with .NET and the Twitter API to simplify the programming tasks and challenges you'll learn throughout the book.

Windows Azure Tools for Microsoft Visual Studio (including the Azure SDK)

You can download this SDK directly from Microsoft at `http://go.microsoft.com/fwlink/ ?LinkId=128752` to enable an integrated environment to develop cloud-based services in a familiar setting in Visual Studio. The SDK examples also include valuable libraries for communicating with Azure Storage, and activating ASP.NET Provider model support for cloud services.

TweetSharp v1.0

You'll need the official first release of TweetSharp, an open source .NET Twitter library that is useful for both beginning Twitter API developers and those who are already experienced (or have read this book) and want to accelerate development time by using TweetSharp to abstract away the details and get a prototype running quickly. You can fetch the latest release by visiting `http://tweetsharp .googlecode.com/downloads`. To use it on your projects, choose Add Reference from your Visual Studio project and select both Dimebrain.TweetSharp.dll and Newtonsoft.Json.dll if you are targeting ASP.NET, and the corresponding Compact and Silverlight suffixed libraries of the same name for mobile and rich development targets, respectively. Figure I-3 shows the TweetSharp page on Google Code, where you can find additional support, releases, and documentation.

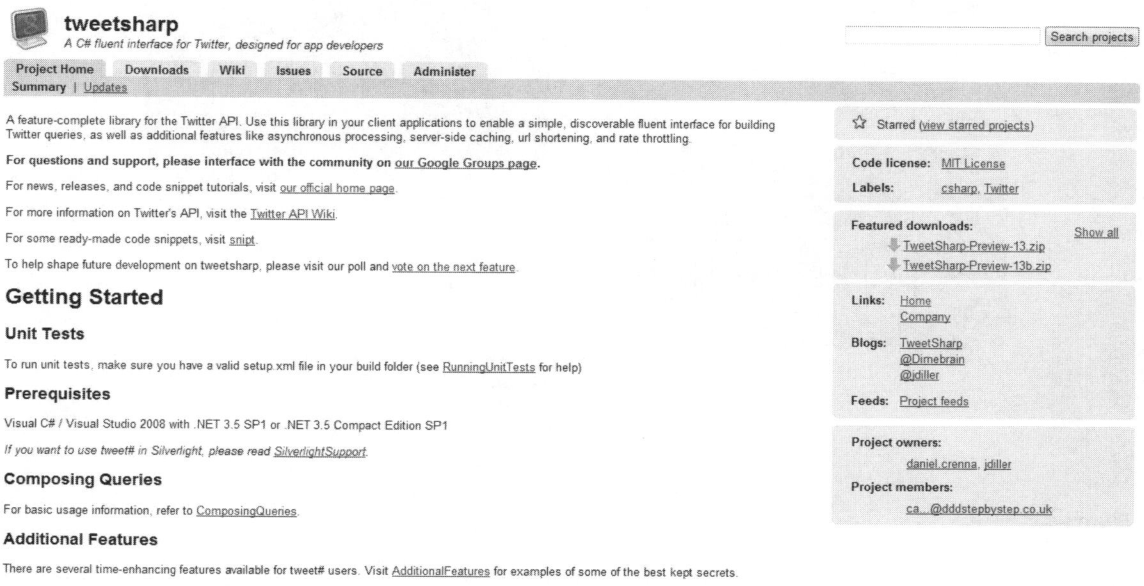

Figure I-3

After installing your environment and its dependencies, you may want to visit `http://www.microsoft.com/azure` to familiarize yourself with the Azure platform and sign up for a Windows Live ID and Microsoft Connect account if you do not have either of these. You will go through the Azure sign up and configuration process in Chapter 10 when learning how to build a cloud-hosted web application, but you will save time if these services are in place.

Debugging HTTP Traffic

The vast majority of your time developing modern web applications is spent consuming external web services. Twitter application development is no exception, and the ability to work with HTTP traffic at a lower level than what's immediately available in the .NET Framework provides valuable insight into what occurs under the hood when you program against the live web. To help you diagnose and understand what you send and receive when communicating with Twitter, you can download and configure Wireshark at `http://wireshark.org`, a free and open source HTTP analysis tool whose homepage is shown in Figure I-4. This section will explain how to use it effectively when consuming the Twitter API.

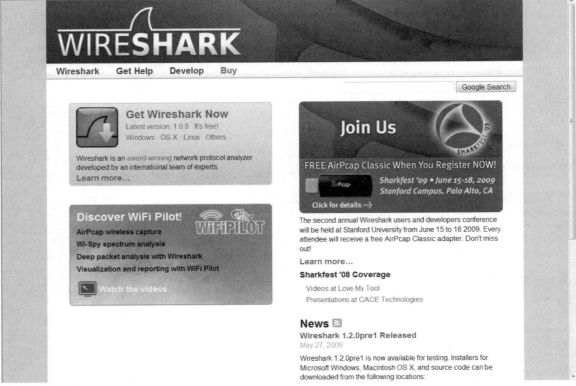

Figure I-4

Configuring Wireshark

Wireshark is a detailed and comprehensive tool, and as such requires customization to filter out all traffic other than what aids your development efforts with Twitter. To trace Twitter HTTP traffic in Wireshark exclusively, first locate the network adapter that is associated with your live Internet connection, as highlighted in Figure I-5. You can reach the dialog displayed by visiting the Capture menu and choosing Interfaces . . . from the options provided.

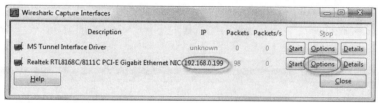

Figure I-5

Clicking the Options button for the network adapter you intend to trace will bring you to a form where it is possible to focus tracing efforts on a single domain. Following the example in Figure I-6, specifying host twitter.com and clicking Start will begin a new session for Twitter.

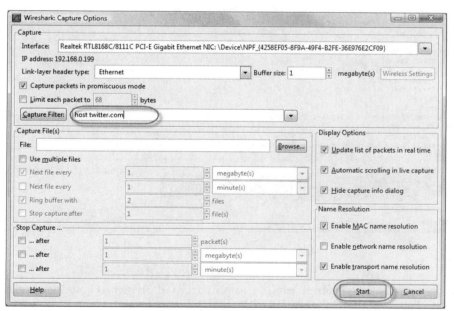

Figure I-6

Introduction

Wireshark will now display all communication occurring between your network card and
`http://twitter.com`. The next step is to further constrain these results by protocol, so that only HTTP
requests and responses are shown, to avoid viewing raw TCP traffic that occurs frequently when
establishing connections. To accomplish this, Figure I-7 illustrates applying a visual filter, specifying
`http.request || http.response` as a filter expression.

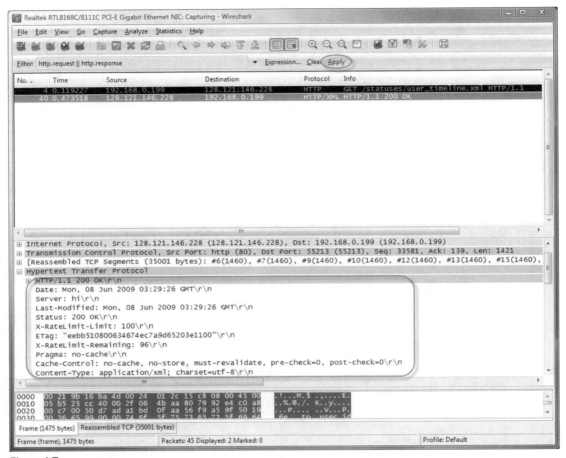

Figure I-7

After the filter expression is enabled using the Apply command, Twitter API traffic is displayed
conveniently. Figure I-7 shows the HTTP GET request to Twitter for statuses on a user's timeline,
followed by the HTTP response from Twitter containing special headers and the XML message result.
You will learn how to interpret this data in Chapter 1, but for now, you can set up Wireshark so that
you're ready to get into the details at a lower level. Whenever you encounter unexpected behavior,
remember that you have an excellent diagnostic tool at your disposal.

Summary

You set up a development environment to build, run, and modify the examples in this book to build your own Twitter applications in ASP.NET, Silverlight 3, and Windows Azure, as well as monitor and troubleshoot the Twitter API with an HTTP traffic monitoring tool. You used the new Microsoft Web Platform Installer to streamline your configuration experience, installing most key components of your environment in one place. In the first chapter, you'll begin at the beginning, with HTTP web programming and the services model that embraces it. You're ready to build your next Twitter application!

Conventions

To help you get the most from the text and keep track of what's happening, we've used a number of conventions throughout the book.

Notes, tips, hints, tricks, and asides to the current discussion are offset and placed in italics like this.

As for styles in the text:

❑ We *highlight* new terms and important words when we introduce them.

❑ We show keyboard strokes like this: Ctrl+A.

❑ We show file names, URLs, and code within the text like so: `persistence.properties`.

❑ We present code in two different ways:

```
We use a monofont type with no highlighting for most code examples.
We use gray highlighting to emphasize code that is of particularly importance in
the present context.
```

Source Code

As you work through the examples in this book, you may choose either to type in all the code manually or to use the source code files that accompany the book. All of the source code used in this book is available for download at `http://www.wrox.com`. Once at the site, simply locate the book's title (either by using the Search box or by using one of the title lists) and click the Download Code link on the book's detail page to obtain all the source code for the book.

Because many books have similar titles, you may find it easiest to search by ISBN; this book's ISBN is 978-0-470-53132-7.

Once you download the code, just decompress it with your favorite compression tool. Alternately, you can go to the main Wrox code download page at `http://www.wrox.com/dynamic/books/download.aspx` to see the code available for this book and all other Wrox books.

Errata

We make every effort to ensure that there are no errors in the text or in the code. However, no one is perfect, and mistakes do occur. If you find an error in one of our books, like a spelling mistake or faulty piece of code, we would be very grateful for your feedback. By sending in errata you may save another reader hours of frustration and at the same time you will be helping us provide even higher quality information.

To find the errata page for this book, go to www.wrox.com and locate the title using the Search box or one of the title lists. Then, on the book details page, click the Book Errata link. On this page you can view all errata that has been submitted for this book and posted by Wrox editors. A complete book list including links to each book's errata is also available at www.wrox.com/misc-pages/booklist.shtml.

If you don't spot "your" error on the Book Errata page, go to www.wrox.com/contact/techsupport.shtml and complete the form there to send us the error you have found. We'll check the information and, if appropriate, post a message to the book's errata page and fix the problem in subsequent editions of the book.

p2p.wrox.com

For author and peer discussion, join the P2P forums at p2p.wrox.com. The forums are a Web-based system for you to post messages relating to Wrox books and related technologies and interact with other readers and technology users. The forums offer a subscription feature to e-mail you topics of interest of your choosing when new posts are made to the forums. Wrox authors, editors, other industry experts, and your fellow readers are present on these forums.

At http://p2p.wrox.com you will find a number of different forums that will help you not only as you read this book, but also as you develop your own applications. To join the forums, just follow these steps:

1. Go to p2p.wrox.com and click the Register link.
2. Read the terms of use and click Agree.
3. Complete the required information to join as well as any optional information you wish to provide and click Submit.
4. You will receive an e-mail with information describing how to verify your account and complete the joining process.

   You can read messages in the forums without joining P2P but in order to post your own messages, you must join.

Once you join, you can post new messages and respond to messages other users post. You can read messages at any time on the Web. If you would like to have new messages from a particular forum e-mailed to you, click the Subscribe to this Forum icon by the forum name in the forum listing.

For more information about how to use the Wrox P2P, be sure to read the P2P FAQs for answers to questions about how the forum software works as well as many common questions specific to P2P and Wrox books. To read the FAQs, click the FAQ link on any P2P page.

Professional
Twitter® Development
With Examples in .NET 3.5

1

Working with RESTful Services

The Twitter API is the Schrödinger's cat of web service APIs. Until you call it, you never know if it's alive or dead. Sometimes the mere act of calling it is enough to kill it.

— **Scott Koon**, *Witty*

Before you can learn to run with the Twitter API, you first must walk with the web. The Representational State Transfer (REST) pattern, and the *RESTful* services that follow its principles, provide an intuitive layer over traditional HTTP programming that is a widely adopted standard among modern web sites, and Twitter is no exception. In this chapter you will learn how to consume REST services with .NET, some nuances of the Hypertext Transfer Protocol (HTTP) programming model, and how they fit together. This will prepare you to take on the Twitter API at its deepest levels, using all options available to you to control your development experience and get the most out of your custom applications.

What is REST?

REST is a philosophy of web architecture, derived from a service-oriented approach and characterized by a transparent interface over HTTP. REST is designed to demonstrate a low barrier to entry for web developers, and encourages the design of scalable, discoverable web programming. REST itself is not a protocol or a messaging system; everything needed to consume REST services is found in existing technologies. Commonly, REST principles behave like web services, adopting their nature to cleanly separate the implementation details of a resource from the client that consumes it; there is a clear boundary between client and server, with only the representation of a resource shared between them. This approach is in contrast to the well-established Remote Procedure Call (RPC) design with SOAP, which seeks to erase the boundary between external resources and internal callers with well articulated proxies, effectively treating remote resources as if they were local equivalents. That said, many REST principles are amenable to RPC patterns. Figure 1-1 illustrates the conceptual difference between RPC and REST services from a method invocation standpoint; in the RPC scenario, remote methods are treated as native, local methods through the use of a proxy, whereas web service calls have clear boundaries, and local calls must consume remote calls and handle processing internally.

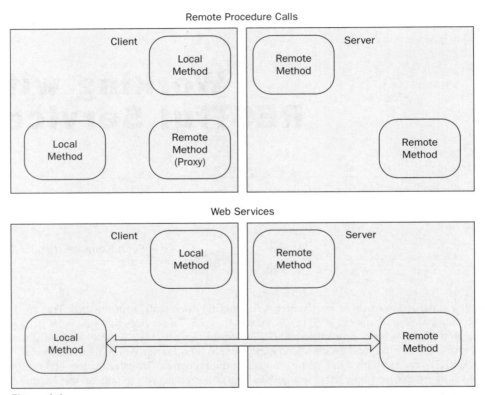

Figure 1-1

Web Services vs. Remote Service Calls (RPC)

XML is a broad language with natural suitability for encoding messages, SOAP is a protocol, and REST is a set of principles, which means none of these are strictly tied to HTTP to transport their operations. Using Remote Procedure Calls (RPC) to provide local methods via proxies for remote services, rather than web services themselves, is a valid approach with XML, SOAP, or REST. XML-RPC, SOAP-RPC, and REST-RPC are all very real, valid implementations of their respective protocols, as are XML Web Services, SOAP Web Services, and REST Web Services.

The REST Paradigm

Essentially, REST allows you to work with raw HTTP messaging by mapping HTTP method verbs to actions you wish to perform with the target application and its resources. It is also a set of principles and practices that help ensure a stateless, scalable, and predictable experience for web developers and users.

REST Means Resources

Let's step into the metaphysical for just a moment. Who are you? What are you? Are you a software developer, or are you a human? Are you both? Are you neither? If I'm looking at your resume, I'm seeing a very different side of you than if you were my friend and I was visiting you from out of town. Who you really are, and how you are represented based on the context, are two very different things. The separation between *state* (your actual self), and *representation* (your resume, or your charming personality) is what distinguishes REST services from XML or SOAP-based web services and particularly those that work with RPC; rather than focusing on providing lengthy metadata or schema to represent returning data as one version of the truth on either side of the client and server, representation is flexible and varied. The state of you, your body, is a *resource* (anyone in Human Resources understands this). The *representation* of you as your resume is only one of out of many alternate possibilities. With a RESTful service, you are capable of sending requests for *resources* and receiving back a *representation* that changes based on how you phrased the request. "Can I have your resume?" will elicit a different response than "Can I come to your wedding?"; both responses might come in the form of a paper document, but the contents of each won't resemble each other.

Online, resources normally take the form of content: web pages, pictures, and videos are representations of the underlying *resources* that are retrieved when you ask for them; the resource itself might be "my cat," represented by a photo gallery, video library, or Twitter account (even pets are on Twitter now). Asking for a resource is not more difficult than opening up a browser and typing in a URL (Universal Resource Locator) and waiting for a response. URLs are technically a subset of a larger concept known as Universal Resource Indicators (URIs); both serve the same purpose of providing a common path to information resources wherever they reside, while URLs are constrained to common web protocols like `http://`, `https://`, `ftp://`, and `mailto:`. As an example, `file://` is a valid URI but not a valid URL, and a good thing too, as `file://` points to private file resources on your local hard drive! A visual example of the differences between URIs and URLs is shown in Figure 1-2.

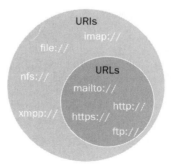

Figure 1-2

REST Means Addressability

Following on the concept of resources, the principle of addressability simply means that every resource that makes up your application must have at least one URI.

Often, a compliment for good web design is *hackability*, or the ability for a user to guess how to reach certain pages on a web site just by reading where they currently sit in the page hierarchy. A hackable and intuitive URI is a core tenet of RESTful service design. Similarly, Twitter provides several "alias" methods that map to official methods; this is one strategy for providing several ways to accomplish the same task, by predicting URIs that developers might assume already exist to interact with resources, and implementing them as pass-through to their actual locations.

> `http://twitter.com/users/dimebrain.xml` will take you to the author's Twitter page, but this is not a supported Twitter API method; it's actually an alias to the correct `http://twitter.com/users/show.xml?screen_name=dimebrain` method.

Another RESTful principle involves where you can find addressable resources. One obvious place is on the web site you're interacting with: `http://twitter.com/statuses/public_timeline.xml` is exactly where you'll find a list of public statuses in XML format, but a true RESTful service will provide URIs in the response itself. If you look at tweets on the public timeline, you will see that you can then find the link to each user profile and their latest status. You are performing "state transfer" from one URI to the next; this is REST.

Example

```
GET: http://twitter.com/statuses/public_timeline.xml
<?xml version="1.0" encoding="UTF-8"?>
<statuses type="array">
    <status>
        <created_at>Thu Apr 09 00:54:15 +0000 2009</created_at>
        <id>1480413065</id>
        <text>?????????????</text>
        <source>&lt;a href=&quot;http://twitterfox.net/&quot;&gt;TwitterFox&lt;/a&gt;
        </source>
        <truncated>false</truncated>
        <in_reply_to_status_id />
        <in_reply_to_user_id />
        <favorited>false</favorited>
        <user>
        <id>8846542</id>
        <name>igaiga07</name>
        <screen_name>igaiga07</screen_name>
        <description>Web?????</description>
        <location>Japan</location>
        <profile_image_url>http://static.twitter.com/images/default_
profile_normal.png
        </profile_image_url>
        <url></url>
```

```
            <protected>false</protected>
            <followers_count>358</followers_count>
      </user>
      </status>
      <...>
   </statuses>
```

With each tweet returned in this representation of public timeline statuses, you have four new URIs to explore:

- ❑   `http://twitter.com/statuses/show/1480413065.xml`

- ❑   `http://twitter.com/users/show/8846542.xml`

- ❑   `http://static.twitter.com/images/default_profile_normal.png` (image)

- ❑   `http://twitterfox.net` (external)

REST Means Formats

Since REST services define resources by addressing them in at least one way, and you know that resources can exist in many incarnations or representations, then formats are essentially one part of a URI that needs to change in order to produce a different representation of a resource, all things being equal. A format, in HTTP terms, is the expected content type of the representation you're after. The Twitter API, for example, represents many of its resources in both Extensible Markup Language (XML) and JavaScript Simple Object Notation (JSON). To choose between the two, you only have to change the format extension at the end of the URI path.

```
http://twitter.com/statuses/public_timeline.xml
http://twitter.com/statuses/public_timeline.json
```

REST Means Stateless

REST favors stateless operation; everything required to correctly identify and retrieve the resource representation should accompany the URI and HTTP request parameters. A natural side effect of stateless services is improved scalability, as neither the client nor the server need to carry persisted information for each user, and both can optimize their operation knowing at all times how to proceed with a request. Many web applications still use some form of state in the form of a session, passed to the client by ID in a response cookie. Twitter's API is currently stateless; session identifiers are passed to you in responses, but the session is empty. In the future, Twitter may provide stateful session enhancements to create new application development possibilities.

REST Means a Uniform Interface

One of the more recognizable features of RESTful services is the mapping of available actions on resources to HTTP method verbs. These mappings closely resemble familiar Create, Retrieve, Update, and Delete operations on databases (CRUD) and provide a hint about the object-oriented, persistable nature of an application's resources behind the server. The HTTP method verbs related to REST actions are a sub-set of those available. Table 1-1 describes the relationship between HTTP verbs and RESTful actions.

Table 1-1: Mapping HTTP Method Verbs to REST Actions

HTTP Method/ Verb	REST Action
GET	Fetch a representation of a resource
POST	Creates a new resource, or updates an existing one
PUT	Creates a new resource, or updates an existing one via providing a URI to the existing resource, or a placeholder URI for the intended new resource.
DELETE	Destroys a resource

HTTP v1.1 specification: `http://www.ietf.org/rfc/rfc2616`

With the exception of POST, all REST-mapped method verbs are safe and idempotent; calling them multiple times does not alter their behavior or the resulting effect on the server. This means attempting to update or delete the same resource multiple times will not cause other resources to update or delete.

Using this subset of HTTP verbs is characteristic of RESTful service interfaces, but you are still capable of using the remaining HTTP verbs in your applications. This Table 1-2 provides the remaining HTTP verbs that participate in RESTful service calls.

Table 1-2: Non-REST HTTP Method Verbs

HTTP Method Verb	Description
OPTIONS	Fetches a response from the server with representative headers describing the request options available for the given URI.
HEAD	Fetches only the header information for the underlying URI; useful for determining server responsiveness prior to further calls.
TRACE	Asks the server to return the message originally sent back to the calling client in order to diagnose issues.
CONNECT	Used to signal a proxy that can also support tunneling (such as HTTPS).

HTTP v1.1 specification: `http://www.ietf.org/rfc/rfc2616`

HTTP and URIs

Now that you understand the principles behind REST, the next step is to get familiar with how REST calls are processed, using HTTP to transport messages from client to server, and URIs as addresses pointing to the available actions clients can perform against server resources.

The Anatomy of a URI

The addressability principle of a RESTful service, you have learned, is fulfilled with a URI. While the URI is conceptually simple, it does have a few moving parts that are worthy of discussion.

.NET eases the process of working with URIs with the specialized `System.Net.Uri` class. It is useful to know how a URI is structured, particularly when you need to deal with encoding, escaping, and normalizing as you will in Chapter 7 when implementing OAuth. Fortunately, you have plenty of tools at your disposal to make short work of this task. While all URIs start as a string similar to typing a URL into a browser, you can pass that string into the `Uri` class, which will handle parsing your intended resource address, making portions of it available for processing; `Uri` also has a collection of static methods that provide convenience methods for validation and creation. The following examples illustrate how to construct a `Uri` from various sources.

Create a New URI from a String

```
string url = "http://twitter.com/statuses/public_timeline.xml";
Uri uri = new Uri(url);
Console.WriteLine(uri.AbsoluteUri);
```
```
http://twitter.com/statuses/public_timeline.xml
```

Create a New URI from Component Instances

```
string host = "http://twitter.com";
string path = "/statuses/public_timeline.xml";

Uri uri = new Uri(host);
uri = new Uri(uri, path);
Console.WriteLine(uri.AbsoluteUri);
```
```
http://twitter.com/statuses/public_timeline.xml
```

Create a New URI using Try Pattern Validation

```
string url = "http://twitter.com/statuses/public_timeline.xml";

Uri uri;
if(Uri.TryCreate(url, UriKind.Absolute, out uri))
{
    Console.WriteLine(uri);
}
```
```
http://twitter.com/statuses/public_timeline.xml
```

Validating that a URI String is Well Formed and Relative vs. Absolute

```
string url = "/statuses/public_timeline.xml";
if(Uri.IsWellFormedUriString(url, UriKind.Absolute))
{
    Console.WriteLine(url);
}

if (Uri.IsWellFormedUriString(url, UriKind.Relative))
{
    Console.WriteLine(url);
}
/statuses/public_timeline.xml
```

Several Uri class properties map to subsections of a given URI string. Each section of a URI has a formal identification, even though we tend to treat them as unique and atomic. With Uri, you have easy access to these portions without resorting to parsing the values out yourself. The Uri class itself is illustrated as a class diagram in Figure 1-3.

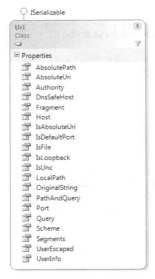

Figure 1-3

In addition to the class diagram, Table 1-3 maps Uri properties to relevant sections of a real URI, so you can get acquainted with the parts of URI referred to throughout this book.

Table 1-3: `System.Net.Uri` **and URIs**

Uri Class Property	URI
AbsolutePath	http://twitter.com/**statuses/user_timeline**.xml?screen_name=wrox&page=3
AbsoluteUri	**http://twitter.com/statuses/user_timeline.xml?screen_name=wrox&page=3**
Authority	http://**twitter.com**/statuses/user_timeline.xml?screen_name=wrox&page=3
Fragment	http://apiwiki.twitter.com/REST+API+Documentation**#StatusMethods**
Host	http://**twitter.com**/statuses/user_timeline.xml?screen_name=wrox&page=3
LocalPath	http://twitter.com/**statuses/user_timeline**.xml?screen_name=wrox&page=3
PathAndQuery	http://twitter.com/**statuses/user_timeline.xml?screen_name=wrox&page=3**
Port	http://twitter.com:**80**/statuses/user_timeline.xml?screen_name=wrox&page=3
Query	http://twitter.com/statuses/user_timeline.xml**?screen_name=wrox&page=3**
Scheme	**http**://twitter.com/statuses/user_timeline.xml?screen_name=wrox&page=3
Segments	http://twitter.com[**/**][**statuses/**][**user_timeline**].xml?screen_name=wrox
UserInfo	http://**username:password**@twitter.com/statuses/user_timeline.xml

Escaping and Encoding with `Uri` and `HttpUtility`

Since URIs point to resources and have a formal anatomy, some restrictions are applied to ensure there is no room for ambiguity when interpreting where a URI address ultimately points. One example is the restricted use of the / character, which breaks up a URI into separate segments; if you wanted to create a path where / was a part of the resource's name rather than a segment delimiter, you would meet with failure. A URI isn't more than a string of characters, which must have some rigid delimiting in place so that it resolves correctly any time the specification is followed. Table 1-4 arranges the relationship between reserved and unreserved characters depending on where they sit in the complete URI.

Table 1-4: Restricted Characters in a URI

Reserved Characters	URI Reserved Characters
: / ? # [ ] @	! $ & ' ( ) * + , ; =

URI specification: http://www.ietf.org/rfc/rfc3986

Reserved characters are not permitted anywhere in the URI, while URI reserved characters are not permitted in the *scheme, authority,* or *path segments* of a URI but may appear in the *query or fragment.*

With so many restrictions on what is permitted in a URI, how could you use HTTP for RESTful services and maintain any level of human expression or flexibility without symbols like "?" or "!", or present descriptive phone or currency data without "(", "$", and ")"? When you need to send reserved characters as data in a URI string, you must *escape* them.

URI escaping is a form of encoding. Technically, escaping characters is a sub-set of encoding, a broader term meaning any process of changing the representation of bits from one system to another. Specifically, escaping URIs means you must replace offending reserved characters with their *percent-encoded* equivalents. Percent-encoding is an algorithm which produces a short string that begins with %, and then converts the source reserved character from ASCII into a two-digit hexadecimal value. This carries with it the requirement that % has its own percent-encoded equivalent to avoid ambiguity. The following data in Table 1-5 represents the final escaped output of reserved URI characters.

Table 1-5: URI Escape Codes

Reserved Character	Escape Code	Reserved Character	Escape Code
(space)	%20	?	%3F
#	%23	@	%40
$	%24	[	%5B
%	%25	\	%5C
&	%26	]	%5D
/	%2F	^	%5E
:	%3A	`	%60
;	%3B	{	%7B
<	%3C	|	%7C
=	%3D	}	%7D
>	%3E	~	%7E

URI specification: http://www.ietf.org/rfc/rfc3986

Unreserved characters in a URI may be used anywhere in the address without requiring escaping. The unreserved characters are the alphabet in upper and lower case, all numeric digits, and the special characters - . _~. Feel free to use these anywhere. You may also escape them, though it is not a requirement and servers will treat escaped unreserved characters as if they were unescaped.

What does the escaping of reserved characters in a URI have to do with the Twitter API? Since the API is RESTful, you use it to create new resources, like tweets, on Twitter's servers, passing our data in the URI. Let's sneak a peek at the API call that updates a user's status.

`http://twitter.com/statuses/update.xml?status=This contains <special>`
`characters!` If you sent this API call as-is, you would receive a 400 Bad Request response from Twitter; it's not a well-formed URI. First, you've added spaces to this URI and you know spaces are reserved, as are the "<" and ">" characters. The "!" is permissible here, because it is part of the URI query and not in one of the URI component sections like the authority or segments.

To send this request you must first escape it. In .NET, you have two supported options to perform this task: use the `Uri` class you've already learned about, or `System.Web.HttpUtility`.

Got Hash Tags?

The `Uri.EscapeUriString` method, and the `Uri` class itself when instantiated with a URL string, will recognize the hash tag symbol ("#") as the query fragment rather than a reserved character for encoding. If you are planning to escape a URI for posting a Twitter update that includes a hash tag, you need to replace any leftover #'s with %23 yourself.

```
string urlWithHashTags =
  "http://twitter.com/statuses/update.xml?Phew! #relief";
string url = new Uri(urlWithHashTags).ToString().Replace("#",
"%23");
```

`HttpUtility` contains two methods, `UrlEncode` and `UrlDecode`, for the purposes of encoding and decoding URL string data between ASCII and percent-encoded values.

```
string url = "http://twitter.com/statuses/update.xml?status=This has <special>
characters!";

Console.WriteLine(HttpUtility.UrlEncode(url));
http%3a%2f%2ftwitter.com%2fstatuses%2fupdate.xml%3fstatus%3dThis+has+%3cspecial%3e+
characters!
```

It appears that `HttpUtility`'s encoding method does not know how to differentiate between what is part of the URI and what is a reserved character in a place it shouldn't be; it just escapes whatever string input you provide it. Now that you've escaped this entire URI, is it valid?

```
string url = "http://twitter.com/statuses/update.xml?status=This has <special>
characters!";

Uri uri = new Uri(url);
```

If you executed the code above, `Uri` would raise the `UriFormatException`, explaining that it couldn't determine the required format; it can't tell if you're trying to pass it a relative URI such as a path and query with some escaped characters, as opposed to an absolute URI that is fully escaped, even when reserved characters are rightfully placed. If you tried to send the string above as is in a web request, it would fail, again with a 400 Bad Request message.

You should avoid escaping reserved characters that are where they should be, and this means if you want to use `HttpUtility`, you have to do the heavy lifting of deciding when and when not to escape specific characters in a URL prior to sending it in a web request.

`Uri`'s `EscapeUriString` and `UnescapeUriString` static methods allow you to perform the same task as `HttpUtility`, except with sensitivity to the components of a URI.

```
string url = "http://twitter.com/statuses/update.xml?status=This has <special>
characters!";
Console.WriteLine(Uri.EscapeUriString(url));
```

```
http://twitter.com/statuses/update.xml?status=This%20has%20%3Cspecial%3E%20characters!
```

Now this URI is properly escaped, containing no reserved characters where they don't belong, and ready for addressing in a web request. You can also pass the unescaped URL string into the constructor of the `Uri` class to automatically escape the string when used as a class instance.

HttpUtility and the URI Specification

There are other reasons to use `Uri` and not `HttpUtility`; if you compare the outputs of both, you will notice that `Uri` escape codes are uppercase, while `HttpUtility`'s are lowercase. According to RFC 3986, the specification that describes URI escaping, both upper and lower casing is valid, but uppercase is preferred for consistency. You'll learn in Chapter 7 that uppercase escaping is actually a requirement of OAuth, and using `HttpUtility`'s methods will cause your authentication code to fail. You might also notice that `HttpUtility` doesn't escape spaces, but instead replaces them with the "+" sign. A "+" itself is reserved in the component parts of a URI as it is a URI reserved character, but is otherwise unreserved when used elsewhere, such as the query. Therefore passing in an unescaped "+" sign in a URI query rather than %20 and expecting it to behave like a space rather than a literal "+" breaks the URI specification.

You might not notice this behavior when working with the Twitter API, as the majority of time you require spaces in a URI are when posting status updates, where the URI query is technically submitted in a POST request with a content type of `application/x-www-urlencoded`, the format of which uses "+" to denote spaces. To work effectively with external systems and technologies over the web, it helps to ensure you are performing requests correctly. Perhaps `HttpUtility` should have its name changed to `HttpPostUtility`.

URI specification: `http://www.ietf.org/rfc/rfc2616.txt`

W3C HTML 4.01 specification for application/x-www-urlencoded: `http://www.w3.org/TR/html401/interact/forms.html#h-17.13.4.1`

In general, using `Uri` will ensure your web service calls are properly escaped according to a recognized standard, and will function in your Twitter applications and authentication code. It is also easier to use than manually parsing URIs and encoding with `HttpUtility`, and provides object-oriented features for inspecting specific parts of a URI.

The Anatomy of HTTP Requests and Responses

You're getting closer to a broad understanding of how REST is envisioned, and how resources are addressed. Now you can explore the messages passed between the client and the server owning the address to the desired resource. The world's most popular REST client is a web browser. Underneath the browser's slick exterior is a regular passing of request and response messages, a constant conversation that might resemble a digital version of the card game "Go Fish!," but with trillions of cards. HTTP requests and responses are the questions and answers of the web.

HTTP v1.1

There are several tables in this section representing a very broad sample of the HTTP programming model. This information is not exhaustive, but should help you form an opinion about what you can do with HTTP and what you can look for in the Twitter API. Throughout this book, only HTTP v1.1 is used and assumed, as it is the enabling technology behind REST-based services on the web and is the commonly accepted architecture of today's Internet.

Requests

Every request begins with a declaration of the HTTP method or verb, the relative URI path to the resource requested, including any query data, and the version of the HTTP specification expected by the client originating the request. This is known as the *Request Line*. An HTTP GET request to `http://twitter.com/statuses/public_timeline.xml` is sent as string information in a particular format, shown below.

```
GET /statuses/public_timeline.xml HTTP/1.1
Host: twitter.com
```

For typical GET requests, this is often enough information to obtain a response from the host server. However, you have more options available, in the form of request headers, to control and direct the information you request, either for processing, performance, or security reasons. Headers are case insensitive name-value pairs provided after the essential URI information and preceded by a blank line. Headers are presented as meta-data to accompany the request. The following is a list of some of the more common and useful headers and their usage, though there are others. In addition, servers may accept custom request header information that is specific to the application in use; Twitter accepts some custom headers that you will learn in Chapter 8.

Table 1-6 represents most of the headers that are applicable to either a request or a response.

Table 1-6: Selected General Headers for HTTP 1.1

Header	Usage
Cache-Control	Defines the caching scheme in place to direct the server to send a stored response, or generate a new one.
Connection	Since HTTP v1.1, all connections are inherently "keep-alive," or, they persist after they are created. Sending "close" as the value of this header will set the expectation the connection will not live on after a response is received
Date	The date and time when the request was issued, or the response was received. This is expressed in an HTTP date format according to RFC 1123, an example of which is "Sun, 06 Nov 1994 08:49:37 GMT "; the date should always display as universal time.
Pragma	Helpful when dealing with servers that do not support HTTP 1.1, this header is used to send optional directives to a server. The most common example is "no-cache," which is used as a backwards compatible stand-in for the HTTP 1.1 Cache-Control header's value of the same name when requesting that a client send a request for a resource to the server even when it may possess a valid cached copy.
Transfer-Encoding	Identifies whether or not a request or response has deliberately changed its own message encoding, so that it is able to safely reach its destination, informing the recipient that it must decode the message itself before it can process its contents.

HTTP v1.1 specification: `http://www.ietf.org/rfc/rfc2616.txt`

Our interest in RESTful services in this book is primarily as a consumer of services rather than a provider. Watching incoming HTTP responses for these general headers is useful for tracing application performance in terms of request round-trips, open connections, and, more commonly, how returning content expects to live in the form of cached copies after a response has returned.

Request headers help control when and in what form server data is returned to the client. Often, web service issues stem from a mismatch in the various ways messages are encoded, transmitted, and processed using many of the headers in Table 1-7.

Table 1-7: Selected Request Headers for HTTP 1.1

Header	Usage
Accept	A filter expression for the types of media (MIME types) that the client can accept from the server for a resource's representation
Accept-Charset	A filter expression for the types of character sets accepted from the server for a request
Accept-Encoding	A filter expression for the types of encoding accepted from the server for a request; this header is commonly used for declaring support for `gzip` or `deflate` compression encoding algorithms.
Accept-Language	A filter expression for the types of languages acceptable to the client; this is useful for localized applications.
Authorization	This header contains the authentication scheme and any credentials required to access a protected resource.
Expect	This header is paired with the 100-continue behavior to indicate to a server that the client is expecting an acknowledgment when making calls to the serve.
From	This header adds additional information about the originator identity of the request.
Host	This header is required for all requests, and indicates the authority, or domain, of the server the request is intended for.
If-Match	This header provides an ETag value to indicate that the request should only return the resource that is matched to the provided ETag. If the server copy of the resource has changed since the original ETag was provisioned, those changes are reflected in the response.
If-Modified-Since	This header provides a date value to indicate that the server should only return the addressed resource if it has changed since the date provided.
If-None-Match	Similar to If-Match, this header provides a series of ETag values, indicating that the server should only return the resource if none of the tags provided currently apply to the resource. If none apply, the most recent resource is returned by the server.
If-Unmodified-Since	The client
Max-Forwards	Used to limit the number of proxies or gateways a request should cross when using the TRACE or OPTIONS method verbs.
Proxy-Authorization	This header contains the authentication scheme and any credentials required to access a protected resource, when there is a proxy between the client and the destination server for whom the credentials are for.
Referer	If the request received the URI address from another service, it may provide that referring URI in this header, to provide helpful information to the server about the proliferation of resource addresses.
User-Agent	This header identifies the client making the request in a descriptive manner. It's up to the server to define when and how to handle this value.

HTTP v1.1 specification: `http"//www.ietf.org/rtf/rfc2616.txt`

Request headers are easy to add or change on your .NET request objects, whether you are using `WebClient` or `HttpWebRequest`. Figure 1-4 shows a class diagram illustrating the `HttpWebRequest` object.

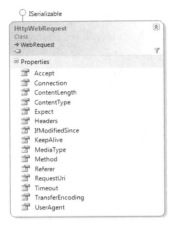

Figure 1-4

The `HttpWebRequest` object model surrounding headers is fairly confusing; on the one hand, the bulk of all headers are provided through the `Headers` property as a `WebHeaderCollection`, however there are several properties that map directly to specific headers in the request. This is due to the fact that some headers are restricted from direct access. If a header is restricted, you must set it through the specific property provided for it (if there is one) to avoid raising an exception; otherwise, you can set one of the recognized headers through the collection itself. Table 1-8 demonstrates which headers are unavailable for modification.

Table 1-8: Restricted Headers

.NET Restricted Header	HttpWebRequest Property
Accept	`Accept` and `MediaType`
Connection	`Connection`
Content-Length	`ContentLength`
Content-Type	`ContentType`
Date	None; this is set during instance initialization
Expect	`Expect`
Host	None; you must provide this through the constructor URL
If-Modified-Since	`IfModifiedSince`
Range	None
Referer	`Referer`
Transfer-Encoding	`TransferEncoding`
User-Agent	`UserAgent`

The `Authorization` header is restricted in Silverlight, reflecting the fact that cross-domain web requests must obey the browser security model. This means that an exception is thrown if you attempt to change or add an `Authorization` header directly in Silverlight using `WebClient` or `HttpWebRequest`; if you have cross-domain permission to access a service, however, it must not be protected by HTTP authentication; instead, you would likely provide an API key or other credential directly in the URI. Since Twitter is not cross-domain enabled, you will learn how build and communicate with a Windows Azure proxy in Chapter 12.

Responses

Similar to requests, every response begins with an important informational line, known as the *status line*.

```
HTTP/1.1 401 Unauthorized
```

In the status line example above, you know the HTTP version is used, that the response failed, returning a status code of 401, and that this corresponds to a refusal to authorize the request. The following list in Table 1-9 is a selection of common status codes returned in REST service replies. These statuses map to common REST actions, although every server ultimately decides how and with what status to reply to incoming requests.

Table 1-9: A Selection of Response Status Codes for HTTP 1.1

Status Code	Reason Phrase	Usage
Informational Message Range		
100	Continue	A receipt of acknowledgement that the server can process the request as received.
Successful Message Range		
200	OK	The request was successfully processed.
201	Created	The request was successfully processed, and the end result was the creation of a new resource.
202	Accepted	The request was successful, but no returned data is available yet as the request may be queued or currently processing.
204	No Content	The request was successful, and no returned data is valid for this operation.
205	Reset Content	The request was successful, and no returned data is valid for this operation; however, the underlying resource has changed as a result of the operation.

Table 1-9 (continued)

Status Code	Reason Phrase	Usage
206	Partial Content	The request was successful, but the data returned represents only part of the original resource as opposed to the whole. The range of the partial data returned is defined in a response header.
Redirection Message Range		
300	Multiple Choices	The resource as addressed exists in multiple representations, but the representation wasn't provided.
301	Moved Permanently	The resource as addressed exists, but the address provided is no longer correct. The proper address is provided in a response header.
302	Found	The resource as addressed exists on the server, but in a different location. The real location is provided in a response header.
303	See Other	The resource as addressed exists in more than one location, and the address given is not the preferred location. The preferred location is provided in a response header.
304	Not Modified	The original request used a modification header, and the resource has not changed since the date specified in that header.
Client Error Message Range		
400	Bad Request	The resource address provided was malformed.
401	Unauthorized	The resource as addressed is protected, and the request provided missing or incorrect credentials required to work with it.
403	Forbidden	The resource as addressed in the request exists, but the client is not permitted to access it.
404	Not Found	The resource as addressed in the request provided does not exist on the server.
405	Method Not Allowed	The resource as addressed exists, but does not support the HTTP method intended for use in the request.

Status Code	Reason Phrase	Usage
406	Not Acceptable	The request included an Accept header, and the server cannot produce a representation of the resource addressed in any format the client can accept.
407	Proxy Authentication Required	The request was sent through a proxy, and the proxy wasn't able to authenticate the originating client with the server; the request never reached the server.
408	Request Time-out	The request did not complete sending to the server in the time the server requires.
410	Gone	The request attempted to access a resource that used to exist, but no longer exists.
413	Request Entity Too Large	The request's content length is larger than the server will accept.
417	Expectation Failed	The request expected the server to return 100 Continue as a response, but the server does not support that behavior.
Server Error Message Range		
500	Internal Server Error	The server experienced a fault when attempting to process the request.
503	Service Unavailable	The server is down due to maintenance or capacity issues. If known, the time to resolution is sent in the response's Retry-After header.

HTTP v1.1 specification: `http://www.ietf.org/rfc/rfc2616.txt`

Often, more is needed for the client to determine why the request failed and take steps to correct the content of a follow-up request. Since HTTP responses are messages following the same format as HTTP requests, they may provide additional information in a collection of headers. Here in Table 1-10 are some of the more commonly encountered response headers used in web programming.

Table 1-10: Selected Response Headers for HTTP 1.1

Header	Usage
Age	Provides a server's estimate of how long the resource has lived in its cache, if it resides there.
ETag	Provides a form of unique identifier issues by the server for the given request.
Location	If the server does not return content, but knows where that content is stored, it may send the known URI in this header.
Proxy-Authenticate	This response header provides the client with the available authentication schemes available for use on the server, when the client making the request is communicating through a proxy.
Retry-After	Provides a server's estimate of when.
Server	This header identifies the server sending the response in a descriptive manner. It's up to the client to define when and how to handle this value.
Vary	Lets a requesting client know what parts of their request were used to determine the resulting content.
WWW-Authenticate	This response header provides the client with the available authentication schemes available for use on the server, when the client making the request is communicating through a proxy.

HTTP v1.1 specification: http://www.ietf.org/rfc/rfc2616.txt

Planning Features using HTTP Headers

Coordinating your application's behavior with certain request and response headers, and response status codes is good practice. If the goal of a responsive web application is to spend bandwidth only when absolutely necessary, knowing how to reduce that traffic whenever possible is a fundamental part of fulfilling that goal. You will learn the specific header and status code options available to you for tuning your Twitter API development in Chapter 8, but you can prepare for thinking in terms of HTTP request optimization now by understanding how request and response headers can work together. Table 1-11 gives a few examples to get you thinking in terms of how you can form your HTTP messages for most effect.

Table 1-11: Features of HTTP Headers

Feature Type	Strategy
Traceability	When a resource is created, updated, or deleted, check if the response contains the target resource for immediate processing, or a detailed error message indicating any transaction history (i.e., `404` if the resource never existed vs. `410` if the resource was deleted prior to the request).
Polling	When a server returns an error, check the `Retry-After` response header, in case the server is able to provide a good time to resend the request rather than polling at ineffective intervals.
Caching	Using a combination of the `ETag` returned in a response and an `If-None-Match` on the client, bandwidth is reduced when a server knows it can send a `304 Not Modified` status, rather than re-fetching a resource that the client already has in its current form.
Caching	Using `If-Modified-Since` on the client provides an opportunity for the server to return `304 Not Modified` if the resource hasn't changed since the date provided, which would come from a client's own last cached time.
Compression	Attempting, whenever possible, to send `gzip` or `deflate` compression in `Accept-Encoding`, so that the server can send substantially smaller resource documents the client can decompress on receipt.

Both the client and the server need to participate fully in these negotiations in order to work as expected. You will get a better understanding working with an API of what is possible.

Twitter and REST

While quite close to a faithful implementation, Twitter's API is not completely faithful to the RESTful practice of leveraging the HTTP spec as a programming layer. Instead, Twitter's API was designed to provide the ease of use and addressability benefits of REST, but must also remain sensitive to the compatibilities of a large number of third party platforms where developers are building their Twitter applications. Twitter's API is therefore "pragmatically RESTful," rather than explicitly so. Breaking from a strict REST design is not uncommon on the web; some principles are discarded where they conflict with the goals of the application as a whole. The following is a list of some known Twitter deviations from REST concepts, to help you understand where what you have learned about REST may not line up with your experiences developing against Twitter:

❑ All responses to API requests that are successful return a status code of `200`; a true REST service would return status code `201` for POST calls, providing the URI to the newly created resource in the response's `Location` header.

❑ The Twitter API does not return status code `204` for empty collections or no-op calls, or `205` for successful updates or deletes. Rather than use these status codes as stand-in for void-returning methods, Twitter always returns a resource element as a confirmation of an action, whether that resource was created or destroyed, with status code `200`.

❑   If a call to the DELETE or POST method verb can't complete because the resource used to exist but was already deleted, Twitter just returns status code `404` indicating the resource was not found, rather than sending `410` indicating the resource was present previously, but was actively deleted.

❑   Twitter does not support the OPTIONS or HEAD method verbs against any of its URIs.

This is not an exhaustive list, and may change in the future. What won't change any time soon are the ubiquitous use of REST and HTTP, and the foundations of HTTP message passing on the web. If you haven't already, spend some time reading the HTTP v1.1 specification. Besides providing excellent review material for designing or consuming RESTful services, it also has a demystifying effect on web programming in general.

Communicating with the Web and .NET

The .NET Framework provides a rich set of classes for interacting online, both in the context of web applications, and in desktop, console, and mobile applications through native HTTP and TCP communication support. In this section, you will learn how to use the most common .NET tools for web communication, all of which play a key role in your Twitter application development.

`WebClient`, `HttpWebRequest` *and* `HttpWebResponse`

If you've worked with the web in any capacity in .NET, you are likely familiar with the `HttpWebRequest` and `HttpWebResponse` classes; they are the workhorse of web communication in the .NET Framework, especially on the desktop, where programming against the web must come in the form of simulated framework support rather than first class server-side processing. That support comes in the form of the `HttpWebRequest` and `HttpWebResponse` classes, with `WebClient`, `Uri`, and `HttpUtility` classes playing supporting roles.

> **If you want to run the code examples listed in this section right away, make sure you skim over the section Twitter vs. NET in this chapter first to pick up some necessary information on how to set up your requests for success.**

Simplifying Web Communication with `WebClient`

.NET's `WebClient` class is designed to frame web requests with familiar language, and uses `HttpWebRequest` and `HttpWebResponse` under the hood to achieve it. Supporting sequential and asynchronous operation, `WebClient` is simple to configure and use. The following code will use an instance of `WebClient` to download Twitter's *public timeline*, the most recent tweets posted by any user of Twitter who chooses to make their updates public.

```
WebClient client = new WebClient();
byte[] data = client.DownloadData("http://twitter.com/statuses/public_timeline.xml");
```

You still need to convert the downloaded data from bytes to a string to interpret the results (in this case I asked for the XML representation) using this approach.

```
string results = Encoding.UTF8.GetString(data);
Console.WriteLine(results);
```

You can also use WebClient to access the public timeline resource as a stream.

```
WebClient client = new WebClient();
Stream stream = client.OpenRead("http://twitter.com/statuses/public_timeline.
json");

using(StreamReader sr = new StreamReader(stream))
{
    string results = sr.ReadToEnd();
    Console.WriteLine(results);
}
```

If you are building a desktop application and do not want to block your application's UI thread while processing a request with Twitter, you will need to implement an asynchronous fetching strategy. WebClient allows you to set up asynchronous operations using the .NET event handling model.

```
public void DownloadDataAsyncTest()
{
    AutoResetEvent block = new AutoResetEvent(false);

    Uri uri = new Uri("http://twitter.com/statuses/public_timeline.xml");

    WebClient client = new WebClient();
    client.DownloadDataCompleted += client_DownloadDataCompleted;
    client.DownloadDataAsync(uri, block);

    block.WaitOne();
}

static void client_DownloadDataCompleted(object sender,
DownloadDataCompletedEventArgs e)
{
    string results = Encoding.UTF8.GetString(e.Result);
    Console.WriteLine(results);

    if(e.UserState is AutoResetEvent && e.UserState != null)
    {
        ((AutoResetEvent) e.UserState).Set();
    }
}

public void OpenReadAsyncTest()
{
    AutoResetEvent block = new AutoResetEvent(false);

    Uri uri = new Uri("http://twitter.com/statuses/public_timeline.xml");
```

```
        WebClient client = new WebClient();
        client.OpenReadCompleted += client_OpenReadCompleted;
        client.OpenReadAsync(uri, block);

        block.WaitOne();
    }

    void client_OpenReadCompleted(object sender, OpenReadCompletedEventArgs e)
    {
        using (StreamReader sr = new StreamReader(e.Result))
        {
            string results = sr.ReadToEnd();
            Console.WriteLine(results);
        }

        if (e.UserState is AutoResetEvent && e.UserState != null)
        {
            ((AutoResetEvent)e.UserState).Set();
        }
    }
```

The DownloadDataAsync and OpenReadAsync methods do not provide an overload to pass in a simple string, so you will need to have a valid URI handy to make use of them.

So far, we have only covered reading and downloading data from a URI, which is equivalent to HTTP GET methods. With HTTP GET, everything the server needs to process the request is directly available in the URI. Using HTTP POST, however, requires you send additional data along with the request. Using WebClient, this means switching from a download (GET) to an upload (POST) frame of mind. To post a tweet using WebClient, you will need to send credentials as well. You will learn more about credentials in the next section, but for now all you need to know is that to perform private functions, such as updating your Twitter status or profile information, you must also provide a username and password to prove you are the account holder.

```
        string url = "http://twitter.com/statuses/update.xml";
        string data = "status=I'm uploading a string!";

        WebClient client = new WebClient();
        client.Credentials = new NetworkCredential(USERNAME, PASSWORD);

        string result = client.UploadString(url, data);
        Console.WriteLine(result);
```

An important distinction to make when sending a post request, like the one above to update your status, is that you need to split the URL between the resource and the query string, not only to satisfy the method signature of WebClient's UploadString method, but also because it is structured correctly to match an HTTP POST's behavior. The query string of a post request is sent as post parameters and converted into binary data, rather than as part of the request URI. If you inspect the outgoing HTTP POST request and compare it to a GET request containing a query string, you will notice the difference.

Wireshark

Wireshark is an excellent network traffic monitoring program which you may have installed while setting up your environment in the first chapter. Throughout the book, where you see detailed HTTP message information passed between client and server, this is the output that is directly available to you using `Wireshark`, which you learned how to configure for Twitter traffic in the *Getting Started* section at the beginning of the book. There are other popular options for a tool like this, such as `Fiddler` or `netmon`. Use whatever you like, but do use one; not only will you increase your understanding of HTTP programming and the server you are testing against, you will also spot potential opportunities for optimization or correction much sooner than if you are trying to resolve problems at a much higher level. Remember, you're just passing messages back and forth; it's helpful to take peek in the envelope from time to time.

```
GET /statuses/public_timeline.xml?page=3 HTTP/1.1
    Request Method: GET
    Request URI: /statuses/public_timeline.xml?page=3
    Request Version: HTTP/1.1
Host: twitter.com

POST /statuses/update.xml HTTP/1.1
    Request Method: POST
    Request URI: /statuses/update.xml
    Request Version: HTTP/1.1
Authorization: Basic YWxseW91cmJhc2U6YXJlYmVsb25ndG91cw==
Host: twitter.com
Content-Length: 30
```

You can also post parameters with `WebClient` using a `NameValueCollection`, which might make it easier for your application to track and use multiple post parameters in the same request. This is the equivalent code for the string-based post method.

```csharp
string url = "http://twitter.com/statuses/update.xml";

NameValueCollection postParameters = new NameValueCollection();
postParameters.Add("status", "I'm uploading a name value collection!");

WebClient client = new WebClient();
client.Credentials = new NetworkCredential(USERNAME, PASSWORD);

byte[] data = client.UploadValues(url, postParameters);
string result = Encoding.UTF8.GetString(data);
Console.WriteLine(result);
```

These posting methods similarly support asynchronous operation with consistent method signatures.

```
public void UploadValuesAsyncTest()
{
    AutoResetEvent block = new AutoResetEvent(false);

    Uri uri = new Uri("http://twitter.com/statuses/update.xml");

    NameValueCollection postParameters = new NameValueCollection();
    postParameters.Add("status", "I'm uploading asynchronously!");

    WebClient client = new WebClient();
    client.Credentials = new NetworkCredential(USERNAME, PASSWORD);
    client.UploadValuesCompleted += client_UploadValuesCompleted;

    client.UploadValuesAsync(uri, null, postParameters, block);

    block.WaitOne();
}

void client_UploadValuesCompleted(object sender, UploadValuesCompletedEventArgs e)
{
    string results = Encoding.UTF8.GetString(e.Result);
    Console.WriteLine(results);

    if (e.UserState is AutoResetEvent && e.UserState != null)
    {
        ((AutoResetEvent)e.UserState).Set();
    }
}
```

WebClient also supports uploading files, a useful feature for using Twitter's API to update a user's profile image and background. It is not possible to send arbitrary multi-part forms with WebClient, but UploadFile performs the task of preparing files for posting. Due to Twitter's encoding requirements, you will need to use the multi-part form techniques in Chapter 7 to post images to Twitter.

```
Uri uri = new Uri("http://twitter.com/statuses/update.xml");

WebClient client = new WebClient();
client.Credentials = new NetworkCredential(USERNAME, PASSWORD);
byte[] data = client.UploadFile(uri, "profile.jpg");

string result = Encoding.UTF8.GetString(data);
Console.WriteLine(result);
```

Optimizing with `WebClient`

You'll soon learn that there are a few optimizations you can make with `HttpWebRequest` that are not available with the `WebClient` class. You can choose to use `HttpWebRequest` to retain more control over your HTTP programming experience, or you can derive a new `WebClient` class and override its `GetWebRequest` and `GetWebResponse` methods to edit the underlying request and response objects.

```
protected override WebRequest GetWebRequest(Uri address)
{
    var request = (HttpWebRequest) base.GetWebRequest(address);
    // your request modification and optimization here
}

protected override WebRequest GetWebResponse(Uri address)
{
    var response = (HttpWebResponse) base
        .GetWebResponse(address);
    // your response modification and handling here
}
```

The `WebClient` class provides a simple interface for web communication, and it is possible to design and develop many Twitter applications using only the `WebClient` class.

Enhanced Control with `HttpWebRequest` and `HttpWebResponse`

While `WebClient` provides a simplified programming model, you may need more control over the requests you send to Twitter and other web APIs. This includes manipulating the request and response headers you picked up earlier in this chapter to conform to a server peculiarity, or optimize a request. For these kinds of tasks, you can use `HttpWebRequest` and `HttpWebResponse`.

With `HttpWebRequest`, only the stream-based style of message handling is supported. While the semantics of calling the request itself are very similar to WebClient, the main difference is that the HttpWebRequest class exposes many additional features and headers of the request, allowing you to customize it to suit your needs. This means you can adjust the caching headers, set timeouts and authentication handling, and construct multi-part form posts.

```
string url = "http://twitter.com/statuses/public_timeline.xml";
HttpWebRequest request = (HttpWebRequest)WebRequest.Create(url);

using (WebResponse response = request.GetResponse())
{
    using (var reader = new StreamReader(response.GetResponseStream()))
    {
        Console.WriteLine(reader.ReadToEnd());
    }
}
```

Asynchronous operation is slightly more difficult to implement than the WebClient equivalent, but manageable. Rather than subscribing to an event, you need to provide all of the required state to the Begin-prefixed methods.

```
public void HttpWebRequestGetAsyncTest()
{
    AutoResetEvent block = new AutoResetEvent(false);

    const string url = "http://twitter.com/statuses/public_timeline.xml";
    HttpWebRequest request = (HttpWebRequest)WebRequest.Create(url);

    object[] state = new object[] {request, block};
    request.BeginGetResponse(BeginGetResponseStreamCompleted, state);

    block.WaitOne();
}

static void BeginGetResponseStreamCompleted(IAsyncResult result)
{
    object[] state = (object[])result.AsyncState;
    WebRequest request = (WebRequest)state[0];
    AutoResetEvent block = (AutoResetEvent)state[1];

    using (var response = request.EndGetResponse(result))
    {
        using (var reader = new StreamReader(response.GetResponseStream()))
        {
            Console.WriteLine(reader.ReadToEnd());
            block.Set();
        }
    }
}
```

For finer control over asynchronous HTTP posts, you can also obtain an asynchronous handle for the operation that obtains a new Stream for HttpWebRequest writing. This will allow you to process the request and decide whether to continue on to write the post parameters into the request before sending, or abort the request before a request is actually sent to the server.

```
public void HttpWebRequestPostAsyncTest()
{
    AutoResetEvent block = new AutoResetEvent(false);

    // create a new request
    const string url = "http://twitter.com/statuses/update.xml?status=tweet!";
    HttpWebRequest request = (HttpWebRequest)WebRequest.Create(url);
    request.Method = "POST";
    request.Credentials = new NetworkCredential(USERNAME, PASSWORD);
    request.ServicePoint.Expect100Continue = false;

    // prepare POST data
    request.ContentType = "application/x-www-form-urlencoded";
    byte[] content = Encoding.UTF8.GetBytes(url);
    request.ContentLength = content.Length;
```

```
        object[] state = new object[] { request, content, block };
        request.BeginGetRequestStream(BeginGetRequestStreamCompleted, state);

        block.WaitOne();
    }

    static void BeginGetRequestStreamCompleted(IAsyncResult result)
    {
        object[] state = (object[])result.AsyncState;
        WebRequest request = (WebRequest)state[0];
        byte[] content = (byte[]) state[1];
        AutoResetEvent block = (AutoResetEvent)state[2];

        // you have the opportunity here to avoid making the request
        using (var stream = request.EndGetRequestStream(result))
        {
            state = new object[]{request, block};
            stream.Write(content, 0, content.Length);
            request.BeginGetResponse(BeginGetResponseStreamCompleted, state);
        }
    }

    static void BeginGetResponseStreamCompleted(IAsyncResult result)
    {
        object[] state = (object[])result.AsyncState;
        WebRequest request = (WebRequest)state[0];
        AutoResetEvent block = (AutoResetEvent)state[1];

        using (var response = request.EndGetResponse(result))
        {
            using (var reader = new StreamReader(response.GetResponseStream()))
            {
                Console.WriteLine(reader.ReadToEnd());
                block.Set();
            }
        }
    }
}
```

You were able to correct the Expect100Continue issue when making posts with Twitter in the example above by changing the property on the request instance rather than through ServicePointManager. HttpWebRequest instances always point to an internal ServicePoint instance. ServicePoint is a class that manages all connection information between your application and a URI resource address. Rather than exist only for the lifetime of an HttpWebRequest, the ServicePoint is managed by the ServicePointManager class and shares information it knows about a given URI with any future HttpWebRequest instances that are created for the same URI.

Accessing the Web from Inside Compiled Assemblies

If you write reusable class libraries that make HTTP requests in .NET, you need to know that referencing these libraries in ASP.NET requires the proper trust on the part of your hosting provider. This is due to the security policy behind the `WebPermission` class. Depending on your hosting service provider, this could present a challenge, as hosting services are typically run in partial trust, and rightfully so. You can, however, configure your assemblies to operate in medium trust by adding the `AllowPartiallyTrustedCallers` attribute to your assembly:

```
[assembly: AllowPartiallyTrustedCallers]
```

By default, the medium trust configuration file includes a mask, `$OriginalUrl$`, that allows you to provide an authorized URL in your application's `web.config` file. To allow access to any URL on a domain, you can provide a regular expression rather than a static path.

```
<system.web>
    <trust level="Medium" originUrl="http://twitter\.com/.*" />
</system.web>
```

Your host provider may not use the default configuration. If that is the case, you can contact them to request adding connect permissions to additional web addresses.

Going Low Level with Sockets and `TcpClient`

Previously you learned that HttpWebRequest, while offering a flexible and convenient abstraction over and above raw HTTP communication, restricts access to some vital headers, and otherwise obfuscates what is actually occurring underneath. You find yourself in a situation where you really want low level control over your web communication. Taking things a step further down, the `TcpClient` class will allow you to open raw socket connections and pass your HTTP messages through it. This code example demonstrates sending an HTTP POST over a socket connection.

```
public class TcpClientTests
{
    public void TcpClientPostTest()
    {
        string url = "http://twitter.com/statuses/update.xml?status=tweet!";
        Uri uri = new Uri(url);

        // build an HTTP POST message
        StringBuilder sb = new StringBuilder();
        sb.AppendFormat("POST {0}{1} HTTP/1.1", uri.LocalPath, uri.Query);
        sb.Append(Environment.NewLine);
        sb.AppendFormat("Host: {0}", uri.Host);
```

```csharp
        sb.Append(Environment.NewLine);
        sb.AppendFormat("Date: {0}", DateTime.Now.ToString("r"));
        sb.Append(Environment.NewLine);
        sb.AppendFormat("Authorization: Basic {0}", GetAuthToken());
        sb.Append(Environment.NewLine);
        sb.Append(Environment.NewLine);

        string message = sb.ToString();
        Console.WriteLine(message);

        // open a socket connection
        using (TcpClient client = new TcpClient(uri.Host, uri.Port))
        {
            NetworkStream stream = client.GetStream();

            SendMessage(stream, message);

            while (!stream.DataAvailable)
            {
                Thread.Sleep(500);
            }

            using (var reader = new StreamReader(stream))
            {
                Console.WriteLine(reader.ReadToEnd());
            }
        }
    }

    private static string GetAuthToken()
    {
        string auth = String.Format("{0}:{1}", USERNAME, PASSWORD);
        byte[] bytes = Encoding.UTF8.GetBytes(auth);
        return Convert.ToBase64String(bytes);
    }

    private static void SendMessage(Stream stream, string message)
    {
        byte[] bytes = Encoding.ASCII.GetBytes(message);
        stream.Write(bytes, 0, bytes.Length);
        stream.Flush();
    }
}
```

It should go without saying that this form of posting HTTP messages comes with no guarantees, but it does provide the most flexibility in terms of controlling exactly what is sent in each request.

Handling Exceptions

One feature of RESTful services is their use of HTTP response codes to notify clients when something has gone wrong. Unfortunately, the underlying .NET architecture does its job well, and raises a WebException whenever an HttpWebResponse returns an RFC-mandated error response code rather than OK (200) or another response that is information, successful, or redirected. The end result is that you are left with an exception, not a detailed description of the problem, as described by Twitter and returned in the response.

Fortunately, every WebException contains a WebResponse inside it. Accessing the stream from this response, where the previous attempt raised an exception, will result in retrieving the response you were after. You may also find it helpful to case the WebResponse to an HttpWebResponse, as that class provides more HTTP specific diagnostic information, such as the response status code returned. The following code demonstrates this technique.

```
try
{
    String url = "http://twitter.com/statuses/universal_timeline.xml";
    WebClient client = new WebClient();
    client.Credentials = new NetworkCredential(USERNAME, PASSWORD);
Stream stream = client.OpenRead(url);

    using (StreamReader sr = new StreamReader(stream))
    {
        string results = sr.ReadToEnd();
        Console.WriteLine(results);
    }
}
catch (WebException ex)
{
    using (Stream stream = ex.Response.GetResponseStream())
    {
        using (StreamReader reader = new StreamReader(stream))
        {
            string result = reader.ReadToEnd();

            // 404 - Twitter is not available on other planets (yet)
            Console.WriteLine(result);
        }
    }
}
```

WCF and REST Wrappers

One method of HTTP communication in .NET we are overlooking here is WCF. With WCF, it is possible to create a strongly typed wrapper around all of the representations of a RESTful resource, including the Twitter API.

❏ You can use WCF's proxy generation features to create data classes out of representative XML, such as the object responses for statuses, direct messages, and users returned by Twitter.

❏ You can use .NET 3.5's `UriTemplate` to define the inputs for the Twitter API's feature set in a generic way, replacing placeholders with the parameters of your client method signature.

❏ You can configure WCF to use `WebHttpBinding`, a simplified binding for communicating with HTTP and *POX (plain old XML)*.

WCF as a web client communication option is not included in this book for two reasons. The first is that WCF clients are not sensitive to REST design without some lengthy configuration; you can use `WebHttpBinding` to enable consumption of REST services, but there is no native support for what REST services actually do, such as relying on the HTTP response status codes to provide better result details; similar to `HttpWebRequest`, WCF services will treat these informative REST messages like errors, at least without programmer intervention, which causes the WCF service itself to fail.

The second reason not to cover building REST wrappers using WCF is that this style of client design is at an even higher level of abstraction than using `WebClient`, because you are effectively using it to write methods on objects that perform the same functionality as a request to a URI using one of the other approaches shown in this book. Using a wrapper around an API has its advantages, and you will learn how to use TweetSharp, itself a wrapper around Twitter, to drastically reduce the amount of time it takes to develop Twitter applications. The purpose of this chapter, however, is to provide you with the skills, and perhaps the confidence, to know exactly what is happening between your application and the RESTful service it consumes, not to learn the implementation details of WCF REST clients.

If you are interested in using WCF to wrap REST APIs, Chapter 10 of Jon Flanders' *RESTful .NET* (O'Reilly, 2008) provides a good overview of the process involved.

HTTP Basic Authentication

HTTP basic authentication is one of a variety of ways available to provide more secure web communication by helping determine whether the web user attempting to perform an action on a web site is in fact the person he or she claims to be. The concept of a username and password has existed since the birth of the web, and basic authentication is supported by practically every web browser with even marginal user adoption. Today, Twitter supports basic authentication at a minimum, as well as *OAuth*, Twitter's recommended and emerging standard. You will apply the *OAuth 1.0 specification* to your Twitter applications and learn the pitfalls of basic authentication in Chapter 7.

Username and Password

A user's username and password are passed together, along with the authentication scheme, in your request's Authorization header. To ensure that all characters are properly transferred, the username and password are delimited together with a colon, and then *Base64* encoded. It is important to note that while Base64 encoding isn't human readable, it is *not* secure, since reversing the encoding is straightforward in most programming frameworks. The following example demonstrates the ease of converting to and from Base64 encoded values.

```
string username = "username";
string password = "password";

// convert username and password to Base64
string auth = String.Format("{0}:{1}", username, password);
byte[] bytes = Encoding.UTF8.GetBytes(auth);
string token = Convert.ToBase64String(bytes);

Console.WriteLine(token);
dXNlcm5hbWU6cGFzc3dvcmQ=

// convert Base64 back to username and password
bytes = Convert.FromBase64String(token);
auth = Encoding.UTF8.GetString(bytes);

Console.WriteLine(auth);
username:password
```

In .NET, the `HttpWebRequest` class provides a general-purpose authentication mechanism through `ICredential` that allows you to forego setting the authorization header or Base64 encoding the username and password yourself. By creating a new instance of `System.Net.NetworkCredential` and setting it as the value of your request's `Credentials property`, basic authentication is implemented for you, as per this snippet.

```
string url = "http://twitter.com/statuses/public_timeline.rss";
HttpWebRequest request = (HttpWebRequest)WebRequest.Create(url);
request.Credentials = new NetworkCredential(username, password);

using (WebResponse response = request.GetResponse())
{
    using (StreamReader reader = new StreamReader(response.GetResponseStream()))
    {
        Console.WriteLine(reader.ReadToEnd());
    }
}
```

Realm

You may make a request without authentication to a protected resource and receive a 401 - Unauthorized response. In this response, you will find a header indicating the *realm* where the resource resides. This is an *opaque* string, meaning its value is arbitrary and specific to the server that defines it. Generally, the realm identity is given to protect a group of resources, and any URI defined at a more granular detail in terms of its path (`/birds/endangered` and `birds/endangered/eagle/` as an example) are protected under the same realm. Twitter's API is currently grouped into a single realm.

```
HTTP/1.1 401 Unauthorized
    Date: Wed, 08 Apr 2009 14:16:23 GMT
    Server: hi
    Status: 401 Unauthorized
WWW-Authenticate: Basic realm="Twitter API"
    Cache-Control: no-cache, max-age=1800
    Content-Type: application/xml; charset=utf-8
```

Passing Basic Authentication in a URL

It is possible to attach a username and password directly to a URL:

`http://`***username:password***`@twitter.com/statuses/user_timeline.xml`

If you were to type that URL above, providing your own credentials, into your favorite browser, you would be able to retrieve your protected user timeline in XML format. Keep in mind that passing the URL above to the `WebRequest`'s `Create` method will not result in creating and applying a `Credentials` instance for your request; sending the authorization header along with this URL is a feature of the *browser*, not the URL itself. If you sent a new request with this URL, .NET would strip the authentication information prior to sending the request, and you would receive a 401 response. You could, however, use the `UserInfo` property of the `Uri` class instantiated with your URL, and build a `NetworkCredential` instance for your request from that information.

Working with Proxies, Gateways, and Firewalls

No conversation about web communication is complete without discussing requests that must travel through a proxy, gateway, or firewall. A proxy is an alternate domain that a web service can use to address a resource. Often, proxies are configured at corporate sites to enhance security and block certain site traffic; yes, even Twitter at some companies. Since proxies are quite common and useful for corporate oversight and privacy, adding proxy support to your Twitter applications might be a popular feature.

Gateways are much easier to handle than proxies; you don't need to do anything at all. Since a gateway is a form of transparent proxy, web service consumers, like your application, do not need to know their addresses; if Twitter uses a gateway behind the scenes, it's not up to you to track it down.

You might have an idea about the existence of proxies already, based on the header topics covered earlier in the chapter. Generally, if you use `HttpWebRequest` it is easy to configure proxies without the need to negotiate the proxy communication yourself. However, one interesting characteristic of `HttpWebRequest` is that it will use Internet Explorer's's proxy information by default, even if you never thought to change this proxy information yourself. Here are a few helpful instructions to ensure you're always using the correct proxy settings when making requests with `HttpWebRequest`.

```
// Creating a request as you normally would
HttpWebRequest request = (HttpWebRequest)WebRequest.Create(URL);
request.Method = "POST";
request.Headers["Authorization"] = String.Format("Basic {0}", TOKEN);
request.ServicePoint.Expect100Continue = false;
request.PreAuthenticate = true;

// You need to explicitly set the proxy to null
// to avoid using the default proxy for all calls
request.Proxy = null;

// The default browser might not be IE; this proxy is
// derived from IE, the system browser, explicitly
request.Proxy = WebRequest.GetSystemWebProxy();

// This is the value that all requests are initially set to, and if it is
// explicitly set, IE will not become the default if it is unspecified elsewhere
// you could also configure the default proxy through this static property
request.Proxy = WebRequest.DefaultWebProxy;

// If you previously specified a proxy, those settings are reflected here by
default,
// otherwise the default is IE's current proxy values
IWebProxy proxy = request.Proxy;

// Creating a new proxy is similar to adding the same information to a request
request.Proxy = new WebProxy("http://myproxy.com");
request.Credentials = new NetworkCredential(USERNAME, PASSWORD);
```

Twitter vs. .NET

While .NET provides robust web communication classes, Twitter does not respond exactly how .NET's default configuration expects. The end result for your application is unnecessary web traffic, or refusal from the API to process your requests. Fortunately you can work around this behavior by spending time understanding what is happening underneath the hood of HttpWebRequest and Twitter itself. You can incorporate these behaviors into your request utility to get the results and performance you need.

Expect100Continue

You may have lots of success in building your application, only to have Twitter stop you in your tracks when you attempt to update a status (send a tweet), the API's most important method. Rather than tweeting like you expect, Twitter responds with a 417 error. The following output shows the end result of a call with default .NET behavior still in place.

Example

```
POST: http://twitter.com/statuses/update.xml?status=tweet!
<!DOCTYPE HTML PUBLIC "-//IETF//DTD HTML 2.0//EN">
<html><head>
<title>417 Expectation Failed</title>
</head><body>
<h1>Expectation Failed</h1>
<p>The expectation given in the Expect request-header
```

```
    field could not be met by this server.</p>
    <p>The client sent<pre>
        Expect: 100-continue
    </pre>
    but we only allow the 100-continue expectation.</p></body></html>
```

This side effect is the result of two things. First, when a `ServicePoint` instance for the URI you are posting to is first instantiated, its initial value for the `Expect100Continue` property is set to `true`. Second, Twitter does not support Expect100Continue behavior in general, so it must be disabled for any requests that post data to the API. You can find more details on this thread in the API developer discussion group: `http://groups.google.com/group/twitter-development-talk/browse_thread/thread/7c67ff1a2407dee7`

The `Expect100Continue` property tells the `HttpWebRequest` to add the value '100-continue' to the outgoing request's "expect" header. This asks the server to send back an HTTP response with a response code of 100 prior to your `HttpWebRequest` sending the actual payload. This is an optimization that makes sense for many other services, since you may want to avoid sending a large payload to a server if it will not process it; expecting a form of promise that your request will succeed makes a lot of sense. However, with a service like Twitter, designed for real time use and under constant load, it also makes sense to avoid the extra overhead of sending you an acknowledgment for every request; since Twitter makes good use of caching, and the API is rate limited, abuse scenarios are limited, and the time it takes to return a 100 response back to you is better used giving you want you wanted in the first place.

ServicePointManager.Expect100Continue and WebClient

If you are using the `WebClient` class rather than `HttpWebRequest` to make calls to the Twitter API, you must disable the expectation header using the static `ServicePointManager.Expect100Continue` property. The reason is that `WebClient` does not provide access to the internal `HttpWebRequest` it manages underneath, so there is no way to access the URI-bound service point from your client instance as-is.

Since you know that `ServicePoint` data is shared for subsequent requests to the same URI, it may suit your application better to set `Expect100Continue` as `false` through the static `ServicePointManager.Expect100Continue` property, disabling it for all newly `ServicePoint` to URI mappings. If you need to make other service calls where this behavior is a benefit, you can disable the matching `ServicePoint` for your particular request through the instance itself:

```
HttpWebRequest request = (HttpWebRequest)WebRequest.Create(url);
request.ServicePoint.Expect100Continue = false;
```

UseNagleAlgorithm

Requests you send to Twitter are typically very short; only profile methods that allow you to post binary data have potentially significant payloads. Therefore, you may benefit from disabling Nagle algorithm-based optimization, which delays sending TCP traffic until enough is available. Since Nagle optimization is enabled on requests by default, disabling it will avoid the overhead when you know requests from your application to Twitter occur in short, frequent bursts.

> ### *ServicePointManager.UseNagleAlgorithm* **and** *WebClient*
>
> Similar to `Expect100Continue`, you need to use the static `ServicePointManger.UseNagleAlgorithm` property if you intend to use `WebClient` for your application.

`NetworkCredential` *and Pre-authentication*

Your next challenge is reducing unnecessary bandwidth between Twitter and your application. While not an issue with public, unauthenticated calls, without considering the nuances of .NET web authentication you could end up *silently doubling* the number of API roundtrips you generate using some API methods. Consider the following code that posts a tweet.

```
string url = "http://twitter.com/statuses/update.xml?status=tweet!";

// build a request
HttpWebRequest request = (HttpWebRequest)WebRequest.Create(url);
request.Credentials = new NetworkCredential(USERNAME, PASSWORD);
request.Method = "POST";
request.ServicePoint.Expect100Continue = false;

// create POST content
request.ContentType = "application/x-www-form-urlencoded";
byte[] content = Encoding.UTF8.GetBytes(url);
request.ContentLength = content.Length;

using (var stream = request.GetRequestStream())
{
    stream.Write(content, 0, content.Length);

    using (var response = request.GetResponse())
    {
        using (var reader = new StreamReader(response.GetResponseStream()))
        {
            Console.WriteLine(reader.ReadToEnd());
        }
    }
}
```

If you run this code, Twitter will post a new tweet to your account, and return the XML representation of that new tweet, to prove it was a success and to allow you to process it immediately in your own application if needed. What it won't tell you is that this one function, thanks to `HttpWebRequest`, required two separate calls to the API. The following trace shows the results of a deceptively successful HTTP POST request.

```
POST /statuses/update.xml?status=tweet! HTTP/1.1
    Content-Type: application/x-www-form-urlencoded
    Host: twitter.com
    Content-Length: 52
    Connection: Keep-Alive

HTTP/1.1 401 Unauthorized
    Status: 401 Unauthorized
    WWW-Authenticate: Basic realm="Twitter API"
    Cache-Control: no-cache, max-age=1800
    Content-Type: application/xml; charset=utf-8
    Content-Length: 155
    Vary: Accept-Encoding
    Connection: close

POST /statuses/update.xml?status=tweet! HTTP/1.1
    Content-Type: application/x-www-form-urlencoded
    Authorization: Basic YWxseW91cmJhc2U6YXJlYmVsb25ndG91cw==
    Host: twitter.com
    Content-Length: 74

HTTP/1.1 200 OK
    Status: 200 OK
    Content-Type: application/xml; charset=utf-8
    Content-Length: 1679
    Vary: Accept-Encoding
    Connection: close
```

You specified a username and password using the NetworkCredential class, attached it to your post, and the end result was that you sent two separate requests to Twitter; one that fails because it has no authentication attached, and an identical request that succeeds, this time with the expected authorization header.

The reason for this stems from the fact that the NetworkCredential class is a general-purpose object for multiple password-based authentication schemes. For example, it is used in .NET for basic, digest, NTLM and Kerberos authentication. Furthermore, the Credential property on your HttpWebRequest instance is not a NetworkCredential, but an ICredential, whose GetCredentials method could resolve to any of the supported authentication types. This means that your request has no way of knowing what credentials are demanded by the service its calling, until that service challenges the request by failing. If you look at the first response in the trace above, you'll notice this: WWW-Authenticate: Basic realm="Twitter API". This header is the information the request needs to know to send the username and password you provided as Basic authorization, and not another type.

Your next thought may be to use the provided PreAuthenticate property on your HttpWebRequest. The PreAuthenticate property instructs your request to avoid waiting for the authorization challenge before sending credentials *after the authentication scheme is established*.

```
// build a request with pre-authentication
HttpWebRequest request = (HttpWebRequest)WebRequest.Create(url);
request.Credentials = new NetworkCredential(USERNAME, PASSWORD);
request.Method = "POST";
request.ServicePoint.Expect100Continue = false;
request.PreAuthenticate = true;
```

Now when you make the same request to the Twitter domain, you will still receive a 401 response the first time, which your request will answer with your credentials. Any subsequent requests from you to Twitter will include the authorization header; congratulations, you've greatly reduced the amount of traffic required to make an API call!

You can do better. Since you know at any given time what authentication scheme to attempt against the Twitter API, you can avoid the initial authentication challenge and always send the authorization header when making requests. To do this, you need to bypass using `NetworkCredential` and set the authorization header yourself. Since you've already learned how to form the basic authentication token, this is not a difficult task.

```
// create a basic auth token
string auth = String.Format("{0}:{1}", USERNAME, PASSWORD);
byte[] bytes = Encoding.UTF8.GetBytes(auth);
string token = Convert.ToBase64String(bytes);

// set the header manually to avoid the challenge
HttpWebRequest request = (HttpWebRequest)WebRequest.Create(url);
request.Headers["Authorization"] = String.Format("Basic {0}", token);
```

```
POST /statuses/update.xml?status=tweet! HTTP/1.1
    Content-Type: application/x-www-form-urlencoded
    Authorization: Basic YWxseW91cmJhc2U6YXJlYmVsb25ndG91cw==
    Host: twitter.com
    Content-Length: 52

HTTP/1.1 200 OK
    Status: 200 OK
    Content-Type: application/xml; charset=utf-8
    Content-Length: 1657
    Vary: Accept-Encoding
    Connection: close
```

Now your Twitter API calls can be as lean as possible, requiring only one request per API response! If you had elected to allow .NET to send handshake data in the first request, you could run into unexpected results. For example, Twitter uses an API method to determine how many calls in the current hour an account is allowed to make, and that method requires credentials; if the first call from .NET results in an authentication failure, as it would without setting the authorization header explicitly in the first request, the data returned by the method is always for the default, unauthenticated IP address of the method you called, not the account you intended to use, which may throw off your calculations or introduce a bug that's difficult to diagnose.

Creating a Request Utility

Since service calls are similarly structured, they are a great candidate for automation. One of the tangible benefits of using a third-party library to wrap the Twitter API is the ability to abstract away the details of sending, receiving, and processing HTTP messages. Even without using a library, it is not a difficult task to write your own general purpose tool to wrap web service calling functions, so you can focus on the Twitter API and your application design.

Let's build that tool right now, laying a foundation for your discovery of the Twitter API in the next chapter. Our goal is to design a convenient set of methods that allow you to make HTTP requests to a server from your calling application in a way that is intuitive and helps you focus on the task at hand of consuming data from remote web sources.

PHP developers have long enjoyed access to cURL, a convenient and powerful API for this exact purpose. The `WebClient` class is arguably a decent equivalent wrapper for .NET, but you could go further to make your learning experience with web communication even simpler, as well as provide utility functions for the applications you build. Paying homage to cURL, we'll call our project 'NUrl,' a set of .NET 3.5 extension methods to make it easy to make web requests. Then when you write your unit tests to learn the Twitter API or build your next Twitter application, you can write this:

```
"http://twitter.com/statuses/public_timeline.rss".Get();
```

Instead of this:

```
var url = "http://twitter.com/statuses/public_timeline.rss";
var request = (HttpWebRequest)WebRequest.Create(url);
using (WebResponse response = request.GetResponse())
{
    using (var reader = new StreamReader(response.GetResponseStream()))
    {
        Console.WriteLine(reader.ReadToEnd());
    }
}
```

You already know what's needed to write a robust set of methods for web operations against Twitter's API. NUrl will use `HttpWebRequest` for HTTP GET, POST, PUT, and DELETE. Feel free to use `WebClient` in your applications, but based on the specific considerations you've learned when working with the Twitter API, using `HttpWebRequest` is the recommended approach.

URI Validation

Before a URL is passed on to functions, it is validated, and, if necessary, its contents are escaped correctly. If the URL is not valid, or a bad parameter was passed in, an exception is thrown. Notice that we're using `Uri` to attempt to create an absolute URI from the provided string input. Escaping is handled when the request is instantiated. This code validates a URL.

```
public static string ValidateUrl(this string url)
{
    if (String.IsNullOrEmpty(url))
    {
        throw new ArgumentException("No URL provided", "url");
    }

    if (Uri.IsWellFormedUriString(url, UriKind.Absolute))
    {
        return url;
    }

    Uri uri;
    Uri.TryCreate(url, UriKind.Absolute, out uri);

    if (uri != null)
    {
        return url;
    }

    throw new ArgumentException("Malformed URL provided", "url");
}
```

Exception Handling

You also need a reliable way to look past any REST-based response codes that are returned in the HttpWebResponse and treated like exceptions. Based on what you know about how WebExceptions are thrown, a short utility method is all you need to ensure you get the specific error results rather than an exception, without changing the expectation of the utility methods. This example handles response codes returned from a REST service.

```
private static string HandleWebException(WebException ex)
{
    if (ex.Response is HttpWebResponse && ex.Response != null)
    {
        var stream = ex.Response.GetResponseStream();
        using (var reader = new StreamReader(stream))
        {
            var result = reader.ReadToEnd();
            return result;
        }
    }

    throw ex;
}
```

Basic Authorization

Internally, when preparing a REST service call to use basic authentication, you can use two short utility methods that take care of converting string input to and from Base64 encoding. Their use isn't required to use NUrl, but they are useful methods to have on hand. These extension methods handle Base64 encoding.

```
public static string Base64Encode(this string input)
{
    byte[] data = Encoding.UTF8.GetBytes(input);
    return Convert.ToBase64String(data);
}

public static string Base64Decode(this string input)
{
    byte[] data = Convert.FromBase64String(input);
    return Encoding.UTF8.GetString(data);
}
```

HTTP GET

Performing HTTP GET requests is fairly straightforward, as there is no content body to write to the stream before sending the message. The Get method should support basic authentication as well as public calls. This set of methods provides sequential HTTP GET support.

```
public static string Get(this string url)
{
    var request = CreateGetRequest(url);

    return ExecuteGet(request);
}

public static string Get
(this string url, string username, string password)
{
    string pair = String.Concat(username, ":", password);
    string token = pair.Base64Encode();

    var request = CreateGetRequest(url);
    request.Headers["Authorization"] =
        String.Format("Basic {0}", token);

    return ExecuteGet(request);
}

private static WebRequest CreateGetRequest(string url)
{
    url = ValidateUrl(url);

    var request = (HttpWebRequest)WebRequest.Create(url);
    request.Method = "GET";

    return request;
}

private static string ExecuteGet(WebRequest request)
{
    Console.WriteLine("GET: {0}", request.RequestUri);

    try
    {
        using (var response = request.GetResponse())
```

```
        {
            var stream = response.GetResponseStream();
            using (var reader = new StreamReader(stream))
            {
                return reader.ReadToEnd();
            }
        }
    }
    catch (WebException ex)
    {
        return HandleWebException(ex);
    }
}
```

Rounding out the HTTP GET functionality is support for asynchronous operation. To do this, we'll create a new event handler and argument class, so that callers can define what happens when a request completes in familiar terms, passing in a method that matches a signature with the event data raised during the asynchronous operation. You can create the following class to provide event arguments to support asynchronous operations.

```
public class WebResponseEventArgs : EventArgs
{
    public Uri Uri { get; set; }
    public string Response { get; set; }
}
```

These methods will add additional support for asynchronous methods for HTTP GET requests.

```
public static IAsyncResult GetAsync(this string url,
Action<WebResponseEventArgs>
                            callback)
{
    WebRequest request = CreateGetRequest(url);

    return ExecuteGetAsync(request, callback);
}

public static IAsyncResult GetAsync(this string url,
                        string username,
                        string password,
                        Action<WebResponseEventArgs>
                            callback)
{
    string pair = String.Concat(username, ":", password);
    string token = pair.Base64Encode();

    WebRequest request = CreateGetRequest(url);
    string header = String.Format("Basic {0}", token);
    request.Headers["Authorization"] = header;

    return ExecuteGetAsync(request, callback);
}
```

```
    private static IAsyncResult ExecuteGetAsync(WebRequest request,
    Action<WebResponseEventArgs>
                                callback)
{
    Console.WriteLine("GET: {0}", request.RequestUri);

    return
        request.BeginGetResponse(
            result => RaiseWebResponse(request,
    result,
    callback), null);
}

    private static void RaiseWebResponse(WebRequest request,
    IAsyncResult result,        Action<WebResponseEventArgs>
    callback)
{
    var args = new WebResponseEventArgs { Uri = request.RequestUri };
    try
    {
        var response = request.EndGetResponse(result);
        var stream = response.GetResponseStream();
        using (var reader = new StreamReader(stream))
        {
            args.Response = reader.ReadToEnd();
        }
    }
    catch (WebException ex)
    {
        args.Response = HandleWebException(ex);
    }

    callback.Invoke(args);
}
```

HTTP POST

With Get support up and running you can focus on Post. You know posts are considered unsafe; as they could, and often do, affect the state of the server with each call. Sequential and asynchronous support for HTTP POST via the Post method is listed below.

```
using System;
using System.IO;
using System.Net;
using System.Text;

namespace Wrox.Twitter.NUrl
{
    partial class NUrl
    {
        public static string Post(this string url)
        {
            byte[] content;
```

```
        var request = CreatePostRequest(url, out content);

        return ExecutePost(request, content);
    }

    public static string Post(this HttpWebRequest request, byte[] content)
    {
        request.Method = "POST";
        request.ContentType = "application/x-www-form-urlencoded";
        request.ContentLength = content.Length;

        return ExecutePost(request, content);
    }

    public static string Post(this string url,
                              string username,
                              string password)
    {
        byte[] content;
        var request = CreateAuthPostRequest(username,
                                            password,
                                            url,
                                            out content);

        return ExecutePost(request, content);
    }

    public static IAsyncResult PostAsync(this string url,
                                         Action<WebResponseEventArgs>
                                             callback)
    {
        byte[] content;
        var request = CreatePostRequest(url, out content);

        return ExecutePostAsync(request, content, callback);
    }

    public static IAsyncResult PostAsync(this string url,
                                         string username,
                                         string password,
                                         Action<WebResponseEventArgs>
                                             callback)
    {
        byte[] content;
        var request = CreateAuthPostRequest(username,
                                            password,
                                            url,
                                            out content);

        return ExecutePostAsync(request, content, callback);
    }
```

```csharp
private static string ExecutePost(WebRequest request, byte[] content)
{
    Console.WriteLine("POST: {0}", request.RequestUri);

    try
    {
        using (var stream = request.GetRequestStream())
        {
            stream.Write(content, 0, content.Length);

            using (var response = request.GetResponse())
            {
                using (
                    var reader =
                        new StreamReader(response.GetResponseStream()))
                {
                    var result = reader.ReadToEnd();
                    return result;
                }
            }
        }
    }
    catch (WebException ex)
    {
        return HandleWebException(ex);
    }
}

private static IAsyncResult ExecutePostAsync(WebRequest request,
                                             byte[] content,
                                             Action
                                                 <WebResponseEventArgs>
                                                 callback)
{
    Console.WriteLine("POST: {0}", request.RequestUri);

    var state = new object[] {request, content, callback};

    return request.BeginGetRequestStream(
        BeginGetRequestStreamCompleted, state);
}

private static WebRequest CreatePostRequest(string url,
                                            out byte[] content)
{
    url = ValidateUrl(url);

    var request = (HttpWebRequest) WebRequest.Create(url);
    request.Method = "POST";
    request.ContentType = "application/x-www-form-urlencoded";
    content = Encoding.UTF8.GetBytes(url);
    request.ContentLength = content.Length;
```

```
            return request;
        }

        private static WebRequest CreateAuthPostRequest(string username,
                                                        string password,
                                                        string url,
                                                        out byte[] content)
        {
            var pair = String.Concat(username, ":", password);
            var token = pair.Base64Encode();

            var request = CreatePostRequest(url, out content);

            var header = String.Format("Basic {0}", token);
            request.Headers["Authorization"] = header;
            return request;
        }
    }
}
```

HTTP PUT

The PUT method has the same structure as POST, as it is intended to upload data to a resource address. You can simply transpose the POST functionality to add PUT support to the library. Here are the sequential and asynchronous support methods for HTTP PUT.

```
using System;
using System.IO;
using System.Net;
using System.Text;

namespace Wrox.Twitter.NUrl
{
    partial class NUrl
    {
        public static string Put(this string url)
        {
            byte[] content;
            WebRequest request = CreatePutRequest(url, out content);

            return ExecutePut(request, content);
        }

        public static string Put(this string url,
                                 string username,
                                 string password)
        {
            byte[] content;
            WebRequest request = CreateAuthPutRequest(username,
                                                      password,
                                                      url,
                                                      out content);
```

```csharp
        return ExecutePut(request, content);
}

public static IAsyncResult Put(this string url,
                               Action<WebResponseEventArgs>
                                   callback)
{
    byte[] content;
    WebRequest request = CreatePutRequest(url, out content);

        return ExecutePutAsync(request, content, callback);
}

public static IAsyncResult Put(this string url,
                               string username,
                               string password,
                               Action<WebResponseEventArgs>
                                   callback)
{
    byte[] content;
    WebRequest request = CreateAuthPutRequest(username,
                                              password,
                                              url,
                                              out content);

        return ExecutePutAsync(request, content, callback);
}

private static string ExecutePut(WebRequest request, byte[] content)
{
    Console.WriteLine("PUT: {0}", request.RequestUri);

    try
    {
        using (Stream stream = request.GetRequestStream())
        {
            stream.Write(content, 0, content.Length);

            using (WebResponse response = request.GetResponse())
            {
                using (
                    StreamReader reader =
                        new StreamReader(response.GetResponseStream()))
                {
                    string result = reader.ReadToEnd();
                    return result;
                }
            }
        }
    }
    catch (WebException ex)
    {
        return HandleWebException(ex);
    }
```

```
        }

        private static IAsyncResult ExecutePutAsync(WebRequest request,
                                                    byte[] content,
                                                    Action
                                                         <WebResponseEventArgs>
                                                    callback)
        {
            Console.WriteLine("POST: {0}", request.RequestUri);

            object[] state = new object[] {request, content, callback};

            return request.BeginGetRequestStream(
                BeginGetRequestStreamCompleted, state);
        }

        private static WebRequest CreatePutRequest(string url,
                                                    out byte[] content)
        {
            url = ValidateUrl(url);

            HttpWebRequest request = (HttpWebRequest) WebRequest.Create(url);
            request.Method = "PUT";
            request.ContentType = "application/x-www-form-urlencoded";
            content = Encoding.UTF8.GetBytes(url);
            request.ContentLength = content.Length;

            return request;
        }

        private static WebRequest CreateAuthPutRequest(string username,
                                                    string password,
                                                    string url,
                                                    out byte[] content)
        {
            string pair = String.Concat(username, ":", password);
            string token = pair.Base64Encode();

            WebRequest request = CreatePutRequest(url, out content);

            string header = String.Format("Basic {0}", token);
            request.Headers["Authorization"] = header;
            return request;
        }
    }
}
```

HTTP DELETE

Like PUT, DELETE is a simple adjustment to the HTTP verb declaration for an HTTP GET, as it does not require uploading of additional data other than specifying the URI of the resource you intend to delete. Therefore, you can use the existing features of Get to build out the Delete methods, shown here.

```
using System;
using System.IO;
using System.Net;

namespace Wrox.Twitter.NUrl
{
    partial class NUrl
    {
        public static string Delete(this string url)
        {
            WebRequest request = CreateDeleteRequest(url);

            return ExecuteDelete(request);
        }

        public static string Delete(this string url,
                                    string username,
                                    string password)
        {
            string pair = String.Concat(username, ":", password);
            string token = pair.Base64Encode();

            WebRequest request = CreateDeleteRequest(url);
            string header = String.Format("Basic {0}", token);
            request.Headers["Authorization"] = header;

            return ExecuteDelete(request);
        }

        public static IAsyncResult DeleteAsync(this string url,
                                        Action<WebResponseEventArgs>
                                            callback)
        {
            WebRequest request = CreateDeleteRequest(url);

            return ExecuteDeleteAsync(request, callback);
        }

        public static IAsyncResult DeleteAsync(this string url,
                                        string username,
                                        string password,
                                        Action<WebResponseEventArgs>
                                            callback)
        {
            string pair = String.Concat(username, ":", password);
            string token = pair.Base64Encode();
```

```csharp
        WebRequest request = CreateDeleteRequest(url);
        string header = String.Format("Basic {0}", token);
        request.Headers["Authorization"] = header;

        return ExecuteDeleteAsync(request, callback);
    }

    private static string ExecuteDelete(WebRequest request)
    {
        Console.WriteLine("DELETE: {0}", request.RequestUri);

        try
        {
            using (WebResponse response = request.GetResponse())
            {
                var stream = response.GetResponseStream();
                using (StreamReader reader = new StreamReader(stream))
                {
                    return reader.ReadToEnd();
                }
            }
        }
        catch (WebException ex)
        {
            return HandleWebException(ex);
        }
    }

    private static IAsyncResult ExecuteDeleteAsync(WebRequest request,
                                         Action<WebResponseEventArgs>
                                                  callback)
    {
        Console.WriteLine("DELETE: {0}", request.RequestUri);

        return
            request.BeginGetResponse(
                result => RaiseWebResponse(request, result, callback), null);
    }

    private static WebRequest CreateDeleteRequest(string url)
    {
        url = ValidateUrl(url);

        HttpWebRequest request = (HttpWebRequest)WebRequest.Create(url);
        request.Method = "DELETE";

        return request;
    }
}
}
```

Running NUrl on the Command Line

You can run the NUrl code as a command line utility for quick access to the Twitter API, in addition to using the extension methods in your own code to drive your service calls. The usage for NUrl is basic; pass in the HTTP method, the username and password if applicable, and a resource address.

```
> NUrl.exe get http://twitter.com/statuses/public_timeline.xml

> NUrl.exe post username:password http://twitter.com/statuses/
update.xml?status=tweet!
```

Summary

This chapter was intense; you may have come from a background in Windows or ASP.NET programming that kept you far away from HTTP programming; this is not a bad thing, since productivity is quite important in software development. However, becoming a student of REST is an excellent way to get back to the heart of the web, while learning to use or build scalable, simple services. Here's a short review of what you learned:

❑   REST is a set of principles for designing and building web services using HTTP that map HTTP verbs to object-oriented persistence principles, define every resource as addressable, and support operation with multiple representations of a given resource, where the returning data provides new URIs to further information or actions

❑   The HTTP 1.1 specification is a rich, thorough programming model for working with the web. By coordinating request and response headers, and responding to status codes returned by the target server, you can build applications that are sensitive to bandwidth and recover intelligently from the unexpected.

❑   You learned how to send and receive HTTP messages from the most helpful abstraction to low level message passing, using `WebClient`, `HttpWebRequest`, and `TcpClient`.

❑   Twitter's API is pragmatically RESTful, but does not follow the HTTP specification exactly; you will also need to make adjustments to the default .NET web request behavior to successfully consume the Twitter API and decrease bandwidth by avoiding authentication challenge and response.

❑   You built a utility class to perform URI validation, exception handling, and HTTP requests that you can use in your Twitter application development, and anywhere else RESTful services are consumed.

It's not possible to cover the entirety of sockets, HTTP 1.1, REST, and .NET's classes for web communication in one chapter, but you should now have a better understanding of the web as a simple passing of messages, REST as a collection of good principles for building quality web services, and .NET's `WebClient` and `HttpWebRequest` as helpful tools for both. Sitting on top of this understanding is the Twitter API, a RESTful service that you are now ready to master.

In the next chapter, you will learn how to consume the Twitter API and understand what features are available to you when building your applications.

2

The Twitter REST API

> *"Twitter is a succinct concept so its API is small and compact. That makes it very approachable by a broad range of developers. A weekend hobbyist can easily tinker around with it and have something up and running in a few hours while a professional can use the API's simplicity as a building block to create interesting variations and extensions of the service."*
>
> **Lee Brenner,** *blu*

In Chapter 1, you learned how a RESTful service is organized, and how to write web queries using the `System.Net` namespace. You will build on this knowledge by utilizing the NUrl tool to communicate with the Twitter API.

Obtaining a Twitter Account

If you haven't already done so, now is a good time to sign up for a Twitter account. An account allows you to access the authenticated portions of the API, which make up a considerable amount of the features available for use. Signing up for an account is straightforward; just open your browser to `http://twitter.com/signup` and follow the on-screen prompts. Figure 2-1 shows a typical signup page.

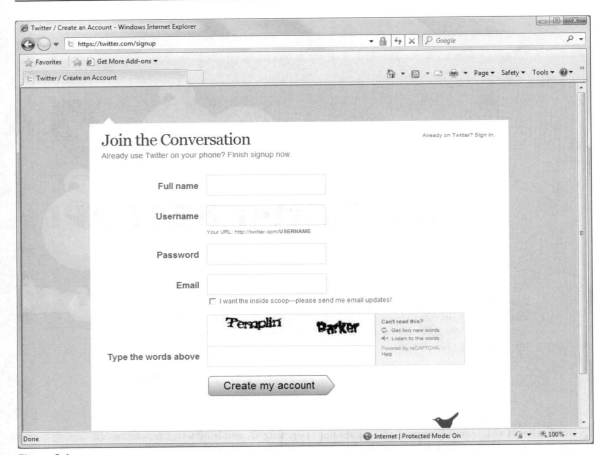

Figure 2-1

This chapter breaks down how Twitter itself is structured, the anatomy of the REST API, how Twitter objects are represented in returned data, and how to send and receive data using the Twitter API. Each API call includes a typical usage scenario, as well as any special considerations you need to make when building your application to use the method. This will give you a solid grasp on the API for real-world use.

Overview

Learning an API is always a combination of visualization, information, and practice. In this book are examples of all three. At the beginning of each resource feature section, you will find a diagram laying out the API's landscape in a visual way, so you can tell at a glance how to structure your resource requests. Each API method is documented in detail, including an example of what kind of problem it could solve. To round it off, the source code includes a Windows application that allows you to select and explore the API and call it directly, so you can experiment with various method verbs, parameters, formats, and error information. By making use of all three, you should round out your understanding of the API and be able to visualize what kind of programs you will need to write and assemble to execute your application's vision.

Using the TwitterExplorer Application

The source code for the book includes a Windows Form application, written using the NUrl tool you built in Chapter 1, to provide a convenient way to experiment with the API calls found in this chapter. Running TwitterExplorer while working through these examples will help you associate each call to its expected inputs and outputs, and the source code will help familiarize yourself with the NUrl utility you built in Chapter 1, which you may use and extend to suit your own project needs.

Resources

Following your understanding of REST, Twitter breaks down its feature space as resources, with each functional area separated by a noun. Actions you can take on a resource follow the resource name in the URI path. The following is a general outline of each resource available to you.

Statuses

Statuses are the heart of Twitter and consist of 140 characters of arbitrary text. When someone mentions "tweets," they are referring to statuses. The 140 character limit applies to the entire message, including any metadata or recipients the user provides. The statuses resource provides some facility for the social graph, allowing you to retrieve the friends and followers of a given user along with those users' most recent status.

While the root noun for friend and follower methods is *statuses*, it makes more sense to include these methods with the *users* noun; Twitter references these methods in the *users* resource in the REST documentation itself, in case you have trouble locating them elsewhere. You can find the latest documentation at `http://apiwiki.twitter.com/Twitter-API-Documentation`.

Users

Users are the folks on Twitter that are making use of the system, providing you with both data to harvest, and challenges to solve. A user is always bundled together with their latest status update.

Direct Messages

Direct messages are statuses that only appear to the user recipient you define when they are created. Even though they are functionally no different than plain *statuses*, this resource provides features for organizing direct messages sent and received, as well as helping ensure private information isn't accidentally shared with the entire planet.

Friendships

Friendships define the social graph of participant users as well as the possible interactions available between each participant. Though not immediately obvious when using Twitter's own web site to interact with others, friendships are not equivalent to following users, which includes device updates in addition to user timeline updates, which befriending provides. In other words, befriending a user produces that user's updates in your friends timeline, but will not result in receiving that user's updates to any registered devices, similar to your mobile phone. Friendships, combined with device notifications, are the strictest sense of "following" another user, according to the Twitter API.

Social Graph

Applications that are designed to find value in the Twitter social graph are constrained by the API's 200 result limit when retrieving friends or followers; users with thousands of followers require hundreds of API calls, which is impractical for the vast majority of user accounts who are constrained to 100 API requests per hour. To help provide a solution to this challenge, Twitter provides social graphing resources, allowing you to quickly compare a list of all friends or followers by their unique identifier, against your own user cache (I'll discuss caching in more detail in Chapter 7). Designing for a global user cache is a little extra work up front, but will yield many more feature options in your development projects.

Accounts

The accounts area contains all the administrative features of Twitter's web site, which allow you to build applications that keep your users within your application to update their profile bio, photos, colors, and background. It also provides information on the participant's current rate limits, to help you make intelligent decisions about when to send requests and keep your application responsive.

Favorites

Referring to statuses, a participant may indicate favorite statuses for review later or for another purpose. This area provides the ability to classify statuses as favorites, or cancel previously favorite statuses. From an application design point of view, it is difficult to view favorites in parallel; because it is only possible to obtain favorites at a user-level, finding those who have chosen to favorite a specific status as a favorite requires a global user cache.

Notifications

Provided that the participant is already friends with a given user, these methods allow subscription management for specified users' updates. This means updates are published to the user's registered devices. Currently only mobile phones are available for notification subscription.

Blocks

Because all communication is not always welcome, blocking allows a participant to choose to avoid viewing any status updates from a given user, even if that user is referencing the participant in some way. Although your application may want to handle status update filtering in some other way, blocking another user will also remove that user from the participant's followers or friends list, if applicable.

Help

Currently, this area provides a single, unrated method that allows you to test the heartbeat of Twitter's API. This is useful for deciding how and when to notify a user about the health of the system when using your application.

Representations

Twitter provides several representational formats through the API. These formats allow you some flexibility in how you process or respond to information when making requests, and take the form of pseudo-objects that portray the various entities that make up Twitter as an application itself.

Formats

Twitter supports eXtensible Markup Language (XML) and JavaScript Simple Object Notation (JSON) throughout the REST API at a minimum, with some resources available as syndicated in either RSS or Atom formats.

Elements

Twitter responds to API calls with data in the requested format, but that data also represents an underlying object model, which is useful for your application for visualization and feature definition. As an example, here is the response to a GET call to show a specific user's profile, in XML format. The following and notifications elements in the output XML are deprecated, so they will not return a value.

```
GET: http://twitter.com/users/show/Dimebrain.xml
<user>
  <id>11173402</id>
  <name>Daniel Crenna</name>
  <screen_name>dimebrain</screen_name>
  <location>Canada</location>
  <description>Daniel Crenna builds social software.</description>
<profile_image_url>image.png</profile_image_url>
  <url>http://www.dimebrain.com</url>
  <protected>false</protected>
  <followers_count>305</followers_count>
  <profile_background_color>050f10</profile_background_color>
  <profile_text_color>333333</profile_text_color>
  <profile_link_color>0084B4</profile_link_color>
  <profile_sidebar_fill_color>e0e0e0</profile_sidebar_fill_color>
  <profile_sidebar_border_color>000000</profile_sidebar_border_color>
  <friends_count>227</friends_count>
  <created_at>Fri Dec 14 18:48:52 +0000 2007</created_at>
  <favourites_count>49</favourites_count>
  <utc_offset>-14400</utc_offset>
  <time_zone>Atlantic Time (Canada)</time_zone>
  <profile_background_image_url>background.png</profile_background_image_url>
  <profile_background_tile>false</profile_background_tile>
  <statuses_count>750</statuses_count>
  <notifications />
  <following />
  <status>
    <created_at>Sat Apr 04 16:47:33 +0000 2009</created_at>
    <id>1452248860</id>
    <text>This is an example of an XML response from Twitter.</text>
    <source>web</source>
    <truncated>false</truncated>
    <in_reply_to_status_id>1452238970</in_reply_to_status_id>
    <in_reply_to_user_id>14660297</in_reply_to_user_id>
    <favorited>false</favorited>
    <in_reply_to_screen_name>John_Papa</in_reply_to_screen_name>
  </status>
</user>
```

It is easy to infer the object model for both users, and statuses, using this XML representation. Later in the Twitter Objects section of this chapter you will learn the Twitter object model in detail, as well as build data classes suitable for use in your own projects. These objects will come in handy in Chapter 3, where you will learn how to convert data from its REST representation as previously shown, to convenient data classes to program against.

Authenticating Users

Users of Twitter, and ultimately your application, provide credentials that you must pass along to Twitter in a web service call, in the form of *Basic authentication*, an insecure username and password pair, or *OAuth* authentication, an encrypted token and secret bound to the user's explicit authorization for a specific application.

If you are using Basic authentication, it is better to avoid requiring local storage of a user's credentials. Sometimes storing passwords is unavoidable, such as when building client applications that would otherwise require the user to provide their username and password on every application startup. If you feel you must store passwords, your application is a good candidate for OAuth because the user's true Twitter credentials are never seen in your code, and stored tokens and their secrets are specific to your application and revocable at any time.

> *A detailed explanation of integrating OAuth in your applications is provided in Chapter 6. Tips on storing sensitive user data is provided in Chapter 7.*

API Rate Limits

Rate limiting is both a security device and a bandwidth governor for Twitter. If a malicious program was developed unannounced, it could rapidly spam or phish accounts, or impersonate real people at a much more alarming rate than if their mayhem was limited to a certain number of requests per hour. The typical Twitter user, at least using the Twitter site itself, rarely needs that much API leverage, and it helps Twitter measure the overall effect of a growing user base.

The Twitter API provides two very different rate-limiting scenarios: accounts or IP addresses that are limited to 100 API calls per hour, and white-listed accounts or IP addresses that are limited to 20,000 API calls per hour. This is clearly a large gap between two distinct levels of service. It is helpful to think of the standard accounts as "consumers," and white-listed accounts as "producers" in the Twitter universe. For example, if you built a Twitter client—software that assists everyday users with their Twitter tasks—you could feasibly build your application to consume only the user's credentials and rate limit, because all API calls would originate from the consumer's account. If you decide to make an unauthenticated call to an API method on behalf of a user, then that call will always count against the IP address and not the

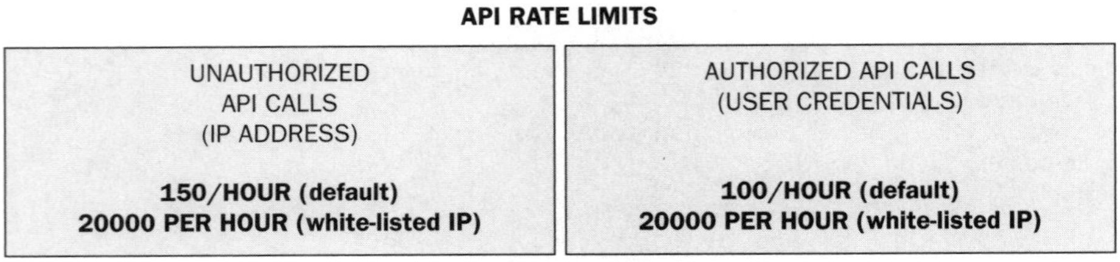

API RATE LIMITS

UNAUTHORIZED API CALLS (IP ADDRESS)	AUTHORIZED API CALLS (USER CREDENTIALS)
150/HOUR (default) **20000 PER HOUR (white-listed IP)**	**100/HOUR (default)** **20000 PER HOUR (white-listed IP)**

Figure 2-2

user's account — the request provides no authorization credentials. Figure 2-2 shows a visual cue for how rate limiting is partitioned by the API.

However, providing advanced features often requires building custom processes that mine Twitter for extra value for your application, such as a global user cache or per-user analysis of friends and followers. In those cases, it is generally best to obtain a dedicated Twitter account for your application, and apply for white-listing by visiting `http://twitter.com/help/request_whitelisting`. That way, if your features grow to the point of needing more horsepower, you have an account that does the job, while your users keep their simple, unrestricted experience.

Twitter Features

An API by definition provides an interface for you to develop applications against. Twitter's API exposes most of the features seen on the Twitter site itself, and *dogfoods* the API by using it in their own work. What you can do with an API helps shape your vision for your application — as a way to accomplish common tasks quickly, as well as as a good indicator of what feels missing and how your application could step in to fulfill that missing link. You are ready to start building applications with the Twitter API. As each feature is documented and discussed, symbols will appear representing whether the particular REST method requires user authentication ([A]), or is rate limited ([R]) by Twitter.

Statuses

Statuses, or tweets, are the most important feature of Twitter, as all functionality and appeal revolves around the ability to send status updates to interested participants. There are a number of different ways of looking at statuses through the API, but their data representation is always the same.

> ### A Quick Glossary of Twitter Status Special Characters
>
> When confined to 140 characters, people still need ways to communicate context and audience. Twitter provides a basic set of status characters that are essentially symbols that users and application developers should recognize.
>
> ❏ **Hashtags (#)**
>
> Any string of text preceded by the # character indicates a topic or channel of conversation, i.e., #haiku or #teaparty. These hashtags are searchable using the Search API, and their results are provided in near real time. This feature helps create Twitter community games, such as #followfriday, where users recommend their favorite followers to others.
>
> ❏ **Mentions (@)**
>
> You can refer to another user by screen name by preceding that user's name with the @ character. These mentions of others are picked up by the Twitter REST and Search APIs, allowing others to loosely view a conversation between two people, and for users to quickly find questions, praise, or criticism meant for them.

A Quick Glossary of Twitter Status Special Characters (*Continued*)

❑   Stock Tickers ($)

Twitter's Search API and site recognize stock symbols preceded by the $ sign. This was first popularized by StockTwits.com, and Twitter supported its use by making it easier to search in real time.

❑   **Your Application's Symbol (?)**

Because Twitter updates are plain text, you could create your own set of symbols that your application is designed to recognize and act on, helping add more value to status updates for your own use. Keep in mind that your special characters won't mean anything to other applications, so do this only when it serves a real purpose — if only to prevent alienating users of your application by requiring updates with meanings that aren't easily guessed. A Quick Glossary of Twitter Status Special Characters

---

Public Timeline

The public timeline is the raw global public stream of available tweets. The public timeline is most useful for applications that perform analysis of customer sentiment or social conscience, as opposed to applications and custom clients that assist users maximize their Twitter experience. If your goal is to search Twitter as a whole, you are likely better served by the Search API covered in Chapter 4, as opposed to shouldering the burden of text analysis on your own code and the public timeline. Still, the public timeline is a provocative stream of data that you could process and present in many interesting ways.

> **Relative Method URL:** /statuses/public_timeline.{format}
>
> **HTTP Methods:** GET
>
> **REST Formats:** XML, JSON, RSS, Atom
>
> **Optional Parameters:** None
>
> **Data Representation:** A collection of status objects (20 at a time)

Example

```
GET: http://twitter.com/statuses/public_timeline.xml
```

> **Special Considerations:** The public timeline request is cached for 60 seconds on Twitter's servers. This means attempting to pull data from this resource faster than the refresh rate is a waste of resources. Because this timeline is public, it does not include statuses for users who have elected to protect their updates from public scrutiny.

Sequencing and Pagination

Some API methods support pagination and sequencing through optional parameters. These are essential features for status timelines, as you must often present and synchronize long results of tweets in a user interface. It is important to note that methods with pagination are expensive; users with many followers or updates, for example, will require multiple calls to fulfill scenarios such as listing every follower or tweet for a given user.

Sequencing

Sequencing is supported with `since_id` and `max_id`; these parameters take the ID of the anchor status, and all tweets matching the query parameters before (`max_id`) or after (`since_id`) the given status ID are shown. If the query used has further constraints, using sequencing may result in returning less than the expected number of tweets, if any. For example, attempting to return only updates occurring after a more recent tweet (`since_id`), but asking for it on a page (`page`) well into the past, will yield no results.

Pagination

Pagination can affect both the number of statuses returned in a query, and the location of the results returned in the larger set. Pagination is controlled using `page` and `count` parameters. The page parameter is 1-based, so requests for `page=1` will return the first page of a result. If `page` and `count` are used in combination, the result returned assumes that pages not returned contain the same number as specified in `count`. For example, `page=3&count=100` would return results assuming page 1 and page 2 both had 100 results, prior to the results you would receive.

Friends Timeline [A] [R]

The friends timeline is a coalesced view of all statuses of the target user, and those users that he or she follows. This is identical to Twitter's home page when you are logged in. You are able to request the friends timeline for other users as well, provided you are authenticated. By default, the friends timeline returns the most recent 20 statuses on the timeline, and customized results are possible through the pagination and sequence parameters.

Relative Method URLs:

/statuses/friends_timeline.{format} (*for the authenticating user*)

/statuses/friends_timeline/{id/screen_name}.{format} (*for another user*)

HTTP Methods: GET

REST Formats: XML, JSON, RSS, Atom

Optional Parameters (sequencing, pagination):

`since_id , max_id, count, page`

Data Representation: A collection of status objects (20 by default, 200 maximum)

Example

`GET: http://twitter.com/statuses/friends_timeline.json?page=2&count=100`

Special Considerations: When using the friends timeline with a combination of `since_id` or `max_id` and `count`, the number of results returned applies to the *top of a result list*, without considering the direction of your tweets. For example, if you wanted to retrieve all the statuses since a given status ID, and asked for a `count` of 100 statuses in the response, the 100 statuses you received would not be in ascending order from the given status ID up to the total `count` request, but would instead derive from the very end of the entire result set, therefore making it possible to produce gaps in your results if you are not structuring your application to stitch timelines together from multiple calls using `since_id`.

Disambiguating Screen Names and IDs

It is possible to run into trouble when calling API methods assuming that users cannot choose screen names that are completely numeric. If you wanted to fetch the most recent tweets from the user Dimebrain, one documented way to do so would be to HTTP GET `http://twitter.com/statuses/user_timeline/`**Dimebrain**`.xml`

Following the same example, what if you wanted to do the same for the user "519"? `http://twitter.com/statuses/user_timeline/`**519**`.xml` would actually return the user "amanda_peters" who has the ID 519. This misfire was caused by how the URI is set up to accept either a screen name or an ID, in place of the ID parameter; presented with a numeric value, there is no way to tell if it is one or the other, and the default behavior assumes an ID.

To get around the issue without requiring an extra API call to retrieve 519's true ID, some methods provide support to pass additional parameters to the API to disambiguate between ID and name. These parameters are `user_id` and `screen_name`. When these parameters are used, the URI is modified by not passing the ID in the URI itself, but instead relying on one of these parameters.

`http://twitter.com/statuses/user_timeline/`**519**`.xml`

becomes

`http://twitter.com/statuses/user_timeline.xml?screen_name=`**519**

User Timeline [A] [R]

The friends timeline is a coalesced view of all statuses of the target user, and those users that he or she follows. This is identical to Twitter's home page when you are logged in. You are able to request a friends timeline for other users as well, provided you are authenticated. If no additional parameters are provided, the method will return the authenticating user's timeline, common for client applications where a user is logging in to see updates to which they are subscribed.

Relative Method URLs:

/statuses/user_timeline.{format} *(for the authenticating user)*

/statuses/user_timeline/{id | screen_name}.{format} *(for another user)*

HTTP Methods: GET

REST Formats: XML, JSON, RSS, Atom

Optional Parameters (disambiguation, sequencing, and pagination):

user_id, screen_name, since_id, max_id, page, count

Data Representation: A collection of status objects (20 by default, 200 maximum)

Example

```
GET: http://twitter.com/statuses/user_timeline/Dimebrain.xml
```

Special Considerations: If you are attempting to retrieve every tweet for a given user, you must use the page parameter and increment the page until you no longer receive any results. It might be useful to guess the number of pages required based on the total number of statuses posted by the user in question, but this is not a reliable number. Each call to retrieve a new page counts against your rate limit.

```
const double tweetsPerPage = 20; // can be changed using count parameter

var screenName = "Dimebrain";
var updatesCount = 821; // get this through another API call

var pages = (double)updatesCount / tweetsPerPage;
var last = (int) Math.Floor(pages); // last "full page" of tweets

var query = string.Format(
  "http://twitter.com/statuses/user_timeline.xml?screen_name={0}&page={1}",
screenName, last);

var response = query.Get(USERNAME, PASSWORD);
```

Show [A] [R]

The show method is used to retrieve a single, specific status based on the provided ID.

Relative Method URL: /statuses/show/{id}.{format}

HTTP Methods: GET

REST Formats: XML, JSON

Optional Parameters: None

Data Representation: A single status object

Example

```
GET: http://twitter.com/statuses/show/1526311087.xml
```

Special Considerations: This call only requires authentication if the author of the status you are attempting to retrieve has protected updates, though it is rate limited to the requesting IP address even if you do not use authentication, so it may suit your purposes better to authenticate regardless of the author's protection status. It is also not an efficient way to retrieve statuses, as it requires one API call per status and advance knowledge of the status ID. This method is not rate limited and requires no authentication, however, so you may find it useful as a backup strategy for API-starved applications when you already have a cache of status IDs from which to fetch.

Update [A]

Status updates are the participatory action of the Twitter API. Updates always come from an authenticated user, and are not rate limited. To facilitate threaded conversations, the in_reply_to_status_id parameter is used to indicate to which status the current update is in reference.

Relative Method URL: /statuses/update.{format}?status={status}

HTTP Methods: POST

REST Formats: XML, JSON

Optional Parameters: in_reply_to_status_id

Data Representation: A single status object for the posted update

Example

```
POST: http://twitter.com/statuses/update.xml?status=Sounds like a
plan!&in_reply_to_status_id=1526311087
```

Special Considerations: The API will not permit duplicate status updates as a way to mitigate spam, so you should ensure that updates are unique on your end before sending the request, to reduce unnecessary traffic, otherwise the API will simply return the previous duplicate status. Whenever possible, use the in_reply_to_status_id, as it provides invaluable context for displaying threaded conversations, which is a popular and expected feature for most Twitter client applications. To use in_reply_to_status_id correctly, the status update that intends to reply to the original status must mention the original message's author somewhere in the message body. If you don't mention the author, the property is ignored altogether.

Mentions [A] [R]

This feature returns statuses where the authenticated user's screen name is referenced with the "@" symbol.

Relative Method URL: /statuses/mentions.{format} *(for the authenticating user)*

HTTP Methods: GET

REST Formats: XML, JSON, RSS, Atom

Optional Parameters (sequencing and pagination):

since_id, max_id, page, count

Data Representation: A collection of status objects (20 by default, 200 maximum)

Example

GET: **http://twitter.com/statuses/mentions.xml**

Special Considerations: This method is not equivalent to the statuses that are direct public replies to the authenticated user; it is a superset of both the direct replies, and any statuses where the user is mentioned using '@.' If you only want to retrieve replies, or only statuses that start with the user reference, you can use the Search API's from operator.

The Search API is covered in Chapter 4.

Destroy [A] [R]

This method destroys a specific status by ID.

Relative Method URL: /statuses/destroy/{id}.{format} *(for authenticated user)*

HTTP Methods: POST, DELETE

REST Formats: XML, JSON

Optional Parameters: None

Data Representation: A single status representing the successfully destroyed status

Example

DELETE: **http://twitter.com/statuses/destroy/1528649353.json**

Special Considerations: Deleting a status only removes it from all timelines; it is still possible to find deleted updates through the Search API. If your application deals with sensitive information, you should take extra precautions to communicate this fact to your users. Remember that you cannot delete statuses that the authenticating user did not author.

The Search API is covered in Chapter 4.

Users

Users are the consumers of the social objects in your applications. Twitter's concept of a user is fairly sparse, following in the spirit of its design.

Friends *[A]* *[R]*

This method provides enumeration on the users the authenticated user, or the specified user, is following.

> **Relative Method URLs:**
>
> /statuses/friends.{format} *(for the authenticating user)*
>
> /statuses/friends/{id/screen_name}.{format} *(for another user)*
>
> **HTTP Methods:** GET
>
> **REST Formats:** XML, JSON
>
> **Optional Parameters (disambiguation, sequencing, pagination):**
>
> `user_id, screen_name, page`
>
> **Data Representation:** A collection of user objects (100 at a time)

Example

> GET: `http://twitter.com/statuses/friends.json?screen_name=wrox`

> **Special Considerations:** There is no way to increase the yield of friends from this method, which makes it impractical for trying to retrieve a users' complete list of friends. To accomplish this, you should use the social graphing methods combined with a global user cache, and fill that cache data with the results of this method running on your own application account. Otherwise, fetching the intended user's data first to retrieve the raw count of friends will help use only as many calls as required.

Followers *[A]* *[R]*

This method provides enumeration on the users that are following the authenticated user, or the specified user.

> **Relative Method URLs:**
>
> /statuses/followers.{format} *(for the authenticating user)*
>
> /statuses/ followers /{id/screen_name}.{format} *(for another user)*
>
> **HTTP Methods:** GET
>
> **REST Formats:** XML, JSON
>
> **Optional Parameters (disambiguation, sequencing, pagination):**
>
> `user_id, screen_name, page`
>
> **Data Representation:** A collection of user objects (100 at a time)

Example

```
GET: http://twitter.com/statuses/followers.json?id=wrox
```

Special Considerations: The same considerations for friends apply for followers. The following code might help you think about enumerating friends and followers and the number of API calls involved.

```
const double followersPerPage = 100;

string screenName = "Dimebrain";
double followersCount = 351; // get this number from another call

double pages = followersCount / followersPerPage;
int loops = (int)Math.Ceiling(pages);

for(int i = 1; i < loops; i++)
{
    string query = string.Format(
    "http://twitter.com/statuses/followers.xml?screen_name={0}&page={1}",
    screenName, i);

    Console.WriteLine(query.Get(USERNAME, PASSWORD));
}
```

Show (A) [R]

This method provides direct access to Twitter's users. It may be called without authentication, but requests for protected users will result in a user object that is missing a most recent status. Similarly, calls to protected users from authenticated accounts that are not friends with the user will also omit any statuses.

Relative Method URLs:

/users/show.{format} *(for the authenticating user)*

/users/show/{id/screen_name}.{format} *(for another user)*

HTTP Methods: GET

REST Formats: XML, JSON

Optional Parameters (disambiguation):

user_id, screen_name

Data Representation: A single user object, with or without most recent status, depending on the protected status and the user's relationship to the authenticating user

Example

```
GET: http://twitter.com/users/show/8460902.xml
```

> **Special Considerations:** Any code that deserializes Twitter's response into a class instance should account for the fact that any given user result may not contain a status, and that this could change whenever the user modifies their privacy settings.

Direct Messages [A] [R]

Direct messages are functionally equivalent to statuses, and differ in that they are intended for a private audience. The Twitter API provides you with some features for tracking messages received and sent by the authenticating user.

Calling the API method without a corresponding action will provide recent direct messages received by the authenticating user.

> **Relative Method URL:** /direct_messages.{format}
>
> **HTTP Methods:** GET
>
> **REST Formats:** XML, JSON, RSS, Atom
>
> **Optional Parameters (sequencing, pagination):**
>
> `since_id, page, count, max_id`
>
> **Data Representation:** A collection of direct message objects (20 by default, 200 maximum)

Example

```
GET: http://twitter.com/direct_messages.rss?page=2&count=50
```

Sent [A][R]

This method retrieves direct messages sent by the authenticating user.

> **Relative Method URL:** /direct_messages/sent.{format}
>
> **HTTP Methods:** GET
>
> **REST Formats:** XML, JSON
>
> **Optional Parameters (sequencing, pagination):**
>
> `since_id, page, count`
>
> **Data Representation:** A collection of statuses (20 by default, 200 maximum)

Example

```
GET: http://twitter.com/direct_messages/sent.xml
```

Special Considerations: Only `since_id` is provided, which means pagination can only occur in one direction; you may need to use `count` to achieve more results than necessary for backward traversal with minimal calls required.

New [A]

New direct messages are issued through this method. Although you can send direct messages using the statuses/update method by preceding the message text with a "D," this method provides safe access to this functionality to reduce the number of tweets sent with an "outside voice."

Relative Method URL: /direct_messages/new.{format}?user={id/screen_name}&text={text} *(for the authenticating user)*

HTTP Methods: POST

REST Formats: XML, JSON

Optional Parameters: None

Data Representation: A single direct message object successfully sent through the API

Example

```
POST: http://twitter.com/direct_messages/new.xml?user=wrox&text=Writing a book is
hard work!
```

Special Considerations: Unlike status updates, direct messages are personal and prone to being sensitive in nature for spam-conscious users; keep direct messages relevant and avoid overuse. There is no disambiguation support for direct_messages, so you will need to resolve numerically named users' true ID before sending direct messages to them.

Destroy [A] [R]

This method destroys a direct message specified by ID.

Relative Method URL: /direct_messages/destroy/{id}.{format}

HTTP Methods: POST, DELETE

REST Formats: XML, JSON

Optional Parameters: None

Data Representation: A single direct message representing the deleted direct message

Example

```
POST: http://twitter.com/direct_messages/destroy/12345.xml
```

> **Special Considerations:** Because direct messages are not searchable, deleting them here is permanent. Keep in mind that users may set up their Twitter accounts to receive direct messages by email, in which case a copy of the message is sent to the recipient immediately.

Friendships

Friendships are the web users weave around who they trust, who they're interested in hearing from, and who they want to have conversations with. Twitter is a wholly permission-based system, and friendship isn't necessarily reciprocal; you befriend who you want to hear from or "follow."

Create [A]

This method provides the ability to create a new asymmetrical friendship from the authenticated user to another user.

> **Relative Method URL:** /friendships/create/{id/screen_name}.{format}
>
> **HTTP Methods:** POST
>
> **REST Formats:** XML, JSON
>
> **Optional Parameters:** `follow=true`
>
> **Data Representation:** A single user object, befriended by the method call

Example

```
POST: http://twitter.com/friendships/create
```

> **Special Considerations:** Friendships are not the whole story for following a user's notifications on Twitter. Besides the common timeline statuses which show up when a friendship is created between the authenticating user and another user, it is also possible to follow a user's updates on a mobile device. This functionality is available from the notifications/follow method covered in the dedicated Notifications section of the API later in this chapter, as well as through the optional `follow=true` provided here, which performs both tasks simultaneously. Also, disambiguation is not supported for numerical screen names, so you will need to retrieve the user's ID before calling this method in those cases.

Destroy [A]

Friendships are cancelled using this method.

> **Relative Method URL:** /friendships/destroy/{id/screen_name}.{format}
>
> **HTTP Methods:** POST, DELETE

REST Formats: XML, JSON

Optional Parameters (disambiguation): user_id, screen_name

Data Representation: A single user object whose friendship is cancelled by the method call

Example

```
DELETE: http://twitter.com/friendships/destroy/BritneySpears.xml
```

Special Considerations: There are no side effects to this method, i.e., if a symmetrical friendship exists between two users, only the authenticated user's intent for friendship is removed during this call. The social side effects, of course, could last a lifetime.

Exists (A) [R]

This method allows you to test for the existence of friendship between two users.

Relative Method URL:
/friendships/exists.{format}?user_a={id/screen_name}&user_b={id/screen_name}

HTTP Methods: GET

REST Formats: XML, JSON

Optional Parameters: None

Data Representation: A plain text "true" or "false" indicating the result of the friendship test

Example

```
GET: http://twitter.com/friendships/exists.
xml?user_a=Dimebrain&user_b=BritneySpears
```

Special Considerations: Remember, friendships are not necessarily symmetrical, so it does not follow that if user A is a friend of user B, then user B must also be a friend of user A; if you need to verify symmetrical relationships, you need to call the inverse method.

Social Graphing

One of the recent additions to the API was added to address a specific developer issue; social graphing methods allow you to obtain a complete list of every ID for an authenticated user's friends or followers in one API call. Although that information alone is not terribly useful, it does enable global caching scenarios that let your code quickly compare "pick lists" of IDs against an internal database, and quickly determine if a user has gained or lost friends and followers — useful analytics for many Twitter business applications.

Friends (A) [R]

This method provides a complete list of IDs for the users the authenticating user follows as friends.

> **Relative Method URLs:**
>
> /friends/ids.xml *(for the authenticating user)*
>
> /friends/ids/{id/screen_name} *(for another user)*
>
> **HTTP Methods:** GET
>
> **REST Formats:** XML, JSON
>
> **Optional Parameters (disambiguation):**
>
> user_id, screen_name

Example

```
GET: http://twitter.com/friends/ids/wrox.xml
```

> **Data Representation:** A collection of numeric IDs referencing the IDs of the specified (or authenticated) user's friends.

Followers (A) [R]

This method provides a complete list of IDs of users following the authenticating user.

> **Relative Method URLs:**
>
> /followers/ids.xml *(for the authenticating user)*
>
> /followers/ids/{id/screen_name} *(for another user)*
>
> **HTTP Methods:** GET
>
> **REST Formats:** XML, JSON
>
> **Optional Parameters (disambiguation):**
>
> user_id, screen_name
>
> ```
> GET: http://twitter.com/followers/ids/wrox.xml
> ```
>
> **Data Representation:** A collection of numeric IDs referencing the IDs of the specified (or authenticated) user's followers

Account

The account feature space of the API is articulated by methods to change the settings of a user's account, just as a user would change them manually by visiting http://twitter.com and logging in. This opens up some options for your application to provide custom Twitter account "skinning," from backgrounds to profile pictures to layout colors. Account methods also include session management and rate limit querying.

Verify Credentials [A]

This method gives you an inexpensive and unlimited way to check a user's authentication credentials before moving on to true authenticated methods. This is useful for client applications during a user's initial setup, or applications that begin processing multiple requests automatically after credentials are passed in. Rather than take the hit of failing authentication, which logs against the unauthenticated rate limit and could cause side effects for authentication-optional methods, use this method instead to be sure proper credentials are supplied.

> **Relative Method URL:** /account/verify_credentials.{format}
>
> **HTTP Methods:** GET
>
> **REST Formats:** XML, JSON
>
> **Optional Parameters:** None
>
> **Data Representation:** A single user object representing the successfully authenticated user

Example

```
GET: http://twitter.com/account/verify_credentials.xml
```

End Session [A] [R]

Developing applications with background processes could rely on session state to coordinate multiple processing. This method is meant to force ending a user's authenticated session state on Twitter. Currently, Twitter does not make use of the session created on the server and terminated by this method.

> **Relative Method URL:** /account/end_session.{format}
>
> **HTTP Methods:** POST
>
> **REST Formats:** XML, JSON
>
> **Optional Parameters:** None
>
> **Data Representation:** An error message object indicating the authenticated user is logged out

Example

```
POST: http://twitter.com/end_session.xml
```

> **Special Considerations:** This method does not serve much more of a purpose than forcing users to log in to Twitter on their next page visit. Look to the future for when session state is utilized for this method to shine.

Update Delivery Device [A] [R]

This method allows specifying which user device will receive updates from users flagged for notification by the authenticating user.

Relative Method URL: /account/update_delivery_device.{format}?device={sms/none}

HTTP Methods: POST

REST Formats: XML, JSON

Optional Parameters: None

Data Representation: A single user object representing the authenticated user with updated device settings

```
POST: http://twitter.com/account/update_delivery_device.xml?device=sms
```

Special Considerations: Although the official documentation provides an additional device parameter, IM, instant messaging device updates are disabled indefinitely.

If you are looking for XMPP-style push updates for your Twitter application, check out Chapter 8.

Update Profile Colors [A] [R]

This method allows direct manipulation of a user's profile page styles on Twitter's site.

Relative Method URL: /account/update_profile_colors

HTTP Methods: POST

REST Formats: XML, JSON

Optional Parameters (profile color style info):

```
profile_background_color, profile_text_color, profile_link_color,
profile_sidebar_fill_Color, profile_sidebar_border_color
```

Data Representation: A single user object representing the authenticated user with updated profile style settings

Example

```
POST: http://twitter.com/account/update_profile_colors
.xml?profile_text_color=f3edff&profile_background_color=190e39&profile_link_color=80647A
```

Special Considerations: Do not include the customary "#" when entering colors in the style parameters. Colors are represented by their hexadecimal RGB values. A great site for finding stylish color combinations is http://www.colorhunter.com.

Update Profile Image [A] [R]

This method provides a means of updating the authenticating user's Twitter profile image displayed on their web timeline pages.

Relative Method URL: /account/update_profile_image.{format}

HTTP Methods: POST (multi-part form binary data)

REST Formats: XML, JSON

Optional Parameters: None

Data Representation: A single user object representing the authenticated user with an updated profile image

Example

```
POST: http://twitter.com/account/update_profile_image.xml
```

Special Considerations: A multi-part form post containing raw binary data of the desired image must accompany this message. You cannot supply a URL to an image hosted elsewhere.

Details on how to prepare multi-part form requests for Twitter is covered in Chapter 7.

Update Profile Background Image [A] [R]

This method provides a means of updating the authenticating user's Twitter background image displayed on their web timeline pages. If tile=true is included as a parameter, Twitter will treat the background image as a tile, and repeat it along its x and y axes.

Relative Method URL: /account/update_profile_background_image.{format}

HTTP Methods: POST (multi-part form binary data)

REST Formats: XML, JSON

Optional Parameters: tile=true

Data Representation: A single user object representing the authenticated user with an updated profile background image

Example

```
POST: http://twitter.com/account/update_profile_background_image.xml?tile=true
```

Special Considerations: A multi-part form post containing raw binary data of the desired image must accompany this message. You cannot supply a URL to an image hosted elsewhere.

Details on how to prepare multi-part form requests for Twitter is covered in Chapter 7.

Rate Limit Status (A)

Checking the rate limit for a given user is essentially determining what a user is still able to do in the given timeframe based on their levels of activity. Rate limit data is most useful in algorithms that attempt to queue and release API calls intelligently to cover the allowed usage in the allotted hour while minimizing the impact on functionality for higher priority features of your application. If authentication credentials are omitted in the request, the originating IP's API limit is reported instead.

Chapter 7 includes example code for an API call priority queue.

Relative Method URL: /account/rate_limit_status.{format}

HTTP Methods: GET

REST Formats: XML, JSON

Optional Parameters: None

Data Representation: A special rate limit object containing details of how many API calls are available in the current hour, and when the limit will refresh

Example

```
GET: http://twitter.com/account/rate_limit_status.xml
```

Special Considerations: If you do not provide credentials, the rate limit status falls back to the rate limit of the IP address your request originates from. If your API call fails due to bad credentials, you will still receive the rate limit results for the unauthenticated IP address. If you use a white-listed account and consistently receive a much lower rate limit, it is likely due to stealth authentication failures, which can be cured by following advice on `NetworkCredential` in Chapter 1. In Chapter 7's Working with Twitter Constraints, you will find an alternative method of obtaining the rate limit status by inspecting the HTTP response headers that are returned with the response for any rate limited API call you make.

Update Profile [A] [R]

This method allows you to update biographical information for the user that is displayed on their Twitter home page. This is useful for applications that work like a complete front end for Twitter, including user management profile operations.

Relative Method URL: /account/update_profile.{format} *(for the authenticating user)*

HTTP Methods: POST

REST Formats: XML, JSON

Optional Parameters (profile elements):

```
name, email, url, location, description
```

Data Representation: A single user object representing the authenticated user with updated profile parameters

Example

```
POST: http://twitter.com/account/update_profile.xml?name=Daniel
Crenna&url="http://dimebrain.com"&location="Canada"
```

Special Considerations: Although Twitter does not currently support location-aware application development, you can approximate it in your own application by updating the participating users' profile location with custom information, such as a latitude and longitude. Of course, you shouldn't do this without the user's permission.

Favorites

Favorites are a form of social voting, or "vote to promote" system. Favorites are useful as a personal bookmarking system, or they may fulfill some other user-generated purpose for notable status updates.

The friends timeline is a coalesced view of all statuses of the target user, and those users that he or she follows. This is identical to Twitter's home page when you are logged in. You are able to request the friends timeline for other users as well, provided you are authenticated.

Relative Method URLs:

/favorites.{format} *(for the authenticating user)*

/favorites/{id/screen_name}.{format} *(for another user)*

HTTP Methods: GET

REST Formats: XML, JSON, RSS, Atom

Optional Parameters (paging): page

Data Representation: A collection of favorited status objects (20 at a time) Example

GET: `http://twitter.com/favorites.xml`

Special Considerations: Favorites are generally underused by Twitter users and applications. You could incorporate them as a great community voting system or game of tag, or find another novel use for flagging users' statuses. That said, it is challenging to use favorites beyond the needs of the authenticating user, because tracking favorites in an application requires manually traversing a user's favorites and cross-referencing them with other users. It is a daunting task, for example, to attempt to find all users who selected a given status as a favorite, as that would require checking the favorites of every user in the system.

Create [A] [R]

This method adds the specified status by ID to the authenticated user's list of favorite updates.

Relative Method URL: /favorites/create/{id}.{format}

HTTP Methods: POST

REST Formats: XML, JSON

Optional Parameters: None

Data Representation: A single status object representing the favorite status addition

Example

```
POST: http://twitter.com/favorites/create/911038129.xml
```

Destroy [A] [R]

This method removes the specified status by ID to the authenticated user's list of favorite updates.

Relative Method URL: /favorites/destroy/{id}.{format}

HTTP Methods: POST, DELETE

REST Formats: XML, JSON

Optional Parameters: None

Data Representation: A single status object representing the status that fell from favor

Example

```
DELETE: http://twitter.com/favorites/destroy/1532044978.xml
```

Notifications

The /notifications methods perform a function similar to /friendships, except notifications works on existing friendships and includes the explicit subscription of updates from enabled devices over and above showing the specified user's updates on the friends timeline.

Follow [A] [R]

This method provides the ability to "follow" a user by adding them to the authenticated user's subscriptions for their updates on any enabled devices.

Relative Method URL: /notifications/follow/{id/screen_name}.{format}

HTTP Methods: POST

REST Formats: XML, JSON

Optional Parameters: None

Data Representation: A single user object representing the newly followed user

Example

```
POST: http://twitter.com/notifications/follow/Dimebrain.xml
```

Special Considerations: The authenticated user must already have a friendship with the specified user, otherwise an error is returned. You must first use /friends/create to establish a relationship prior to using this method.

Leave [A] [R]

The friends timeline is a coalesced view of all statuses of the target user, and those users that he or she follows. This is identical to Twitter's home page when you are logged in. You are able to request the friends timeline for other users as well, provided you are authenticated.

> **Relative Method URL:** /notifications/leave/{id/screen_name}.{format}
>
> **HTTP Methods:** POST
>
> **REST Formats:** XML, JSON
>
> **Optional Parameters:** None
>
> **Data Representation:** A single user object representing the newly abandoned user

Example

```
POST: http://twitter.com/notifications/leave/SocialGuru.xml
```

> **Special Considerations:** The authenticated user must already have a friendship with the specified user, otherwise an error is returned. You must first use /friends/create to establish a relationship prior to using this method.

Blocks

Not every relationship is meant to be. These methods provide a simple interface for removing users from timelines and notifications in a semi-permanent way, as shown in.

Create [A] [R]

This method creates a new block for the authenticated user.

> **Relative Method URL:** /blocks/create/{id/screen_name}.{format}
>
> **HTTP Methods:** POST
>
> **REST Formats:** XML, JSON
>
> **Optional Parameters:** None
>
> **Data Representation:** A single user object representing the user blocked by the call

Example

```
POST: http://twitter.com/blocks/create/spammersteve.xml
```

Exists [A] [R]

This method tests whether the authenticated user is currently blocking the specified user.

Relative Method URLs: /blocks/exists/{id/screen_name}.{format}

/blocks/exists.{format}?{user_id/screen_name}

HTTP Methods: POST

REST Formats: XML, JSON

Optional Parameters (disambiguation): `user_id, screen_name`

Data Representation: A single user object representing the user that is blocked by the authenticating user. If a block does not exist for the specified user on the authenticating user's account, Twitter returns an HTTP 404 error.

Example

```
GET: http://twitter.com/blocks/exists.json?screen_name=phishingfred
```

Blocking [A] [R]

This method returns the users the authenticating user is currently blocking, either in full user data representations and twenty at a time, or a complete list of IDs.

Relative Method URLs:

/blocks/blocking.{format}

/blocks/blocking/ids.{format}

HTTP Methods: GET

REST Formats: XML, JSON

Optional Parameters (paging): `page`

Data Representation: A collection of users (20 per page) if the call does not specify IDs, and a complete list of all user IDs if it is specified

Example

```
GET: http://twitter.com/blocks/blocking.json?page=3
```

Destroy [A] [R]

This method reverses a new block against a user by the authenticated user.

Relative Method URL: /blocks/destroy/{id/screen_name}.{format}

HTTP Methods: POST

REST Formats: XML, JSON

Optional Parameters: None

Data Representation: A single user representing the user unblocked by the call

Example

```
POST: http://twitter.com/blocks/destroy/relevantrita.xml
```

Special Considerations: Unblocking a user does not "re-follow" them, which would require establishing a new friend connection with friendships/create or notifications/follow.

Help

Twitter's API specifies a simple help section that currently contains a single method to test the responsiveness of the Twitter service. You can use this method as defined to help guarantee that further calls are possible for your application.

Test

This method is a heartbeat for the API itself. Use it to see whether Twitter has any planned maintenance or if the service is currently unavailable.

Relative Method URL: /help/test.{format}

HTTP Methods: GET

REST Formats: XML, JSON

Optional Parameters: None

Data Representation: A plain string "ok" if the service is active, otherwise, an error object explaining the interruption

Example

```
POST: http://twitter.com/help/test
```

Twitter Objects

Ultimately, whatever format you receive from Twitter containing the data you requested requires processing to make it useful for your application. One characteristic of REST is that representations of data do not attempt to appear as native data to the application calling the service; there is a clear seam between consumer and provider. If you are familiar with web services implemented with RPC, you are accustomed to leaning on the framework for data parsing and deserialization tasks, which are left to you when consuming a REST service. What you need after retrieving a result from Twitter, is a way to convert the response into object instances, useful for data-binding, available for LINQ queries, and otherwise first-class citizens of your application. You will learn several techniques for performing these tasks efficiently and accurately with all supported formats in Chapters 3 and 5. Now you'll gain familiarity with the data model itself, what it represents, and what the Twitter object model might look like after it takes class form in your application.

Statuses

In object terms, a Twitter status is not complicated; it follows a persistable model by providing an ID and a timestamp indicating when it was created on the server. It also provides some properties about which application was used to create it, who the intended audience or conversation thread was, as well as a reference to the user who authored the status. In the following example output, the API is used to fetch a specific status, and you can see that the user element is nested within the main status element, which gives you a hint about how you can map this nested relationship as an object with a reference to a user instance.

Example

```
GET: http://twitter.com/statuses/show/1425448269.xml
<?xml version="1.0" encoding="UTF-8"?>
<status>
  <created_at>Tue Mar 31 16:49:10 +0000 2009</created_at>
  <id>1425448269</id>
  <text>Tomorrow I begin writing my book on Twitter application development for @
wrox, exciting times ahead</text>
  <source>&lt;a href="http://www.atebits.com/software/tweetie/"&gt;Tweetie&lt;/
a&gt;</source>
  <truncated>false</truncated>
  <in_reply_to_status_id></in_reply_to_status_id>
  <in_reply_to_user_id></in_reply_to_user_id>
  <favorited>false</favorited>
  <in_reply_to_screen_name></in_reply_to_screen_name>
  <user>
    <id>11173402</id>
    <name>Daniel Crenna</name>
    <screen_name>dimebrain</screen_name>
    <location>Canada</location>
    <description>Daniel Crenna builds social software.</description>
    <profile_image_url>image.png</profile_image_url>
    <url>http://www.dimebrain.com</url>
    <protected>false</protected>
```

```
    <followers_count>310</followers_count>
    <profile_background_color>050f10</profile_background_color>
    <profile_text_color>333333</profile_text_color>
    <profile_link_color>0084B4</profile_link_color>
    <profile_sidebar_fill_color>e0e0e0</profile_sidebar_fill_color>
    <profile_sidebar_border_color>000000</profile_sidebar_border_color>
    <friends_count>229</friends_count>
    <created_at>Fri Dec 14 18:48:52 +0000 2007</created_at>
    <favourites_count>50</favourites_count>
    <utc_offset>-14400</utc_offset>
    <time_zone>Atlantic Time (Canada)</time_zone>
    <profile_background_image_url>background.png </profile_background_image_url>
    <profile_background_tile>false</profile_background_tile>
    <statuses_count>758</statuses_count>
    <notifications />
    <following />
  </user>
</status>
```

Because you know the user element will become its own object, our object model for a status in .NET is clean and compact.

How Long Is the 140-Character Limit on Twitter Messages?

It depends. You might hear that Twitter limits all statuses to 140 characters. In reality, it limits statuses to 140 bytes. The difference comes from the fact that Twitter messages are UTF-8 encoded (the Unicode character set), which opens up the possibility for multi-byte characters. One popular application of these character symbols is the site http://tinyarro.ws, which shrinks URLs using Unicode symbols. Unfortunately, these characters require 3 bytes of information to encode, and count as 3 "characters" of Twitter's status limit. Many client applications don't recognize this, and will post statuses that are longer than 140 bytes, resulting in a tweet that is truncated when it is stored by Twitter.

The elements of a status object are provided in Table 2-1. Be sure to familiarize yourself with each element and its description, as it is easy to infer behavior from the element names that may not exist, specifically those related to reply elements or the favorited element. Table 2-1 describes the elements you can expect on status representations.

Table 2-1: Twitter Status Elements

Element Name	Description
created_at	The time the status was created, in *Coordinated Universal Time (UTC)*.
id	The unique identifier for the status.
text	The message content, which appears in its URI escaped format.
source	Third-party applications, similar to the one you'll write, are able to provide information to identify them to Twitter. This element provides what application the user was using to create the status.
truncated	A Boolean value indicating whether or not the status was truncated when it was created (it was longer than 140 bytes).
in_reply_to_status_id	The ID of the status this status is in reference to, to aid with threaded conversations.
in_reply_to_user_id	The ID of the user who created the status this status replies to; this is not the same thing as mentioning a user in a status, it only applies to the referenced reply status, if any.
in_reply_to_screen_name	The screen name of the user who created the status this status replies to; this is not the same thing as mentioning a user in a status, it only applies to the referenced reply status, if any.
favorited	A Boolean value indicating whether this status appears in the authenticated user's list of favorites. This element cannot track if the status is a favorite in another user's list of favorites, or who those users are.

Users

Twitter's user representation is very similar to the status; in fact it is reversed, with the status element nested inside the user element. Sending an API call to retrieve a famous celebrity on Twitter confirms this. You can infer a classic "has-a" object relationship between the user and the status with this information.

Example

```
http://twitter.com/users/show/BritneySpears.xml
```

```xml
<?xml version="1.0" encoding="UTF-8"?>
<user>
  <id>16409683</id>
  <name>Britney Spears</name>
  <screen_name>britneyspears</screen_name>
```

```
        <location>Los Angeles, CA</location>
        <description>Yes! This is the real Britney Spears! We've got updates from her
team, her website and yes, even Britney herself!</description>
        <profile_image_url>image.png</profile_image_url>
        <url>http://www.britneyspears.com</url>
        <protected>false</protected>
        <followers_count>938533</followers_count>
        <profile_background_color>0099B9</profile_background_color>
        <profile_text_color>3C3940</profile_text_color>
        <profile_link_color>0099B9</profile_link_color>
        <profile_sidebar_fill_color>95E8EC</profile_sidebar_fill_color>
        <profile_sidebar_border_color>5ED4DC</profile_sidebar_border_color>
        <friends_count>77545</friends_count>
        <created_at>Mon Sep 22 20:47:35 +0000 2008</created_at>
        <favourites_count>0</favourites_count>
        <utc_offset>-28800</utc_offset>
        <time_zone>Pacific Time (US &amp; Canada)</time_zone>
        <profile_background_image_url>background.png</profile_background_image_url>
        <profile_background_tile>false</profile_background_tile>
        <statuses_count>117</statuses_count>
        <notifications>false</notifications>
        <following>false</following>
        <status>
            <created_at>Thu Apr 16 19:17:30 +0000 2009</created_at>
            <id>1535996874</id>
            <text>Congratulations to @marypascoe on winning the first pair of tickets to
Britney&#8217;s LA show tonight.  Who will be next? -Adam Leber (Manager)</text>
            <source>web</source>
            <truncated>false</truncated>
            <in_reply_to_status_id></in_reply_to_status_id>
            <in_reply_to_user_id></in_reply_to_user_id>
            <favorited>false</favorited>
            <in_reply_to_screen_name></in_reply_to_screen_name>
        </status>
</user>
```

You can now picture the Twitter object model as a relationship between users and statuses.

There are a fair number of elements to make up a Twitter user, as detailed profile elements are returned for every representation; this is to aid developers who want to work with the user's own preferences to tune their application appearance. You may benefit from adopting a fairly lazy persistence strategy here, as user profile information can change often, and is available on most API calls with users. Caching stale information could get in your way. Table 2-2 provides the description of each user data element.

Table 2-2: Twitter User Elements

Element Name	Description
created_at	The time the user was created, in Coordinated Universal Time (UTC).
id	The unique identifier for the user.
name	The user's name; this is meant to function as a "real name" for the user's account, which is not visible as part of the URL.
screen_name	The user's screen name; also the name of the Twitter account referenced in a user's page URL. A user is able to change this value at any time, so it is not a reliable indicator of user identity.
location	The location of the user, in free form text. The location is searched during Search API and calls for rough geo-location approximation, but there is no support for geo-location in the API. This is not a validated field.
description	Also referred to as the "bio" field on Twitter's site, this is a 160-character field for a user's biographical information, or other descriptive text.
url	This could be the user's company site, blog, or another URL.
protected	A user has the option of protecting their status updates from people they have not authorized. This means their statuses do not appear in the public timeline and are unavailable during API calls, i.e., if you attempt to retrieve the user object for a protected user, the call will succeed but the user object will not contain a nested status. This Boolean field indicates whether the user protects their updates.
followers_count	How many followers the user currently attracts.
friends_count	This is the number of people this user has subscribed to, to receive their status updates on the friends timeline.
favourites_count	Watch the spelling on this one, as it is not due to localization. This is the number of statuses the specified user has favorited.
statuses_count	The number of status updates a user has made in total. This number reduces when a user deletes statuses.
utc_offset	This is the offset, in seconds, between the user's registered time zone and UTC time.
time_zone	The user's registered timeline. This element is only available for updates on Twitter's site, and not through the API.
notifications	This Boolean field is set to true if the authenticated user is receiving notifications from the user in the representation. This is set to false if the API call was unauthenticated.

Element Name	Description
following	This Boolean field is set to true if the authenticated user is following the user in the representation. This is set to false if the API call was unauthenticated.
profile_image_url	This is the URL to the user's profile image on Twitter's static file servers.
profile_background_image_url	This is the URL to the user's background image on Twitter's static file servers.
profile_background_color	This is a hex string representation of the user's profile background color.
profile_text_color	This a hex string representation of the user's profile foreground text color.
profile_link_color	This a hex string representation of the user's profile anchor link color.
profile_sidebar_fill_color	This a hex string representation of the user's profile sidebar background color.
profile_sidebar_border_color	This a hex string representation of the user's profile border color.

It's worth remembering that if a user has decided to protect their updates, and the user your code is executing for is not authorized to see those updates, the data representation will not include a status. In an object model, this means you should take care not to assume that a `TwitterUser` instance's `Status` property will contain a value.

Direct Messages

Direct messages are structurally similar to statuses, but include additional context, such as the sender and recipient of the message, who appear as nested user objects. This context is integral, as direct message text doesn't need to contain user references, and the API method call to send them specifies the recipient in URL parameters.

Example

```
POST: http://twitter.com/direct_messages/new.xml?user=Dimebrain&text=I love your book!
<?xml version="1.0" encoding="UTF-8"?>
<direct_message>
<id>86818523</id>
<sender_id>28865870</sender_id>
<text>I love your book!</text>
<recipient_id>11173402</recipient_id>
<created_at>Mon Apr 06 01:43:36 +0000 2009</created_at>
<sender_screen_name>prodevbook</sender_screen_name>
```

```
<recipient_screen_name>dimebrain</recipient_screen_name>
<sender>
  <id>28865870</id>
  <name>prodevbook</name>
  <screen_name>prodevbook</screen_name>
  <...>
</sender>
<recipient>
  <id>11173402</id>
  <name>Daniel Crenna</name>
  <screen_name>dimebrain</screen_name>
  <...>
</recipient>
</direct_message>
```

The user information in the previous example is abbreviated, but both `sender` and `recipient` nested elements contain all the user elements you constructed for the `TwitterUser` class. The relationship between all three is definable in your object model, which is starting to take shape.

The elements that make up a direct message are simple and informative, relating to the parties involved and the message content. Table 2-3 describes the elements provided within a direct message node.

Table 2-3: Twitter Direct Message Elements

Element Name	Description
created_at	The time the direct message was created, in Coordinated Universal Time (UTC).
id	The unique identifier for the direct message.
text	The direct message content; similar to statuses, this will reach you as URL escaped text.
recipient_id	The ID of the user that received the direct message.
recipient_screen_name	The ID of the user that received the direct message.
recipient	A complete user object representing the user that received the direct message.
sender_id	The ID of the user who sent the direct message.
sender_screen_name	The screen name of the user who sent the direct message.
sender	A complete user object representing the user that sent the direct message.

Rate Limit Status

The API call that provides an authenticated user's current Twitter service usage returns a custom object with a few elements that will help you determine when to send API calls on your user's behalf. You will work with this object in Chapter 7.

Example

```
GET: http://twitter.com/account/rate_limit_status.xml
<?xml version="1.0" encoding="UTF-8"?>
<hash>
  <reset-time-in-seconds type="integer">1239976922</reset-time-in-seconds>
  <remaining-hits type="integer">100</remaining-hits>
  <hourly-limit type="integer">100</hourly-limit>
  <reset-time type="datetime">2009-04-17T14:02:02+00:00</reset-time>
</hash>
```

The rate limit object is a little different than other returned representations as it is placed in a hash element, rather than its own object. Containing value types exclusively, this object is a good candidate to work as a `struct` in your object model.

You should be aware that the rate limit status object does not include the time the limit was tested, or the user or IP address it applies to, so it is most safely used as a non-persisted, periodic check when you know the context of the result. Table 2-4 describes the elements for a rate limit representation in detail.

Table 2-4: Twitter Rate Limit Status Elements

Element Name	Description
reset-time	The date and time when the user or IP's rate is set to restore. The format for this element is a custom Twitter timestamp, which you will learn about in the next section.
reset-time-in-seconds	The UNIX epoch time the user or IP's rate is set to restore. This is not the number of seconds until the rate will restore, it is equivalent to the value of reset-time.
hourly-limit	This is how many API calls the user or IP may make in an hour of activity.
remaining-hits	This is how many API calls a user or IP address has left in the current hour. This number is based on a rolling 60-minute window, rather than resetting at the beginning of an hour.

Errors

The data that Twitter returns when something goes wrong is short and sweet, containing the URI resource producing the error, and an informational message explaining what went wrong. The following is a representative example for the output when calling any authenticated API method with incorrect credentials.

```
<?xml version="1.0" encoding="UTF-8"?>
<hash>
   <request>/account/verify_credentials.xml</request>
   <error>Could not authenticate you.</error>
</hash>
```

Table 2-5 provides a description of the elements found in an error hash.

Table 2-5: Twitter Error Elements

Element Name	Description
request	The request URI you called that resulted in an error.
error	A description of the error as reported by Twitter.

Although the error data is useful for logging, it does not provide a safe way for you to provide your own messages in your application's UI, other than attempting to parse the error element. If the error message changes over time, your application could miss errors, producing unexpected results.

Working with the API

You now possess a comprehensive account of the API methods available to you, the data they return, and some considerations for their limits. With that, you are ready to look closer at the API, practice using it, and learn a few finer points.

Twitter's `DateTime` Format

Unfortunately, how Twitter represents a timestamp is different, depending on whether you're looking at a REST API representation, a Search API representation, or requested rate limit details. Fortunately, conversion in .NET is possible using custom formatting expressions. The following code will help you convert any Twitter date element into a `DateTime` instance.

REST API

These dates appear in the returned objects' `create_at` element.

```
const string input = "Fri Dec 14 18:48:52 +0000 2007";

const string format = "ddd MMM dd HH:mm:ss zzzzz yyyy";
var date = DateTime.ParseExact(input, format, CultureInfo.InvariantCulture,
DateTimeStyles.AdjustToUniversal);

Console.WriteLine(date);
```
```
14/12/2007 6:48:52 PM
```

Search API

These dates appear in the returned search statuses' `created_at` element.

```
const string input = "Tue, 13 Jan 2009 18:10:17 +0000";

const string format = "ddd, dd MMM yyyy HH:mm:ss zzzzz";
var date = DateTime.ParseExact(input, format, CultureInfo.InvariantCulture,
DateTimeStyles.AdjustToUniversal);

Console.WriteLine(date);
13/01/2009 6:10:17 PM
```

Rate Limit Status

These dates appear in the `reset_time` field when calling the `account/rate_limit_status` method.

```
const string input = "2009-04-17T14:02:02+00:00";

const string format = "yyyy-MM-ddTHH:mm:sszzzzzzz";
var date = DateTime.ParseExact(input, format, CultureInfo.InvariantCulture,
DateTimeStyles.AdjustToUniversal);

Console.WriteLine(date);
```

17/04/2009 2:02:02 PM The date is also represented in the `reset_time_in_seconds`, as the number of seconds since precisely midnight on January 1, 1970 (this is also known as *Unix Epoch Time*). When converted to a `DateTime` instance, it should match the `reset_time` field exactly.

```
const long input = 1239976922;

var date = new DateTime(1970, 1, 1);
date = date.AddSeconds(input);

Console.WriteLine(date);
17/04/2009 2:02:02 PM
```

Configuring a Custom Application Source

One of the marketing tools available to Twitter application developers is the ability to identify your applications to the world whenever a user sends a public message using one of them. To take advantage of this feature today, you must use OAuth authentication, as discussed in Chapter 6. In the past, application developers using Basic authentication applied directly to Twitter to procure a custom identity; those with compelling reasons for not adopting OAuth may contact Twitter directly to request this feature.

Source Parameter and User Agent

Application identity is provided in the status object representations in the form of the `source` element covered earlier. This element takes the form of an HTML link to a URL of your choice, which is usually the page you want existing and potential new users to go to learn about or download your application. The details you provide when you configure your application to use OAuth authentication are what appear in the `source` element when users use your application. Figure 2-3 shows the identity of your application as defined on a custom Twitter application's settings page.

Figure 2-3

Another way of identifying your application, though not as glamorous as `source`, is the "User-Agent" header. This header is found on both `WebClient` and `HttpWebRequest` instances' header collections, as it is part of the HTML 1.1 specification. Setting this header's value to the name of your application will help Twitter analyze your search traffic, in case your application is popular enough to need white listing with the Search API. You'll learn more about the Search API in Chapter 4.

Optional Headers

You may optionally provide specialized Twitter headers when sending a request to the API. Although these headers are not currently used to identify your application, they may serve a purpose in the future. If you want to provide as much information as possible to Twitter when your application executes, add these headers to your `HttpWebRequest` or `WebClient`. Table 2-6 shows the proper header names and their expected values.

Table 2-6: Twitter Client Request Headers

HTTP Header	Description
X-Twitter-Client	The name of your Twitter application.
X-Twitter-URL	The URL to your application's web site.
X-Twitter-Version	The calling version of your application.

These headers are not officially used to designate your application; instead, the source parameter sent with your request for REST API calls, and the request's user agent for Search API calls, are used to identify your application to these services.

Handling Errors

Perhaps the most famous visual depiction of Twitter, the *fail whale* that is displayed when something goes wrong on Twitter's side is the best indication that an API call that is met with an error is directly tied to the service's availability. The error image is shown in Figure 2-4.

Figure 2-4

When you don't get the result you want, Twitter is usually trying to do more than throw up its hands and give up. In Chapter 1, you learned how to get between an `HttpWebException` and capture the response data representing the error. Now you have the ability to discover the various ways Twitter can fail, either due to a malformed request, missing authentication, or service interruption. Unfortunately, because errors are returned as simple XML hashes containing the failing API request and a descriptive message, it is too risky to create strongly typed `Exception` classes in place of every possible error, because any change to the description of the problem would break your code. However, you can get a sense of the REST-based error code returned in the HTTP response to know how to respond to your users in the event of a problem. Table 2-7 provides a breakdown of the error response codes returned by Twitter; use these to branch your code based on possible error states.

Table 2-7: Twitter Errors

HTTP Response Code	Description
200 (OK)	This result indicates a successful API call. If it is a GET, the results were retrieved as expected. If it was a POST, the underlying state of the server successfully changed to suit the method.
304 (Not Modified)	This result indicates that the API call would explicitly return no results. Typically this occurs when you send a request with a since_id parameter, and no entities (statuses or direct messages) with a higher status currently exist.
400 (Bad Request)	This result occurs when the IP address or User account (when credentials are provided) is past its rate limit. You can continue to use account/rate_limit_status to determine when API usage will restore, or switch from IP to User limiting, or vice versa.
401 (Not Authorized)	This error occurs when the credentials provided, either via Basic or OAuth authorization, are incorrect for the given user.
403 (Forbidden)	This result is reserved for when Twitter receives an API call that it refuses to fulfill. Examples of this error occurring include attempting to remove a friendship that doesn't exist, or create a friendship that already exists.
404 (Not Found)	When a resource request is well-formed, but the resource specified doesn't exist, this error is returned. Typically this will occur when requesting the user profile of a user that doesn't exist, or attempting to pull a status or direct message that was previously deleted.
406 (Not Acceptable)	This request occurs when you attempt to retrieve a representation from an API, citing an unsupported format for that method.
500 (Internal Server Error)	This result occurs when your API call results in a server error. These are atypical and indicate a problem on Twitter's side.
502 (Bad Gateway)	Service interruptions, scheduled or natural, are indicated with this error status. This is the error message that will return in the event of a *fail whale* due to over capacity.
503 (Service Unavailable)	This result occurs when Twitter is over capacity (i.e., *fail whale is presented to the user*).

http://apiwiki.twitter.com/HTTP-Response-Codes-and-Errors

Requesting Data from Twitter

Now that you have a complete picture of how to use .NET to consume RESTful web services, and how the Twitter API is arranged, where and when should you call the API to retrieve data? Your Twitter application might be an ASP.NET Web Forms or MVC web project, a Silverlight rich client, a WPF smart client, or even a simple console application. Depending on the scenario, you will have different requirements, and restrictions, on how you make calls against the Twitter API, or any RESTful service over HTTP.

The code you have worked with so far is suitable for any application running .NET in full trust. You can make `HttpWebRequests` freely in your desktop applications or web applications in full trust. If you are developing for a shared web hosting environment, which are frequently configured for medium trust, you will need to add the Twitter domain in your medium trust `WebPermission` policy, or request its addition from your hosting provider; additional information on this task is available in the excerpt *Using the WebPermission Setting in ASP.NET Partial Trust* by Stefan Schakow (`http://www.wrox.com/WileyCDA/Section/Using-the-WebPermission-Setting-in-ASP-NET-Partial-Trust.id-291738.html`).

Web Requests on the Client Side

Calling the Twitter API directly from browser-based applications using jQuery (or another JavaScript framework) or the Silverlight networking stack in your ASP.NET application is a trickier situation. Any code that executes in a web browser must follow the browser security model. This means that service calls originating from a browser application may only call the same domain that the application itself is served from; this excludes all third-party web services such as Twitter.

Things aren't so restricted in the rich world of Silverlight and Flash-based sites. These rich plugins have access to a stronger networking stack, and provided the domain gives explicit permission to do so, it is possible to make cross-domain calls in Silverlight. Servers give permission for cross-domain calls by publishing a policy file. Silverlight publishes a `clientaccesspolicy.xml` to allow Silverlight clients full access to the remote site; if this file isn't available, it can also use Flash's `crossdomain.xml` file, provided that the site serving the `crossdomain.xml` policy file allows access from all remote sites, not just the application you're building.

Unfortunately, if you navigate to Twitter's policy for Flash-based applications, you will see that only internal Twitter sites are granted cross-domain access. The file is described in the following code.

Example

```
http://twitter.com/crossdomain.xml

<cross-domain-policy xsi:noNamespaceSchemaLocation="http://www.adobe.com/xml/
schemas/PolicyFile.xsd">
<allow-access-from domain="twitter.com"/>
<allow-access-from domain="api.twitter.com"/>
<allow-access-from domain="search.twitter.com"/>
<allow-access-from domain="static.twitter.com"/>
<site-control permitted-cross-domain-policies="master-only"/>
<allow-http-request-headers-from domain="*.twitter.com" headers="*" secure="true"/>
</cross-domain-policy>
```

In Chapter 3, you will see an example of client-side script execution using JSONP and Silverlight, and you could use jQuery to make JSONP calls to the Twitter API as well, but both of these methods are limited in their capacity by browser security, at least without an application proxy. In short, you may only make calls to the API that use the HTTP GET verb in a browser and those methods you wish to use with Basic authentication must specify the credentials *inside the URL itself*. This is not a secure way to share credentials, as they are sent as plain text. You are recommended to use a proxy between your application and Twitter, whether that's a WCF service set up on your own server or an Azure-hosted proxy, to consume Twitter data. You will work with proxies in the Extended Topics section of this book, making their use second nature in your Twitter development.

Summary

This is a chapter that you may need to review often to keep yourself aware of what methods are available for your Twitter applications. Make sure to visit the book's web site, as the Twitter team's agile development practices could result in frequent updates to the API, and you'll want to get the latest changes to this chapter to stay up to date. Here is a brief overview of the core concepts you learned in this chapter:

❏ The Twitter API is a RESTful service that provides methods to work with the core resources of the Twitter service: statuses, users, direct messages, friendships, user accounts, favorites, message notifications, and community management.

❏ You understand Twitter's rate limiting structure, authentication requirements, and what is required to work with timed data, errors, and client-side restrictions.

❏ You have a comprehensive list of all Twitter's methods, what representation formats they support, the data they return and any additional information to consider when building an application that utilizes those methods. You also have a practice application to help you learn the API and use the utility code covered in Chapter 1.

❏ You have an idea of what Twitter's data representations would look like as .NET objects so that you could work with them in your application after they are converted from your target format.

Now you are ready to learn how to work with the data Twitter returns in each of the API methods, to bring that data into your application in a way that you are most familiar: as .NET classes. To do that, you need to know your options for parsing XML and JSON data on the server side. You will also learn how to use Twitter's undocumented JSONP support to respond to callbacks on the client side, without an application proxy.

3

Working with XML, JSON, and JSONP

"*Twitter is a succinct concept so its API is small and compact. That makes it very approachable by a broad range of developers. A weekend hobbyist can easily tinker around with it and have something up and running in a few hours while a professional can use the API's simplicity as a building block to create interesting variations and extensions of the service.*"

Lee Brenner, *blu*

In this chapter you get productive using multiple methods in .NET for parsing XML and JSON responses from the Twitter API. Depending on your project and environment, you may need to choose one of these methods over another. You also learn how to utilize Twitter's support for JSONP callbacks on the client-side, enabling interesting read-access scenarios for Twitter widgets in both Silverlight and JQuery. The ability to move data from Twitter API's representative formats to class instances you built in Chapter 2 will help you get your applications up and running quickly and in familiar territory.

Working with XML Responses

XML is a ubiquitous language for web communication. Following that reputation, there are many ways to consume XML data supported by the .NET Framework. You may have a preference for the method you choose, but the end result is always the same, taking the representational XML retrieved from Twitter and converting into convenience classes you can use to program your applications against.

Using LINQ to XML

LINQ to XML was introduced with C# 3.0 and the .NET Framework 3.5. It allows you to work with XML documents as if they were classes, walking the XML graph by calling extension methods on its elements. The advantage of this approach is that all XML processing occurs directly in calling code, which does not require decorating your target classes with unnecessary attributes, promoting a Plain Old CLR Objects (POCO) design where developers need only define objects as properties and behavior rather than providing additional context such as how and where to persist instances of the object.

To use LINQ to XML, you first need to convert an XML string or file into an XDocument instance, which provides the starting point for calling extension methods on the XML graph.

```
// load from a file
XDocument document = XDocument.Load("user.xml");

// load from a string
string response = "<?xml version=\"1.0\" encoding=\"UTF-8\"?>...";
XDocument document = XDocument.Load(new StringReader(response));
```

Now you are free to look up element nodes in the XDocument on the successfully loaded instance. In this case, you need to obtain the root element node for the response representing a Twitter user.

```
// find the 'user' element in the XML document
XElement user = document.Element("user");
if(user == null)
{
    // handle that this XML document has no 'user' element
}
```

If an XElement is not found to match the string provided, it returns null, which you should anticipate in your own code; because you know that making a web request to Twitter could return the results you expect but it could also return an error, testing for the case of a null element is a simple and effective way to work with conversion exceptions higher up in your code. The XElement class contains a Value property, which returns the inner text of the XML element it represents, which means the value is always a string rather than a typed object.

```
XElement user = document.Element("user");
string screenName = user.Element("screen_name").Value;
```

Because LINQ to XML returns null rather than raise exceptions when it can't find the nodes you specify, it is helpful to write a bit of code to get between the element and your declaration, so you can deal with empty strings rather than null objects and guarantee that your calls always return a string value you can work with.

```
private static string GetElementValue(XContainer parent, XName child)
{
    // ensure a search for a element always returns a string value
    var element = parent.Element(child);
    return element == null ? string.Empty : element.Value;
}
```

One disadvantage of using LINQ to XML is that because all parsing occurs explicitly, code can run long when parsing multiple elements. In addition, because you are working exclusively with text data, you need code in place to convert strings to various types. In this case, a few helper methods for int, long, and bool to accompany extension methods for Twitter date conversion are sufficient for Twitter's object model needs. In these examples, the TryParse pattern is used to avoid catching exceptions on bad input values.

```
private static bool ToBoolean(string value)
{
    if (string.IsNullOrEmpty(value))
    {
        return false;
    }

    // Twitter sometimes returns 0 when it means "true"; it's a bug
    if(value.Equals("0"))
    {
        return true;
    }

    bool result;
    return bool.TryParse(value, out result) ? result : false;
}

private static int ToInt32(string value)
{
    if(string.IsNullOrEmpty(value))
    {
        return 0;
    }

    int result;
    return int.TryParse(value, out result) ? result : 0;
}

private static long ToInt64(string value)
{
    if (string.IsNullOrEmpty(value))
    {
        return 0;
    }

    long result;
    return long.TryParse(value, out result) ? result : 0;
}
```

Now you can safely provide default values for string you need to convert to int, long, and bool data types. Here are the extension methods you will re-use to convert from Twitter's API dates to DateTime instances.

```
using System;
using System.Globalization;

namespace Wrox.Twitter.Objects
{
    public static class TwitterExtensions
    {
        public const string RestDateFormat =
            "ddd MMM dd HH:mm:ss zzzzz yyyy";

        public const string SearchDateFormat =
            "ddd, dd MMM yyyy HH:mm:ss zzzzz";

        public static DateTime FromRestDate(this string input)
        {
            return ConvertDate(input, REST_DATE_FORMAT);
        }

        public static DateTime FromSearchDate(this string input)
        {
            return ConvertDate(input, SEARCH_DATE_FORMAT);
        }

        private static DateTime ConvertDate(string input, string format)
        {
            DateTime date = DateTime.ParseExact(input,
                                                format,
                                                CultureInfo.InvariantCulture,
                                                DateTimeStyles.AdjustToUniversal);
            return date;
        }
    }
}
```

Finally, you can write a method that takes the more generic XContainer representing an arbitrary block of XML containing multiple elements, and parse each of the known Twitter user elements from a root user node with the following code.

```
private static TwitterUser AsUser(XContainer document, string name)
{
    var user = document.Element(name);
    if(user == null)
    {
        return null;
    }

    // user elements
    var createdDate = GetElementValue(user, "created_at");
    var id = GetElementValue(user, "id");
    var screenName = GetElementValue(user, "screen_name");
    var location = GetElementValue(user, "location");
    var description = GetElementValue(user, "description");
    var url = GetElementValue(user, "url");
    var friendsCount = GetElementValue(user, "friends_count");
```

```
var followersCount = GetElementValue(user, "followers_count");
var favoritesCount = GetElementValue(user, "favourites_count");
var statusesCount = GetElementValue(user, "statuses_count");
var isProtected = GetElementValue(user, "protected");
var utcOffset = GetElementValue(user, "utc_offset");
var timeZone = GetElementValue(user, "time_zone");
var hasNotifications = GetElementValue(user, "notifications");
var isFollowing = GetElementValue(user, "following");

// profile elements
var imageUrl = GetElementValue(user, "profile_image_url");
var backgroundColor = GetElementValue(user, "profile_background_color");
var backgroundImageUrl = GetElementValue(user, "profile_background_image_url");
var linkColor = GetElementValue(user, "profile_link_color");
var textColor = GetElementValue(user, "profile_text_color");
var sidebarFillColor = GetElementValue(user, "profile_sidebar_fill_color");
var sidebarBorderColor = GetElementValue(user, "profile_sidebar_border_color");
var backgroundTile = GetElementValue(user, "profile_background_tile");

return new TwitterUser
{
    CreatedDate = createdDate.FromRestDate(),
    Id = Convert.ToInt32(id),
    Name = screenName,
    Location = location,
    Description = description,
    Url = url,
    FriendsCount = ToInt32(friendsCount),
    FollowersCount = ToInt32(followersCount),
    FavoritesCount = ToInt32(favoritesCount),
    StatusesCount = ToInt32(statusesCount),
    IsProtected = ToBoolean(isProtected),
    UtcOffset = utcOffset,
    TimeZone = timeZone,
    HasNotifications = ToBoolean(hasNotifications),
    IsFollowing = ToBoolean(isFollowing),
    ProfileImageUrl = imageUrl,
    ProfileBackgroundColor = backgroundColor,
    ProfileBackgroundImageUrl = backgroundImageUrl,
    ProfileLinkColor = linkColor,
    ProfileTextColor = textColor,
    ProfileSidebarBorderColor = sidebarBorderColor,
    ProfileSidebarFillColor = sidebarFillColor,
    IsProfileBackgroundTiled = ToBoolean(backgroundTile),
    Status = AsStatus(user, "status")
};
}
```

One of the relationships you already know about is the nested representations provided for users and statuses; a user representation contains a nested status, and a status representation contains a nested user. In the previous code listing, you are calling the AsStatus method and passing in the name of the XML element you expect to contain the block of XML representing the user's latest status update.

```csharp
private static TwitterStatus AsStatus(XContainer document, string name)
{
    var status = document.Element(name);
    if (status == null)
    {
        return null;
    }

    var createdDate = GetElementValue(status, "created_at");
    var id = GetElementValue(status, "id");
    var text = GetElementValue(status, "text");
    var source = GetElementValue(status, "source");
    var isTruncated = GetElementValue(status, "truncated");
    var inReplyToStatusId = GetElementValue(status, "in_reply_to_status_id");
    var inReplyToUserId = GetElementValue(status, "in_reply_to_user_id");
    var inReplyToScreenName = GetElementValue(status, "in_reply_to_screen_name");
    var isFavorited = GetElementValue(status, "favorited");

    return new TwitterStatus
    {
        CreatedDate = createdDate.FromRestDate(),
        Id = ToInt32(id),
        Text = text,
        Source = Uri.UnescapeDataString(source),
        IsTruncated = ToBoolean(isTruncated),
        IsFavorited = ToBoolean(isFavorited),
        InReplyToStatusId = ToInt64(inReplyToStatusId),
        InReplyToUserId = ToInt32(inReplyToUserId),
        InReplyToScreenName = inReplyToScreenName,
        User = AsUser(status, "user")
    };
}
```

Because you structured your conversion methods well, the previous code that converts the nested user inside the status element is reusing the same code listed previously. You can reuse the code even further in your conversion method for direct messages, directing the user conversions to the nested sender and recipient elements, shown next.

```csharp
private static TwitterDirectMessage AsDirectMessage(XContainer message)
{
    var createdDate = GetElementValue(message, "created_at");
    var id = GetElementValue(message, "id");
    var text = GetElementValue(message, "text");

    var recipientId = GetElementValue(message, "recipient_id");
    var recipientScreenName = GetElementValue(message, "recipient_screen_name");
    var senderId = GetElementValue(message, "sender_id");
    var senderScreenName = GetElementValue(message, "sender_screen_name");

    return new TwitterDirectMessage
    {
        CreatedDate = createdDate.FromRestDate(),
        Id = ToInt64(id),
        Text = text,
```

```
            RecipientId = ToInt64(recipientId),
            RecipientScreenName = recipientScreenName,
            Recipient = AsUser(message, "recipient"),
            SenderId = ToInt64(senderId),
            SenderScreenName = senderScreenName,
            Sender = AsUser(message, "sender")
        };
    }
```

For now, when building a Twitter objects converter for XML, you can simply return null in this case, to function similar to C#'s as keyword. Here is the code you need to handle conversion of collections, rather than single objects, for API calls that return groups of objects.

```
    private static IEnumerable<TwitterStatus> AsStatuses(XContainer document, string
    name)
    {
        var collection = document.Element("statuses");
        if (collection == null)
        {
            yield break;
        }

        var statuses = collection.Elements("status");
        if (statuses == null || statuses.Count() == 0)
        {
            yield break;
        }

        foreach (var status in statuses)
        {
            yield return AsStatus(status, "status");
        }
    }

    private static IEnumerable<TwitterStatus> AsUsers(XContainer document, string name)
    {
        var collection = document.Element("users");
        if (collection == null)
        {
            yield break;
        }

        var users = collection.Elements("user");
        if (users == null || users.Count() == 0)
        {
            yield break;
        }

        foreach (var user in users)
        {
            yield return AsStatus(user, "user");
        }
    }
```

```
private static IEnumerable<TwitterDirectMessage> AsDirectMessages(
        XContainer document)
{
    var collection = document.Element("direct-messages");
    if (collection == null)
    {
        yield break;
    }

    var messages =
        collection.Elements("direct_message");
    if (messages == null || messages.Count() == 0)
    {
        yield break;
    }

    foreach (var message in messages)
    {
        yield return AsDirectMessage(message);
    }
}
```

If you're coming from a long history of handling serialization with XML in .NET, you may find that LINQ to XML offers a striking simplicity and power when transforming XML representations from the Twitter API. If you are in an environment that cannot support LINQ, or are interested in rounding out your knowledge of .NET's XML support, you can continue to the next section to learn a more mature, though less rich, XML serialization strategy in the .NET Framework.

Using XML Attributes and XmlSerializer

Prior to the introduction of LINQ to XML, the most common way of converting XML into objects was through the use of XmlSerializer and attribute decorations on a class. This method has the advantage of automating more of the serialization process, but also requires modifications to your C# classes to provide meta-data around the names and types of properties to handle special cases with XML representations you didn't create with an XML Schema Definition (XSD), which is the case when consuming Twitter data. The following code shows the TwitterUser class annotated with XML attributes.

```
using System;
using System.Xml.Serialization;

namespace Wrox.Twitter.XmlWithXmlSerializer.Objects
{
    [XmlType(TypeName = "user")]
    public class TwitterUser
    {
        [XmlElement("id")]
        public int Id { get; set; }
```

```csharp
[XmlElement("followers_count")]
public int FollowersCount { get; set; }

[XmlElement("name")]
public string Name { get; set; }

[XmlElement("description")]
public string Description { get; set; }

[XmlElement("profile_image_url")]
public string ProfileImageUrl { get; set; }

[XmlElement("url")]
public string Url { get; set; }

[XmlElement("protected")]
public bool IsProtected { get; set; }

[XmlElement("screen_name")]
public string ScreenName { get; set; }

[XmlElement("location")]
public string Location { get; set; }

[XmlElement("status")]
public TwitterStatus Status { get; set; }

[XmlElement("friends_count")]
public int FriendsCount { get; set; }

[XmlElement("profile_background_color")]
public string ProfileBackgroundColor { get; set; }

[XmlElement("utc_offset")]
public string UtcOffset { get; set; }

[XmlElement("profile_text_color")]
public string ProfileTextColor { get; set; }

[XmlElement("profile_background_image_url")]
public string ProfileBackgroundImageUrl { get; set; }

[XmlElement("time_zone")]
public string TimeZone { get; set; }

[XmlElement("favourites_count")]
public int FavouritesCount { get; set; }

[XmlElement("profile_link_color")]
public string ProfileLinkColor { get; set; }

[XmlElement("statuses_count")]
public int StatusesCount { get; set; }
```

```
        [XmlElement("profile_sidebar_fill_color")]
        public string ProfileSidebarFillColor { get; set; }

        [XmlElement("profile_sidebar_border_color")]
        public string ProfileSidebarBorderColor { get; set; }

        [XmlElement("profile_background_tiled")]
        public bool IsProfileBackgroundTiled { get; set; }

        // Twitter returns empty elements, requiring nullable values here
        [XmlElement("notifications", IsNullable = true)]
        public bool? HasNotifications { get; set; }

        // Twitter returns empty elements, requiring nullable values here
        [XmlElement("following", IsNullable = true)]
        public bool? IsFollowing { get; set; }

        [XmlElement("created_at")]
        public DateTime CreatedDate { get; set; }
    }
}
```

After declaring the XML attributes for this class, deserialization is run using the following code.

```
using System;
using System.IO;
using System.Xml.Serialization;
using Wrox.Twitter.XmlWithXmlSerializer.Objects;

var xml = File.ReadAllText("Representations/user.xml");

var serializer = new XmlSerializer(typeof(TwitterUser));
var reader = new StringReader(xml);
var user = (TwitterUser)serializer.Deserialize(reader);

Console.WriteLine(user.ScreenName);
```

Rather than producing the desired results, the code, when executed, will throw an
InvalidOperationException. This is due to an issue working with Twitter's DateTime representation
as well as the presence of nullable types in Twitter's XML response without XSD info describing the
empty tags may contain nullable data. This is a common XML serialization issue; when you don't have
control over the data returned from an API call, you need to make concessions. XmlSerializer does
not support Nullable<T> natively; because Twitter's API can return empty Boolean XML elements,
such as for the notifications and following elements on a user representation, you need to hook up

support for yourself using a common workaround pattern. To implement this pattern for `DateTime` values, you can change your classes to reflect the following example:

```
[XmlElement("created_at")]
private string CreatedDateImpl { get; set; }

public DateTime CreatedDate
{
    get
    {
        return String.IsNullOrEmpty(CreatedDateImpl)
                ? new DateTime()
                : CreatedDateImpl.FromRestDate();
    }
    set
    {
        const string format = TwitterExtensions.RestDateFormat;
        CreatedDateImpl = value.ToString(format);
    }
}
```

After making these changes to Twitter objects that use `DateTime`, these classes will properly handle the deserialization of date values even though they use an additional property. To support nullable types where Twitter returns a blank XML tag, the following further adjustments to `TwitterUser` are made:

```
// Twitter returns empty elements, requiring nullable values here
[XmlElement("notifications")]
public string NotificationsImpl { get; set; }

[XmlIgnore]
public bool HasNotifications
{
    get
    {
        if(String.IsNullOrEmpty(NotificationsImpl))
        {
            NotificationsImpl = "false";
        }
        return Convert.ToBoolean(NotificationsImpl);
    }
    set
    {
        NotificationsImpl = value.ToString();
    }
}

// Twitter returns empty elements, requiring nullable values here
[XmlElement("following", IsNullable = true)]
public string FollowingImpl { get; set; }

[XmlIgnore]
public bool? IsFollowing
```

```
{
    get
    {
        if (String.IsNullOrEmpty(FollowingImpl))
        {
            FollowingImpl = "false";
        }
        return Convert.ToBoolean(FollowingImpl);
    }
    set
    {
        FollowingImpl = value.ToString();
    }
}
```

With nullable type support in place, and some documentation for developers using classes that use additional properties to skirt XML serialization concerns, Twitter objects returned as XML representations are converted to .NET classes.

Working with JSON Responses

Although JSON, as a data format, has some ancillary benefits over XML—such as its compact size and parsing speed—it is also valuable as a dynamic scripting language, able to execute code generated on a server directly in a browser as JavaScript. Because JSON is JavaScript, it bypasses the browser security model that prevents JavaScript downloaded from an external site to execute, because parsing an incoming JSON payload will execute the JavaScript inline. JSON's dynamic nature has helped boost its popularity, particularly among RESTful API developers. Similar to XML, your task is to parse JSON returned from Twitter into data classes you can bind or interact with to build your applications. In .NET, there are two prominent ways to achieve this.

Using ASP.NET AJAX's `JavaScriptSerializer`

`System.Web.Script.Serialization` (found in `System.Web.Extensions.dll`) is a namespace that was introduced with ASP.NET AJAX that contains a number of classes to help work with modern web applications on the client-side. One of these classes is the `JavaScriptSerializer`, which bounced in and out of obsolescence, but is back as a fully supported class as of .NET 3.5 SP1. With `JavaScriptSerializer`, you are given a simple interface for round-trip serialization of JSON data. Similar to using XML serialization without customization, the `JavaScriptSerializer` suffers from naming convention ambiguity, and an inability to easily configure custom `DateTime` serialization. Despite this, you can actually produce some results without raising exceptions when the following standard code is executed.

```
using Wrox.Twitter.NUrl;
using Wrox.Twitter.NUrl.Objects;

// retrieve a JSON user representation
var json = "http://twitter.com/users/Dimebrain.xml".Get();
```

```
// create a new serialization instance
var serializer = new JavaScriptSerializer();

// convert from JSON to a mapped Twitter object
var user = serializer.Deserialize<TwitterUser>(json);

Console.WriteLine(user.Location);
Ottawa
```

If you're using the Twitter classes you built in Chapter 2, how was the `JavaScriptSerializer` able to deserialize results from an API call without any customization? The truth is that the serialization process is able to map simple properties that happen to line up, such as `Location` to `location` and `Description` to `description`, but in more complex scenarios such as converting a custom format string into a `DateTime` instance, or mapping `ScreenName` to `screen_name`, the serializer simply ignores the properties altogether. If you were to inspect the deserialized instance of `TwitterUser` at runtime, most of its `string` properties are `null`, and value types such as `DateTime` and `Boolean` remain in their default initialized state.

To compensate for the default behavior, and the fact that you cannot control the structure of JSON data returned by the Twitter API, you will need to build your own support to handle mapping non-standard JSON property elements to your Twitter class properties. Fortunately, `JavaScriptSerializer` uses an abstract companion class, the `JavaScriptConverter`, to allow you to exert more control over the serialization process in a reusable way. Taking a page from XML serialization in .NET, you can start by declaring a few custom attributes that will allow you to mark up your original Twitter classes with mapping information from the JSON representation to the effected property. These attributes are simple and described here:

```
using System;

namespace Wrox.Twitter.JsonWithJavaScriptSerializer
{
    [AttributeUsage(AttributeTargets.Property)]
    public class JsonElementAttribute : Attribute
    {
        public string Name { get; private set; }

        public JsonElementAttribute(string name)
        {
            Name = name;
        }
    }
}
```

The first attribute is used to decorate a class property that maps to a simple JSON element. The next attribute, following, is used to indicate that a class property is a complex, custom type with its own JSON property attributes.

```
using System;

namespace Wrox.Twitter.JsonWithJavaScriptSerializer
{
    [AttributeUsage(AttributeTargets.Property)]
    public class JsonTypeAttribute : Attribute
    {
        public string Name { get; private set; }

        public JsonTypeAttribute(string name)
        {
            Name = name;
        }
    }
}
```

Now you can use these attributes to provide the meta-data necessary to inform a custom serialization converter that you want to change the default behavior for how properties are discovered and used to serialize your objects. The following code demonstrates what the TwitterUser class would look like with this additional information. The CreatedDate property is commented out, currently, because it requires special treatment

```
using System;
using Wrox.Twitter.JsonWithJavaScriptSerializer.Objects;

namespace JsonWithJavaScriptSerializer.Objects
{
    public class TwitterUser
    {
        [JsonElement("id")]
        public int Id { get; set; }

        [JsonElement("followers_count")]
        public int FollowersCount { get; set; }

        [JsonElement("name")]
        public string Name { get; set; }

        [JsonElement("description")]
        public string Description { get; set; }

        [JsonElement("profile_image_url")]
        public string ProfileImageUrl { get; set; }

        [JsonElement("url")]
        public string Url { get; set; }

        [JsonElement("protected")]
        public bool IsProtected { get; set; }

        [JsonElement("screen_name")]
        public string ScreenName { get; set; }
```

```
    [JsonElement("location")]
    public string Location { get; set; }

    [JsonType("status")]
    public TwitterStatus Status { get; set; }

    [JsonElement("friends_count")]
    public int FriendsCount { get; set; }

    [JsonElement("profile_background_color")]
    public string ProfileBackgroundColor { get; set; }

    [JsonElement("utc_offset")]
    public int UtcOffset { get; set; }

    [JsonElement("profile_text_color")]
    public string ProfileTextColor { get; set; }

    [JsonElement("profile_background_image_url")]
    public string ProfileBackgroundImageUrl { get; set; }

    [JsonElement("time_zone")]
    public string TimeZone { get; set; }

    [JsonElement("favourites_count")]
    public int FavoritesCount { get; set; }

    [JsonElement("profile_link_color")]
    public string ProfileLinkColor { get; set; }

    [JsonElement("statuses_count")]
    public int StatusesCount { get; set; }

    [JsonElement("profile_sidebar_fill_color")]
    public string ProfileSidebarFillColor { get; set; }

    [JsonElement("profile_sidebar_border_color")]
    public string ProfileSidebarBorderColor { get; set; }

    [JsonElement("profile_background_tile")]
    public bool IsProfileBackgroundTiled { get; set; }

    [JsonElement("notifications")]
    public bool HasNotifications { get; set; }

    [JsonElement("following")]
    public bool IsFollowing { get; set; }

    //[JsonElement("created_at")]
    //public DateTime CreatedDate { get; set; }
```

```
        }
    }
```

The `TwitterUser` class now has mapping information embedded into its class structure, including declaring the nested `TwitterStatus` as a custom complex type rather than a simple property element, though you are not quite ready to handle `DateTime` conversion in the next step. To build a converter class for use with a serializer, you must first derive from the abstract JavaScript converter class, and implement each of its required methods. You can start by stubbing out a `MappingJavaScriptConverter` class to handle the task of lining up the attributes declared on your Twitter objects to their corresponding JSON element values.

```csharp
using System;
using System.Collections.Generic;
using System.Web.Script.Serialization;

namespace Wrox.Twitter.JsonWithJavaScriptSerializer.Converters
{
    internal partial class MappingJavaScriptConverter : JavaScriptConverter
    {
        public override object Deserialize
            (IDictionary<string, object> dictionary,
             Type type,
             JavaScriptSerializer serializer)
        {
            throw new NotImplementedException();
        }

        public override IDictionary<string, object> Serialize
            (object obj,
             JavaScriptSerializer serializer)
        {
            throw new NotImplementedException();
        }

        public override IEnumerable<Type> SupportedTypes
        {
            get { throw new NotImplementedException(); }
        }
    }
}
```

Each of the required methods in a custom converter provides enough context within their respective method signatures to accomplish your goals. The `Deserialize` method provides the target deserialization type, the serializer used, and a property bag of JSON element names with their associated JSON values. Simple types are represented by their .NET counterparts, such as `string` and `int`, while more complex types are represented as JSON results for further deserialization. The Serialize method requires you to prepare a similar dictionary of elements and their values given an instance of a .NET object with the accompanying serializer. Finally, the `SupportedTypes` enumeration lets you specify the custom types your serialization code applies to, though if you are writing generic handling code as is the case here, you can return a collection containing only a type of `object` to cancel this restriction.

To map properties to their JSON equivalents, you must use .NET's reflection features, not only to obtain the runtime value of the `JsonElement` and `JsonType` attribute names you declared, but also to ensure your code is reusable with any class by reflecting on the property names defined on the target type, to map them to your attributes and set their value when creating a new, deserialized instance. To increase the performance of code that makes regular use of reflection, it is wise to cache the results of the mapping logic that matches the value given in a mapping attribute to the name of a property. The code covering this aspect of `MappingJavaScriptConverter` is listed here:

```
using System;
using System.Collections.Generic;
using System.Reflection;
using System.Web.Script.Serialization;

namespace Wrox.Twitter.JsonWithJavaScriptSerializer.Converters
{
    internal partial class MappingJavaScriptConverter : JavaScriptConverter
    {
        // only use reflection once when mapping properties to attributes
        protected static readonly
            IDictionary<Type, IDictionary<string, string>> _propertyMap =
                new Dictionary<Type, IDictionary<string, string>>();

        // a collection of which JSON values are really custom types is also
        // a good candidate for caching
        protected static readonly
            IDictionary<Type, IDictionary<string, Type>> _typeMap =
                new Dictionary<Type, IDictionary<string, Type>>();

        public override IEnumerable<Type> SupportedTypes
        {
            get
            {
                return new List<Type>
                    {
                        // all types are supported
                        typeof (object)
                    };
            }
        }

        public override object Deserialize(
            IDictionary<string, object> dictionary,
            Type type,
            JavaScriptSerializer serializer)
        {
            // check if this type needs mapping
            EnsureTypeIsMapped(type);

            // create a type with custom mappings
            return DeserializeByMapping(type, dictionary);
        }

        private static object DeserializeByMapping(Type type,
```

```
                                            IDictionary<string, object>
                                            dictionary)
{
    var instance = Activator.CreateInstance(type);
    foreach (var key in dictionary.Keys)
    {
        if (!_propertyMap[type].ContainsKey(key))
        {
            // skip unmapped properties
            continue;
        }

        // find the correct mapping to the type
        var mapping = _propertyMap[type][key];

        // look up the mapping on the type
        var property = type.GetProperty(mapping);

        // check if this element is another type
        object value;
        if (_typeMap[type].ContainsKey(key))
        {
            // get the target type, mapping if needed
            var target = _typeMap[type][key];
            EnsureTypeIsMapped(target);

            // get the manifest of nested type values
            var manifest =
                (IDictionary<string, object>) dictionary[key];

            // recursively deserialize the nested type
            value = DeserializeByMapping(target, manifest);
        }
        else
        {
            // get the value of the JSON property
            value = dictionary[key];
        }

        if (!property.PropertyType.Equals(value.GetType()))
        {
            // don't try to set an incompatible type
            continue;
        }

        // set the mapped property value on new instance
        property.SetValue(instance, value, null);
    }

    return instance;
```

```csharp
    }

    private static void EnsureTypeIsMapped(Type type)
    {
        if (_propertyMap.ContainsKey(type))
        {
            // no work to do
            return;
        }

        // add this type to the map
        var mapping = new Dictionary<string, string>();
        var types = new Dictionary<string, Type>();

        _propertyMap.Add(type, mapping);
        _typeMap.Add(type, types);

        var properties = type.GetProperties();
        foreach (var property in properties)
        {
            // does this property have special markup?
            MapElement(mapping, property);

            // is this property a nested type?
            MapType(types, mapping, property);
        }
    }

    private static void MapElement(IDictionary<string, string> mapping,
                                   PropertyInfo property)
    {
        var elements =
            property.GetCustomAttributes(
                typeof (JsonElementAttribute),
                true);

        if (elements.Length != 1)
        {
            return;
        }

        // this JSON element is a custom mapped property
        var element = (JsonElementAttribute) elements[0];
        mapping.Add(element.Name, property.Name);
    }

    private static void MapType(IDictionary<string, Type> types,
                                IDictionary<string, string> mapping,
                                PropertyInfo property)
    {
        var attributes =
```

```
                    property.GetCustomAttributes
                        (typeof (JsonTypeAttribute),
                        true);

            if (attributes.Length != 1)
            {
                return;
            }

            // this JSON element is another custom type
            var element = (JsonTypeAttribute) attributes[0];
            mapping.Add(element.Name, property.Name);
            types.Add(element.Name, property.PropertyType);
        }
    }
}
```

Although reflection code is sometimes confusing, you are doing very little beyond creating in-memory dictionaries that store the JSON element name relative to the class property name, and setting the value of public properties to match the values provided in the serialization dictionary. The interesting parts of this code include the fact that you must track custom types as well as simple .NET types, and recursively call the same deserialization logic when you encounter custom types. This is because the value of the serialized dictionary type is more JSON, not a .NET class, and it must use the same conversion process repeatedly until all class types are represented by .NET objects. Since serialization stems from previously converted types, in scenarios where you are transforming values from an *opaque* data source, the code to complete this class with serialization logic is simple in comparison.

```
using System;
using System.Collections.Generic;
using System.Reflection;
using System.Web.Script.Serialization;

namespace Wrox.Twitter.JsonWithJavaScriptSerializer.Converters
{
    internal partial class MappingJavaScriptConverter : JavaScriptConverter
    {
        public override IDictionary<string, object> Serialize
            (object obj,
            JavaScriptSerializer serializer)
        {
            var type = obj.GetType();
            EnsureTypeIsMapped(type);

            IDictionary<string, object> result =
                new Dictionary<string, object>();
            foreach (var property in type.GetProperties())
            {
                if (!_propertyMap[type].ContainsKey(property.Name))
                {
```

```
                // skip unmapped properties
                continue;
            }

            // get the correct mapping name to serialize
            var mapping = _propertyMap[type][property.Name];

            // get the value of the instance property
            var value = property.GetValue(obj, null);

            result.Add(mapping, value);
        }

        return result;
    }
  }
}
```

Depending on how you elect to save class instances of Twitter objects you generate from API calls, you may not require serialization from classes back into their representative JSON data. Now that you have a converter ready to work with non-standard JSON element naming, you can register it when you build a `JavaScriptSerializer` instance, and invoke the serializer as you would normally.

```
using Wrox.Twitter.NUrl;
using Wrox.Twitter.JsonWithJavaScriptSerializer.Objects;

// retrieve a JSON user representation
var json = "http://twitter.com/users/Dimebrain.xml".Get();

// create a new serialization instance
var serializer = new JavaScriptSerializer();

// add the custom mapping converter to the serializer
serializer.RegisterConverters(new List<JavaScriptConverter>
                              {
                                      // add your custom converter
                                      new MappingJavaScriptConverter()
                              });

// convert from JSON to a mapped Twitter object
var user = serializer.Deserialize<TwitterUser>(json);

Console.WriteLine(user.Location);
Console.WriteLine(user.CreatedDate);
Dimebrain
01/01/0001 12:00:00 AM
```

After running the deserialization with your custom converter, the resulting `TwitterUser` instance now contains the correct values for all the non-standard mappings in a Twitter JSON representation. Unfortunately it's not complete because the `CreatedDate` property requires custom `DateTime` deserialization, similar to the challenges you've already faced with XML. To solve that challenge, you can take a similar approach to the MappingJavaScriptConverter, by deriving that class and building on the additional DataTime logic to create a TwitterConverter class.

```
using System;
using System.Collections.Generic;
using System.Linq;
using System.Reflection;
using System.Web.Script.Serialization;
using Wrox.Twitter.JsonWithJavaScriptSerializer.Objects;
using Wrox.Twitter.Objects;

namespace Wrox.Twitter.JsonWithJavaScriptSerializer.Converters
{
    internal partial class TwitterConverter : MappingJavaScriptConverter
    {
        public override IEnumerable<Type> SupportedTypes
        {
            get
            {
                return new List<Type>
                    {
                        typeof (TwitterStatus),
                        typeof (TwitterUser),
                        typeof (TwitterDirectMessage),
                        typeof (TwitterRateLimitStatus)
                    };
            }
        }

        public override object Deserialize(
            IDictionary<string, object> dictionary,
            Type type,
            JavaScriptSerializer serializer)
        {
            if (dictionary == null)
            {
                return null;
            }

            // deserialize based on custom mapping
            var instance = base.Deserialize(dictionary, type, serializer);

            // find DateTime properties on the real object to convert
            MapDateTime(dictionary, type, instance);

            return instance;
        }

        private void MapDateTime(IDictionary<string, object> dictionary,
                                 Type type,
                                 object instance)
        {
            foreach (var property in type.GetProperties())
```

```csharp
        {
            var nestedType = MapNestedType(type,
                                           property,
                                           dictionary,
                                           instance);

            if (nestedType != typeof (DateTime))
            {
                // skip non-DateTime properties
                continue;
            }

            // map dictionary name back to real property
            foreach (var entry in _propertyMap[type])
            {
                if (!entry.Value.Equals(property.Name))
                {
                    continue;
                }

                // get JSON element value
                var value = dictionary[entry.Key].ToString();

                // convert and set to DateTime
                var dateTime = value.FromRestDate();

                // set value to converted real DateTime
                property.SetValue(instance, dateTime, null);
            }
        }
    }
}

private Type MapNestedType(Type type,
                           PropertyInfo property,
                           IDictionary<string, object> dictionary,
                           object instance)
{
    var nestedType = property.PropertyType;
    if (SupportedTypes.ToList().Contains(nestedType))
    {
        foreach (var entry in _propertyMap[type])
        {
            if (!entry.Value.Equals(property.Name))
            {
                continue;
            }

            var nestedInstance = property.GetValue(instance, null);
            if (nestedInstance == null)
            {
                // avoid null instances of nested types
                continue;
            }
```

```
                  var nestedDictionary =
                      (IDictionary<string, object>) dictionary[entry.Key];
                  MapDateTime(nestedDictionary, nestedType, nestedInstance);
              }
          }
          return nestedType;
      }

      public override IDictionary<string, object> Serialize
          (object obj, JavaScriptSerializer serializer)
      {
          // you can leave this implementation for when it's needed
          throw new NotImplementedException();
      }
   }
}
```

Completing the conversion process for `DateTime` is much easier due to having utility extension methods for converting Twitter's REST date formats readily available from your previous work, as well as reusing

---

James Newton-King's JSON.NET

To address the .NET Framework's lack of a LINQ to JSON counterpart to LINQ to XML—so far the simplest and cleanest approach to consuming external data you've seen—James Newton-King established the JSON.NET open source project to provide you with a fast, convenient LINQ library for handling serialization of both JSON to objects, and XML to JSON. Following a similar structure to the attribute-based annotation style covered in this section, you would declare the characteristics of the JSON representation in your class code:

```
using System;
using Newtonsoft.Json;

[JsonObject(MemberSerialization.OptIn)]
public class TwitterRateLimitStatus :
{
    [JsonProperty("remaining_hits")]
    public int RemainingHits
    {
        get; set;
    }

    [JsonProperty("hourly_limit")]
    public int HourlyLimit
    {
        get; set;
```

```
            }

            [JsonProperty("reset_time_in_seconds")]
            public long ResetTimeInSeconds
            {
                get; set;
            }

            [JsonProperty("reset_time")]
            [JsonConverter(typeof(TwitterDateTimeConverter))]
            public DateTime ResetTime
            {
                get; set;
            }
    }
```

After declaring the type, properties, and any custom converters such as the
`TwitterDateTimeConverter` in this hypothetical example, you would then use a
strongly typed conversion class to perform the deserialization:

```
    using Newtonsoft.Json;
    using Wrox.Twitter.NUrl;

    var response =
    "http://twitter.com/account/rate_limit_status.json".Get();
    var rateLimitStatus =
    JsonConvert.Deserialize<TwitterRateLimitStatus>(json);
```

You can download JSON.NET from `http://codeplex.com/json`.

the mapping logic recently created. You still need to ensure that nested complex types are handled
correctly, and at first glance, this seems an inordinate amount of code to produce a simple result, but
there is no way for generic code to anticipate custom `DateTime` formats or non-standard element names,
and if it tried to do so, it would likely produce more problems in the long run. Fortunately, this kind of
conversion task is only written once, and changed very little.

It's important to note, however, that you will need to keep on top of any changes in the data formats
returned from Twitter, as ignoring these changes would result in some properties suddenly reverting
back to default or uninitialized values when the underlying mapping changes. You may have additional
ideas to help you build out your conversion classes to improve their performance or ease of use.

Using WCF's `DataContractJsonSerializer`

Windows Communication Foundation (WCF) is a powerful framework for service-based communication
in .NET. Within WCF there is a large body of serialization techniques for generating proxies for real
objects based on a data contract. You can borrow some of WCF's serialization implementation,

specifically the DataContractJsonSerializer, to perform the task of consuming JSON response from the Twitter API. By now, you know what to expect when performing JSON to object mapping; the first step is to mark up your data classes with the DataContract and DataMember attributes to line up the expected properties. This is what the TwitterUser class will look like after annotation, concessions for DateTime conversion notwithstanding.

```csharp
using System.Runtime.Serialization;

namespace Wrox.Twitter.JsonWithDataContractJsonSerializer.Objects
{
    [DataContract]
    public class TwitterUser
    {
        [DataMember(Name="id")]
        public int Id { get; set; }

        [DataMember(Name = "followers_count")]
        public int FollowersCount { get; set; }

        [DataMember(Name = "name")]
        public string Name { get; set; }

        [DataMember(Name = "description")]
        public string Description { get; set; }

        [DataMember(Name = "profile_image_url")]
        public string ProfileImageUrl { get; set; }

        [DataMember(Name = "id")]
        public string Url { get; set; }

        [DataMember(Name = "protected")]
        public bool IsProtected { get; set; }

        [DataMember(Name = "screen_name")]
        public string ScreenName { get; set; }

        [DataMember(Name = "location")]
        public string Location { get; set; }

        [DataMember(Name = "status")]
        public TwitterStatus Status { get; set; }

        [DataMember(Name = "friends_count")]
        public int FriendsCount { get; set; }

        [DataMember(Name = "profile_background_color")]
        public string ProfileBackgroundColor { get; set; }

        [DataMember(Name = "utc_offset")]
        public string UtcOffset { get; set; }

        [DataMember(Name = "profile_text_color")]
        public string ProfileTextColor { get; set; }
```

```
[DataMember(Name = "profile_background_image_url")]
public string ProfileBackgroundImageUrl { get; set; }

[DataMember(Name = "time_zone")]
public string TimeZone { get; set; }

// The favourites_count element is spelled with the UK variant
// in the Twitter API; watch out for it!
[DataMember(Name = "favourites_count")]
public int FavoritesCount { get; set; }

[DataMember(Name = "profile_link_color")]
public string ProfileLinkColor { get; set; }

[DataMember(Name = "statuses_count")]
public int StatusesCount { get; set; }

[DataMember(Name = "profile_sidebar_fill_color")]
public string ProfileSidebarFillColor { get; set; }

[DataMember(Name = "profile_sidebar_border_color")]
public string ProfileSidebarBorderColor { get; set; }

[DataMember(Name = "profile_background_tiled")]
public bool IsProfileBackgroundTiled { get; set; }

[DataMember(Name = "notifications")]
public bool HasNotifications { get; set; }

[DataMember(Name = "following")]
public bool IsFollowing { get; set; }

// You can't handle dates yet, but will soon
// [DataMember(Name = "created_at")]
public DateTime CreatedDate { get; set; }

    }
}
```

Working with the object as is, the following code deserializes the object from a JSON representation:

```
using System;
using System.IO;
using System.Runtime.Serialization.Json;
using System.Text;
using Wrox.Twitter.JsonWithDataContractJsonSerializer.Objects;

// retrieve a JSON user representation
var json = File.ReadAllText("Representations/user.json");

TwitterUser user;
// open a stream to the JSON text for serialzation
```

```
using (var ms = new MemoryStream(Encoding.Unicode.GetBytes(json)))
{
    var type = typeof (TwitterUser);

    // create a new serializer for a Twitter user
    var serializer = new DataContractJsonSerializer(type);

    // deserialize using the type's data contract
    user = (TwitterUser) serializer.ReadObject(ms);
}

Console.WriteLine(user.ScreenName);
Console.WriteLine(user.CreatedDate);
Dimebrain
01/01/0001 12:00:00 AM
```

Even though `DataContractJsonSerializer` is able is handle nested types by default, it employs a Microsoft-based workaround for JSON `DateTime` literal data, and as a sealed class, is unavailable for extension. To get around this limitation, you can deserialize incoming `DateTime` data from Twitter as a plain string, and use the correct property to convert the value manually. To do this, you need to implement a way to convert from a `DateTime` back to a Twitter-based string to provide a setter method, and change the `TwitterUser` class implementation, shown next:

```
[DataMember(Name = "created_at")]
private string DateTimeSpecified { get; set; }

public DateTime CreatedDate
{
    get
    {
        return DateTimeSpecified.FromRestDate();
    }
    set
    {
        var dateTime = value.ToString(TwitterExtensions.RestDateFormat);
        DateTimeSpecified = dateTime;
    }
}
```

The handling of date values aside, the `DataContractJsonSerializer` is an efficient and simplified way to consume JSON data from Twitter, compared to the `JavaScriptSerializer`. You now have options for handling data in both major REST representational formats, which should ease your Twitter application development. Although working with the specifics of multiple serialization strategies is taxing, these skills transfer well to any further social software you build that makes heavy use of third-party APIs that require XML and JSON, which is arguably all of them.

Calling Back to Client Code with JSONP

So far, you have learned how to parse JSON as a data format, but not to take advantage of its dynamic execution capability in the browser. To achieve some dynamic behaviors with the Twitter REST API, you can take advantage of JSON with padding, or *JSONP*, which allows you to wrap a JSON response from a server in an event handler that is executed dynamically in the browser. Twitter supports JSONP by providing a callback parameter on non-protected API resources. What the callback parameter provides is a simple wrapper around the JSON response that names the callback method defined on the client-side to handle that response. If you look at the JSON response to this Twitter API call, you will see that a callback was used to wrap a user representation.

```
http://twitter.com/users/Dimebrain.json?callback=jsonLoad
jsonCallback(
{"notifications":false,
 "profile_background_color":"050f10",
 "description":"Daniel Crenna builds social software...",
 "utc_offset":-18000,
 "screen_name":"dimebrain",
 "profile_text_color":"333333",
 "following":false,
 "favourites_count":77,
 "profile_link_color":"0084B4",
 "url":"http://www.dimebrain.com",
 "name":"Daniel Crenna",
 "statuses_count":980,
 "protected":false,
 "status": ...,
 "profile_background_tile":false,
 "profile_sidebar_fill_color":"e0e0e0",
 "followers_count":408,
 "profile_background_image_url":"...",
 "time_zone":"Eastern Time (US & Canada)",
 "friends_count":323,
 "profile_sidebar_border_color":"000000",
 "location":"Ottawa",
 "id":11173402,
 "created_at":"Fri Dec 14 18:48:52 +0000 2007",
 "profile_image_url":"..."}
```

While constituting a simple change to the JSON output and by providing a suitable callback in your client-side JavaScript, it is possible to inject the REST API call with its callback parameter into the body of your page. By returning a call to the event handler, the result is cross-site JSON code executing dynamically in the browser.

Using Silverlight

Thanks to Silverlight's robust support for interaction with the browser host layer, you can write a simple wrapper to support JSONP callbacks that raise an event when a padded JSON response is returned from Twitter, and evaluate the handler script dynamically. Your first task is to ensure that the page hosting your Silverlight control is equipped with a JavaScript callback to handle an incoming JSON response, as well as the JavaScript that enables JSON itself. To do this, you can write methods to load the necessary script files from an assembly stream, injecting each script as a block at the bottom of the current HTML page.

```csharp
using System;
using System.Collections.Generic;
using System.IO;
using System.Reflection;
using System.Windows.Browser;

namespace Wrox.Twitter.CrossDomainTwitter.Json
{
    public static partial class JsonExtensions
    {
        private static bool _initialized;

        public static void InjectIntoPage(this string script)
        {
            script.InjectIntoPage("text");
        }

        public static void InjectIntoPage(this string script, string property)
        {
            /*
             * <script type="text/javascript">
             * [your JavaScript here]
             * </script>
             */
            var tag = HtmlPage.Document.CreateElement("script");
            tag.SetAttribute("type", "text/javascript");
            tag.SetProperty(property, script);
            HtmlPage.Document.DocumentElement.AppendChild(tag);
        }

        private static void LoadScript(string path)
        {
            // Remember to mark your script files as embedded resources
            var assembly = Assembly.GetExecutingAssembly();
            using (var stream = assembly.GetManifestResourceStream(path))
            {
                if (stream == null)
                {
                    throw new ArgumentException(
                        "Unable to locate JavaScript to inject");
                }

                using (var reader = new StreamReader(stream))
                {
                    var script = reader.ReadToEnd();
                    script.InjectIntoPage();
```

```
                    }
            }
    }

    public static void Initialize()
    {
        // This script is available at www.json.org/json2.js
        LoadScript("Wrox.Twitter.CrossDomainTwitter.Scripts.json2.js");

        // This script contains your JavaScript to handle callbacks
        LoadScript("Wrox.Twitter.CrossDomainTwitter.Scripts.hooks.js");

        // Set a global ID to interact with this Silverlight instance
        var id = HtmlPage.Plugin.Id;
        var script = string.Format("setHost('{0}');", id);
        script.InjectIntoPage();

        initialized = true;
    }
}
}
```

With the prerequisite scripts in place, you are ready to build a bridge to respond to JSON callbacks from Twitter. The callback method itself is responsible for informing your Silverlight control instance that there is data to process. The contents of the hooks.js, shown here, contains the callback handling logic as well as a method to set the Silverlight control instance's ID globally so that it is accessible when raising scriptable events.

```
var $id;

function setHost(id) {
    // set a global identifier for the Silverlight instance
    $id = id;
}

function jsonCallback(jsonData) {
    // find the global ID of the Silverlight plugin
    var id = $id;

    // fetch the Silverlight plugin from the DOM
    var silverlight = document.getElementById(id);

    // parse the incoming callback JSON data
    var response = JSON.stringify(jsonData);

    // raise the Silverlight plugin's JsonEvent
```

```
        // and pass the JSON response to this scriptable type
        if (silverlight) {
            silverlight.Content.JsonEvent.Received(response);
        }
    };
```

This JavaScript method tells some, but not all, of the story behind responding to a client-side JSON event. First, there is a global identifier needed to find the element ID of the Silverlight control instance on the HTML page. Second, you are raising a `Received` event on a custom `JsonEvent` class to pass the arriving JSON response up to your Silverlight code. To write Silverlight class code that is available to you on the client-side via JavaScript, you need to specify the `ScriptableType` and `ScriptableMember` attributes on the intended classes. In this case, a custom `JsonEvent` class needs these methods to enable the previous scenario, and is shown in the following:

```
using System;
using System.Windows.Browser;

namespace Wrox.Twitter.CrossDomainTwitter.Json
{
    [ScriptableType]
    public class JsonEvent
    {
        public static event EventHandler<JsonEventArgs> Responded;

        public static void OnResponded(string response)
        {
            if (Responded != null)
            {
                Responded(null, new JsonEventArgs(response));
            }
        }

        [ScriptableMember]
        public void Received(string json)
        {
            OnResponded(json);
        }
    }

    public class JsonEventArgs : EventArgs
    {
        public string Response { get; private set; }

        public JsonEventArgs(string data)
        {
            Response = data;
        }
    }
}
```

Now your callback code, when presented with JSON, will pass that response to Silverlight, which will in turn raise an event that you can respond to, bringing rich support for Twitter API calls directly to Silverlight on the client-side, with no server interaction required. To finish this feature, you need to similarly inject the API call as a script block with an external source, which is the heart of JSONP functionality; downloading any JavaScript from an external source evaluates that script at runtime, and it contains calls to methods on your client-side—which is how dynamic execution occurs. Here are a set of methods that provide a `Get` feature similar to NUrl, but instead invoke a JavaScript method to inject your API call in the host HTML.

```csharp
using System;
using System.Collections.Generic;
using System.IO;
using System.Reflection;
using System.Windows.Browser;

namespace Wrox.Twitter.CrossDomainTwitter.Json
{
    public static partial class JsonExtensions
    {
        private static readonly Dictionary<string, object> _scriptables =
            new Dictionary<string, object>();

        private static bool _initialized;

        public static void Get(this string url, string callback)
        {
            // Ensure the URL is well formed
            url = ValidateUrl(url);

            // Ensure pre-requisite scripts exist
            if (!_initialized)
            {
                Initialize();
            }


            // Protect access to the dictionary from multiple
            // threads at a time
            lock (_scriptables)
            {
                // Register scriptables so that you can raise JSON events
                if (!_scriptables.ContainsKey("JsonEvent"))
                {
                    var jsonEvent = new JsonEvent();
                    HtmlPage.RegisterScriptableObject("JsonEvent", jsonEvent);
                    _scriptables.Add("JsonEvent", jsonEvent);
                }
            }

            // Add the JSONP callback parameter
            var uri = new Uri(url);
            url = uri.Query.Contains("?")
                        ? url + "&"
                        : url + "?";
            url = String.Concat(url, "callback=", callback);
```

```
        // Inject the API call into the page as an external source
        url.InjectIntoPage("src");
    }

    private static string ValidateUrl(string url)
    {
        if (String.IsNullOrEmpty(url))
        {
            throw new ArgumentException("No URL provided", "url");
        }

        if (Uri.IsWellFormedUriString(url, UriKind.Absolute))
        {
            return url;
        }

        Uri uri;
        Uri.TryCreate(url, UriKind.Absolute, out uri);

        if (uri != null)
        {
            return url;
        }

        throw new ArgumentException("Malformed URL provided", "url");
    }
}
}
```

To send a cross-site JSONP call to Twitter from your Silverlight code, you can now use a simple extension method, specifying the desired callback to use. Here is the code for a simple Silverlight page that posts the returned JSON data as a browser window alert:

```
using System.Windows.Browser;
using Wrox.Twitter.CrossDomainTwitter.Json;

namespace Wrox.Twitter.CrossDomainTwitter
{
    public partial class MainPage
    {
        public MainPage()
        {
            InitializeComponent();

            Loaded += MainPage_Loaded;
```

```
        }

        static void MainPage_Loaded(object sender, System.Windows.RoutedEventArgs e)
        {
            // Wire up the handler when JSON is returned from Twitter
            JsonEvent.Responded += JsonEvent_Responded;

            // Define the Twitter API call
            var url = "http://twitter.com/users/Dimebrain.json";

            // Send a JSON request using the 'jsonCallback' handler
            url.Get("jsonCallback");
        }

        static void JsonEvent_Responded(object sender, JsonEventArgs e)
        {
            // report the results as a browser alert
            HtmlPage.Window.Alert(e.Response);
        }
    }
}
```

Although it is simple to Twitter API calls with JSONP, you need to consider the security implications. Not only are you sending plain text credentials in the URL of any authenticated API calls, but you are also limited in what areas of the API you can access without using a proxy between your client facing code and a server making HTTP requests on your behalf.

Security Restrictions with JSONP

As Chapter 1 outlined, browser security restrictions prevent you from complete client-side access to Twitter's API, or any external web service that does not originate from your server. In Silverlight, this restriction comes in the form of tight control over the `HttpWebRequest` and `TcpClient` classes; while you are able to easily set the authorization headers on either of these on the server to provide API credentials, you will instead raise exceptions whenever you attempt to do this from a Silverlight control instance. Whether you try to provide a `NetworkCredential`, set the headers explicitly, or event attempt to set internal state with reflection, you will not succeed in making a cross-site request unless the service you are calling explicitly allows it using a `clientaccesspolicy.xml` or `crossdomain.xml` file. In Twitter's case, only their own servers are allowed cross-domain access, as listed here or by visiting `http://twitter.com/crossdomain.xml`.

```
<cross-domain-policy
xsi:noNamespaceSchemaLocation="http://www.adobe.com/xml/schemas/PolicyFile.xsd">
<allow-access-from domain="twitter.com"/>
```

```
<allow-access-from domain="api.twitter.com"/>
<allow-access-from domain="search.twitter.com"/>
<allow-access-from domain="static.twitter.com"/>
<site-control permitted-cross-domain-policies="master-only"/>
<allow-http-request-headers-from domain="*.twitter.com" headers="*" secure="true"/>
</cross-domain-policy>
```

With these restrictions in place, you are not able to perform any HTTP POST or DELETE methods against the API in general, or provide authentication in service calls. However, JSONP *does* allow you, thanks to the user information component of the URI specification, to make authorized API calls using Basic authentication by providing your credentials at the beginning of an API request. To access protected resources from a JSONP request, you can modify the Silverlight example code to provide user credentials, as written here:

```csharp
using System;
using System.Windows;
using System.Windows.Browser;
using Wrox.Twitter.CrossDomainTwitter.Json;

namespace Wrox.Twitter.CrossDomainTwitter
{
    public partial class MainPage
    {
        public MainPage()
        {
            InitializeComponent();

            Loaded += MainPage_Loaded;
        }

        private static void MainPage_Loaded(object sender, RoutedEventArgs e)
        {
            // Using HTTP GET with authorization in the URL
            JsonEvent.Responded += JsonEvent_Responded;

            // Prepare user credentials
            var username = Uri.EscapeDataString("prodevbook");
            var password = Uri.EscapeDataString("wroxblox!");
            var pair = string.Concat(username, ":", password);

            // Provide the user credentials at the beginning of a protected API call
            var url =
                string.Format(
                    "http://{0}@twitter.com/statuses/user_timeline.json", pair);

            // Make the protected call with JSONP
            url.Get("jsonCallback");
        }
    }
}
```

Calling JSONP Services in ASP.NET AJAX

If you are not using Silverlight, but rather an ASP.NET application of some variety, it is still possible to handle JSONP callbacks in the browser in the same manner as you've learned here, though the manner in which you make a client-side web service is understandably written in JavaScript rather than in server-side code. Here is a JavaScript equivalent for injecting an API call with a callback parameter at runtime:

```javascript
function jsonLoad(url, callback) {
    var script = document.createElement('script');
    script.type = 'text/javascript';
    script.src = url;

    if (callback) {
        script.src += hasParameters(url) ? '&' : '?';
        script.src += 'callback=' + callback;
    }

    var head = document.getElementsByTagName('head')[0];
    head.appendChild(script);
};

function hasParameters(url) {
    url = url.replace(/[\[]/, "\\[").replace(/[\]]/, "\\]");
    var pattern = "[\\?]\w+=([^&#]*)";
    var regex = new RegExp(pattern);
    var results = regex.exec(url);

    return results != null;
}
```

```csharp
        private static void JsonEvent_Responded(object sender, JsonEventArgs e)
        {
            HtmlPage.Window.Alert(e.Response);
        }
    }
}
```

Twitter applications designed to live on the browser with minimal user interaction are good candidates for leveraging Twitter's JSONP support; widgets that search the public timeline fit this description.

Summary

You now have what you need to develop against most of Twitter's REST API and convert the resulting responses into meaningful data for your application. You are likely more aware now that although REST provides clear separation between web services and application logic, many of the implementation details of dealing with that separation and transforming REST representations is left up to you. There are plenty of classes to support these transformation tasks, but issues such as cyclical references, custom type conversion and `DateTime` formats, and heterogeneous mapping of properties to data elements often confuse the issue and require decorating otherwise clean class implementations in favor of adding support for corner cases. After working through this chapter, however, you have learned:

❑   How to parse XML responses using `XmlSerializer` and LINQ to XML.

❑   How to write customer serialization code to process JSON with ASP.NET's `JavaScriptSerializer`, and WCF's `DataContractJsonSerializer` classes.

❑   The fine print surrounding the limitations of the browser security model, and how those constraints affect consuming the Twitter REST API in client-side code.

The next chapter covers the Twitter Search API, a near real-time service you can consume with RSS and Atom syndication, in addition to JSON, to write responsive, world-aware applications that combine data from multiple sources.

The Twitter Search API

"The Twitter Search API is pretty useful — you can search on complex terms, filter by date ranges, and return the results as an RSS feed. Also good — it pretty much never goes offline [insert your own joke about the fail whale here]. We used it to pull relevant tweets to display in a Silverlight client for the PDC08 and MIX09 web sites.

Although search.twitter.com *never seems to go offline, you do have to watch out for latency, especially during peak events. We saw latency of 10 to 15 minutes during MIX09, which might have had to do with the fact that SXSW was going on at the same time."*

Jon Galloway, *Witty*

This chapter dives into the Search API, explores its similarities and differences with the REST API, goes into detail about search operators and parameters, and offers recommendations for how to best construct your search queries and handle incoming results from the API.

Overview

Today, Twitter's search functionality is contained within a distinct and separate API that is behaviorally inconsistent with the REST API, but offers simple and powerful real-time search capabilities. The look into the history behind the fracture of Twitter's API into two distinct offerings reveals that *Summize*, a "conversational search engine" company in Virginia, was acquired by Twitter and its API was migrated to http://search.twitter.com. It offers very few resource methods compared to the REST API, but the power of search lies in the speed it has to index real-time content from Twitter, as well as its support for logical search operators and parameters to fine-tune incoming results. The Search API is broken down into two feature spaces, described here.

Search

Searching Twitter is, more accurately, searching publically accessible status updates for specific content. Those users who choose to protect their updates do not appear in search results, and you cannot search for users or direct messages. It's worth noting that search indexing will capture status updates that a user decides to delete later, making any publically posted message on the service effectively intractable. If you are building applications to leverage Twitter for business purposes, it won't hurt to make that characteristic of the search indexing to your user base.

Trends

Another side of the Search API, trend features, allows you to detect dominating conversational topics on Twitter at large, broken down into current, daily, and weekly relevance. If you're building an application to scoop stories of interest or tailor content for a real-time experience, you will spend a lot of time with this simple feature.

API Rate Limits

The Search API is rate limited by IP address, and does not require credentials, though the actual hourly rate limit imposed by IP is not disclosed. Typically, you should not run into any problems with fair and moderate use of the API. If you are making extensive use of search in your applications, you can follow the white-listing process to deregulate your API calls from a specific IP location.

Twitter Search's `DateTime` Format

Because the Search API is a heterogeneous system, it uses its own date formats that contrast with the REST API; the most common Search API date format was covered earlier in Chapter 2. In fact, incorporating search functionality using syndicated content (RSS or Atom formats) brings an additional two date representation into your applications, bringing the total to four. Working with search trends requires yet another set of date formats. You will learn the new syndicated date formats when you put them to use in Chapter 5, however the trends formats are covered in the Search Objects and Converting Queries and Trends sections in this chapter.

Search Features

Twitter's Search API powers both the `http://search.twitter.com` micro-site, as well as the embedded real-time search features provided within your own Twitter home page. Unlike the REST API, you are able to filter results from the source in interesting ways. All API calls share `http://search.twitter.com` as their root URL path.

Search

Search allows you to construct a query and receive the results of that query ordered from the most recent status update. The power of search is realized with the combination of operators and parameters to narrowly define criteria, as well as a results wrapper object to assist with paging results.

> **Relative Method URL:** /search.{format}
>
> **HTTP Methods:** GET

REST Formats: JSON, Atom

Optional Parameters: Search operators and parameters (see next section)

Data Representation: A collection of search objects wrapped in a meta-level query object (15 nested statuses at a time by default, 100 maximum)

Example

```
GET: http://search.twitter.com/search.rss?q=wrox
```

Current Trends

Current trends provide details for the top 10 trending topics on Twitter, either by text reference or hashtag channel inclusion.

Relative Method URLs: /trends.{format}

/trends/current.{format}

HTTP Methods: GET

REST Formats: JSON

Optional Parameters: `exclude`

Data Representation: A Twitter trend results object (returning the top 10 results for the current date and time)

Example

```
GET: http://search.twitter.com/trends/current.json
```

Special Considerations: If you use /trends/current, the as_of element returning the time sensitivity of your result will use UNIX epoch time to represent the date and time; if you use /trends, as_of will fall back to the Search API's date format. In addition, the JSON schema returned uses a different element model and naming convention. For consistency with the other trend methods, it is better to stick to the most qualified /trends/current URL. In addition, the exclude parameter may only specify one value, hashtags, which instructs the API to remove all results from trends that include the hashtag channel modifier.

Daily Trends

Daily trends provide details on the top 20 trending topics on Twitter for a given date or today's date by default, broken down by hour.

Relative Method URL: /trends/daily.{format}

HTTP Methods: GET

REST Formats: JSON

Optional Parameters: `date, exclude`

Data Representation: A Twitter trend results object (returning the top 20 results for each hour)

Special Considerations: To specify a trend by `date`, use the *YYYY-MM-DD* format. In addition, the `exclude` parameter may only specify one value, `hashtags`, which instructs the API to remove all results from trends that include the hashtag channel modifier.

Weekly Trends

Weekly trends provide details on the top 30 trending topics on Twitter for a given week, broken down by date from a given start date, or the first date in the current week by default.

> **Relative Method URL:** /trends/daily.{format}
>
> **HTTP Methods:** GET
>
> **REST Formats:** JSON
>
> **Optional Parameters:** `date, exclude`
>
> **Data Representation:** A Twitter trend results object (returning the top 30 results for each day)

Example

```
GET: http://search.twitter.com/trends/weekly.json?date=2009-06-06&exclude=hashtags
```

Special Considerations: To specify a trend by `date`, use the *YYYY-MM-DD* format. In addition, the `exclude` parameter may only specify one value, `hashtags`, which instructs the API to remove all results from trends that include the hashtag channel modifier.

Search Operators

A search operator is a symbol that is part of your query URL parameter, rather than a distinct URL parameter passed in support of the original expression. Search operators allow you to craft expressions that target specific content on Twitter. Twitter's particular operator set includes standard Boolean logic as well as specific operators for the service. To compose a search query, you can combine any number of search operations and pass them as a URL parameter labeled `q`. You should ensure the value of your complete query is properly URL escaped.

Boolean Logic

You may logically separate statements to relax or tighten your search results. Twitter Search supports scoping arguments using parentheses, but does not provide SQL-like grouping on results. `SF (jobs OR tech)` return results containing both `SF` and `jobs` together, or `SF` and `tech` together.

AND (implicit)

By default, words combined in a query are logically combined with an implicit `AND` operator. You should not provide the `AND` explicitly or it will become a value in your search.

OR (explicit)

You may use OR to obtain results containing any words connected by this operator. You *must* include OR as uppercase, or it will become a discrete value in your search, which will yield many more status updates from Oregon than you may have intended. To search for Oregon's abbreviation, use an exact phrase.

Exact Phrase

Specifying search parameters in quotations will ensure your results contain the exact results you are looking for. Exact phrase matching is case insensitive. This is useful if you are looking for common words, but need them arranged in a specific order, i.e., `"that's what she said"`.

Exclusions

The true power of Twitter Search lies in your ability to control what results you don't see, not simply what results you want to see. To slice data in relation to the absence of certain words, add a minus sign before and adjacent to the word itself. You may want to see results using a specific word, but without including specific uses of that word. You can do that combining exclusions with exact phrases, i.e., `pants -"pants on fire"` will scrub your results of a particular cliché.

Hashtags

Hashtags are Twitter users best strategy to break up their communication into meaningful channels, similar to a radio frequency. If you only want to tune in to a conversation that uses a human-powered taxonomy, you can provide the full name of the channel including its # prefix as part of your query along with any other expressions. To search for folks who forgot to include the hashtag but were likely intending to post to the channel, you could try the query `swineflu -#swineflu`.

Referencing Users

A common requirement for Twitter applications is to detect and respond to conversations. To accomplish this, you can use special operators along with user screen names to search for messages to, from, and mentioning other users.

From

Use `from:` in front of a screen name to constrain your results to a particular author. The query `#tweetsharp from:Dimebrain OR from:jdiller OR from:JakCharlton` will return recent updates in the TweetSharp project channel, but only those written by one of its contributors.

To

To find statuses directed to a particular account, use `to:` as a prefix to the recipient screen name. Twitter search defines messages directed to a particular user based on where the user reference is found in the status update. For a message to belong to a recipient, it must reference the user, using the @ symbol, at the beginning of the message body; if the message is for more than one user, as long as each referenced user is listed before any message content, using `to:` will uncover them.

References

In contrast with using the `to:` operator, if you only provide the full text for a user reference, which is the @ symbol prefixing a valid screen name, you can obtain search results where a specific user is mentioned. On Twitter's own site, this is equivalent to the *Mentions* feature. This is a great way to keep up with conversations relating to a specific Twitter account. Another helpful query is to find people who meant to reach you, but didn't reference you properly. To make sure no follower is left behind, try `Dimebrain -@dimebrain -from:Dimebrain`, where `Dimebrain` is the account you wish to check for errant references.

User Sentiment

Some Twitter application ideas shine when they can test the sentiments of users in real-time, whether they are fans and foes of your product or cause, or if they are actively seeking advice. Twitter provides some operators to help with this task.

Positivity

Adding `:)` to your query is not only cute; it also helps Twitter filter results according to a best guess whether the content of the message is positive. Even though it also returns smiley faces literally, it is not the limit of this sentiment operator, as it will attempt to determine the overall mood of the actual content of the text.

Negativity

Similar to the positivity operator, negativity looks for disparaging comments surrounding your query and is activated using the `:(` operator. It is fairly effective, but sentiment operators should be part of your efforts—rather than the only method—to determine sentiment, as results are sometimes inaccurate. For example, the `:P` digital smiley, which is often associated with good humor, is sometimes detected as a negative reaction.

Question

Users that are asking a question are found using the `?` operator. Providing just `?` will turn Twitter Search into an instant Q&A platform, though it is most useful combined with multiple operators to find specific inquiries.

Timelines

You may further constrain your query by providing time-bound limits, which is useful for limiting search results to specific time periods whether past or present.

Since

The `since:` operator takes a date formatted as *yyyy-MM-dd*, ensuring no search results appear that did not occur until on or after the given date. Because Twitter is near real-time, unless you are specifying a very recent date and expect to find limited results based on the rest of your query, this operator may appear to have no effect—there might be plenty of recent results to obtain.

Until

The `until:` operator takes a date formatted as *yyyy-MM-dd*, ensuring no search results appear that are after the given date. This is useful for time boxing results, though you cannot request a date that is further than a month away from the current date, otherwise you will receive an HTTP 404 response indicating that no results are found.

Context

Outside of search, you may want to see specific context with your results. The Search API allows you to specify some contextual operators to help locate application demographics and user linking behavior. These contextual operators additionally limit results to a past seven-day window.

Links

Adding the operator expression `filter:links` to your query will result in restricting your results to those that contain valid URLs. This is useful for locating messages that refer other users to off-site content.

Source

The `source:` operator allows you to filter results based on the Twitter application that the user's message originated from. This is obviously useful for tracking usage of your application, as well as those of your competition. You must provide the common name for the application as recognized by Twitter, i.e., `source:motto` would restrict results to users who use the *motto* Twitter client.

Search Parameters

After a query is expressed, you can add additional URL parameters to tune the results of the search further, outside the scope of raw message content. The following search parameters are supported.

Geo Location

Twitter does not provide arbitrary geocoding capability natively, but it does allow you to perform basic location geocode limiting using the user's self-reported profile location. Specifically, this means Twitter maps a plain text city or other locale to latitude and longitude coordinates internally, and provides the `geocode` parameter to query against real coordinates you provide. Although some custom applications update the user's profile location on the user's behalf, changing it to specific coordinates, this functionality is not performed by Twitter itself. To search for messages within a geo location, you provide the actual latitude and longitude, as well as the distance tolerance in miles (`mi`) or kilometers (`km`), separated by commas. This example would return all results for the word fun within 100 miles of Ottawa, Canada.

Example

```
GET: http://search.twitter.com/search.json?q=fun&geocode=45.4215,-75.691894,
100mi
```

You can find a variety of online sources for mapping real world addresses to geo coordinates, such as `http://www.batchgeocode.com`.

Pagination

The Search API uses a default count of 15 results per page per query. You can use page and rpp, similar to the REST API's page and count parameters to retrieve more results. The rpp parameter sets the desired results per page and is limited to a maximum of 100 results. The page and rpp parameters in combination cannot provide more than 1,500 results based on the implied usage. This means that you cannot add the URL parameter values page=16&rpp=100 to your query and get a meaningful result, because this would imply 16 * 100 = 1600 total search results. If you are looking to cover a wide range of statuses you may want to take advantage of the since: query operator or the since_id query parameter to set your search within a specific time, though Twitter limits how far into the past your queries can reach, and this limit is a dynamic number based on performance factors of the service as a whole.

Timelines

One of the more useful Search API parameters for keeping up with frequent updates is since_id. You can use this parameter to filter your query to only return results that occur after a specific status's creation, defined by ID. This means that your application can internally track the last status retrieved, and provide that status' ID as the since_id parameter value, ensuring that you only retrieve messages you don't already have.

Callbacks

Covered in detail in Chapter 4, the Search API supports JSONP callbacks by specifying the name of the client-side *padding* function to invoke via the callback query parameter.

Globalization

Twitter is useful in any language, and provides a way to constrain queries to include a specific language using the lang parameter. You need to specify the two-letter language code as outlined by ISO 639-1 as the URL parameter value, i.e., lang=en. Examples include en (English), es (Spanish), and fr (French). You can find a complete list of language codes at http://en.wikipedia.org/wiki/List_of_ ISO_639-1_codes.

Search Objects

Twitter's Search API currently supports representations in the JSON format only. To accommodate this constraint, you can use one of the JSON to object conversion methods from Chapter 3. To work with both search queries and trends effectively, you can use both JavaScriptSerializer and DataContractJsonSerializer approaches.

Queries

The Search API in non-syndicated formats returns a detailed wrapper object providing both the results of the query and context around the query itself, to help with further searches and reporting. The nested statuses in a search result are slightly modified versions of the TwitterStatus object, and contain some important representational differences.

Example

```
GET: http://search.twitter.com/search.json?q=from:wrox
{"results":
 [
    {"text":"Bill Evjen interview on ASP.NET, books, MVC vs webforms, ASP.NET 3.5
SP1 at dzone.com: http:\/\/bit.ly\/7GW5J",
      "to_user_id":null,
        "from_user":"wrox",
           "id":1708585886,
        "from_user_id":83334,
        "iso_language_code":"en",
        "source":"&lt;a
href=&quot;http:\/\/www.tweetdeck.com\/&quot;&gt;TweetDeck&lt;\/a&gt;",

"profile_image_url":"http:\/\/s3.amazonaws.com\/twitter_production\/profile_
images\/196512481\/0470257024_normal.jpg",
        "created_at":"Tue, 05 May 2009 18:30:38 +0000"},
        {"text":"RT @philderksen: @robertschultz My company just received Wrox's
asp.net mvc 1.0 book also. Good stuff so far.",
        "to_user_id":null,
        "from_user":"wrox",
        "id":1708496138,
        "from_user_id":83334,
        "iso_language_code":"en",
        "source":"&lt;a
href=&quot;http:\/\/www.tweetdeck.com\/&quot;&gt;TweetDeck&lt;\/a&gt;",

"profile_image_url":"http:\/\/s3.amazonaws.com\/twitter_production\/profile_
images\/196512481\/0470257024_normal.jpg",
        "created_at":"Tue, 05 May 2009 18:20:28 +0000"},
        {"text":"Sympathy and best wishes to any of my Microsoft friends affected
by today's additional layoffs.",
        "to_user_id":null,
        "from_user":"wrox",
        "id":1708399840,
        "from_user_id":83334,
        "iso_language_code":"en",
        "source":"&lt;a
href=&quot;http:\/\/www.tweetdeck.com\/&quot;&gt;TweetDeck&lt;\/a&gt;",

"profile_image_url":"http:\/\/s3.amazonaws.com\/twitter_production\/profile_
images\/196512481\/0470257024_normal.jpg",
        "created_at":"Tue, 05 May 2009 18:09:40 +0000"}
 ],
 "since_id":0,
 "max_id":1708585886,
 "refresh_url":"?since_id=1708585886&q=from%3Awrox",
 "results_per_page":3,
 "next_page":"?page=2&max_id=1708585886&rpp=3&q=from%3Awrox",
 "completed_in":0.058115,
 "page":1,
 "query":"from%3Awrox"}
}
```

A possible object model for a `TwitterSearchResult` wrapper and its nested `TwitterSearchStatus` collection results are displayed in Figure 4-1.

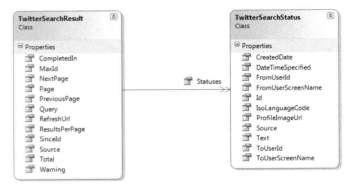

Figure 4-1

A breakdown of the elements returned in the JSON response for query results are outlined in Table 4-1.

Table 4-1: Twitter Search Query Elements

Element Name	Description
since_id	If a `since_id` parameter value was specified in the original request, it is provided here.
max_id	This element describes the most recent status by ID retrieved with these results.
refresh_url	Provides a convenience string fragment representing the query string you can send back to Twitter to get the results of the same query expression, but for statuses created after the ID defined by `max_id`. This simplifies retrieving a continuous stream of results for the given query.
results_per_page	This element returns the number of actual updates provided by the query.
next_page previous_page	Provides a convenience string fragment representing the query string you can send back to Twitter to get the results of the same query expression when there are more results available in either direction. You can use a combination of `next_page` and `previous_page` to provide pagination for your application. Perhaps more importantly, these elements won't contain data when no further results are available, allowing you to write logic that loops through results until no subsequent pages are found.

Element Name	Description
completed_in	This element tracks Twitter's search performance by providing a floating point value indicating the number of seconds it took Twitter to process the results.
page	The current page of results the output references.
query	The query expression used to make the original Search API call, without parameters.
results	A nested element collection of status updates that represents the actual content of the search results.

Although search results contain a form of status, it is not the same collection of elements you assembled into the TwitterStatus object in Chapter 2. In Figure 4-2, you can see the difference between the TwitterSearchStatus, returned in search results, and TwitterStatus, returned in REST API calls.

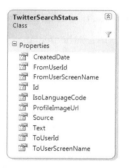
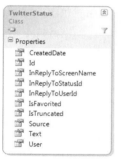

Figure 4-2

The TwitterSearchStatus object provides a source language, and gains some additional insight into the recipient of the message, because TwitterStatus is only informed about the recipient user if the status itself is in reply to a particular message. However, the FromUserId and ToUserId properties reference the internal IDs for users as they existed for the original search service provided by *Summize* before it was purchased by Twitter. This means that these values currently hold little value to you, and obtaining the user's actual ID will require you to make additional REST API calls. Details about the elements returned for search statuses are found in Table 4-2.

Table 4-2: Twitter Search Status Elements

Element Name	Description
created_at	The date and time the status was created, expressed in the Twitter Search API date format.
id	The unique ID corresponding to the true status representation on Twitter.
from_user_id	The internal Search API ID for the user who sent the original message. *This value has no meaning for you.*
from_user	The screen name for the user who sent the original message. This is useful for obtaining more user details about the sender via the REST API if needed.
to_user_id	The internal Search API ID for the user who received the original message. *This value has no meaning for you.*
to_user	The screen name for the user who received the original message. This is useful for obtaining more recipient user details via the REST API if needed.
text	The full-text content of the status.
source	The URL to the Twitter application used to send the message.
iso_language_code	The two-letter language code for the declared language of the message based on sending users' profiles.

Trends

The object model for trends has subtle variations that make it difficult to deserialize into objects without a custom converter and the `JavaScriptSerializer` class. Specifically, the date and times that separate trends into their appropriate *buckets* are generated as JSON properties. Because you cannot provide a real class property for every possible date and time, you must design your trend classes differently. In addition, the date and time formats and schema used for trend results are not consistent.

Examples

Due to API evolution, there is a difference in schema output for the original top 10 `trends` URL, and the updated, explicit `trends/current` resource. They are provided in the following code for comparison.

```
GET: http://search.twitter.com/trends.json
{"as_of":"Tue, 05 May 2009 20:04:26 +0000",
 "trends":
 [{"name":"Dom DeLuise","url":
    "http:\/\/search.twitter.com\/search?q=%22Dom+DeLuise%22"},
   {"name":"Arsenal","url":"http:\/\/search.twitter.com\/search?q=Arsenal+OR+%23arse
nal"},
   {"name":"Happy Cinco De
Mayo","url":"http:\/\/search.twitter.com\/search?q=%22Hap
py+Cinco+De+Mayo%22+OR+%22Cinco+De+Mayo%22"},
   {"name":"Swine Flu","url":"http:\/\/search.twitter.com\/search?q=%22Swine+Flu%22"},
```

```
{"name":"#packrat","url":"http:\/\/search.twitter.com\/search?q=%23packrat"},
{"name":"#railsconf","url":"http:\/\/search.twitter.com\/search?q=%23railsconf"},
{"name":"Apple","url":"http:\/\/search.twitter.com\/search?q=Apple+OR+%23apple"},
{"name":"H1N1","url":"http:\/\/search.twitter.com\/search?q=H1N1"},
{"name":"KFC","url":"http:\/\/search.twitter.com\/search?q=KFC"},
{"name":"Star Trek","url":"http:\/\/search.twitter.com\/search?q=%22Star+Trek%22"}]
```

GET: http://search.twitter.com/trends/current.json

```
{"as_of":1241553544,
 "trends":
 {"2009-05-05 19:59:04":
 [{"query":"\"Dom DeLuise\"",
   "name":"Dom DeLuise"},
  {"query":"Arsenal OR #arsenal",
   "name":"Arsenal"},
  {"query":"\"Happy Cinco De Mayo\" OR \"Cinco De Mayo\"",
   "name":"Happy Cinco De Mayo"},
  {"query":"\"Swine Flu\"","name":"Swine Flu"},
  {"query":"#packrat","name":"#packrat"},
  {"query":"#railsconf","name":"#railsconf"},
  {"query":"Apple OR #apple","name":"Apple"},
  {"query":"H1N1","name":"H1N1"},
  {"query":"KFC","name":"KFC"},
  {"query":"\"Star Trek\"","name":"Star Trek"}]
 }
}
```

The formats vary, but both schemas provide a relevant SearchDate, providing context for when the query was made, as well as the trend name and a way to find the trending topic using further Search API calls. The original schema uses the complete HTML link to the Twitter site's search query, while the updated schema gives you just the query you need to pass to the Search API to work with the trend data. You can design an object model that harmonizes both of these examples, shown in Figure 4-3.

Figure 4-3

Trends are indexed by the date and time they are relevant; as trends wax and wane in popularity, and based on the time scope you chose, these lists will contain different numbers of results and use different raw date and time formats. Specifically, weekly trends will include timestamps that reference dates but no time, daily trends will truncate their date and times based on hours, and current trends will provide the time the query was searched. In Table 4-3, each of the trend elements is described.

Table 4-3: Twitter Search Trends Elements

Element Name	Description
as_of	The timestamp for the time the query was received by the Search API.
trends	An inner collection of trending topics, indexed by relevant date and/or time.

Further details around the nested trend elements are provided in Table 4-4.

Table 4-4: Twitter Search Trend Elements

Element Name	Description
{dynamic date}	This element name changes based on the time slice of the current collection of top trends. It could be in any of yyyy-MM-dd (*weekly*), yyyy-MM-dd HH:mm (*daily*), or yyyy-MM-dd HH:mm:ss (*current*) date formats.
query	For trends/current, trends/daily, and trends/weekly methods, this element provides the query expression that identifies a trending topic. Usually this is a single word or hashtag, but can include additional operators.
name	This element provides the plain name of the trending topic, as displayed on Twitter.com.

Converting Queries and Trends

Because query and trend results do not line up well with the equivalent methods in the REST API, you can use the following code examples to help make short work of the various nuances of date formats and nested conversion. This example provides a custom JavaScriptConverter for use with JavaScriptSerializer for converting results to trends:

```
using System;
using System.Collections;
using System.Collections.Generic;
using System.Web.Script.Serialization;
using Wrox.Twitter.Objects;
using Wrox.Twitter.TwitterSearchObjects.Objects;
```

```
namespace Wrox.Twitter.TwitterSearchObjects.Converters
{
    public class TwitterTrendsConverter : JavaScriptConverter
    {
        public override IEnumerable<Type> SupportedTypes
        {
            get
            {
                return new[]
                        {
                            typeof (TwitterSearchTrends)
                        };
            }
        }

        public override object Deserialize(
            IDictionary<string, object> dictionary,
            Type type,
            JavaScriptSerializer serializer)
        {
            if (dictionary == null)
            {
                return null;
            }

            var searchTrends = new TwitterSearchTrends();

            object value;
            if (dictionary.TryGetValue("trends", out value))
            {
                // there are two possible trend schemas depending on the URL
                if (value is Dictionary<string, object>)
                {
                    // parse the search date from the as_of element
                    var unixTime = Convert.ToInt64(dictionary["as_of"]);
                    var searchDate = unixTime.FromUnixTime();
                    searchTrends.SearchDate = searchDate;

                    var entries = (Dictionary<string, object>) value;
                    foreach (var entry in entries)
                    {
                        // parse the dynamic DateTime as the relevant date,
                        // which could be based on the current date and time,
                        // a date with multiple times (for daily trends), or
                        // a date without time (for weekly trends)
                        var relevantDate = entry.Key.FromTrendsDate();

                        // convert child array into trend objects
                        var trendList = (ArrayList) entry.Value;
                        ConvertTrendArrayList(trendList,
                                              searchTrends,
                                              relevantDate);
                    }
```

```
            }
            else if (value is ArrayList)
            {
                // parse the date from the as_of element
                var relevantDate =
                    dictionary["as_of"].ToString().FromSearchDate();

                // the relevant date is also the search date in this case
                searchTrends.SearchDate = relevantDate;

                // convert child array into trend objects
                var trendList = (ArrayList) value;
                ConvertTrendArrayList(trendList, searchTrends, relevantDate);
            }
        }

        return searchTrends;
    }

    private static void ConvertTrendArrayList(ArrayList trendList,
                                              TwitterSearchTrends trends,
                                              DateTime relevantDate)
    {
        // add an indexed entry for this date bucket
        trends.Add(relevantDate, new List<TwitterSearchTrend>());

        foreach (Dictionary<string, object> item in trendList)
        {
            var trend = new TwitterSearchTrend();

            // http://search.twitter.com/trends.json
            // http://search.twitter.com/trends/current.json
            if (item.ContainsKey("name"))
            {
                trend.Name = item["name"].ToString();
            }

            // http://search.twitter.com/trends/current.json
            if (item.ContainsKey("query"))
            {
                trend.Query = item["query"].ToString();
            }

            // http://search.twitter.com/trends.json
            if (item.ContainsKey("url"))
            {
                trend.Url = item["url"].ToString();
            }
```

```
                     // add the deserialized trend to its relevant bucket
                     trends[relevantDate].Add(trend);
                 }
             }

             public override IDictionary<string, object> Serialize
                     (object obj, JavaScriptSerializer serializer) { throw new
         NotImplementedException(); }
         }
     }
```

The `TwitterExtensions` code in use throughout previous chapters is due for an update to provide the `FromTrendsDate` and `FromUnixTime` methods previously featured, allowing safe conversion from multiple possible date formats. This code demonstrates the additional functionality:

```
using System;
using System.Collections.Generic;
using System.Globalization;

namespace Wrox.Twitter.Objects
{
    public static class TwitterExtensions
    {
        public const string TrendsWeeklyDateFormat =
            "yyyy-MM-dd";

        public const string TrendsDailyDateFormat =
            "yyyy-MM-dd HH:mm";

        public const string TrendsCurrentDateFormat =
            "yyyy-MM-dd HH:mm:ss";


        public static DateTime FromTrendsDate(this string input)
        {
            // depending on the call, the trends date format could change
            return ConvertDate(input,
                            new[]
                            {
                                TrendsCurrentDateFormat, TrendsDailyDateFormat,
                                TrendsWeeklyDateFormat
                            });
        }

        public static DateTime FromUnixTime(this long input)
        {
            var date = new DateTime(1970, 1, 1);
            date = date.AddSeconds(input);

            return date;
        }
```

```
            private static DateTime ConvertDate(string input,
                                                IEnumerable<string> formats)
        {
            if (String.IsNullOrEmpty(input))
            {
                return new DateTime();
            }

            foreach(var format in formats)
            {
                // try to parse the current format
                DateTime result;
                if (DateTime.TryParseExact(input,
                                    format,
                                    CultureInfo.InvariantCulture,
                                    DateTimeStyles.AdjustToUniversal, out result))
                {
                    // success
                    return result;
                }
            }

            // Couldn't convert with any provided format
            return new DateTime();
        }
    }
}
```

You can convert to the `TwitterSearchStatus` object using `DataContractJsonSerializer` in a
similar way to REST API objects using the same approach, though it's worth noting that the Search API
may return empty elements rather than omitting elements that do not apply. This interferes with the
deserialization process. To mitigate this, you can declare all value types on the `TwitterSearchStatus`
object as nullable, demonstrated with the following class code:

```
using System;
using System.Runtime.Serialization;
using Wrox.Twitter.Objects;

namespace Wrox.Twitter.TwitterSearchObjects.Objects
{
    [DataContract]
    public class TwitterSearchStatus
    {
        [DataMember(Name = "id")]
        public long? Id { get; set; }
```

```csharp
        [DataMember(Name = "text")]
        public string Text { get; set; }

        [DataMember(Name = "source")]
        public string Source { get; set; }

        [DataMember(Name="to_user_id")]
        public int? ToUserId { get; set; }

        [DataMember(Name = "from_user_id")]
        public int? FromUserId { get; set; }

        [DataMember(Name = "from_user")]
        public string FromUserScreenName { get; set; }

        [DataMember(Name = "to_user")]
        public string ToUserScreenName { get; set; }

        [DataMember(Name = "iso_language_code")]
        public string IsoLanguageCode { get; set; }

        [DataMember(Name = "profile_image_url")]
        public string ProfileImageUrl { get; set; }

        [DataMember(Name = "created_at")]
        public string DateTimeSpecified { get; set; }

        public DateTime CreatedDate
        {
            get
            {
                return DateTimeSpecified.FromSearchDate();
            }
            set
            {
                var dateTime = value.ToString
                    (TwitterExtensions.SearchDateFormat);
                DateTimeSpecified = dateTime;
            }
        }
    }
}
```

Summary

The Search API is capable of providing fast responses to creative and complex requests for real-time data. With it you can find interesting facts, watch local activity, keep tabs on the competition, manage user timelines, improve communication with your application's user base, and fulfill countless other uses:

❏ You learned the small but versatile feature space of the Search API represented by queries and trending topics.

❏ You referenced the Search API's collection of expression operators and URL parameters that offer configurability for your searches including convenient query pagination, geo location, and language filtering.

❏ You worked with JSON elements as .NET objects, and worked out some specific details around dealing with query and trends dynamic results when converting responses into data classes.

In Chapter 5, you will uncover the syndicated content formats available extensively in the Search API, but also in select areas of the REST API, and use them to provide alternative ways of saving and consuming API requests, for applications that provide feeds for users, as well as lightweight or optimized applications that don't require complete Twitter object graphs to function well.

5

Working with RSS and Atom Syndication

"Twitter's support for the RSS and Atom formats really broadens where you can incorporate Twitter data. Want to keep an eye on an interesting topic? Subscribe to a search in your RSS reader. Want to combine, filter, or remix your twitter stream? Feed it into Yahoo Pipes and slice and dice it to your heart's content."

Kevin Dente, *Witty*

Similar to XML and JSON introduced, with the Twitter REST API, this chapter goes in to better detail about how to handle *Really Simple Syndication (RSS)* and Atom feeds, both valid return formats when communicating with Twitter, and available extensively through the Search API. In this chapter you learn how to consume RSS and Atom feeds to develop applications that use near real-time search results from Twitter.

Syndication on the Web

The spirit of web syndication, and the technology that arrived in the late 1990s to facilitate it, is the idea that content on a page is more valuable to everyone if it's portable, not just between web sites but between any technology that wants to present it. Web consumers needed a better way to assemble all the content they cared about in one place (imagine if you still had to visit each and every web site you were interested in just to see if it had updated!), and content creators needed a better way to share their content with other web sites easily and under clear license, but also reach wider audiences beyond their web presence.

There are two syndication formats supported by the majority of web applications and feed reader applications: RSS 2.0 and Atom 1.0. A rich history of development and debate exists between both formats, though both attempt to provide the same solution in a different way. Generally, the Atom format provides more extensibility, better handling of content delivery, and interoperability with other XML namespaces and URIs. The wide adoption of both formats ensures you are free to use either when creating applications that provide syndication for your users. You may, however, have a preference for one or the other for consuming Twitter based on the content Twitter returns in both formats.

Feed Objects

With the exception of the structure of the data returned, both RSS and Atom are XML formats. The important difference for your usage is that the data returned by Twitter in RSS or Atom is not a representation of the real resource entities you're expecting from XML or JSON formats, but rather a summary of the most essential information for those entities, with additional URI links to retrieve the information in the way you have up to this point. Depending on how you design your application, working with summary information may introduce an advantage for you, because transferring large object graphs of Twitter entities in XML or JSON requires more bandwidth in general.

RSS 2.0

RSS output is structured around a *channel* of information containing a collection of *items*. Here is a representative example of a single Twitter status returned in RSS format, based on a user timeline API call.

```xml
<?xml version="1.0" encoding="UTF-8"?>
<rss version="2.0" xmlns:atom="http://www.w3.org/2005/Atom">
  <channel>
    <title>Twitter / dimebrain</title>
    <link>http://twitter.com/dimebrain</link>
    <atom:link type="application/rss+xml" rel="self" href="http://twitter.com/
statuses/user_timeline/Dimebrain.rss?count=1"/>
    <description>Twitter updates from Daniel Crenna / dimebrain.</description>
    <language>en-us</language>
    <ttl>40</ttl>
    <item>
      <title>dimebrain: @jdiller Make sure you really stick it to the author. Being
pedantic also helps.</title>
      <description>dimebrain: @jdiller Make sure you really stick it to the author.
Being pedantic also helps.</description>
      <pubDate>Thu, 30 Apr 2009 02:08:50 +0000</pubDate>
      <guid>http://twitter.com/dimebrain/statuses/1655219639</guid>
      <link>http://twitter.com/dimebrain/statuses/1655219639</link>
    </item>
  </channel>
</rss>
```

One interesting observation about Twitter's RSS output is that it uses the Atom namespace to provide the API method URI used to return the current results. Table 5-1 provides a breakdown of what data is available to you when consuming RSS.

Table 5-1: RSS Output

XML Element	Description
`<channel>`	
`<title>`	The service source (Twitter) and the user's screen name.
`<link>`	The public URI to the user's timeline page on Twitter.
`<description>`	The original Twitter API query method used to obtain this result.
`<language>`	The real name and screen name of the user, with Twitter context.
`<ttl>`	The four-letter cultural code for the user's profile specified language.
	The *Time to Live* for this feed; it is a request to keep hits to the API to update feed data to within one request per the number of minutes specified in this element.
`<item>`	
`<title>`	The screen name and message content for a given status or direct message.
`<description>`	The screen name and message content for a given status or direct message. (identical to the previous entry)
`<pubDate>`	The published date of the status or direct message enclosed in the `item` element.
`<guid>`	A URI to a permanent location for the status or direct message. In this case, it points to Twitter's page for the status. The URI includes the status or direct message ID.
`<link>`	A URI to a permanent location for the status or direct message. In this case, it points to Twitter's page for the status. The URI includes the status or direct message ID. (identical to the previous entry)

Based on this example output, to fit the RSS specification, there is a fair bit of duplicate data in the feed. Although full user profile data is absent from this feed, you are still able to obtain the user's full name, screen name, and the status content and ID, perhaps using regular expressions to parse out the values.

Depending on your needs, this may be enough to run your application, or you may need to make follow-up API calls to fill in the missing information. The URIs referenced in the output are less useful to you, as they refer to Twitter's own web site rather than raw API data. Mapping these elements to an object model might look like what is shown in Figure 5-1.

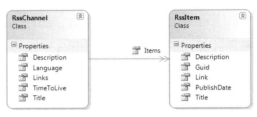

Figure 5-1

Atom 1.0

Turning to the Atom format, the output is similar to RSS in that it is structured as syndicated content, and the following example shows a representative Atom response to a Twitter API request for a status.

```xml
<?xml version="1.0" encoding="UTF-8"?>
<feed xml:lang="en-US" xmlns="http://www.w3.org/2005/Atom">
  <title>Twitter / dimebrain</title>
  <id>tag:twitter.com,2007:Status</id>
  <link type="text/html" rel="alternate" href="http://twitter.com/dimebrain"/>
  <link type="application/atom+xml" rel="self" href="http://twitter.com/statuses/
user_timeline/Dimebrain.atom?count=1"/>
  <updated>2009-05-01T01:01:16+00:00</updated>
  <subtitle>Twitter updates from Daniel Crenna / dimebrain.</subtitle>
    <entry>
      <title>dimebrain: Looking to compare notes with others whose WPF
prototypes run like a bicycle in Win7 but a jet on Vista.</title>
      <content type="html">dimebrain: Looking to compare notes with others
whose WPF prototypes run like a bicycle in Win7 but a jet on Vista.</content>
      <id>tag:twitter.com,2007:http://twitter.com/dimebrain/statuses/1663923737</id>
      <published>2009-04-30T23:15:57+00:00</published>
      <updated>2009-04-30T23:15:57+00:00</updated>
      <link type="text/html" rel="alternate" href="http://twitter
.com/dimebrain/statuses/1663923737"/>
      <link type="image/png" rel="image" href="profileImage.png"/>
      <author>
        <name>Daniel Crenna</name>
        <uri>http://www.dimebrain.com</uri>
      </author>
    </entry>
</feed>
```

You will notice that the format of dates in this Atom example differ from the dates for the same API call returned previously in RSS format. Twitter will move toward a consistent date representation in the future, but today, you need to adjust your own code to account for this fact, or standardize on a single feed format to consume the API. In this case, the Search API's date format is used for Atom feeds, even for REST API calls. Table 5-2 provides the data available within an Atom feed.

Table 5-2: Atom Output

XML Element	Description
	<feed>
<title>	The service source (Twitter) and the user's screen name.
<id>	A unique identifier for the feed, always the same value in this case, and the year indicator is a reflection of when the Atom functionality was released into production.
<link>[1]	The public URI to the user's timeline page on Twitter.
<link>[2]	The original Twitter API query method used to obtain this result.
<updated>	The date and time the API was called to retrieve this result.
<subtitle>	The real name and screen name of the user, with Twitter context.
	<entry>
<title>	The screen name and message content for a given status or direct message.
<content>	The screen name and message content for a given status or direct message (identical to the previous element, except for the declared content type).
<id>	A unique identifier for the status or direct message includes a URI to the status or direct message, on Twitter, which includes its ID.
<published>	The date the original status or direct message was published.
<updated>	The date the original status or direct message was updated, which is always identical to the published date.
<link>[1]	A URI to the status or direct message's permanent location on the Twitter site, which includes the ID.
<link>[2]	A URI to the user's profile photo.
<author>	Additional elements for author data, namely his or her profile URL and real name.

The Atom feed suffers from similar data duplication issues found with the previous RSS example due to feed validation conformance. It also includes an unnecessary updated element, when Twitter statuses and direct messages are inherently *atomic*; there is no concept of updating either with the API. The Atom feed provides the date and time of when your API call was made, which is not provided with RSS. Due to formatting, Atom content is roughly 75 percent larger in size than RSS, which, if you're conscious about bandwidth usage, may not justify a few additional data elements of context; the date the search was performed, and URIs to the user's profile URL and profile image. Similar data classes to describe an Atom feed in objects could resemble the following class diagram as shown in Figure 5-2.

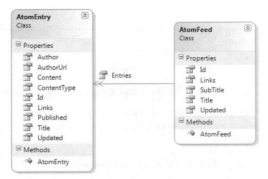

Figure 5-2

Even though there is much larger discussion yet to take place about the importance of RSS, Atom, and syndication as a whole, for the purposes of Twitter application development it is helpful to consider these as additional formats, judged solely on their merits in providing the right data to your application. If the features you intend to provide are sparse, or if you will provide your own feeds to users that combine the results of multiple search queries, then consuming API calls in RSS or Atom formats may provide the performance or simplicity you need. In the next section, the details of mapping this content to classes, and extracting the relevant Twitter information from either format, are covered using two strategies available in the .NET 3.5 Framework.

Consuming Feeds

Ultimately, consuming syndicated content through a feed is no different than making a REST call for a resource in XML or JSON, and the Twitter API is no exception. The effective difference is that the format itself, although XML based, is specific to syndication services in RSS, Atom, or another format. Similar to the multiple strategies for transforming XML and JSON data in Chapter 3, this chapter covers two specific strategies in .NET for consuming syndicated content: using LINQ to XML to manually walk a graph of XML elements, and the more robust WCF Syndication Services for automating the consumption of feed data. Both methods allow for quick transformation of syndicated content, with the intent to repurpose it into your own applications.

Why Syndication?

Before diving into the implementation details of data conversion of yet another REST format, it might help to know what value syndication has over standard XML or JSON types, which arguably arrive as more or less complete representations of the underlying entities they represent—you already have a clear path to obtaining complete Twitter objects for users, statuses, and direct messages. Syndication data, on the other hand, takes the form of what is essentially a summarized collection of links to those representations, which must undergo conversion in those formats when requested. Chapter 1 informs you that this is a fundamental principle of RESTful services, but it seems anti-climatic to offer an RSS and Atom feed to data that is more easily processed as XML or JSON. To help answer that question, examine the following properties of RSS or Atom formats:

❑   They are generally publically consumed; though an API call for an XML collection of recent user tweets is equivalent to the same request as an RSS feed, a feed is consumable by a wide range of consumer applications without requiring additional software or remembering a URL.

❑   They are presented as a digest of resource locations rather than raw data, making them more efficient for retrieving large numbers of tweets when you are only interested in basic meta-data and the content of the messages.

❑   They are easier to transform into your own feeds if your application provides syndicated content for its users.

Though retrieving complete user and status representations is simple and direct for shallow applications that don't cache data, you may find that as you begin to build more complex designs and move away from the discovery phase of your Twitter development process, that syndication formats offer an efficient and ubiquitous way to present and remix streams of Twitter data. The following sections provide you with tools for consuming RSS and Atom formats retrieved from the Twitter REST and Search APIs.

With LINQ to XML

After Chapter 3, there are no surprises with LINQ to XML's flexible method for controlling every aspect of parsing XML data. To convert from XML to the AtomFeed class declared earlier, you can follow the same approach as converting from XML to Twitter objects, though you will need to add one additional component to your utility classes; XML namespaces. When declared as they are on syndicated output, scope element names to the logical namespace hierarchy they belong to. If no namespace is declared, as is the case with Twitter objects in XML format, all element names are locally based. In the case of Atom, elements are returned under the http://www.w3.org/2005/Atom namespace; any attempt to fetch them using XContainer's Element method will return null. The following code performs the task of mapping raw Atom output to the AtomFeed and AtomEntry classes:

```
using System;
using System.Collections.Generic;
using System.Xml.Linq;
using Wrox.Twitter.FeedsWithLinqToXml.Objects;
using Wrox.Twitter.NUrl;
using Wrox.Twitter.Objects;

namespace Wrox.Twitter.FeedsWithLinqToXml
{
    internal partial class Program
    {
        private static void Main()
        {
            var atom =
                "http://search.twitter.com/search.atom?q=from:biz"
                .Get();

            var feed = ToAtomFeed(atom);
            Console.WriteLine(feed.Title);
            foreach (var entry in feed.Entries)
```

```
                        {
                            Console.WriteLine("{0}:{1}", entry.Author, entry.Content);
                        }
                        Console.ReadLine();
            }

            private static AtomFeed ToAtomFeed(string atom)
            {
                var feed = (XContainer) XElement.Parse(atom);

                // you must declare a namespace to access elements that declare one
                var title = GetAtomElementValue(feed, "title");
                var id = GetAtomElementValue(feed, "id");
                var subTitle = GetAtomElementValue(feed, "subtitle");
                var links = GetAtomElementAttributeValues(feed, "link", "href");
                var entries = GetAtomElements(feed, "entry");

                var atomFeed = new AtomFeed
                                {
                                    Title = title,
                                    Id = id,
                                    SubTitle = subTitle
                                };

                foreach (var link in links)
                {
                    var uri = new Uri(link);
                    atomFeed.Links.Add(uri);
                }

                // populate the feed with entries
                PopulateAtomEntries(atomFeed, entries);
                return atomFeed;
            }

            private static void PopulateAtomEntries(AtomFeed atomFeed,
                                                    IEnumerable<XElement> entries)
            {
                foreach (var entry in entries)
                {
                    // convert entry element values
                    var title = GetAtomElementValue(entry, "title");
                    var content = GetAtomElementValue(entry, "content");
                    var id = GetAtomElementValue(entry, "id");
                    var published = GetAtomElementValue(entry, "published");
                    var links = GetAtomElementAttributeValues(entry, "link", "href");

                    // convert the author element values
                    var author = GetAtomElement(entry, "author");
                    var authorName = GetAtomElementValue(author, "name");
                    var authorUrl = GetAtomElementValue(author, "uri");

                    // create a new atom entry instance
                    var atomEntry = new AtomEntry
```

```
                {
                    Title = title,
                    Content = content,
                    Id = id,
                    // Atom uses the rate limit status date format for REST,
                    // rather than the REST date format you normally use,
                    // but the standard Search date if search is used
                    // Published = published.FromXmlHashDate(),
                    Published = published.FromAtomSearchDate(),
                    Author = authorName,
                    AuthorUrl = new Uri(authorUrl)
                };


                foreach (var link in links)
                {
                    var uri = new Uri(link);
                    atomEntry.Links.Add(uri);
                }

                atomFeed.Entries.Add(atomEntry);
            }
        }
    }
}
```

The helper methods used to parse Atom specifically address the Atom namespace using the Get method on the XName class; where you previously referenced elements simply by name, this static method provides an overload to tie an element name to a namespace. These helper methods are listed in the following code:

```
using System.Collections.Generic;
using System.Xml.Linq;

namespace Wrox.Twitter.FeedsWithLinqToXml
{
    internal partial class Program
    {
        private const string AtomNamespace = "http://www.w3.org/2005/Atom";

        private static string GetAtomElementValue(XContainer parent, string name)
        {
            var child = XName.Get(name, AtomNamespace);
            return GetElementValue(parent, child);
        }

        private static XElement GetAtomElement(XContainer parent, string name)
        {
            var child = XName.Get(name, AtomNamespace);
            var element = parent.Element(child);
            return element;
        }
```

```
private static IEnumerable<XElement> GetAtomElements(XContainer parent,
                                                     string elementName)
{
    var childName = XName.Get(elementName, AtomNamespace);
    return GetElements(parent, childName);
}

private static IEnumerable<string> GetAtomElementAttributeValues(
    XContainer parent, string elementName, string attributeName)
{
    var childName = XName.Get(elementName, AtomNamespace);
    return GetAttributeValues(parent, childName, attributeName);
}

private static IEnumerable<XElement> GetElements(XContainer parent,
                                                 XName child)
{
    var elements = parent.Elements(child);
    if (elements == null)
    {
        yield break;
    }

    foreach (var element in elements)
    {
        if (element == null)
        {
            continue;
        }

        yield return element;
    }
}

private static string GetElementValue(XContainer parent, XName child)
{
    var element = parent.Element(child);
    return element == null ? string.Empty : element.Value;
}

private static IEnumerable<string> GetAttributeValues(XContainer parent,
                                                      XName childName,
                                                      XName
                                                          attributeName)
{
    var elements = parent.Elements(childName);
    if (elements == null)
    {
        yield break;
    }

    foreach (var element in elements)
    {
```

```
        var attribute = element.Attribute(attributeName);
        if (attribute == null)
        {
            continue;
        }

        yield return attribute.Value ?? "";
    }
  }
 }
}
```

Using LINQ to XML is a good choice for quick parsing needs or when control over the content transformation is a top priority. Syndicated content poses no significant challenges beyond its first use to convert Twitter objects, but does come with a problematic introduction of additional date formats. Table 5-3 should help you decide what formatting method is the best choice depending on request made for syndicated content. Although RSS for either API target conforms to the Search API's date format for JSON calls, the Atom format uses the same date format returned in call to /account/rate_limit_ status for REST API calls, but a custom format for Search API calls.

Table 5-3: RSS and Atom Date Formats

Format	Target API	Date Format String
RSS	Any	*ddd, dd MMM yyyy HH:mm:ss zzzzz*
Atom	REST API	*yyyy-MM-ddTHH:mm:sszzzzzz*
Atom	Search API	*yyyy-MM-ddTHH:mm:ssZ*

Although most useful for publishing service endpoints in your code to consumers, WCF's Syndication Services does add native support for parsing RSS and Atom feeds. In the next section you will learn to use higher level classes to automatically handle feed parsing in either format.

Search API's Additional Namespaces

Beyond the fundamental elements provided by RSS and Atom formats, The Search API will also return additional context in other namespaces. These include the OpenSearch technology (http://a9.com/-/spec/opensearch/1.1/), Google's Base specification (http://base.google.com/ns/1.0), Yahoo!'s Media RSS (http://search .yahoo.com/mrss/), and Twitter's own contextual namespace (http://api .twitter.com). These namespaces provide more data for search results, including the dimensions and content type returned for the user's profile image, the number of actual results returned by a search query, and important warnings from Twitter itself. To retrieve this additional data, you can use the same techniques described earlier to reference XML elements by their namespace.

With SyndicationFeed *and* SyndicationItem

WCF's robust Syndication Services platform provides two classes, SyndicationFeed and SyndicationItem, available when you reference .NET's System.ServiceModel.Web library, that harmonize the RSS and Atom feed implementation details of channel and feed, and entry and item, respectively, into a single concept. It also provides a way to easily load external feed output existing in either format, parsing and populating these new classes automatically. Figure 5-3 outlines the relationship between these classes.

Figure 5-3

For you, the existence of these classes translates into requiring only one object model to convert syndicated content into something you can use to extract Twitter-specific data. Loading and parsing RSS and Atom content into these classes is straightforward, demonstrated by the following code.

```
// Return the most recent five statuses from a Twitter co-founder's account
var atom = "http://search.twitter.com/search.atom?q=from:biz&rpp=5".Get();

// Wrap the string response in a reader
var source = new StringReader(atom);
```

```
// Create an XML targetted reader
var reader = XmlReader.Create(source);

// Load a new syndicated feed object with an XML reader source
var feed = SyndicationFeed.Load(reader);
```

Now that you have a class representing the syndicated content in either supported format, you can walk the object graph to pick out the Twitter data you need to build your application. The following code takes an Atom feed and parses out selected content into new convenience classes, TwitterFeedResult and TwitterFeedInfo, for this purpose.

```
using System;
using System.IO;
using System.Linq;
using System.ServiceModel.Syndication;
using System.Text.RegularExpressions;
using System.Web;
using System.Xml;
using System.Xml.Linq;
using FeedsWithSyndicationServices.Objects;
using Wrox.Twitter.NUrl;

namespace FeedsWithSyndicationServices
{
    internal class Program
    {
        private const string OpenSearchNamespace =
            "http://a9.com/-/spec/opensearch/1.1/";

        private const string TwitterNamespace =
            "http://api.twitter.com/";

        private static void Main()
        {
            // Return the most recent five statuses from
            // a Twitter co-founder's account
            var atom =
                "http://search.twitter.com/search.atom?q=from:Dimebrain&rpp=5".
                    Get();

            // Wrap the string response in a reader
            var source = new StringReader(atom);

            // Create an XML targetted reader
            var reader = XmlReader.Create(source);

            // Load a new syndicated feed object with an XML reader source
            var feed = SyndicationFeed.Load(reader);

            // You would parse the values you care about from the feed object
            var results = ConvertFromAtomSource(feed);
```

```csharp
        foreach (var item in results.Items)
        {
            Console.WriteLine("{0}:{1}", item.UserScreenName, item.Text);
        }

        Console.WriteLine(results.Subject);
        Console.ReadLine();
    }

    private static TwitterFeedResults ConvertFromAtomSource(
        SyndicationFeed feed)
    {
        // Retrieve the results count from the opensearch namespace
        var itemsPerPage =
            feed.ElementExtensions.ReadElementExtensions
                <string>("itemsPerPage", OpenSearchNamespace).Single();

        // Create a results instance to store summary info
        var results = new TwitterFeedResults
                    {
                        // The time the search was received by Twitter
                        SearchDate = feed.LastUpdatedTime.Date,
                        // The feed subject
                        Subject = feed.Title.Text,
                        // The number of results returned with the feed
                        ResultsCount = Convert.ToInt32(itemsPerPage)
                    };

        foreach (var feedItem in feed.Items)
        {
            // Parse out the status/direct_message ID
            // using a regular expression
            var idMatch = Regex.Match(feedItem.Id, "(?<=:)\\d+");
            var id = Convert.ToInt64(idMatch.Value);

            // Parse out the real name and screen name
            // using a regular expression
            var authorName = feedItem.Authors[0].Name;
            var nameMatch = Regex.Match(authorName, "(?<=\\()[\\w\\s]+");
            var screenNameMatch = Regex.Match(authorName,
                                        "[\\w\\s]+(?=\\s\\()");
            var name = nameMatch.Value;
            var screenName = screenNameMatch.Value;

            // Obtain the URL of the application used to
            // post the message; the default is Twitter.com
            var source =
                feedItem.ElementExtensions.ReadElementExtensions
                    <string>("source", TwitterNamespace).Single();

            // Decode the URL in the source HTML entity
            var html = HttpUtility.HtmlDecode(source);
```

```
                // Find the href link attribute on the source entity
                var href = XElement.Parse(html).Attribute("href");

                // Attempt to parse the URL value from the href tag,
                // falling back to the default Twitter URL
                const string defaultUrl = "http://twitter.com";
                var url = href != null
                              ? href.Value ?? defaultUrl
                              : defaultUrl;

                var item = new TwitterFeedItem
                    {
                        // Set status properties
                        CreatedDate = feedItem.PublishDate.Date,
                        Id = id,
                        Text = feedItem.Title.Text,
                        Source = new Uri(url),
                        // Set user profile properties
                        UserName = name,
                        UserScreenName = screenName,
                        UserProfileUrl = feedItem.Authors[0].Uri,
                        UserImageUrl = feedItem.Links[1].Uri.ToString(),
                    };

                results.Items.Add(item);
            }

        return results;
        }
    }
}
```

SyndicationFeed is a good middle step to avoiding format-specific code when loading documents, but as the previous example demonstrates, it doesn't free you from the need to manually line up data fields for your use; using the same code with an RSS search result would fail, because the data schema differs. It is better to standardize your application on the format that provides the best tradeoff between content and bandwidth, and stick with it. The next section will use SyndicationFeed to build an asynchronous application for monitoring search queries on the desktop.

Synchronizing Applications with Feed Updates

Now that you can successfully convert RSS and Atom syndicated content into classes you can work with in your application, you should get acquainted with the style of programming that working with syndicated content implies. When you develop a Twitter application, you will need to approach it the same way you would if you were building a feed reader, regardless of what REST format you settle on. A feed reader is a piece of news aggregation software that allows a user to collect multiple feeds together, assembling the information they want to receive according to their own tastes.

To the casual user of a feed reader application, RSS, Atom, and other syndication formats look like *push* technologies; updates arrive when they're available, with little or no user interaction necessary to elicit the change. Similarly, your Twitter applications should *appear* to provide fresh updates to conversations your users are engaged in, just when they occur, and otherwise get out of the way. Ultimately, however, syndication involves *pulling* content from the publisher to the consumer, similar to any REST API, making a request and comparing the response with data already stored, to decide what aspect or content in the user's experience should change to match the current reality. Chapter 9 will deal with configuring push-based systems, but in general your applications can use the prevailing approach of data polling to pull updates down from a feed.

When to Pull Data

The *Time to Live (TTL)* property of an RSS feed provides a hint for the preferred maximum number of pull requests made by your application; it is a value, in minutes, for the amount of time your system should wait between polls. Although Twitter provides a TTL value of 40, it's not practical to wait that amount of time for most application scenarios. If you do not want to violate the TTL suggestion, you are better off using XML or JSON for more frequent API calls, and RSS or Atom when remixing several Twitter feeds in a background application, as an example, where time isn't of the essence.

Building a polling system is relatively straightforward, and is made more efficient in terms of the number and frequency of API calls made by leveraging the Search API's fully defined objects available as JSON. In this case, however, you can use syndicated content to quickly obtain essential data to display in a visual application. To implement a simple polling application for Windows, you will first need to set up a `Form` to direct the user's search behavior and a `UserControl` to create tweet messages from. The following listing is for the `UserControl`, showing a simple mapping between the important visual elements of a tweet and the text and author's image, implemented as public properties.

```
using System;
using System.Windows.Forms;

namespace Wrox.Twitter.SynchronizingFeeds
{
    public partial class TweetBox : UserControl
    {
        // provide a status date in case
        // you want to sort on it later
        public DateTime CreatedDate
        {
            get; set;
        }

        // the actual Twitter status content
        public string Tweet
        {
            get
            {
                return txtTweet.Text;
```

```
        }
        set
        {
            txtTweet.Text = value;
        }
    }

    // this string will direct the PictureBox control
    // to update its image from Twitter's static content servers
    public string ImageUrl
    {
        get
        {
            return pbProfileImage.ImageLocation;
        }
        set
        {
            pbProfileImage.ImageLocation = value;
        }
    }

    public TweetBox()
    {
        InitializeComponent();
    }

    // to ensure you find duplicates when using the Contains method,
    // override the default reference equality of this class and provide
    // a better comparison; in this case, comparing status content
    public override bool Equals(object obj)
    {
        var other = obj as TweetBox;
        return other != null && Tweet.Equals(other.Tweet);
    }

    // use the tweet content's hashcode when testing for equality
    public override int GetHashCode()
    {
        return (txtTweet != null ? txtTweet.GetHashCode() : 0);
    }
    }
}
```

In the previous example, a PictureBox and TextBox control are referenced, named pbPictureBox and txtTweet respectively, which you can add to the designer service representing the controls that display the user's image and the relevant search result statuses; you can add these yourself or reference the book's code for this search utility. This TweetBox uses simplistic equality operators to use as a basic check to ensure duplicate tweets aren't inadvertently added to the interface; this is to ensure the user experiences a control that appears to update only with new content, even if the data in the polling operation returned multiple duplicates. In your applications, you will likely need a more robust equality comparison beyond the text content, but it suits your purposes to demonstrate asynchronous polling. Next, you can write the code to perform the task of sorting and adding tweets to a Windows Forms application.

```csharp
    // the pre-formatted query stub, in Atom format
    private const string SearchFormat =
        "http://search.twitter.com/search.atom?q={0}";

    private void PollForTweets(string query)
    {
        // turn on a visual cue that polling is occurring
        Invoke((MethodInvoker)delegate { tsPolling.Visible = true; });

        var request = String.Format(SearchFormat, Uri.EscapeDataString(query));
        var response = request.Get();

        using (var source = new StringReader(response))
        {
            using (var reader = XmlReader.Create(source))
            {
                // load the Atom feed using WCF syndication
                var feed = SyndicationFeed.Load(reader);
                if (feed == null)
                {
                    // skip any issues loading the feed
                    return;
                }

                // reverse direction so fresh tweets stay on top
                var results = feed.Items.ToList();
                for (var i = results.Count - 1; i >= 0; i--)
                {
                    var item = results[i];

                    // this conversion assumes Atom format
                    var tweet = new TweetBox
                    {
                        // map the feed item title to the tweet content
                        Tweet = item.Title.Text,

                        // map the second feed item link to the user's photo
                        ImageUrl = item.Links[1].Uri.ToString(),

                        // Set the timestamp for ordering
                        CreatedDate = item.PublishDate.Date
                    };

                    if (flpTweets.Controls.Contains(tweet))
                    {
                        // don't add a duplicate tweet
                        continue;
                    }

                    // add the new tweet to the box
                    flpTweets.Invoke(
                        (MethodInvoker)
                        (() =>
                          {
                              flpTweets.Controls.Add(tweet);
```

```
                    tweet.BringToFront();
                })));


        }
    }
}

if(!IsDisposed)
{
    // turn off a visual cue to show polling is complete
    Invoke((MethodInvoker)delegate { tsPolling.Visible = false; });
}
}
```

Because the task code is structured to work safely when executing asynchronously within a Forms application, thanks to the `MethodInvoker`'s support for anonymous classes, you can complete this application by hooking up events to begin a polling operation that repeats every five seconds. The code to do this is listed here.

```
using System;
using System.ComponentModel;
using System.IO;
using System.Linq;
using System.ServiceModel.Syndication;
using System.Threading;
using System.Windows.Forms;
using System.Xml;
using Wrox.Twitter.NUrl;

namespace Wrox.Twitter.SynchronizingFeeds
{
    public partial class SynchronizingFeeds : Form
    {
        // the pre-formatted query stub, in Atom format
        private const string SearchFormat =
            "http://search.twitter.com/search.atom?q={0}";

        // use internal state to track if polling is in progress
        private static bool _polling;

        // an asynchronous component to perform polling on a
        // background thread
        private static BackgroundWorker _worker;

        public SynchronizingFeeds() { InitializeComponent(); }

        private void btnSearch_Click(object sender, EventArgs e)
        {
            // alternate between starting and stopping search polling
            if (btnSearch.Text.Equals("Start Polling"))
            {
                StartPolling();
                btnSearch.Text = "Stop Polling";
```

```
            txtQuery.Enabled = false;
        }
        else
        {
            StopPolling();
            btnSearch.Text = "Start Polling";
            txtQuery.Enabled = true;
        }
    }

    private void StartPolling()
    {
        // start a new poller
        _polling = true;
        _worker = new BackgroundWorker
                {
                    WorkerSupportsCancellation = true
                };

        // define an anonymous method to poll and pause
        _worker.DoWork += ((sender, args) =>
                        {
                            while (_polling)
                            {
                                // poll and add new tweets to the view
                                PollForTweets(txtQuery.Text.Trim());

                                // delay for five seconds
                                Thread.Sleep(5 * 1000);
                            }
                        });

        // run the poller in the background
        _worker.RunWorkerAsync();
    }

    private void StopPolling()
    {

        _polling = false;
        _worker.CancelAsync();
        flpTweets.Controls.Clear();
    }
  }
}
```

To use the demo application, set the SynchronizingFeeds project as the default start-up project, and run it. You can type in a search query similar to the query box provided on http://search.twitter.com, and press the button labeled *Start Polling* to begin your asynchronous code. Figure 5-4 shows what the application looks like in action.

Figure 5-4

When polling is engaged, every five seconds, a Search API call is made for your query. Twenty recent results are pulled down to your application and compared with what is currently in the view. If the tweet is not already displayed, it is added to the form. You could improve this application by grabbing more results with the `rpp` parameter to ensure you don't miss tweets from heavily trending search topics, but you can use this application as a starting point to work with feed data on a background thread.

Summary

Syndicated content is an important component of the open web, and a supported REST format for the Twitter API. Even though it shares many characteristics with XML, Twitter's syndication output provides essential content without additional details:

❑ You created RSS and Atom abstraction classes useful for consuming feed data for your application.

❑ You learned the conceptual differences between syndicated content and object graphs, to help with decisions around which formats to use in your specific application.

❑　　You consumed syndicated content from the Twitter Search API using LINQ to XML and WCF's `SyndicationFeed` and `SyndicationItem` classes.

❑　　You constructed a simple feed polling application that updates content asynchronously based on a Search API query.

In Chapter 6, you will learn how to design your applications to use OAuth, the emerging API authorization standard, to surpass the security implications of less secure communication over HTTP. This rounds out your foundational understanding of REST, its formats, and its transport—everything you need to start building professional-quality Twitter applications, which will you learn in the next chapter of this book.

6

Basic Authentication and OAuth

"There have been tons of third party applications built around Twitter but the problem with them is users aren't interested in entering their Twitter username and password to check them out. OAuth changes that by allowing users to grant permission once they've logged into Twitter providing better security."

— **Keith Elder**, *Witty*

Up to this point, you have used Twitter's Basic authentication scheme to make your calls against the API. You're also aware that Twitter prefers OAuth authentication, a new standard created by several prominent social web service developers, and that it may remove support for Basic authentication in the near future. Keep in mind that although it is easy to interchange the concepts of authentication and authorization, OAuth specifically handles the challenge of user authorization of API access. The actual authentication of a user's credentials is delegated to the publisher site, i.e., Twitter, which your application intends to consume.

The Pitfalls of Basic Authentication

Your calls to the Twitter API requiring user credentials utilize *Basic authentication*, a convenient method of passing these credentials over the web to remote sites in an `HttpWebRequest`; this authentication scheme is painless to implement, but it has several serious flaws that you should consider.

User Credentials are Visible

In Chapter 1, you learned how to make authorized web requests using Basic authentication, and learned that the authentication pair you provide in the authorization header, the username and password, is Base64 encoded and inserted directly into the request as plain text. Although this isn't human readable, you also know that converting back to ASCII from Base64 encoded strings is trivial. Anyone monitoring your Twitter network traffic would see the password plainly, illustrated by the following example:

```
GET /statuses/user_timeline.xml HTTP/1.1
Authorization: Basic c2VjcmV0YWdlbnRtYW46MDA3
Host: twitter.com
Connection: Keep-Alive
```

The Base64-encoded authentication pair in the monitored outgoing request is easily decoded with sample code in Chapter 1, revealing the plain text `secretagentman:007`; not exactly secret anymore!

Credentials are Reusable

The ability to easily read credentials from outgoing HTTP traffic is one thing, but Basic authentication also suffers from the fact that the credentials used with one request are reusable for any request for the same user. This is the traditional sense of a username and password, where the same credentials grant unlimited rights to the user's privileges, and provides a hacker with the maximum ability to cause damage to the compromised user account.

Credentials are One-Way

Basic authentication has no sense of which provider a user's credentials are for. This means the provider has no way to automatically intervene on the user's behalf when accounts are compromised. A Princeton study called *Reuse and Recycle: Online Password Management* (and available by visiting http://www .cs.princeton.edu/~sgaw/publications/SOUPS/11-gaw.pdf) found that many people choose to use the same password for multiple sites they visit. The reuse of passwords combined with the atomic nature of user credentials that don't include meta-data about the intended web site target makes it impossible to prevent tampering when a hacker successfully steals a user's password.

Existing Alternatives to Basic Authentication

Basic Authentication's shortcomings are well known, and existing standards are already in place to address the problem of secure transmission of credentials on the web. Two widely adopted approaches, which Twitter does not use, include *HTTPS* and *Digest* authentication.

HTTPS and SSL

One school of thought in security targets the vehicle of transport for messages rather than attempting to obscure the details of a publicly visible message, as is the case when communicating over HTTP. A popular form of transport authentication is a combination of Secure Socket Layers (SSL) layered over HTTP. In general, it is expensive to set up and maintain, due to the external nature of the security certificates that are used to verify that the web application employing *HTTPS*, the protocol that allows protected transports, is the application it claims to be. This is an impediment to many social services that begin as startups with constrained budgets, especially for services wanting to use HTTPS to protect web APIs such as Twitter's REST API, because it would require purchasing a certificate for every user to authenticate them.

Digest Authentication

Another way to compensate for Basic authentication, especially when HTTPS or another transport security mechanism is too financially prohibitive, is to use a form of authentication that introduces unknowns that are not observable in the message body itself. Though you will learn about OAuth in this chapter, Digest authentication is similar to OAuth as it involves introducing secret keys to enhance the level of security over an inherently insecure transport such as HTTP. Digest authentication works by replacing the actual user credentials with an MD5 hash of those credentials. It is coupled with the realm of the requested service, as well as a *nonce*—a randomly generated value that is only used once—and is therefore able to prevent the security implications of credentials that are not tied to the specific request.

When Twitter Was Hacked

In January 2009, several prominent Twitter users, such as Fox News, Britney Spears, and Barack Obama, had their accounts compromised. The attack was carried out by a hacker who uncovered the credentials of a Twitter support employee, and used those credentials to access other accounts using Twitter's internal support tools. The incident created a lot of concern for the security of the Twitter service, providing more incentive to switch to an authentication scheme that would address Basic authentication's short-comings and restore user confidence.

What Is Data Portability?

With the explosion of social sites and services online, a growing concern among heavy users of these kinds of applications, and the developers behind them, has centered on the safety of a user's content and credentials across a multitude of sites, as well as the reusability of user-generated content at each provider site. This spirit of portability has benefits for the user and the provider; if I sign up for a photo-sharing service and upload my entire family album, if that site participates in the technologies and formats of the open web, then I don't need to upload those same photos to another service just to make use of a few features I find compelling. Similarly, if my user-generated data is available to other applications, then I can log in to a service I haven't used in a few months and it is up to date and ready for me, as if I had kept up my activities on the site all along. This is all thanks to the ability to grant applications access to my updated content. One resource available to you to research and get involved in technologies that support data portability is `http://dataportability.org`, as shown in Figure 6-1. This site, and others similar to it, is attempting to spread awareness of technologies and micro-formats that help promote an open web, and protect the users who rely on your applications to enrich their web experience.

Figure 6-1

For the purposes of building Twitter applications, your focus on data portability is more to protect the credentials of your user, who may use several Twitter applications. Whenever a username and password is compromised, either from a malicious Twitter application or through hacking an application using Basic authentication, it unlocks that user's privileges for all the Twitter applications they may use. Your applications, however, can become part of the solution by using OAuth, Twitter's preferred authentication scheme for protecting user credentials over HTTP.

What Is OAuth?

One of the recognized technologies in the data portability movement, according to its own site at `http://oauth.net`, is billed as *"An open protocol to allow secure API authorization in a simple and standard method from desktop and web applications."* The authors of the specifications include developers from well-known social players, past and present, such as Twitter, Google, Flickr, Six Apart, Jaiku, ma.gnolia, and Pownce. These developers came together to find a way to solve the problem of desiring inexpensive and open access to developer APIs that enable you to write applications that bring together features from multiple social services, while maximizing the protection of user credentials and resources from malicious hackers and application developers.

182

User Credentials are Hidden

A user's username and password credentials are never shared with the OAuth consumer, which means that a hacker cannot infer a user's credentials from any of the information provided in a request. Instead, a representative signature derived from specific parameters on the request as well as shared secret keys between the consumer and publisher is sent with each request to verify the request is legitimate.

Credentials are Not Reusable

OAuth employs cryptographic hashing, nonce values, and timestamps to ensure that a prepared set of OAuth credentials is only used for a specific request at a specific time. One of the key benefits of building time sensitivity into signatures is avoiding a *replay attack*, where a malicious observer watches an OAuth request reach a server successfully, and then attempts to send the same credentials with their own request to impersonate the user; a nonce is only usable one time, and timestamps allow the server to compare an incoming request to see if there is enough latency to determine it was not created by the original author.

Credentials are Two-Way

When an OAuth consumer, such as your application, subscribes to a publisher site such as Twitter, a consumer key and secret is issued that specifically identifies your application as the intended custodian for user privileges when they are authorized. This means the credentials provided in an OAuth request are inextricably linked to your application, and cannot be used to access any other application. This linking of consumer and publisher helps the unauthorized use of user credentials if compromised, and also makes it easy to change the key and secret values used to identify your application—should those details find their way into the wrong hands—without causing service outages for your existing users.

The OAuth Specification

The OAuth specification is thorough, detailed, and does not compromise. Although each of the component parts that make up the OAuth process are themselves straightforward, it is easy to miss subtle details, which often lead to complete failure to authenticate your applications. In this section, you learn how to implement the specific aspects of the specification that apply to you. You can read the OAuth v1.0 specification in detail at `http://oauth.net`.

OAuth Consumers and Publishers

The segments of the OAuth specification that apply to you cover consumers and providers. In your scenario, your application is the consumer of OAuth authentication services, and Twitter is the publisher. Your role as a consumer is to provide authentication credentials based on a unique consumer token and secret (similar to a username and password) that identify your application to Twitter. You obtain this initial set of credentials when you configure your application on the Twitter development page.

Encoding

OAuth parameters expect URL encoding. The encoding must be according to the URI specification and not `application/x-www-form-urlencoded`, which means that spaces must encode as `%20` and not +, and all hexadecimal representations must appear in uppercase, i.e., `%2F` and not `%2f`. Because of this, you should use `Uri.EscapeDataString`, rather than `HttpUtility.UrlEncode`.

Generating Timestamps

Every OAuth request must specify the time it was generated explicitly. This is useful to compare the declared time of the request and the time it is received by the publisher; it helps to rule out tampering if the request is received at an unreasonable distance from the time it was reported. OAuth declares timestamps in *Unix Epoch* time, or the number of seconds elapsed since January 1, 1970. To create this timestamp, you can use the following example which converts a `DateTime` instance representing the current date and time into a `TimeSpan` object using implicit conversion.

```
System;

namespace OAuthLibrary
{
    public static class OAuth
    {
        public static long CreateTimestamp()
        {
            var now = DateTime.UtcNow;
            var then = new DateTime(1970, 1, 1);

            var timespan = (now - then);
            var timestamp = (long)timespan.TotalSeconds;

            return timestamp;
        }
    }
}
```

You might notice that the `DateTime` instance is created by accessing the `UtcNow` property rather than `Now`. This is because all OAuth servers operate under the assumption that the time provided is in universal time, rather than the local time of the machine making the request. This is important because your OAuth call might silently fail if the timestamp is far enough away from universal coordinated time that it appears as if it has expired.

Generating Nonces

A *nonce* is a randomly generated alphabetical string that increases the security of hashing algorithms by introducing noise, or *entropy*, in an otherwise linear process. Nonces accompany timestamps as an extra security measure; because a nonce is created for every web request, it is helpful to think of it as a unique request identifier similar to a database ID, that helps distinguish multiple calls with an otherwise identical signature. This is useful to prevent replay attacks and other forms of hacking, and is akin to a one-time password. The following code demonstrates creating a random 12-character nonce.

```
using System.Text;

public static class OAuth
{
    private const string ALPHANUMERIC =
    "abcdefghijklmnopqrstuvwxyzABCDEFGHIJKLMNOPQRSTUVWXYZ0123456789";

    public static string CreateNonce()
    {
        var sb = new StringBuilder();
```

```
var random = new Random();

for(var i = 0; i <= 12; i++)
{
    var index = random.Next(ALPHANUMERIC.Length);
    sb.Append(ALPHANUMERIC[index]);
}

return sb.ToString();
    }
}
```

Generating Signatures

With the timestamp and nonce created, you need to learn how to deliver OAuth information to Twitter in a secure way. This is accomplished by creating a secure signature and passing additional parameters with your web requests. Signature generation is the most error prone and sensitive aspect of OAuth; make one mistake, and the signature created will never match the required parameters, causing authentication to fail. A signature is an cryptographically hashed string representing the entire body of the OAuth authentication message, which means it is impossible to decrypt but its value is still verifiable. Table 6-1 provides all the parameters that are used to create a signature.

Table 6-1: OAuth Signature Components

OAuth Parameter	Description
oauth_consumer_key	This is the public key identifying your application. It is provided by Twitter when you configure your OAuth settings.
oauth_consumer_secret	This is the secret key identifying your application, provided by Twitter when you configure your OAuth settings. This private key is used to create the signature but is never shared when sending requests.
oauth_timestamp	This is the Unix epoch timestamp you generated earlier.
oauth_nonce	This is the nonce string value you generated earlier.
oauth_version	This is the version of the OAuth specification in action; today, Twitter uses the final v1.0 specification, so this value is typically "1.0."
oauth_token	This is the public token used for tracking user authorization. You will learn more about token use in the next section.
oauth_token_secret	This is the secret token used for tracking user authorization. This private token is used to create the signature but is never shared when sending requests.
oauth_signature_method	The chosen method of security used to sign OAuth requests. This can be PLAINTEXT, HMAC-SHA1, or RSA-SHA1. Currently, Twitter supports only the HMAC-SHA1 algorithm.

Generating a signature involves collecting standard information about the outgoing web request, and using this information as a safeguard by including it with the signature along with the OAuth parameters included previously. This collection of information is normalized as a single string value, and is known as the *signature base*. It consists of the following components:

❏   The HTTP method of the outgoing request in all capital letters, followed by a non-encoded & character, followed by

❏   A normalized representation of the target URL, followed by a non-encoded & character, followed by

❏   A concatenated list of all web request parameter pairs, including non-OAuth parameters, sorted by name and then by value.

A normalized URL is one that does not contain query or fragment data, or standard port declarations (port 80 for HTTP and port 443 for HTTPS); it is also presented in lowercase. The following code illustrates how to build a utility method to normalize a URL.

```
using System;

public static class OAuth
{
    public static string NormalizeUrl(string url)
    {
        Uri uri;

        // only work with a valid URL in lowercase
        if(Uri.TryCreate(url, UriKind.Absolute, out uri))
        {
            // only include non-standard ports
            string port = "";
            if(uri.Scheme.Equals("http") && uri.Port != 80 ||
                uri.Scheme.Equals("https") && uri.Port != 443 ||
                uri.Scheme.Equals("ftp") && uri.Port != 20)
            {
                port = ":" + uri.Port;
            }

            // use only the scheme, host, port, and path
            url = uri.Scheme + "://" + uri.Host + port + uri.AbsolutePath;
        }

        return url;
    }
}
```

Normalizing the parameters of a request involves an initial collection of all pre-existing request parameters, adding all public, known OAuth parameters, and sorting the resulting collection by name and then value. After this process is complete, the results are concatenated as a single string of name value pairs. To perform this task, you can use the code in the following listing.

```csharp
using System;
using System.Collections.Generic;
using System.Collections.Specialized;
using System.Linq;
using System.Text;

public static class OAuth
{
    public static string NormalizeRequestParameters
            (NameValueCollection parameters)
    {
        var sb = new StringBuilder();

        var list = new List<NameValuePair>();
        foreach (var name in parameters.AllKeys)
        {
            // escaping occurs both here, and during concatenation
            var value = Uri.EscapeDataString(parameters[name]);
            var item = new NameValuePair {Name = name, Value = value};

            // Ensure duplicates are not included
            if(list.Contains(item))
            {
                throw new ArgumentException(
                    "Cannot add duplicate parameters");
            }
            list.Add(item);
        }

        list.Sort((left, right) =>
                    {
                        if (left.Name.Equals(right.Name))
                        {
                            return left.Value.CompareTo(right.Value);
                        }

                        return left.Name.CompareTo(right.Name);
                    });

        foreach (var item in list)
        {
            sb.Append(item.Name + "=" + item.Value);
            if (list.IndexOf(item) < list.Count - 1)
            {
                sb.Append("&");
            }
        }

        return sb.ToString();
    }
    private class NameValuePair
    {
        public string Name { get; set; }
        public string Value { get; set; }
```

```
            public bool Equals(NameValuePair other)
            {
                return Equals(other.Name, Name) &&
                        Equals(other.Value, Value);
            }

            public override bool Equals(object obj)
            {
                return Equals((NameValuePair) obj);
            }
    }}
```

By assembling all query parameters and public OAuth parameters into a single concatenated string, including a normalized URL and the request's HTTP method, you have constructed the signature base necessary to sign your web requests and use OAuth correctly. The following utility method can perform the final task of bringing all these OAuth processes together to build the signature base.

```
using System;
using System.Text;

public static class OAuth
{
    public static string ConcatenateRequestElements
        (string method, string url, string parameters)
    {
        // URL encode base elements
        url = Uri.EscapeDataString(url);
        parameters = Uri.EscapeDataString(parameters);

        // build signature base according to spec
        var sb = new StringBuilder();
        sb.Append(method.ToUpper()).Append("&");
        sb.Append(url).Append("&");
        sb.Append(parameters);

        return sb.ToString();
    }
}
```

OAuth supports three types of signature encryption: plain strings over HTTPS, HMAC-SHA1, and RSA-SHA1. Twitter, as with many popular web services utilizing OAuth, only supports HMAC-SHA1 encryption. The .NET Framework provides security classes to ease the burden of working with hashing algorithms. Using the signature base and a chosen cryptography service provider, you can create an OAuth signature by generating a key from the consumer and token secrets concatenated together with a & character, and then using that key with the chosen cryptography algorithm to sign the signature base. If you don't have a token secret at the time you need to create a signature, you must still provide a placeholder & between the consumer secret you do have, and an empty string where the token secret would go. The following code shows how to create an OAuth signature using HMAC-SHA1.

```
using System;
using System.Text;
using System.Security.Cryptography;

public static class OAuth
{
    public static string CreateSignature
(string signatureBase, string consumerSecret, string tokenSecret)
    {
        if (tokenSecret == null)
        {
            // the token secret is unknown
            tokenSecret = string.Empty;
        }

        // URL encode key elements
        consumerSecret = Uri.EscapeDataString(consumerSecret);
        tokenSecret = Uri.EscapeDataString(tokenSecret);

        // initialize the cryptography provider
        var key = String.Concat(consumerSecret, "&", tokenSecret);
        var keyBytes = Encoding.UTF8.GetBytes(key);
        var signatureMethod = new HMACSHA1(keyBytes);

        // create a signature with the base and provider
        var data = Encoding.ASCII.GetBytes(signatureBase);
        var hash = signatureMethod.ComputeHash(data);
        var signature = Convert.ToBase64String(hash);

        // You must encode the URI for safe net travel
        signature = Uri.EscapeDataString(signature);
        return signature;
    }
}
```

You now have a set of tools you can use to construct the necessary data required to send an OAuth-authorized request. When you are able to prepare this information, you need to attach it to outgoing requests to participate in an OAuth workflow with Twitter.

Sending OAuth Credentials

There are two options for sending OAuth parameters in your web requests: through the authentication header, similar to how Basic authentication performs, or directly in the URL query string, equivalent to any pre-existing parameters that you are sending outside OAuth. Remember that any parameters you provide in the URL must match the parameters included in the OAuth signature signing process; you cannot add parameters after the fact.

To send OAuth parameters in the authorization header, you must provide the name of the authentication scheme, followed by a list of OAuth key value pairs separated by carriage returns, where the value is enclosed in quotation marks. The following code demonstrates how to set the authorization header with this data for a typical request to retrieve a request token—covered in the next section.

```
var url = "http://twitter.com/oauth/request_token";

// create oauth parameters
var timestamp = OAuth.CreateTimestamp().ToString();
var nonce = OAuth.CreateNonce();
var oauthParameters = new NameValueCollection
{
    {"oauth_timestamp", timestamp},
    {"oauth_nonce", nonce},
    {"oauth_version", "1.0"},
    {"oauth_signature_method", "HMAC-SHA1"},
    {"oauth_consumer_key", "key"}
};

// prepare a signature base
url = OAuth.NormalizeUrl(url);
var parameters = OAuth.NormalizeRequestParameters(oauthParameters);
var signatureBase = OAuth.ConcatenateRequestElements("GET", url, parameters);

// obtain a signature and add it to oauth header parameters
var signature = OAuth.CreateSignature(signatureBase, "secret", null);
oauthParameters.Add("oauth_signature", signature);

// build request authorization header
var header = new StringBuilder();
header.Append("OAuth realm=\"Twitter API\" ");
for(var i = 0; i < oauthParameters.Count; i++)
{
    var key = oauthParameters.GetKey(i);
    var pair = key + "=\"" + oauthParameters[key] + "\"";

    header.Append(pair);
    if(i < oauthParameters.Count - 1)
    {
        header.Append(",");
    }
}

// create a new request and set the authorization header
var request = (HttpWebRequest)WebRequest.Create(url);
request.Headers["Authorization"] = header.ToString();
```

Providing OAuth parameters in the request URL is similar to setting the previous authorization header; you obtain the OAuth parameters and generate a signature in the same way, but add the parameters as name value pairs in the query, as per URI specifications.

```
// build URI
var query = new StringBuilder();
for (var i = 0; i < oauthParameters.Count; i++)
{
    var key = oauthParameters.GetKey(i);
    var pair = key + "=" + oauthParameters[key];
```

```
        query.Append(pair);
        if (i < oauthParameters.Count - 1)
        {
            query.Append("&");
        }
    }

    // URL encode the query
    var queryString = Uri.EscapeDataString(query.ToString());

    // build the URL with query string and use to create a request
    url = String.Concat(url, "?", queryString);
    var request = (HttpWebRequest)WebRequest.Create(url);
```

You can assemble web requests that use OAuth authentication. Now you can participate in the OAuth workflow, exchanging tokens and obtaining user authorization for your application.

OAuth Workflow

The OAuth workflow is a series of automated steps that lead a user to opt-in to give your application privileges to a publisher site, and then convert that explicit authorization into credentials you can pass to the publisher's API to access protected resources. Figure 6-2, from the OAuth specification available at http://oauth.net, illustrates the client and server processes that occur from the time your application starts, and a user completes the authorization process, to what occurs afterward.

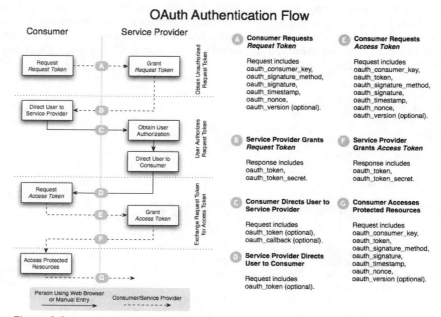

Figure 6-2

Although the OAuth specification encompasses publisher tasks as well, you are concerned only with how to participate in the process to help your user use your application in a safe and secure way. The details of each of the four major steps you'll participate in as a consumer (retrieving a request token, directing your user to the authorization site, exchanging an access token, and finally accessing a protected resource) are covered in detail here.

OAuth Test Servers

Because OAuth is a standardized protocol, you are not limited to Twitter's servers when testing your OAuth implementation. Here are a few OAuth test servers you can use. If you need to find more servers, a quick Google search should provide some current resources.

```
http://term.ie/oauth/example/
```

```
http://oauth-sandbox.mediamatic.nl/
```

```
http://developer.myspace.com/Modules/APIs/Pages/OAuthTool.aspx
(This tool requires a MySpace developer account.)
```

Retrieving an Unauthorized Request Token

The first step in the OAuth workflow is for your code to make an OAuth request to the publisher's request token URL. This request starts the authorization process and lets a publisher know you are trying to secure a connection. The request token is unauthorized because it is too early in the process to obtain a user's authorization to use your application. After this authorization is granted, however, the token you retrieve becomes an authorized token you can exchange for accessing the publisher's resources. You can build a set of reusable methods to structure this request token call and employ the methods you've already created to build a successful OAuth request. Here is what the code for this utility method might look like.

```
using System;
using System.Collections.Specialized;
using System.Net;
using System.Text;
using System.Web;
using Wrox.Twitter.NUrl;

partial class OAuth
{
    public static string GetRequestToken(string url,
                                         string consumerKey,
                                         string consumerSecret)
    {
        // get any parameters in the request body
        // to use in the OAuth signature
        var uri = new Uri(url);
        var parameters = HttpUtility.ParseQueryString(uri.Query);
```

```
// collect the required OAuth signature data to make a request
var oauthParameters = GetOAuthParameters(parameters,
                                         url,
                                         "GET",
                                         consumerKey,
                                         consumerSecret);

// create a new request with OAuth authorization set
var request = BuildOAuthWebRequest(oauthParameters,
                                   url,
                                   null,
                                   null);

// send the request to get back a request token
var token = request.Get();
return token;
    }
}
```

The example demonstrates that an important part of signature generation is including any other parameters defined in the URI in the signature base.

Useful Functions for Sending OAuth Requests

You can add a quick feature upgrade to NUrl, the request library you built in Chapter 2, to allow executing requests directly from the `HttpWebRequest` object rather than a URL, and to help make it easy to send OAuth calls after they are properly created.

```
public static string Get(this HttpWebRequest request)
{
    return ExecuteGet(request);
}
```

You can also use the handy `ParseQueryString` method provided by `HttpUtility` to quickly obtain a collection of request parameters from an existing `Uri`, which you can use to prepare OAuth signatures combining both regular request parameters with OAuth credentials.

```
var uri = new Uri(url);
var parameters = HttpUtility.ParseQueryString(uri.Query);.
```

After you create a collection of OAuth parameters including the new signature, you can build a web request that includes the authorization header, and make the request to retrieve the request token. The following code rounds out this example with the supporting methods used.

193

```csharp
using System;
using System.Collections.Specialized;
using System.Net;
using System.Text;
using System.Web;
using Wrox.Twitter.NUrl;

partial class OAuth
{
    private static HttpWebRequest BuildOAuthWebRequest(
        NameValueCollection oauthParameters,
        string url,
        string httpMethod,
        string realm)
    {
        var header = new StringBuilder();
        header.Append("OAuth ");

        if (!string.IsNullOrEmpty(realm))
        {
            // add realm info if provided
            header.Append("realm=\"" + realm + "\" ");
        }

        for (var i = 0; i < oauthParameters.Count; i++)
        {
            var key = oauthParameters.GetKey(i);
            var pair = key + "=\"" + oauthParameters[key] + "\"";

            header.Append(pair);
            if (i < oauthParameters.Count - 1)
            {
                header.Append(",");
            }
        }

        // create a new request and set the OAuth header
        var request = (HttpWebRequest) WebRequest.Create(url);
        request.Headers["Authorization"] = header.ToString();

        Console.WriteLine(header.ToString());
        return request;
    }

    private static NameValueCollection GetOAuthParameters(
        NameValueCollection requestParameters,
        string url,
        string httpMethod,
        string consumerKey,
        string consumerSecret)
    {
        if (requestParameters == null)
        {
            requestParameters = new NameValueCollection();
        }
```

```
        var timestamp = CreateTimestamp().ToString();
        var nonce = CreateNonce();

        // create oauth requestParameters
        var oauthParameters = new NameValueCollection
                            {
                                {"oauth_timestamp", timestamp},
                                {"oauth_nonce", nonce},
                                {"oauth_version", "1.0"},
                                {"oauth_signature_method", "HMAC-SHA1"},
                                {"oauth_consumer_key", consumerKey}
                            };

        // fold oauth into any existing request request parameters
        foreach (var oauthKey in oauthParameters.AllKeys)
        {
            requestParameters.Add(oauthKey, oauthParameters[oauthKey]);
        }

        // prepare a signature base
        url = NormalizeUrl(url);
        var normalizedParameters =
            NormalizeRequestParameters(requestParameters);
        var signatureBase = ConcatenateRequestElements(httpMethod,
                                                url,
                                                normalizedParameters);

        // obtain a signature and add it to header requestParameters
        var signature = CreateSignature(signatureBase, consumerSecret, null);
        oauthParameters.Add("oauth_signature", signature);

        return oauthParameters;
    }
}
```

When a request token is returned from the server, it comes in the form of a set of name value pairs, specifically oauth_token and oauth_token_secret. You can parse out these values and use them in the later steps of the workflow. Using this utility code, retrieving the request token and its secret is easy.

```
// Twitter's URL for obtaining a request token
const string url = "http://twitter.com/oauth/request_token";

// You get these from your Twitter application's setting page
const string key = "key";
const string secret = "secret";

// make an OAuth call to get a request token using your key and secret
var response = OAuth.GetRequestToken(url, key, secret);

// parse the response values
var collection = HttpUtility.ParseQueryString(response);

// create an anonymous type containing the token parameters
var token = new {Token = collection[0], TokenSecret = collection[1]};
```

Redirecting the User to the Provider Authorization Site

Retrieving the request token is the easiest step in the OAuth workflow; it does not require user interaction. However, the success of OAuth hinges on a user's explicit authorization for your application to access a publisher's services on behalf of the user, but without revealing the user's credentials. To accomplish this, your code must send the user to the publisher itself, where they will enter credentials and accept or deny access privileges to your application. How you perform this step is largely based on your application's architecture; a desktop or mobile application will need to open a new browser instance, whereas an ASP.NET web application could simply redirect the user. Your publisher will provide an authorization URL for this purpose. You need to also provide the request token you obtained in the last step as a query parameter in the outgoing authorization URL; this lets the publisher know that you are engaging the OAuth challenge and response, and what application is attempting to access Twitter on your user's behalf. You will learn how to authorize multiple application types later in the *Walkthroughs* section in this chapter, but for nowthis example code demonstrates how a .NET desktop application could obtain user authorization.

```
// This is the URL Twitter provides for user authorization;
// you must pass the OAuth request token to the URL
var authorizeUrl = "http://twitter.com/oauth/authorize?oauth_token=";

// You would use the request token acquired in the first workflow step
var url = String.Concat(authorizeUrl, Uri.EscapeDataString("oauth_token"));

// This will start the default browser with the constructed URL
Process.Start(url);
```

The result of the call to create a new browser instance is shown in Figure 6-3, showing your custom application as you configured it on Twitter, with options for the user to accept or deny application access.

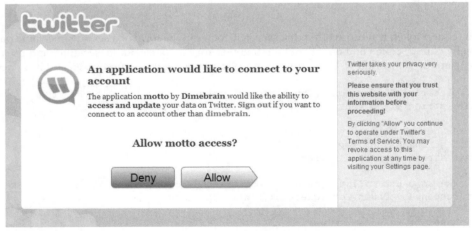

Figure 6-3

One deceptive aspect of this process is that the authorization occurs *out-of-band*; there is nothing left for your application to do. If you are building a desktop application, you need to wait around for the user to complete the authorization process before continuing with an OAuth workflow; you will have no way of confirming when the user is complete, and the user will need to return to your application without assistance. There are user experience concerns with this that you will consider in Authenticating a Desktop, Console, or Mobile Application later in this chapter. If you are building a web application, Twitter will redirect the user for you to a callback URL that you provide in the configuration process.

Exchanging a Request Token for an Authorized Access Token

At this stage in the OAuth workflow, you retrieved a request token, sent your user to the publisher's site, and are waiting to find out if the user accepted or denied your application. Your publisher will provide an access token URL, which you can exchange with the request token you obtained in the first step in the workflow. If the user accepted your request, you will receive an access token, which you can persist if desired, and use repeatedly to access authorized methods on the publisher API. If the user denied your request, the exchange will fail. You can write another utility method to ease the process of exchanging the request token for an access token, using the following code.

```
using System;
using System.Collections.Specialized;
using System.Net;
using System.Text;
using System.Web;
using Wrox.Twitter.NUrl;

partial class OAuth
{
    public static string GetAccessToken(string url,
                                        string consumerKey,
                                        string consumerSecret,
                                        string requestToken,
                                        string requestTokenSecret)
    {
        // get any parameters in the request body
        // to use in the OAuth signature
        var uri = new Uri(url);
        var parameters = HttpUtility.ParseQueryString(uri.Query);

        // collect the required OAuth signature data to make a request
        var oauthParameters = GetOAuthParameters(parameters,
                                        url,
                                        "GET",
                                        consumerKey,
                                        consumerSecret,
                                        requestToken,
                                        requestTokenSecret);

        // create a new request with OAuth authorization set
        var request = BuildOAuthWebRequest(oauthParameters, url, null);

        // send the request to get back a request token
        var token = request.Get();
        return token;
    }
}
```

Looking closer, you'll see that the code to exchange for the access token is almost identical to the code to fetch an unauthorized request token, with the exception of passing the request token to the signature generation utility. To make this method work with a request token, you need to modify the existing helper methods to know to make use of the request token when it is required, but default to existing behavior when it is missing. You can accomplish this with the following modifications.

```
using System;
using System.Collections.Specialized;
using System.Net;
using System.Text;
using System.Web;
using Wrox.Twitter.NUrl;

partial class OAuth
{
    private static NameValueCollection GetOAuthParameters(
        NameValueCollection requestParameters,
        string url,
        string httpMethod,
        string consumerKey,
        string consumerSecret,
        string requestToken,
        string requestTokenSecret)
    {
        if (requestParameters == null)
        {
            requestParameters = new NameValueCollection();
        }

        var timestamp = CreateTimestamp().ToString();
        var nonce = CreateNonce();

        // create oauth requestParameters
        var oauthParameters = new NameValueCollection
                        {
                            {"oauth_timestamp", timestamp},
                            {"oauth_nonce", nonce},
                            {"oauth_version", "1.0"},
                            {"oauth_signature_method", "HMAC-SHA1"},
                            {"oauth_consumer_key", consumerKey}
                        };

        // add the request token if found
        if(!String.IsNullOrEmpty(requestToken))
        {
            oauthParameters.Add("oauth_token", requestToken);
        }

        // fold oauth into any existing request request parameters
        foreach (var oauthKey in oauthParameters.AllKeys)
        {
            requestParameters.Add(oauthKey, oauthParameters[oauthKey]);
        }
```

```
        // prepare a signature base
        url = NormalizeUrl(url);
        var normalizedParameters =
            NormalizeRequestParameters(requestParameters);
        var signatureBase = ConcatenateRequestElements(httpMethod,
                                                        url,
                                                        normalizedParameters);

        // obtain a signature and add it to header requestParameters
        var signature = CreateSignature(signatureBase,
                                        consumerSecret,
                                        requestTokenSecret);
        oauthParameters.Add("oauth_signature", signature);

        return oauthParameters;
    }

    private static NameValueCollection GetOAuthParameters(
        NameValueCollection requestParameters,
        string url,
        string httpMethod,
        string consumerKey,
        string consumerSecret)
    {
        // the original request is now a method overload
        return GetOAuthParameters(requestParameters,
                            url,
                            httpMethod,
                            consumerKey,
                            consumerSecret,
                            null,
                            null);
    }
}
```

Obtaining an access token with your new utility class is as simple as providing the consumer key and secret, along with the request token previously acquired, demonstrated with this code.

```
// at this point you should have sent the user to the authorization page,
// using the request token you retrieved in the first step
var response = OAuth.GetAccessToken(url, key, secret, token, tokenSecret);

// parse the response values
var collection = HttpUtility.ParseQueryString(response);

// create an anonymous type containing the access token parameters
var accessToken = new {Token = collection[0], TokenSecret = collection[1]};
```

Accessing a Protected Resource with an Access Token

You're ready to start using the access token, which provides the publisher with both confirmation of a user's authorization to use your application and which application the authorization is for.

Saving Access Tokens

It's important to note that although the publisher knows which user the access token and secret apply to, it is not obvious from code. If you intend to save the token for reuse, you should pair it with additional user profile information so you don't have to guess who the token belongs to at runtime. If you elect not to save token data, you can repeat the OAuth workflow process each time, but doing so could degrade the user experience.

To access protected resources with an OAuth token, you can use the following code.

```
using System;
using System.Collections.Specialized;
using System.Net;
using System.Text;
using System.Web;
using Wrox.Twitter.NUrl;

partial class OAuth
{
    public static string GetProtectedResource(string url,
                                              string httpMethod,
                                              string consumerKey,
                                              string consumerSecret,
                                              string accesssToken,
                                              string accessTokenSecret)
    {
        // get any parameters in the request body
        // to use in the OAuth signature
        var uri = new Uri(url);
        var parameters = HttpUtility.ParseQueryString(uri.Query);

        // keep a copy of the non-OAuth parameters
        var queryParameters = new NameValueCollection(parameters);

        // collect the required OAuth signature data to make a request
        var oauthParameters = GetOAuthParameters(parameters,
                                                 url,
                                                 httpMethod,
                                                 consumerKey,
                                                 consumerSecret,
                                                 accesssToken,
                                                 accessTokenSecret);

        // if posting, rebuild the URI without the query
        if (httpMethod.ToUpper().Equals("POST"))
        {
            url = String.Concat(uri.Scheme,
                                "://",
                                uri.Authority,
                                uri.AbsolutePath);
        }
```

```csharp
        // create a new request with OAuth authorization set
        var request = BuildOAuthWebRequest(oauthParameters,
                                           url,
                                           null);
        // send the request to get back a request token
        string response = null;
        switch (httpMethod.ToUpper())
        {
            case "GET":
                // using NUrl to send an HTTP GET
                response = request.Get();
                break;
            case "POST":
                request.Method = "POST";
                request.ContentType = "application/x-www-form-urlencoded";

                // collect non-OAuth parameters for the post body
                var sb = new StringBuilder();
                for (var i = 0;
                     i < queryParameters.AllKeys.Length;
                     i++)
                {
                    var key = queryParameters.AllKeys[i];
                    sb.AppendFormat("{0}={1}",
                                    Uri.EscapeDataString(key),
                                    Uri.EscapeDataString(
                                        queryParameters[key]));

                    if (i < queryParameters.Count - 1)
                    {
                        sb.Append("&");
                    }
                }

                // write only the query parameters in the POST body
                var body = sb.ToString();
                var content = Encoding.ASCII.GetBytes(body);
                response = request.Post(content);
                break;
        }

        Console.WriteLine(request.RequestUri.ToString());
        return response;
    }
}
```

Because your queries will typically include more parameters than the OAuth authentication info alone, you will need to provide them for signature signing, but also write them explicitly in an HTTP POST method. With this method in place, accessing protected resources from a desktop application, starting from the beginning of an OAuth workflow, could look similar to the following code example:

```csharp
// This is the URL to retrieve a request token
const string requestUrl = "http://twitter.com/oauth/request_token";
```

```
// This is the URL to exchange the request token for an access token
const string accessUrl = "http://twitter.com/oauth/access_token";

// This is the URL to access a protected resource; in this case,
// the authorized user's timeline
const string userTimeline = "http://twitter.com/statuses/user_timeline.xml";

// This is your application's consumer key
const string key = "key";

// This is your application's consumer secret
const string secret = "secret";

// This is the URL to send a user for authorization
const string authorizeUrl = "http://twitter.com/oauth/authorize?oauth_token=";

// Retrieve and parse the request token
var response = OAuth.GetRequestToken(requestUrl, key, secret);
var collection = HttpUtility.ParseQueryString(response);
var requestToken = new { Token = collection[0], TokenSecret = collection[1] };

// At this point, your application must wait for the user to return
var url = String.Concat(authorizeUrl,
                        Uri.EscapeDataString(requestToken.Token));
Process.Start(url);

// Exchange the request token for the access token after user approval
response = OAuth.GetAccessToken(accessUrl,
                               key,
                               secret,
                               requestToken.Token,
                               requestToken.TokenSecret);
collection = HttpUtility.ParseQueryString(response);
var accessToken = new { Token = collection[0], TokenSecret = collection[1] };

// Get the user timeline using OAuth credentials
response = OAuth.GetProtectedResource(userTimeline,
                                     "GET",
                                     key,
                                     secret,
                                     accessToken.Token,
                                     accessToken.TokenSecret);
```

Now you are ready to build Twitter applications that respect user credentials and instill trust in your user base. OAuth, although strict and comprehensive, is a valuable addition to your web developer skill set in user management, and an important part of your Twitter development portfolio. In the next section you'll learn how to apply OAuth to Twitter applications on the web and on the desktop.

Walkthroughs

The best way to exercise your awareness of OAuth is to use it to authenticate against the Twitter API. You have familiarized yourself with the workflow and are capable of using the tools described earlier to authorize your applications. Now you can use OAuth with an authorized Twitter account to call API methods.

Setting Up Your Twitter Application to Use OAuth

The first step to using OAuth with Twitter is to configure your application, the process that will assign you a consumer key and consumer secret, and allow you to describe your application to others; its icon, what it does, and what access privileges it requires from authorizing users. This process begins when you log in to your Twitter account and access the Connections tab on your Settings page, as Figure 6-4 illustrates.

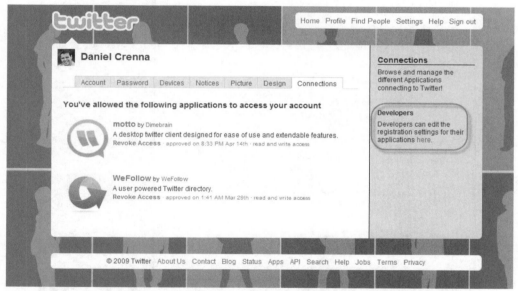

Figure 6-4

Every Twitter user has a similar page which provides them with a list of all third-party Twitter applications that are authorized to use the user's account; hopefully yours is among them. On the right-hand sidebar, however, you will have the option of accessing a developer page to configure your own OAuth application. Figure 6-5 provides that page.

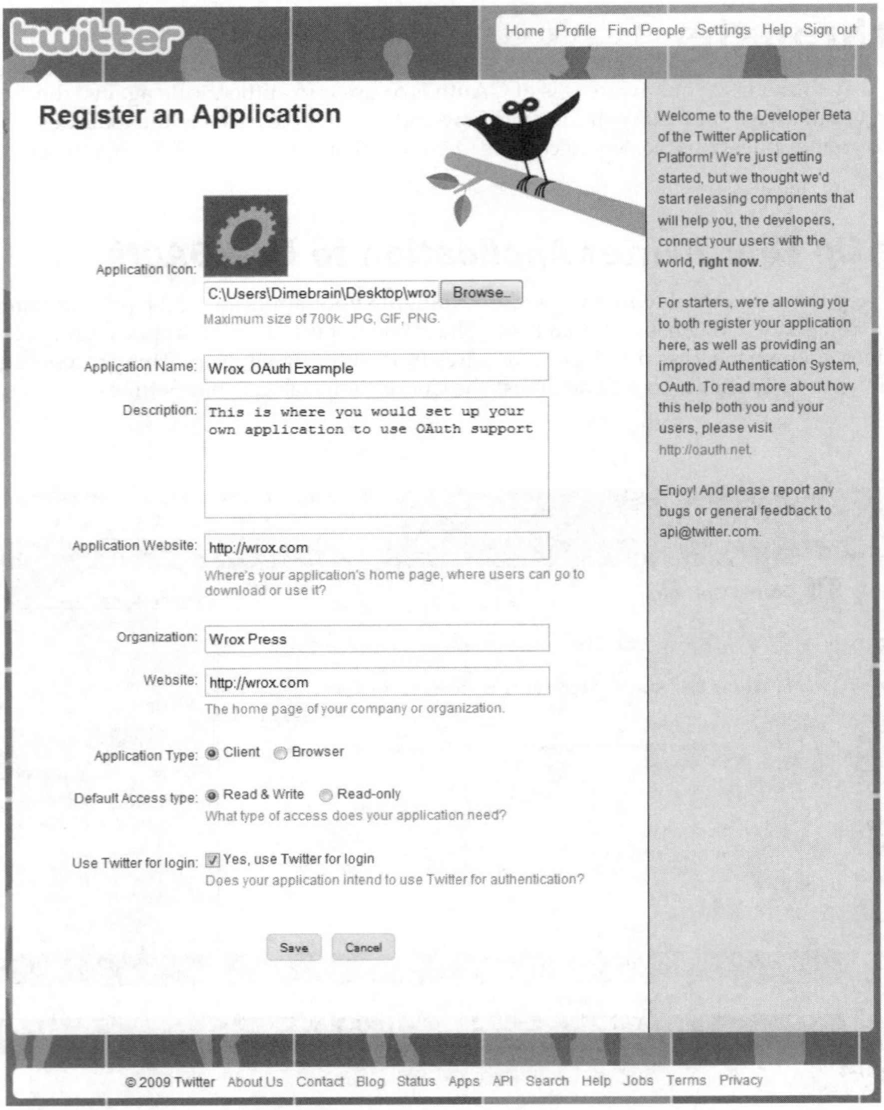

Figure 6-5

The configuration page allows you to provide some useful marketing information about your application, but it also serves as a portal for setting OAuth credentials for use in your application. After you save your application information, you will see as shown in Figure 6-6, which displays your newly provisioned application's OAuth credentials for use in your authentication workflow. You can also reset your consumer key and secret if necessary.

Figure 6-6

Authenticating an ASP.NET Web Application

Because OAuth authorization takes place online, Twitter applications you build as .NET web applications will benefit from a seamless workflow that moves from your site, to Twitter, and back again. The major difference between console and web applications on Twitter's side is the need to provide a callback URL with a web application. When the user has accepted or denied access to your application, Twitter will redirect the user to the URL you provided when configuring your application for web use. Figure 6-7 is an example callback URL.

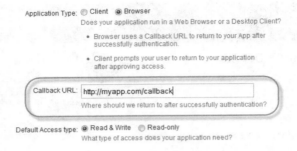

Figure 6-7

Now that a callback URL is in place and after a user authorizes your application, your specified page will receive a request from Twitter. It will provide the request token needed to exchange for an access token provided in the query parameters, which you can parse out and use in your OAuth utility class. Because providing an explicit callback URL does not permit including `localhost` or a non-standard port in the URL description, you will need to deploy your application to a publically accessible URL during your development phase, or modify your machine's HOSTS file to redirect any traffic to the callback URL's domain to your `localhost`. The HOSTS file for the previous callback URL might look like this:

```
# Copyright (c) 1993-2006 Microsoft Corp.
#
# This is a sample HOSTS file used by Microsoft TCP/IP for Windows.
#
# This file contains the mappings of IP addresses to host names. Each
# entry should be kept on an individual line. The IP address should
# be placed in the first column followed by the corresponding host name.
# The IP address and the host name should be separated by at least one
# space.
#
# Additionally, comments (such as these) may be inserted on individual
# lines or following the machine name denoted by a '#' symbol.
#
# For example:
#
#      102.54.94.97     rhino.acme.com          # source server
#       38.25.63.10     x.acme.com              # x client host

127.0.0.1       localhost
::1             localhost
myapp.com       localhost
```

The following listing demonstrates an ASPX page that will look for this token on an incoming request, and if it is not found, will fetch a request token and send the user to Twitter's authorization page. If the token exists, your application will know this is the third step in the workflow, and can exchange the provided token for an access token. When you have the access token, depending on your application's needs, you may want to save it to a session or to your database to avoid the OAuth process in the future.

```
using System;
using System.Configuration;
using System.Web;
using OAuthLibrary;

namespace OAuthWalkthroughWebForms
{
    public partial class _Default : System.Web.UI.Page
    {
        private const string RequestUrl =
            "http://twitter.com/oauth/request_token";

        private const string AccessUrl =
            "http://twitter.com/oauth/access_token";

        private const string AuthorizeUrl =
            "http://twitter.com/oauth/authorize?oauth_token={0}";

        protected void OnLoad(object sender, EventArgs e)
        {
            // add these to web.config or your preferred location
            var consumerKey = ConfigurationManager.AppSettings["consumerKey"];
            var consumerSecret = ConfigurationManager.AppSettings["consumerSecret"]
;

            // look for an access token in the callback
            var requestToken = Request.QueryString["oauth_token"];
            if (requestToken == null)
            {
                requestToken = OAuth.GetRequestToken(RequestUrl,
                                                     consumerKey,
                                                     consumerSecret);
                var collection = HttpUtility.ParseQueryString(requestToken);
                var authorizeUrl = String.Format(AuthorizeUrl,
                                                 collection[0]);

                Response.Redirect(authorizeUrl);
            }
            else
            {
                // oauth is complete and callback is returning
                // the possibly authorized request token
                var collection = HttpUtility.ParseQueryString(requestToken);

                // obtain access token
                var accessToken = OAuth.GetAccessToken(AccessUrl,
                                                       consumerKey,
                                                       consumerSecret,
                                                       collection[0],
                                                       collection[1]);
                collection = HttpUtility.ParseQueryString(accessToken);

                // make a Twitter request with the access token and secret
```

```
                             var url = "http://twitter.com/account/verify_credentials.xml";
                             var verify = OAuth.GetProtectedResource(url,
                                                                     "GET",
                                                                     consumerKey,
                                                                     consumerSecret,
                                                                     collection[0],
                                                                     collection[1]);
                     }
                 }
             }
         }
```

Your understanding of OAuth and a set of useful utility methods are all that is necessary to build OAuth support into an ASP.NET web application. Setting up OAuth for a desktop, console, or mobile application is a similar process with some important differences.

Authenticating a Desktop, Console, or Mobile Application

The loudest complaints around the adoption of and experience using OAuth is from those developing desktop, console, and mobile applications. Because user authorization is explicit and enabled via Twitter's own site, and because Twitter's terms of service (and good manners) prohibit scraping or presenting the site in IFRAMEs, these types of applications require that you redirect the user to a web browser to authorize the application. This workflow is confusing, requires a browser, and forces the user to understand that he needs to return to your application after the authorization phase is complete to use your application. The problem is compounded with mobile applications where the browser experience may interrupt the application or cause additional steps for the user to return to your application. For example, using OAuth with an iPhone application would require you to navigate away from the application to a new browser page, authorize the application, close the browser, and then reopen the application to continue the process—clumsy for the user and troublesome for the developer who has to manage the state of that process. Essentially, a mobile application on any platform is truly a desktop client application for the purposes of engaging in an OAuth workflow that must jump from a browser to a client and back again. Here is the code to write a simple console application using Twitter and OAuth.

```
using System;
using System.Diagnostics;
using System.Web;
using OAuthLibrary;
using OAuthWalkthroughConsole.Properties;

namespace OAuthWalkthroughConsole
{
    class Program
    {
        private const string RequestUrl =
            "http://twitter.com/oauth/request_token";

        private const string AccessUrl =
            "http://twitter.com/oauth/access_token";

        private const string AuthorizeUrl =
```

```
                  "http://twitter.com/oauth/authorize?oauth_token={0}";

        static void Main()
        {
            Console.WriteLine("Welcome to the OAuth Console Walkthrough");
            Console.WriteLine();

            // you can get these from app.config or another source
            var consumerKey = Settings.Default.ConsumerKey;
            var consumerSecret = Settings.Default.ConsumerSecret;

            // get an unauthorized request token
            var requestToken = OAuth.GetRequestToken(RequestUrl,
                                                     consumerKey,
                                                     consumerSecret);
            var collection = HttpUtility.ParseQueryString(requestToken);

            // send the user to the authorization site out of band
            var authorizationUrl = String.Format(AuthorizeUrl, collection[0]);
            Process.Start(authorizationUrl);

            // wait for the user to return to the site
            Console.WriteLine(
                "Press any key to continue after " +
                "authorizing this application...");
            Console.ReadKey();

            // exchange the request token for an access token
            var accessToken = OAuth.GetAccessToken(AccessUrl,
                                                   consumerKey,
                                                   consumerSecret,
                                                   collection[0],
                                                   collection[1]);
            collection = HttpUtility.ParseQueryString(accessToken);

            // access a protected API call on Twitter
            var query = "http://twitter.com/statuses/user_timeline.xml";

            var userTimeline = OAuth.GetProtectedResource(query,
                                                          "GET",
                                                          consumerKey,
                                                          consumerSecret,
                                                          collection[0],
                                                          collection[1]);

            Console.WriteLine(userTimeline);
            Console.WriteLine();

            Console.WriteLine("Press any key to exit the walkthrough.");
            Console.ReadKey();
        }
    }
}
```

Remember that with non-browser applications, you need to identify your OAuth application as a *Client* rather than a *Browser* application to prevent Twitter from sending your users to a callback URL, though you may desire using a callback page to provide more direction for your users to return to your application. Figure 6-8 demonstrates how the user must authorize your application's privileges while the application itself waits around for the event to occur.

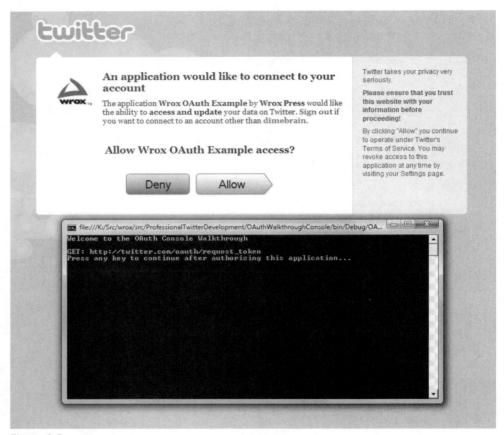

Figure 6-8

Now that you can use OAuth authentication effectively with both browser and client-based applications, you will learn a few takeaways for how to improve the client-based user experience when users are left up to their own devices to authorize and return to your application.

Improving the User Authorization Experience for Desktop Applications

Historically, sending your users on an errand without clear direction and helpful suggestions results in losing that user whether to distraction or frustration. OAuth, although an effective safeguard for your user's data, does not lend itself to a seamless user experience for non-browser–based applications. Fortunately, Google has spent a great deal of time researching the implications of desktop applications using OAuth for federated login strategies. Even though you can't get around the need to switch contexts, you can help the user along with a careful choice of words on your client's sign-in page. Figure 6-9 shows a mock up for a login UI, based loosely on Google's federated login, and might help clarify the intent of your application to your users.

Figure 6-9

With this login design, the following things are clear to the user:

❏ The user needs a Twitter account to move forward with your application,

❏ If the user does not have a Twitter account, your application will assist the user with setting up a new account, likely redirecting them to Twitter's signup page,

❏ The user has no opportunity to enter a password directly with your application, but you will assist them with entering their password on Twitter, and finally,

❏ The user is able to save their access token using your desktop application, so that future access will benefit from automated authorization, bypassing this login screen entirely.

For more information on Google's user experience research, you can visit `http://sites.google.com/site/oauthgoog/UXFedLogin/desktopapps`.

In addition, you may want to provide Twitter with a customized callback URL page to provide a friendly screen instructing the user that the final step in the authorization process is to return the application itself and, likely, press a button to declare they are ready to proceed.

Summary

In this chapter, you covered how to prepare and execute OAuth web requests successfully. You are prepared to use Twitter's preferred authentication strategy to keep your applications current and your users' credentials safe. Specifically, you covered the following concepts and skills:

❏ You learned the security risk created by using Basic authorization over HTTP.

❏ You learned the benefits and spirit of the Data Portability movement.

❏ You covered the OAuth specification in detail, learning how to write code for timestamps and nonce generation, handle URI escaping, use HMAC-SHA1 encryption to sign OAuth requests, and configure HttpWebRequest to send OAuth credentials.

❏ You learned the OAuth workflow process, how tokens are requested and exchanged based on user authorization on the publisher site, and how an access token is used to access protected REST resources.

❏ You walked through the process of using OAuth authentication with web and desktop applications, and learned about some of the challenges of structuring your user experience around OAuth for applications that aren't hosted on the web.

In the next chapter, you will learn how to get the most of your development experience building Twitter applications on the .NET platform, including performance, asynchronous tasks, third-party services integration, and unit testing.

Maximizing Performance and Functionality

"The Twitter API is discoverable, intuitive, and easy to use, but don't overuse it or you will quickly find yourself up against the Twitter rate limits! It might surprise you how quickly API requests add up, so it's best to determine the frequency of your application calls early in the development cycle. When you do get around to calculating frequency, don't forget that some requests require more than one API call in order to build a complete result set. Neglect this point and your frequency projections could be way off and your users will suffer."

Ben Griswold, *Witty*

The Twitter API has limits, and a developer should know those limits to get the most out of their applications. This chapter covers caching, dealing with users with large numbers of friends and followers, and leveraging existing third-party Twitter services to extend the functionality of your projects. Some time will be spent describing a technique for mocking web service calls so that you can develop a Twitter application even when you're offline.

Caching

When working with API rate limits, it's important to reduce the frequency of calls made, especially when your requests are initiated on behalf of your users, either with their credentials or through OAuth. Twitter's API is structured so that data that relates to a user, such as his or her friends, followers, or recently received direct messages, are only accessible while impersonating the content owner's account. Because the vast majority of Twitter users are not developers who have white-listed IP addresses or accounts, this means that your application must remain responsive and useful despite a limitation of making 100 API calls per user per hour. Your white-listed account can make many more requests, but those requests cannot access private data, and as your application grows in popularity, you may need to take further steps to ensure your 20,000 API calls are enough for all purposes. This careful balance between user and application API limits is one of the more challenging aspects of an otherwise clear and productive developer experience working on Twitter applications. The next section deals with caching, storing commonly accessed data, whether on the user's machine or on your own server or other globally accessible storage, so that unnecessary API calls are reduced to a minimum. An aggressive caching strategy that accounts for the nature of real-time systems and their frequent updates is a good foundation on which to build Twitter applications that don't break or offer relevant data when under heavy usage.

User Photos

Twitter provides static URLs to profile images. Over time, the bandwidth cost of retrieving these images will add up, and you can improve the visual performance of your application by caching user photos on your users' machines — saving them on your server isn't practical, because the images are already stored at a location that's optimized for static delivery — it would shift the burden to your own servers rather than alleviating the problem of bandwidth consumption. Generally speaking, a user doesn't change their profile image too often, so you can get away with a more aggressive caching policy.

Preparing for Thread Safety and Exception Handling

Any time you need to design caches, the challenge of thread safety and exception handling inevitably appear. When writing to disk, it is important to ensure your code has a way to resume if any errors occur, as well as protect against attempting to read or write data from the same file handle from multiple threads. If you are not an experienced asynchronous programmer, get the basics of your caching logic implemented first, and then look for potential problems when accessing your code from multiple threads. While thread safety can potentially alter how you should approach these caching designs, it is better to build your confidence and experience in this area before attempting to anticipate potential issues. In general, you should always provide exception handling for all of your application logic, catching the specific exception and reporting or recovering from the fault. The next few caching examples are presented first as simple, logic-based programs, followed by a possible example that is more thread-safe, to give you an idea of what to look for and what is available for change. If you want to really dive into asynchronous programming in .NET, then Jim Duffy's Concurrent Programming on Windows, published by Addison-Wesley, provides a comprehensive manual on the details.

In the following code example, the first 100 followers of a user's account are obtained through an API call, and their respective images are downloaded and cached to disk, using a serializing class that matches the user's profile ID to the image data; you could map to the screen name, but that is another variable parameter which could cause a mismatch if a screen name changes ownership during the process.

```csharp
using System;
using System.Collections.Generic;
using System.IO;
using System.Net;
using System.Web.Script.Serialization;
using Wrox.Twitter.JsonWithJavaScriptSerializer.Converters;
using Wrox.Twitter.JsonWithJavaScriptSerializer.Objects;
using Wrox.Twitter.NUrl;

class Program
{
    private const string Username = "username";
    private const string Password = "password";

    static void Main()
    {
        // Define a one day cache duration, which should satisfy most needs
        var expiration = new DateTime((DateTime.Now + TimeSpan.FromDays(1)).Ticks);

        // Retrieve the first 100 followers for the authenticated account
        var response = "http://twitter.com/statuses/followers.json"
            .Get(Username, Password);

        // Convert the JSON response to a collection of followers
        var followers = DeserializeUsers(response);

        // Cache, or restore from disk, every follower's profile image
        foreach(var follower in followers)
        {
            // Get the user's image, from disk cache or web if the cache is stale
            var image = GetUserImage(follower, expiration);

            // Accessing the image again is guaranteed to come from disk
            image = GetUserImage(follower, expiration);
        }

        Console.WriteLine("All images cached to disk.");
        Console.ReadKey();
    }

    private static byte[] GetUserImage(TwitterUser user, DateTime expiration)
    {
        // Use the user's ID as a file name
        var path = user.Id + ".imagecache";

        // Try to load the image from a disk cache
        if (File.Exists(path))
        {
            // Load the cache entry from disk
            var file = File.OpenRead(path);
            var bytes = new byte[file.Length];
            file.Read(bytes, 0, (int)file.Length);

            // Deserialize the cached image into an entry to inspect
```

```
        var entry = bytes.Deserialize<CacheEntry>();
        if (entry.CreatedDate <= expiration)
        {
            // This image is fresh, just return the data
            return entry.ImageBytes;
        }
    }

    // Download the user's image as raw data and cache it
    return DownloadAndCacheImage(user, path);
}

private static byte[] DownloadAndCacheImage(TwitterUser user, string path)
{
    var client = new WebClient();
    var imageBytes = client.DownloadData(user.ProfileImageUrl);

    // Cache the raw image data in a cache entry
    var cacheEntry = new CacheEntry
    {
        CreatedDate = DateTime.Now,
        ImageBytes = imageBytes,
        ImageUrl = user.ProfileImageUrl
    };

    // Replace any stale disk images
    if(File.Exists(path))
    {
        File.Delete(path);
    }

    // Serialize and cache the entry to disk
    using (var file = File.Create(path))
    {
        var data = cacheEntry.Serialize();
        file.Write(data, 0, data.Length);
    }

    return imageBytes;
}

private static List<TwitterUser> DeserializeUsers(string json)
{
    var serializer = new JavaScriptSerializer();
    serializer.RegisterConverters(new List<JavaScriptConverter>
                        {
                            new TwitterConverter()
                        });

    var users = serializer.Deserialize<List<TwitterUser>>(json);
    return users;
}
}
```

NUrl and the `JavaScriptSerializer` support classes you built in the `JavaScriptSerializer` section in Chapter 3 are used to simplify the calls to Twitter and deserialize the response into objects. In this case, you will need to modify the Twitter objects to allow caching them to disk. To do this, add the `SerializableAttribute` to the class definition of each Twitter object. In the next snippet, the `CacheEntry` class responsible for storing image data and details is defined, and includes the same `SerializableAttribute` that you should add to the Twitter objects.

```
using System;

namespace CachingPhotos
{
    [Serializable]
    public class CacheEntry
    {
        public DateTime CreatedDate { get; set; }
        public string ImageUrl { get; set; }
        public byte[] ImageBytes { get; set; }
    }
}
```

The following utility methods are used to serialize and deserialize a `CacheEntry` object to disk:

```
using System.IO;
using System.Runtime.Serialization.Formatters.Binary;

namespace CachingPhotos
{
    public static class SerializationExtensions
    {
        public static byte[] Serialize<T>(this T instance) where T : class
        {
            byte[] data;
            var formatter = new BinaryFormatter();
            using (var memoryStream = new MemoryStream())
            {
                formatter.Serialize(memoryStream, instance);
                memoryStream.Seek(0, SeekOrigin.Begin);
                data = memoryStream.ToArray();
            }
            return data;
        }

        public static T Deserialize<T>(this byte[] data) where T : class
        {
            if (data.LongLength == 0)
            {
                return default(T);
            }

            var formatter = new BinaryFormatter();
            using (var memoryStream = new MemoryStream(data))
```

```
            {
                var instance = formatter.Deserialize(memoryStream) as T;
                return instance;
            }
        }
    }
}
```

Understanding the logic behind caching photos, you can look for opportunities to introduce thread safety and exception handling to improve the quality of your caching when working with multi-threaded applications. The next example demonstrates the same photo caching program, but introduces synchronization primitives to ensure that only one thread at a time can access a file from the disk cache.

```
using System;
using System.Collections.Generic;
using System.IO;
using System.Net;
using System.Threading;
using System.Web.Script.Serialization;
using Wrox.Twitter.JsonWithJavaScriptSerializer.Converters;
using Wrox.Twitter.JsonWithJavaScriptSerializer.Objects;
using Wrox.Twitter.NUrl;

namespace Wrox.Twitter.CachingPhotos
{
    internal class Program
    {
        private const string Username = "username";
        private const string Password = "password";

        private static void Main()
        {
            // Define a one day cache duration, which should satisfy most needs
            var expiration =
                new DateTime((DateTime.Now + TimeSpan.FromDays(1)).Ticks);

            // Retrieve the first 100 followers for the authenticated sccount
            var response = "http://twitter.com/statuses/followers.json"
                .Get(Username, Password);

            // Convert the JSON response to a collection of followers
            var followers = DeserializeUsers(response);

            // Cache, or restore from disk, every follower's profile image
            foreach (var follower in followers)
            {
                // Get the user's image, from disk cache or web if the cache is stale
                var image = GetUserImage(follower, expiration);

                // Accessing the image again is guaranteed to come from disk
                image = GetUserImage(follower, expiration);
```

```
        }

        Console.WriteLine("All images cached to disk.");
        Console.ReadKey();
}

private static byte[] GetUserImage(TwitterUser user, DateTime expiration)
{
    // Use the user's ID as a file name
    var path = user.Id + ".imagecache";

    // Use a mutex to synchronize access to the file,
    // which allows you to have multiple threads accessing the cache,
    // but only one thread at a time allowed to operate with a given
    // file
    var fileMutex = new Mutex(false, path);
    try
    {
        // Cache's are supposed to be fast, so
        // blocking on a mutex or other primitive
        // for very long is counter-productive.
        // You should consider a shorter timeout,
        // falling back to fetching the resource from
        // the web or skipping the cache.
        fileMutex.WaitOne(Timeout.Infinite);

        // Try to load the image from a disk cache
        if (File.Exists(path))
        {
            // Load the cache entry from disk
            var file = File.OpenRead(path);
            var bytes = new byte[file.Length];
            file.Read(bytes, 0, (int) file.Length);

            // Deserialize the cached image into an entry to inspect
            var entry = bytes.Deserialize<CacheEntry>();
            if (entry.CreatedDate <= expiration)
            {
                // This image is fresh; just return the data
                return entry.ImageBytes;
            }
        }

        // Download the user's image as raw data and cache it
        return DownloadAndCacheImage(user, path);
    }
    catch(IOException)
    {
        // Handle the IO issue here
        return null;
    }
    finally
```

```
                    {
                        // Make sure the mutex is released
                        // even if an exception occurs
                        fileMutex.ReleaseMutex();
                    }
        }

        private static List<TwitterUser> DeserializeUsers(string json)
        {
            var serializer = new JavaScriptSerializer();
            serializer.RegisterConverters(new List<JavaScriptConverter>
                                            {
                                                new TwitterConverter()
                                            });

            var users = serializer.Deserialize<List<TwitterUser>>(json);
            return users;
        }

        private static byte[] DownloadAndCacheImage(TwitterUser user,
                                                    string path)
        {
            // This logic should already be protected by the mutex defined
            // in GetUserImage, but you can obtain it again to be safe
            bool mutexCreated;
            var fileMutex = new Mutex(true, path, out mutexCreated);
            if (mutexCreated)
            {
                fileMutex.ReleaseMutex();

                throw new ApplicationException(
                    string.Format(
                    "The mutex for the file {0} was created more than once.",
                    path));
            }

            try
            {
                var client = new WebClient();
                var imageBytes = client.DownloadData(user.ProfileImageUrl);

                // Cache the raw image data in a cache entry
                var cacheEntry = new CacheEntry
                                    {
                                        CreatedDate = DateTime.Now,
                                        ImageBytes = imageBytes,
                                        ImageUrl = user.ProfileImageUrl
                                    };

                // Replace any stale disk images
                if (File.Exists(path))
```

```
        {
            File.Delete(path);
        }

        // Serialize and cache the entry to disk
        using (var file = File.Create(path))
        {
            var data = cacheEntry.Serialize();
            file.Write(data, 0, data.Length);
        }

        return imageBytes;
    }
    catch(IOException)
    {
        // Handle your IO error here
        return null;
    }
  }
 }
}
```

Statuses and Users

Twitter's primary data elements for users and the statuses they post to the service are great candidates
for caching; statuses are *atomic*, so they never change, and are thus cacheable indefinitely. The user object
is more volatile, because a user can change most of their profile information at any time, though it is not
generally a daily occurrence. Your concern with caching statuses lies mainly in how you want to control
the size of the on-disk cache, for desktop applications, or another storage medium on a web server for
web applications.

Caching vs. Real-Time Relevance

So far, each caching requirement has included consideration for cache *age*, or the
amount of time the cached data is considered relevant. Because Twitter is nearly a
real-time system, it is important that all the data you store have some form of aging
built into it, to avoid losing updates that make a real-time system effective and valuable
for its users.

The following example demonstrates caching public timeline statuses to disk using IsolatedStorage,
where statuses are removed from the cache depending on the total size of the overall data file, and
expiring the oldest status in the cache. The User property of a TwitterStatus object is purposefully
removed from the deserialization result to avoid accidentally reviving stale user data that was relevant
at the time the status was cached. In your applications, you need to resuscitate users another way, and
use the concatenated storage file key to look up the author by ID.

```csharp
using System;
using System.Collections.Generic;
using System.IO;
using System.IO.IsolatedStorage;
using System.Linq;
using System.Web.Script.Serialization;
using Wrox.Twitter.JsonWithJavaScriptSerializer.Converters;
using Wrox.Twitter.JsonWithJavaScriptSerializer.Objects;
using Wrox.Twitter.NUrl;

namespace Wrox.Twitter.CachingUsersAndStatuses
{
    internal class Program
    {
        private static readonly long _storageMaxSize = 2.Megabytes();

        private static void Main()
        {
            // Get the latest public timeline tweets
            var response =
                "http://twitter.com/statuses/public_timeline.json".Get();

            var statuses = DeserializeStatuses(response);
            foreach (var status in statuses)
            {
                // Use the status ID a unique file identifier
                // and hold on to the user ID for mapping to the correct author
                var path = string.Format("{0}_{1}.statuscache", status.Id,
                                         status.User.Id);

                // Avoid relying on possibly stale user data
                status.User = null;

                // Try to load the status from a disk cache
                var result = CacheOrRetrieveStatus(status, path);

                Console.WriteLine(result.Text);
            }

            Console.WriteLine("Cached all fetched public timeline statuses.");
            Console.ReadKey();
        }

        private static TwitterStatus CacheOrRetrieveStatus(TwitterStatus status,
                                                           string path)
        {
            // Get the isolated storage for this applicatino
            var storage =
                IsolatedStorageFile.GetStore(IsolatedStorageScope.User
                                             | IsolatedStorageScope.Assembly,
                                             null, null);

            // Get all statuses currently in the store
            var files = storage.GetFileNames("*.statuscache").ToList();
```

```csharp
        // If the storage is too large, prune the oldest statuses to make space
        while (files.Count > 0 && storage.CurrentSize > (ulong)StorageMaxSize)
        {
            // The files are listed in alphabetic order,
            // locating the oldest statuses at the top of the list
            var fileToRemove = files.FirstOrDefault();
            if (fileToRemove == null)
            {
                throw new ApplicationException(
                    "The isolated storage is full, but not by statuses.");
            }

            try
            {
                storage.DeleteFile(fileToRemove);

                // Retrieve the file list again to account for removals
                files = storage.GetFileNames("*.statuscache").ToList();
            }
            catch (IsolatedStorageException ex)
            {
                // The file is likely open
            }
        }

        var storedFile = storage.GetFileNames(path).SingleOrDefault();
        if (storedFile != null)
        {
            // Load the status from isolated storage
            using (
                var fileStream = new IsolatedStorageFileStream(storedFile,
                                                               FileMode.Open,
                                                               storage))
            {
                var bytes = new byte[fileStream.Length];
                fileStream.Read(bytes, 0, (int) fileStream.Length);

                return bytes.Deserialize<TwitterStatus>();
            }
        }

        // Serialize and cache the status to isolated storage
        using (var fileStream = new IsolatedStorageFileStream(path,
                                                              FileMode.Create,
                                                              storage))
        {
            var data = status.Serialize();
            fileStream.Write(data, 0, data.Length);

            return status;
        }
    }
```

```csharp
        private static List<TwitterStatus> DeserializeStatuses(string json)
        {
            var serializer = new JavaScriptSerializer();
            serializer.RegisterConverters(new List<JavaScriptConverter>
                                            {
                                                new TwitterConverter()
                                            });

            var statuses = serializer.Deserialize<List<TwitterStatus>>(json);
            return statuses;
        }
    }
}
```

Following previous advice, this parallel example shows the same statuses cache, with some consideration for thread safety.

```csharp
internal class Program
{
    // This status cache should permit multiple threads to access
    // it to read data, but only only one thread may write data at
    // any given time. This pattern is possible using .NET's
    // ReaderWriterLockSlim class
    private static readonly ReaderWriterLockSlim _cacheLock =
        new ReaderWriterLockSlim();

    private static readonly long _storageMaxSize = 2.Megabytes();

    private static void Main()
    {
        // Get the latest public timeline tweets
        var response =
            "http://twitter.com/statuses/public_timeline.json".Get();

        var statuses = DeserializeStatuses(response);
        foreach (var status in statuses)
        {
            // Use the status ID a unique file identifier
            // and hold on to the user ID for mapping to the correct author
            var path = string.Format("{0}_{1}.statuscache", status.Id,
                                     status.User.Id);

            // Avoid relying on possibly stale user data
            status.User = null;

            // Try to load the status from a disk cache
            var result = CacheOrRetrieveStatus(status, path);

            Console.WriteLine(result.Text);
        }

        Console.WriteLine("Cached all fetched public timeline statuses.");
        Console.ReadKey();
    }
```

```csharp
private static TwitterStatus CacheOrRetrieveStatus(TwitterStatus status,
                                                   string path)
{
    // Get the isolated storage for this applicatino
    var storage =
        IsolatedStorageFile.GetStore(IsolatedStorageScope.User
                                     | IsolatedStorageScope.Assembly,
                                     null, null);

    // Waits for any thread's writing lock, and then obtains an
    // a reading lock to read data
    _cacheLock.EnterUpgradeableReadLock();
    try
    {
        // Get all statuses currently in the store
        var files = storage.GetFileNames("*.statuscache").ToList();

        // TIP: You might want to consider adding a background task
        // to this cache that ensures there is a minimum amount of
        // free space for the next caching operation

        // WARNING: If you use IsolatedStorage in other areas of your
        // application, you will also need to ensure that that you are
        // synchronzing access to it, so that caches don't compete for
        // reading and writing to the store itself.
        // If the storage is too large, prune the
        // oldest statuses to make space
        while (files.Count > 0 &&
               storage.CurrentSize > (ulong) _storageMaxSize)
        {
            // The files are listed in alphabetic order,
            // locating the oldest statuses at the top of the list
            var fileToRemove = files.FirstOrDefault();
            if (fileToRemove == null)
            {
                throw new ApplicationException(
                    "The isolated storage is full, but not by statuses.");
            }

            try
            {
                // Get write access to the cache
                // before deleting a file
                _cacheLock.EnterWriteLock();

                storage.DeleteFile(fileToRemove);
            }
            catch (IsolatedStorageException)
            {
                // The file is likely open
            }
            finally
```

```
            {
                // You are finished with the exclusive writer lock,
                // so resume using the non-exclusive reader lock
                _cacheLock.ExitWriteLock();

                // Retrieve the file list again to account for removals
                files = storage.GetFileNames("*.statuscache").ToList();
            }
        }

        var storedFile = storage.GetFileNames(path).SingleOrDefault();
        if (storedFile != null)
        {
            // Load the status from isolated storage
            using (
                var fileStream =
                    new IsolatedStorageFileStream(storedFile,
                                                  FileMode.Open,
                                                  storage))
            {
                var bytes = new byte[fileStream.Length];
                fileStream.Read(bytes, 0, (int) fileStream.Length);

                return bytes.Deserialize<TwitterStatus>();
            }
        }

        // Get the write lock on the cache
        cacheLock.EnterWriteLock();

        try
        {
            // Serialize and cache the status to isolated storage
            using (var fileStream = new IsolatedStorageFileStream(path,
                                                                  FileMode
                                                                       .
                                                                       Create,
                                                                  storage)
                  )
            {
                var data = status.Serialize();
                fileStream.Write(data, 0, data.Length);

                return status;
            }
        }
        finally
        {
            // Go back to use the non-exclusive reader lock
            _cacheLock.ExitWriteLock();
        }
    }
```

```
        finally
        {
            // Release the reader lock now that the thread is
            // finished accessing the cache completely
            _cacheLock.ExitUpgradeableReadLock();
        }
    }

    private static List<TwitterStatus> DeserializeStatuses(string json)
    {
        var serializer = new JavaScriptSerializer();
        serializer.RegisterConverters(new List<JavaScriptConverter>
                                    {
                                        new TwitterConverter()
                                    });

        var statuses = serializer.Deserialize<List<TwitterStatus>>(json);
        return statuses;
    }
}
```

Caching user data is a more complex challenge; you want to refer to a cached copy of the user as often as needed, but also ensure that you are not referencing stale data to the extent it's possible. A new CacheEntry class is defined to store users, and is defined in the following snippet.

```
[Serializable]
public class CacheEntry
{
    public DateTime LastAccessedDate { get; set; }
    public TwitterUser User { get; set; }
}
```

The next example shows one possible way to store user data to a disk cache with a generous sliding expiration window. Keep in mind that thread safety concerns for this code are left to you, though you can follow a pattern similar to the previous example to protect writing to the cache, but allow concurrent reads.

```
using System;
using System.Collections.Generic;
using System.IO;
using System.Web.Script.Serialization;
using Wrox.Twitter.CacheUsers;
using Wrox.Twitter.JsonWithJavaScriptSerializer.Converters;
using Wrox.Twitter.JsonWithJavaScriptSerializer.Objects;
using Wrox.Twitter.NUrl;

namespace Wrox.Twitter.CachingUsers
{
    internal class Program
    {
        private const string Username = "username";
        private const string Password = "password";
```

```csharp
        // Define a twelve hour inactivity window before overwriting a cached user
        private static readonly TimeSpan _expiration = TimeSpan.FromHours(12);

        private static void Main()
        {
            // Retrieve the first 100 followers for the authenticated account
            var response =
                "http://twitter.com/statuses/followers.json".Get(Username,
                                                                 Password);

            // Convert the JSON response to a collection of followers
            var followers = DeserializeUsers(response);

            // Cache, or restore from disk, every follower's profile image
            foreach (var follower in followers)
            {
                // Use the user's ID as a file name
                var path = follower.Id + ".usercache";

                var result = FetchOrCacheUser(follower, path);
                Console.WriteLine(result.ScreenName);
            }

            Console.WriteLine("All users cached to disk.");
            Console.ReadKey();
        }

        private static TwitterUser FetchOrCacheUser(TwitterUser user,
                                                    string path)
        {
            // Access the current user entry if it exists
            if (File.Exists(path))
            {
                // Load the cache entry from disk
                var file = File.OpenRead(path);
                var bytes = new byte[file.Length];
                file.Read(bytes, 0, (int) file.Length);

                // Deserialize the cached image into an entry to inspect
                var entry = bytes.Deserialize<CacheEntry>();

                // Base freshness on the duration since the user was accessed
                var elapsed = DateTime.Now.Subtract(_expiration);
                if (entry.LastAccessedDate > elapsed)
                {
                    // Update the last accessed date and re-cache
                    return CacheUser(user, DateTime.Now, path);
                }

                // This image is fresh, just return the data
                return entry.User;
            }
```

```csharp
            // Create an entry to cache for the user
            return CacheUser(user, DateTime.Now, path);
    }

    private static TwitterUser CacheUser(TwitterUser user,
                                         DateTime lastAccessedDate,
                                         string path)
    {
        var cacheEntry = new CacheEntry
                        {
                                LastAccessedDate = lastAccessedDate,
                                User = user
                        };

        // Replace any stale disk users
        if (File.Exists(path))
        {
            File.Delete(path);
        }

        // Serialize and cache the entry to disk
        using (var file = File.Create(path))
        {
            var data = cacheEntry.Serialize();
            file.Write(data, 0, data.Length);

            return cacheEntry.User;
        }
    }

    private static List<TwitterUser> DeserializeUsers(string json)
    {
        var serializer = new JavaScriptSerializer();
        serializer.RegisterConverters(new List<JavaScriptConverter>
                                    {
                                        new TwitterConverter()
                                    });

        var users = serializer.Deserialize<List<TwitterUser>>(json);
        return users;
    }
    }
    }
```

Your caching needs may differ, but these examples should help you get started with caching to disk or IsolatedStorage. The ASP.NET Cache class will provide similar absolute and sliding expirations for your web application caching, though this is an in-memory model, and you may still wish to cache to disk when running web applications.

Working with Twitter Constraints

After learning what is possible with the Twitter API, you will inevitably come up against its limitations when designing and considering the performance impacts of features for a popular Twitter-based application. In the next section you will pick up some helpful advice for steering around some of the constraints that Twitter's own API inflicts on applications that make full use of the API and call it often. You will also find some practices that apply to all kinds of Twitter application ideas.

Storing Authentication Values

Whether you choose to use Basic or OAuth schemes to authorize your application's use with the Twitter API, you are responsible for storing the user's authentication information for recall when making requests. Whether you're developing for the web or Windows, it is good practice to employ some security precautions to help avoid a situation where your user's computer or web account is compromised and his or her Twitter credentials are obtained and used to send malicious messages. For desktop applications, you can leverage the existing DPAPI security features of the .NET Framework; this approach ties the identity of a network user or specific machine to a private RSA encryption key. The advantage to this method is that no additional password is needed to cryptographically hash the contents. The next example demonstrates protecting the username and password of a Twitter user, the values of which are stored in your desktop application's configuration settings:

```
using System;
using Wrox.Twitter.StoringAuthentication.Desktop.Properties;

namespace Wrox.Twitter.StoringAuthentication.Desktop
{
    class Program
    {
        static void Main()
        {
            // You would obtain these values through your
            // application's UI and store them in app.config
            var username = Settings.Default.TwitterUsername;
            var password = Settings.Default.TwitterPassword;

            // Encrypt the currently plaintext credentials
            var encryptedUsername = username.Encrypt();
            var encryptedPassword = password.Encrypt();

            // Store the encrypted values back in app settings, so this
            // user can reconnect automatically on the next login but
            // still protect their data
            Settings.Default.TwitterUsername = encryptedUsername;
            Settings.Default.TwitterPassword = encryptedPassword;
            Settings.Default.Save();

            Console.WriteLine(encryptedUsername);
            Console.WriteLine(encryptedPassword);

            // Decrypt and save credentials again to reset this example
            var decryptedUsername = encryptedUsername.Decrypt();
            var decryptedPassword = encryptedPassword.Decrypt();
```

```
                    Settings.Default.TwitterUsername = decryptedUsername;
                    Settings.Default.TwitterPassword = decryptedPassword;
                    Settings.Default.Save();
                }
            }
        }
```

The previous example is simplified with the help of a set of extension methods for Decrypt and Encrypt operations that accesses System.Web.Security's DPAPI support. To enable security for the roaming user profile, the extension methods are demonstrated here:

```
using System;
using System.Security.Cryptography;
using System.Text;

namespace Wrox.Twitter.StoringAuthentication.Desktop
{
    public static class DpApiExtensions
    {
        public static byte[] Encrypt(this byte[] data)
        {
            if (data.LongLength == 0)
            {
                return data;
            }
            var encrypted = ProtectedData.Protect(data, null,
                                            DataProtectionScope.
                                                CurrentUser);
            return encrypted;
        }

        public static string Encrypt(this string input)
        {
            var bytes = Encoding.Unicode.GetBytes(input);
            var encrypted = bytes.Encrypt();
            var output = Convert.ToBase64String(encrypted);
            Array.Clear(encrypted, 0, encrypted.Length);
            return output;
        }

        public static byte[] Decrypt(this byte[] data)
        {
            if (data.LongLength == 0)
            {
                return data;
            }
            var decrypted = ProtectedData.Unprotect(data, null,
                                            DataProtectionScope.
                                                CurrentUser);
```

```
            return decrypted;
        }

        public static string Decrypt(this string encryptedData)
        {
            try
            {
                var bytes = Convert.FromBase64String(encryptedData);
                var decrypted = bytes.Decrypt();
                var output = Encoding.Unicode.GetString(decrypted);
                Array.Clear(decrypted, 0, decrypted.Length);
                return output;
            }
            catch
            {
                return "";
            }
        }
    }
}
```

For a web application, you could use the same strategy and invoke DPAPI methods to obscure credentials and tokens, but this is more challenging when tying encryption credentials to a roaming profile user, or a specific machine, when you might want to change your server or run your application on a web farm. If you tie encryption to a specific machine and the machine is removed from the equation, your stored account data may exist in an undecipherable form. One creative solution is to tie the encryption mechanism to a machine key and use the same machine key via web.config to ensure any server running your application can reliably encrypt and decrypt user credentials. The next example demonstrates reusing the MembershipProvider class as a surrogate to perform encryption of a user's credentials based on a machine key:

```
using System;
using System.Configuration.Provider;
using System.Text;
using System.Web.Security;

namespace Wrox.Twitter.StoringAuthentication.Web
{
    // Allows you to encrypt and decrypt values bound to a machine key
    public class EncryptionSurrogate : MembershipProvider
    {
        // Create an instance of this class so that the encryption methods are
        // accessible as static methods
        private static readonly EncryptionSurrogate Instance = new
EncryptionSurrogate();

        public override MembershipPasswordFormat PasswordFormat
        {
            // You must specify the Encrypted format for this method to work,
            // as it requires reversal passwords
            get { return MembershipPasswordFormat.Encrypted; }
        }

        public static string EncryptData(string input)
```

```
        {
            try
            {
                var data = Encoding.Unicode.GetBytes(input);

                // Borrow the membership's internal encryption method
                var encrypted = Instance.EncryptPassword(data);

                return Convert.ToBase64String(encrypted);
            }
            catch (ProviderException)
            {
                // Did you forget to define a machine key?
                return input;
            }
        }

        public static string DecryptData(string input)
        {
            try
            {
                var data = Convert.FromBase64String(input);

                // Borrow the membership's internal decryption method
                var decrypted = Instance.DecryptPassword(data);

                return Encoding.Unicode.GetString(decrypted);
            }
            catch (ProviderException)
            {
                // Did you forget to define a machine key?
                return input;
            }
        }

        #region Overrides of MembershipProvider

        public override MembershipUser CreateUser(string username, string password,
string email, string passwordQuestion, string passwordAnswer, bool isApproved,
object providerUserKey, out MembershipCreateStatus status)
        {
            throw new NotImplementedException();
        }

        public override bool ChangePasswordQuestionAndAnswer(string username, string
password, string newPasswordQuestion, string newPasswordAnswer)
        {
            throw new NotImplementedException();
        }

        public override string GetPassword(string username, string answer)
        {
            throw new NotImplementedException();
        }
```

```csharp
        public override bool ChangePassword(string username, string oldPassword,
string newPassword)
        {
            throw new NotImplementedException();
        }

        public override string ResetPassword(string username, string answer)
        {
            throw new NotImplementedException();
        }

        public override void UpdateUser(MembershipUser user)
        {
            throw new NotImplementedException();
        }

        public override bool ValidateUser(string username, string password)
        {
            throw new NotImplementedException();
        }

        public override bool UnlockUser(string userName)
        {
            throw new NotImplementedException();
        }

        public override MembershipUser GetUser(object providerUserKey, bool
userIsOnline)
        {
            throw new NotImplementedException();
        }

        public override MembershipUser GetUser(string username, bool userIsOnline)
        {
            throw new NotImplementedException();
        }

        public override string GetUserNameByEmail(string email)
        {
            throw new NotImplementedException();
        }

        public override bool DeleteUser(string username, bool deleteAllRelatedData)
        {
            throw new NotImplementedException();
        }

        public override MembershipUserCollection GetAllUsers(int pageIndex, int
pageSize, out int totalRecords)
        {
            throw new NotImplementedException();
        }
```

```csharp
public override int GetNumberOfUsersOnline()
{
    throw new NotImplementedException();
}

public override MembershipUserCollection FindUsersByName(string
usernameToMatch, int pageIndex, int pageSize, out int totalRecords)
{
    throw new NotImplementedException();
}

public override MembershipUserCollection FindUsersByEmail(string emailToMatch,
int pageIndex, int pageSize, out int totalRecords)
{
    throw new NotImplementedException();
}

public override bool EnablePasswordRetrieval
{
    get { throw new NotImplementedException(); }
}

public override bool EnablePasswordReset
{
    get { throw new NotImplementedException(); }
}

public override bool RequiresQuestionAndAnswer
{
    get { throw new NotImplementedException(); }
}

public override string ApplicationName
{
    get { throw new NotImplementedException(); }
    set { throw new NotImplementedException(); }
}

public override int MaxInvalidPasswordAttempts
{
    get { throw new NotImplementedException(); }
}

public override int PasswordAttemptWindow
{
    get { throw new NotImplementedException(); }
}

public override bool RequiresUniqueEmail
{
    get { throw new NotImplementedException(); }
}
```

```
public override int MinRequiredPasswordLength
{
    get { throw new NotImplementedException(); }
}

public override int MinRequiredNonAlphanumericCharacters
{
    get { throw new NotImplementedException(); }
}

public override string PasswordStrengthRegularExpression
{
    get { throw new NotImplementedException(); }
}

#endregion
    }
}
```

The `EncryptionSurrogate` class implements two static helper methods used to encrypt and decrypt passwords, and other than specifying the password format, does not implement any other `MembershipProvider` methods. Still, it is a handy way of accessing the machine key without requiring a lot of additional cryptographic code. The next example shows an example machine key in the web. config file; you can visit http://www.orcsweb.com/articles/aspnetmachinekey.aspx for a popular and free way to generate your own machine key, because you need unique values to protect your encryption methods.

```
<configuration>
    <appSettings/>
    <connectionStrings/>
    <system.web>
        <!-- Remember to supply your own unique value for these! -->
        <machineKey
        validationKey='9CDCA73D223DF0F5660A0B2383672F75054CDC25E97DD531D65...'
        decryptionKey='88B25B75F48AE5F7518391B4A85492FA215B175C2514A957'
        validation='SHA1'/>
    </system.web>
</configuration>
```

When you have a machine key defined, you can use the `EncryptionSurrogate` similar to how you'd use the DPAPI encryption strategy in a desktop application — by simply calling the required encryption methods and relying on a portable key to hash the values. This code example shows pseudo code for how to encrypt and decrypt credentials on a web page:

```
using System;
using System.Web.UI;

namespace Wrox.Twitter.StoringAuthentication.Web
{
    public partial class Default : Page
```

```
        {
            protected void Page_Load(object sender, EventArgs e)
            {
                // These sensitive values would come from
                // your application's work flow or input form
                const string username = "username";
                const string password = "password";

                // Use the machine key bound encryptor
                var encryptedUsername = EncryptionSurrogate.EncryptData(username);
                var encryptedPassword = EncryptionSurrogate.EncryptData(password);

                var decryptedUsername =
                    EncryptionSurrogate.DecryptData(encryptedUsername);

                var decryptedPassword =
                    EncryptionSurrogate.DecryptData(encryptedPassword);
            }
        }
    }
```

The due diligence required to do your part to protect credentials will go a long way to help establish trust with your application's user base. Although you cannot anticipate every attack, stealing Twitter credentials, especially when you use OAuth, is not an attractive or fruitful enterprise, so you shouldn't run into this problem. Still, by treating your user's data as sensitive, you will help reduce the risk for everyone involved.

Uploading Files with Multi-Part Form Posts

Twitter's API requires a special raw binary encoding type when using HTTP POST with image files destined for the user's profile and background images. If you intend to provide the ability to adjust these photos directly from your application, you will need to follow fairly rigid multi-part form preparation rules to successfully upload images. The following code example demonstrates the logic necessary to use the ISO-8859-1 encoding type to send raw binary data for Twitter's supported image formats — today they are PNG, GIF, BMP, and JPG.

```
using System;
using System.IO;
using System.Net;
using System.Text;
using Wrox.Twitter.NUrl;

namespace Wrox.Twitter.MultiPartFormRequests
{
    internal class Program
    {
        private const string Password = "password";
        private const string Username = "username";

        private static void Main()
```

```csharp
{
    const string url =
        "http://twitter.com/account/update_profile_background_image.json";

    byte[] imageData;
    var multiPartRequest = BuildMultiPartImagePost(url,
                                                   "coffee-cup.jpg",
                                                   out imageData);

    var response = multiPartRequest.ExecutePost(imageData);

    Console.WriteLine(response);
    Console.ReadKey();
}

protected static HttpWebRequest BuildMultiPartImagePost(string url,
                                                        string path,
                                                        out byte[] bytes)
{
    var boundary = Guid.NewGuid().ToString();
    var request = (HttpWebRequest) WebRequest.Create(url);

    // Add authorization to the request
    var auth =
        Convert.ToBase64String(
            Encoding.UTF8.GetBytes(Username + ":" + Password));

    request.Headers["Authorization"] = "Basic " + auth;
    request.ContentType =
        string.Format("multipart/form-data; boundary={0}", boundary);
    request.Method = "POST";

    var contents = BuildMultiPartFormRequestParameters(boundary, path);
    var payload = contents.ToString();

    // Twitter requires that images are posted as raw binary data
    bytes = Encoding.GetEncoding("iso-8859-1").GetBytes(payload);
    request.ContentLength = bytes.Length;
    return request;
}

protected static StringBuilder BuildMultiPartFormRequestParameters(
    string boundary, string path)
{
    var header = string.Format("--{0}", boundary);
    var footer = string.Format("--{0}--", boundary);
    var contents = new StringBuilder();

    // Add the multi-part header
    contents.AppendLine(header);
```

```
        // Add the file payload
        AppendFileData(contents, path);

        // Add the multi-part footer
        contents.AppendLine(footer);
        return contents;
    }

    private static void AppendFileData(StringBuilder contents, string path)
    {
        // Load the entire image into a buffer
        var fileBytes = File.ReadAllBytes(path);

        // Prepare the file header
        const string fileMask =
            "Content-Disposition: file; name=\"{0}\"; filename=\"{1}\"";
        var fileHeader = String.Format(fileMask, "image", "photo.jpg");
        var fileData =
            Encoding.GetEncoding("iso-8859-1").GetString(fileBytes, 0,
                                                    fileBytes.Length);

        // Append the file header and its content in the multi-part form
        contents.AppendLine(fileHeader);
        contents.AppendLine(string.Format("Content-Type: {0}", "image/jpeg"));
        contents.AppendLine();
        contents.AppendLine(fileData);
    }
}
}
```

Rate Limiting in the Response

To assist with your awareness of a user's current rate limits, the HttpWebResponse returned for an API call that imposes rate limiting will return the current rate for the user who authenticated the call. The rate limits come in the form of custom headers. Table 7-1 displays the relevant rate limit data that you can remove from the response and use to help gauge where your users stand and respond accordingly.

Table 7-1: Rate Limit Data Returned in Response to Rated Requests

Response Header Value	Description
X-RATELIMIT-LIMIT	The account's available API calls per hour.
X-RATELIMIT-REMAINING	The number of remaining API calls available.
X-RATELIMIT-RESET	The time the user's rate limit will reset, expressed in UNIX epoch time.

To use this information in code, you can reuse the object created for rate limit statuses and parse it directly, as demonstrated in the following example program:

```
using System;
using Wrox.Twitter.NUrl;
using Wrox.Twitter.Objects;
using Wrox.Twitter.Objects.Model;

namespace Wrox.Twitter.RateLimitingInResponses
{
    class Program
    {
        private static string Username = "username";
        private static string Password = "password";

        static void Main()
        {
            // Make a rate-limited request
            var url = "http://twitter.com/direct_messages.xml";
            var response = url.Get(Username, Password);

            // Use NUrl to retrieve the last true response
            var httpResponse = NUrl.LastResponse;
            var headers = httpResponse.Headers;

            // Locate the rate limited headers
            var limit = headers["X-RateLimit-Limit"];
            var remaining = headers["X-RateLimit-Remaining"];
            var reset = headers["X-RateLimit-Reset"];

            // Convert the headers into a TwitterRateLimitStatus
            // class, using the FromUnixTime extension from Chapter 2;
            // ResetTime is relative to GMT, so you may need to convert
            // it to local time for display purposes
            var rateLimitStatus =
                new TwitterRateLimitStatus
                    {
                        HourlyLimit = Convert.ToInt32(limit),
                        RemainingHits = Convert.ToInt32(remaining),
                        ResetTimeInSeconds = Convert.ToInt64(reset),
                        ResetTime = Convert.ToInt64(reset).FromUnixTime()
                    };

            Console.WriteLine("{0} / {1}", rateLimitStatus.RemainingHits,
                        rateLimitStatus.HourlyLimit);
            Console.ReadKey();
        }
    }
}
```

Designing Applications with Rate Limits

Your mission to work effectively with rate limits involves more than an aggressive caching strategy and a server dedicated to pulling down updates to keep your user's account API usage light; it also involves planning for when your application will make every API request it needs while it is operating. When rate limits are so important to the overall experience for a user, you need to prioritize background events that update your UI against the user's own desire to invoke features of your application that request data. One effective strategy is to build a generic component that will take the existing rate limit of a user account and determine when to send the rate limited requests you make by storing them in a priority queue; using rate limit information returned in the responses of rated calls, the priority queue can determine when to make a request, and can invoke a callback to pass the results to your application asynchronously when the call is made. As far as your application is concerned, you must simply queue up the feature the user requested and process the response when it's available. This is not always possible and requires some consideration for the user experience, but you can use the following code example as a starting point for your own priority queue for Twitter API requests. The first example demonstrates an example program using the concept of priority queuing. Three tasks are created and added to a queue, and the callback is defined for each task so that they are processed asynchronously as each is executed. The `QueuePriority` enumeration with levels of `Low`, `Medium`, and `High` identifies the level of priority for each task, which is added to an instance of `TwitterRequestQueue`.

```
using System;
using System.Net;
using System.Text;
using System.Threading;

namespace Wrox.Twitter.RateLimitingScheduler
{
    class Program
    {
        private const string Username = "username";
        private const string Password = "password";

        // Create a new request queue for a user
        static readonly TwitterRequestQueue _queue =
            new TwitterRequestQueue(Username, Password);

        // Track the number of completed tasks so the
        // example knows when it is finished
        private static int _completedTasks = 0;
        private static AutoResetEvent _block;

        static void Main()
        {
            // Define a few API calls of varying priority
            const string lowPriority =
                "http://twitter.com/direct_messages.xml";
            const string mediumPriority =
                "http://twitter.com/statuses/user_timeline.xml";
            const string highPriority =
                "http://twitter.com/statuses/followers.xml";
```

```
            // Build requests for the queue
            QueueTask(lowPriority, QueuePriority.Low);
            QueueTask(mediumPriority, QueuePriority.Medium);
            QueueTask(highPriority, QueuePriority.High);

            // Set up a new wait event to track when
            // this example is complete
            _block = new AutoResetEvent(false);
            _block.WaitOne();

            // The example has run all queued tasks
            Console.WriteLine("All tasks completed.");
            Console.ReadKey();
        }

        private static void QueueTask(string url, QueuePriority priority)
        {
            // Create authentication information to reuse with requests
            var auth =
                Convert.ToBase64String(
                    Encoding.UTF8.GetBytes(string.Concat(Username, ":",
Password)));

            // Create a new request and set its authorization
            var request = (HttpWebRequest) WebRequest.Create(url);
            request.Headers["Authorization"] = "Basic " + auth;

            // Queue a new task, defining its callback action
            // in an anonymous method
            _queue.Enqueue(request, priority,
                        webResponseEventArgs =>
                            {
                                Console.WriteLine("Task with " + priority +
                                                    " priority completed.");

                                // End the example when all tasks return
                                _completedTasks++;
                                if (_completedTasks == 3)
                                {
                                    _block.Set();
                                }
                            });
        }
    }
}
```

The first supporting class involved in this example is the PriorityQueue, which uses LINQ to order an internal list when an item is requested from the queue using the Dequeue method, similar to .NET's own Queue class. The code for this class is provided in the following example:

```csharp
using System;
using System.Collections.Generic;
using System.Linq;

namespace Wrox.Twitter.RateLimitingScheduler
{
    public class PriorityQueue<T>
    {
        private readonly IDictionary<T, QueuePriority> _items
            = new Dictionary<T, QueuePriority>(0);

        public void Enqueue(T item, QueuePriority priority)
        {
            if(_items.ContainsKey(item))
            {
                throw new ArgumentException("The item already exists in this
queue.");
            }

            _items.Add(item, priority);
        }

        public T Dequeue()
        {
            var item = SelectNextItem();
            _items.Remove(item);

            return item;
        }

        public T Peek()
        {
            return SelectNextItem();
        }

        private T SelectNextItem()
        {
            // Get the next most important item
            return (from i in _items
                    orderby i.Value descending
                    select i.Key).FirstOrDefault();
        }
    }
}
```

Building on this simple queue implementation, the TwitterRequestQueue class handles API tasks for a specific user whose credentials are passed in the constructor. The TwitterRequest object maintains the state of the HttpWebRequest created for the call and the callback to perform against the response from the API after it is received. The TwitterRequest type that the queue manages is listed in the next snippet.

```
using System;
using System.Net;

namespace Wrox.Twitter.RateLimitingScheduler
{
    public class TwitterRequest
    {
        public HttpWebRequest Request { get; set; }
        public byte[] Content { get; set; }
        public Action<string> Callback { get; set; }
    }
}
```

The `TwitterRequestQueue`, on instantiation, will introduce a background task on a timer that will check the user's rate limit before choosing and executing the next most important request in the queue.

```
using System;
using System.Net;
using System.Threading;
using System.Xml.Linq;
using Wrox.Twitter.NUrl;
using Wrox.Twitter.Objects;
using Wrox.Twitter.Objects.Model;

namespace Wrox.Twitter.RateLimitingScheduler
{
    public class TwitterRequestQueue
    {
        private readonly string _password;
        private readonly string _username;

        // A locking object used for thread safety
        private static readonly object _locker = new object();

        public TwitterRequestQueue(string username, string password)
        {
            _username = username;
            _password = password;

            Queue = new PriorityQueue<TwitterRequest>();

            // Start a new background task that checks the queue
            // for new tasks and compares them against the current rate
            // limit
            var callback = new TimerCallback(
                state =>
                    {
                        // Ensure the rate limit status is valid;
                        // request it if it isn't
                        if (CurrentRateLimitStatus.HourlyLimit == 0)
                        {
                            GetRateLimitByRequest();
                        }
```

```csharp
                    if (CurrentRateLimitStatus.RemainingHits > 0)
                    {
                        // There is enough rate for this task,
                        // so pull it from the queue and process it
                        if (Queue.Peek() != null)
                        {
                            // Don't let other threads run a task if
                            // one is already in progress, to avoid
                            // thread race conditions
                            lock(_locker)
                            {
                                RunTask();
                            }
                        }
                    }
                    else
                    {
                        // The account is currently out of rate,
                        // wait for another opportunity
                        Console.WriteLine("Waiting for API rate limit to
reset...");
                    }
                });


        // Create a new timer instance to run the background
        // task every five seconds
        var timer = new Timer(callback, null,
                        TimeSpan.FromSeconds(0),
                        TimeSpan.FromSeconds(5));
    }

    public PriorityQueue<TwitterRequest> Queue { get; private set; }

    public TwitterRateLimitStatus CurrentRateLimitStatus { get; private set; }

    private void GetRateLimitByRequest()
    {
        var rateLimitRequest =
            "http://twitter.com/account/rate_limit_status.xml"
                .Get(_username, _password);

        var document = XDocument.Parse(rateLimitRequest);
        var hash = document.Element("hash");
        if (hash != null)
        {
            var limit = hash.Element("hourly-limit").Value;
            var remaining = hash.Element("remaining-hits").Value;
            var reset = hash.Element("reset-time-in-seconds").Value;

            UpdateRateLimitStatus(limit, remaining, reset);
        }
    }
```

```csharp
public void Enqueue(HttpWebRequest request, QueuePriority priority,
                    Action<string> callback)
{
    var task = new TwitterRequest
                   {
                       Request = request,
                       Callback = callback
                   };

    Queue.Enqueue(task, priority);
}

private void RunTask()
{
    // Get the next prioritized task
    var task = Queue.Dequeue();

    // Execute the prioritized task
    var httpMethod = task.Request.Method;
    string response;
    switch (httpMethod)
    {
        case "GET":
            response = task.Request.ExecuteGet();
            break;
        case "POST":
            response = task.Request.ExecutePost(task.Content);
            break;
        case "DELETE":
            response = task.Request.ExecuteDelete();
            break;
        default:
            throw new NotSupportedException(
                "Unused HTTP method declared");
    }

    // Invoke the callback for this completed task
    task.Callback.Invoke(response);

    // Use the previous rate limiting example code to
    // set the new rate limit based on the previously
    // completed request
    GetRateLimitByHeader();
}

private void GetRateLimitByHeader()
{
    var httpResponse = NUrl.NUrl.LastResponse;
    var headers = httpResponse.Headers;

    var limit = headers["X-RateLimit-Limit"];
    var remaining = headers["X-RateLimit-Remaining"];
    var reset = headers["X-RateLimit-Reset"];
```

```
          // You might have queued a request that is not
          // rate limited by Twitter; if that's the case,
          // skip this step
          if (limit == null || remaining == null || reset == null)
          {
              return;
          }

          UpdateRateLimitStatus(limit, remaining, reset);
    }

    private void UpdateRateLimitStatus(string limit, string remaining,
                                       string reset)
    {
        CurrentRateLimitStatus =
            new TwitterRateLimitStatus
                {
                    HourlyLimit = Convert.ToInt32(limit),
                    RemainingHits = Convert.ToInt32(remaining),
                    ResetTimeInSeconds = Convert.ToInt64(reset),
                    ResetTime = Convert.ToInt64(reset).FromUnixTime()
                };
    }
  }
}
```

The `TwitterRateLimitStatus` object defined in the Twitter Objects section in Chapter 2 is used to determine whether a user has enough remaining hits to make a call. If the background thread is running for the first time, a separate API call is made to determine the rate limit prior to running any tasks, otherwise, the returning response from the last successful rate limited API request is inspected for Twitter's rate limit information and the current data is updated at that time.

Retrieving Data for Popular Users

If you intend to build applications that many people will use, it's hard to question the value of influential Twitter users, those who have many followers and whose opinion is trusted, using your application. Unfortunately, the Twitter API is most vulnerable when working with users who have many thousands of followers. If you're relying solely on a user account's API limits to operate, and because API calls to get followers and friends are limited to 100 results per page, a popular user with 100,000 followers would require 1,000 API calls, or 10 hours, for your application to have access to the screen names of those they follow, let alone friends! This is clearly not an acceptable amount of time for your application to function at this basic level of data-based usability. Even using a white-listed account or IP, popular users would sap your resources quite heavily to enumerate the data needed. You could always wait for friends and followers to show in the popular user's timeline to fetch the results second-hand, but if you're building anything more complex than a simple Twitter client, you'll want to have a user's social graph in hand. The Twitter API has the social graphing methods to help return a complete list of IDs for friends and followers, but without a cached copy of the user data, this improvement would actually take *more* API calls to use, because you need to make a single request for every ID in the social graph to get the same results that you can get 100 users at a time using the standard methods. To work around this constraint, you can build your own data store that caches users of the entire Twitter service; when a popular user logs on to your application, you can retrieve their complete social graph with two Twitter

API calls and then map the IDs internally to the users you have cached in your repository that is accessible to all users of your application. This concept is known as a *global user cache*, and in the Running a Global User Cache in the Cloud section in Chapter 10, you will work with example code for achieving this in an Azure-hosted web role. For now, the following code example will illustrate the basic components of a global user cache, demonstrated as a console application you could potentially repurpose to run on your server as a Windows Service, ensuring you always have user data for the most demanding users. The CacheEntry to store users is defined first in the following snippet.

```
[Serializable]
public class CacheEntry
{
    public DateTime LastAccessedDate { get; set; }
    public TwitterUser User { get; set; }
}
```

The example assumes you have a Twitter account set up specifically for your application, because this will make it easier to cache only the users that are relevant to your application's user base, as opposed to attempting to cache everyone on Twitter. Because you don't want to hold data as-is for too long to avoid stale user profiles, you should store only what you need to provide a consistent and performant experience for your own users.

```
using System;
using System.Collections.Generic;
using System.Linq;
using System.Threading;
using System.Web.Script.Serialization;
using Wrox.Twitter.JsonWithJavaScriptSerializer.Converters;
using Wrox.Twitter.JsonWithJavaScriptSerializer.Objects;
using Wrox.Twitter.NUrl;
using Wrox.Twitter.Objects;

namespace Wrox.Twitter.GlobalUserCache
{
    internal class Program
    {
        private const string AccountUsername = "username";
        private const string AccountPassword = "password";

        private const string FollowersUrl =
            "http://twitter.com/statuses/followers.json?p={0}&screen_name={1}";

        private const string FriendsUrl =
            "http://twitter.com/statuses/friends.json?p={0}&screen_name={1}";

        // This cache indexes the user's ID with the full data complement,
        // making it easy to compare this list against the social graph
        // API methods that return a raw list of all friend or follower IDs
        private static readonly Dictionary<int, CacheEntry> _cache
            = new Dictionary<int, CacheEntry>();

        private static TwitterRateLimitStatus _currentRateLimitStatus;

        // Define API calls for caching friends and followers
        private static void Main()
```

```
{
        // Get the current count of friends and followers
        // for your application
        var response = "http://twitter.com/account/verify_credentials.json"
            .Get(AccountUsername, AccountPassword);
        var accountUser = DeserializeUser(response);

        // Get the number of friends and followers of your application
        // whose social graphs you intend to cache (100 per page)
        var followerPages =
            Math.Ceiling((double) accountUser.FollowersCount/100);

        // Iterate through all followers of your application,
        // caching followers' friends and followers
        for (var i = 1; i <= followerPages; i++)
        {
            var url = String.Format(FollowersUrl, i,
                                    accountUser.ScreenName);
            response = url.Get(AccountUsername, AccountPassword);

            var followers = DeserializeUsers(response);
            foreach (var follower in followers)
            {
                // Cache this follower's social graph
                CacheSocialGraphForUser(follower);
            }

            // Take a status of the caching operation
            Console.WriteLine(
                "Currently caching {0} graphed users "
                + "from {1} users following @{2}"
                , _cache.Count, accountUser.FollowersCount,
                accountUser.ScreenName);
        }

    Console.WriteLine("Caching of application user graphs completed.");
    Console.ReadKey();
}

private static void CacheSocialGraphForUser(TwitterUser user)
{
    Console.WriteLine("Updating the cache with @{0}'s users",
                      user.ScreenName);

    // Use the specified user to determine the number of friends
    // and followers pages for looping
    var friendPages = Math.Ceiling((double) user.FriendsCount / 100);
    var followerPages = Math.Ceiling((double) user.FollowersCount / 100);

    // Access the user's graph to find users to cache
    CacheUsers(user.ScreenName, friendPages, FriendsUrl);
    CacheUsers(user.ScreenName, followerPages, FollowersUrl);
}
```

```csharp
// Takes the total number of pages for a given API url, and
// caches the results
private static void CacheUsers(string screenName, double totalPages,
                              string apiUrl)
{
    for (var i = 1; i <= totalPages; i++)
    {
        // Get the next page of friends results
        var url = String.Format(apiUrl, i, screenName);
        var result = url.Get(AccountUsername, AccountPassword);
        var users = DeserializeUsers(result);

        foreach (var user in users)
        {
            // Check if the current user is already in the cache,
            // and that the time of cache entry creation
            // was within a day
            var currentEntry =
                _cache.Values.Where(e => e.User.Id.Equals(user.Id))
                    .SingleOrDefault();

            if (currentEntry != null &&
                DateTime.Now.Subtract(
                currentEntry.CreatedDate).Days < 1)
            {
                // User is already cached
                continue;
            }

            if (currentEntry == null)
            {
                currentEntry = new CacheEntry
                    {
                        User = user,
                        CreatedDate = DateTime.Now
                    };

                // Add a cache entry for the user
                _cache.Add(user.Id, currentEntry);
            }
            else
            {
                // Update the user profile data
                currentEntry.User = user;
            }
        }

        // Ensure there is enough rate limit left
        // for the next call, otherwise, wait until the
        // reset time is reached
        // Use NUrl to retrieve the last true response
        EnsureApiLimitRemaining();
    }
}
```

```csharp
private static void EnsureApiLimitRemaining()
{
    var httpResponse = NUrl.NUrl.LastResponse;
    var headers = httpResponse.Headers;

    var limit = headers["X-RateLimit-Limit"];
    var remaining = headers["X-RateLimit-Remaining"];
    var reset = headers["X-RateLimit-Reset"];

    _currentRateLimitStatus =
        new TwitterRateLimitStatus
            {
                HourlyLimit = Convert.ToInt32(limit),
                RemainingHits = Convert.ToInt32(remaining),
                ResetTimeInSeconds = Convert.ToInt64(reset),
                ResetTime = Convert.ToInt64(reset).FromUnixTime()
            };

    if (_currentRateLimitStatus.RemainingHits < 1)
    {
        Console.WriteLine("Waiting for API rate limit to reset...");
        var waitingPeriod =
            DateTime.Now.Subtract(_currentRateLimitStatus.ResetTime);

        Thread.Sleep(waitingPeriod);
    }
}

private static List<TwitterUser> DeserializeUsers(string json)
{
    var serializer = new JavaScriptSerializer();
    serializer.RegisterConverters(new List<JavaScriptConverter>
                                      {
                                          new TwitterConverter()
                                      });

    var users = serializer.Deserialize<List<TwitterUser>>(json);
    return users;
}

private static TwitterUser DeserializeUser(string json)
{
    var serializer = new JavaScriptSerializer();
    serializer.RegisterConverters(new List<JavaScriptConverter>
                                      {
                                          new TwitterConverter()
                                      });

    var users = serializer.Deserialize<TwitterUser>(json);
    return users;
}
        }
    }
}
```

This global caching scheme is designed to find all your application's followers' friends and followers, ensuring your users have fast access to the people that matter to them on Twitter without requiring API hits to do so. If your application or your users are popular, your application's rate limit will quickly deplete, and the program will hibernate for the amount of time specified by the last rate limit data returned on a rated call. After you expose the cached data as a service or in a database, your application will provide a much better experience for your users.

Filtering Data

One of the cornerstones of working with real-time streams of information is the ability to focus only on what interests you at the time. Twitter naturally provides this feature through the following mechanism that is fundamental to the service. When you follow someone, you are asking to include that person's updates in your stream, or timeline, of incoming information. Still, as your users add more and more interesting people to their timeline, it is important to provide them with a means to focus on certain people they follow, or exclude others, either temporarily or permanently, or for certain trending topics or channels. One good example is when monitoring a hashtag channel for incoming updates; some *bot* accounts inject ads for their services in these channels by taking advantage of the fact that channels themselves are public and accessible by merely including the hashtag with a message. It would be great to let your users remove certain accounts from their Twitter timelines when using search, or approve users even when they are mentioned alongside removed users. This next example shows how you can prevent a list of screen names from showing up in results after they are fetched from Twitter using LINQ, while ensuring other users are always displayed:

```
using System;
using System.Collections.Generic;
using System.Linq;
using System.Web.Script.Serialization;
using Wrox.Twitter.JsonWithJavaScriptSerializer.Converters;
using Wrox.Twitter.JsonWithJavaScriptSerializer.Objects;
using Wrox.Twitter.NUrl;

namespace Wrox.Twitter.FilteringTweets
{
    internal class Program
    {
        private const string Password = "username";
        private const string Username = "password";

        private static void Main()
        {
            // This is a list of users you want to exclude
            var blacklist = new[] {"user", "user", "user"};
            // This is a list of users you want to include
            var whitelist = new[] {"user", "user", "user"};

            // Retrieve the first 200 statuses of the authenticating user's
            // friends timeline
            var response = "http://twitter.com/statuses/friends_timeline.json?count=200"
```

```
                    .Get(Username, Password);

            // Deserialize the response payload into objects
            var statuses = DeserializeStatuses(response);

            // Use LINQ to filter users
            var filtered = from s in statuses
                        where
                            // exclude blacklist mentions,
                            ((!blacklist.Any(b => s.Text.Contains("@" + b)) ||
                              // unless a whitelist is mentioned too,
                              whitelist.Any(w => s.Text.Contains("@" + w))) ||
                             // or a whitelist is doing the mentioning
                             whitelist.Contains(s.User.ScreenName)) &&
                            // and exclude all blacklist tweets
                            !blacklist.Contains(s.User.ScreenName)
                        select s;

            // Display the filtered out messages
            var exclusions = statuses.Except(filtered);

            foreach (var status in exclusions)
            {
                Console.WriteLine(status.Text);
            }

            Console.ReadKey();
        }

        private static List<TwitterStatus> DeserializeStatuses(string json)
        {
            var serializer = new JavaScriptSerializer();
            serializer.RegisterConverters(new List<JavaScriptConverter>
                                        {
                                            new TwitterConverter()
                                        });

            var statuses = serializer.Deserialize<List<TwitterStatus>>(json);
            return statuses;
        }
    }
}
```

Keep in mind that there is no *query language* for Twitter data, so all API calls must retrieve the full complement of data as defined by the URL, from which you can fine-tune the results.

Compressing Response Data

Whenever you develop applications that rely on one or more external data publishers, you need to think about the overall cost of bandwidth and the impact of sending and receiving large messages across the network. Even if your application is designed to locate most API calls on the user's side, preventing any traffic costs for your server, large requests will reduce the performance of your application in the eyes of users without the highest *ISP* service levels. Twitter data elements are verbose, and in the case of returning multiple status objects through calls using the XML or JSON representations, will return the complete user profile information for every status in a call, even if those statuses originated from the same author. One classic solution to this problem is to use GZIP or Deflate compression strategies, requesting that the server return the content as compressed data. Luckily, Twitter supports GZIP compression, and it is trivial to enable using the standard `HttpWebRequest` class. The following code example demonstrates enabling GZIP or Deflate compression automatically with .NET objects, though you could manually set the request's `Accept-Encoding` header with the appropriate `gzip, deflate` values, though this would require you to hand-code the decompression method when you receive a response from Twitter in the desired format.

```
using System;
using System.Collections.Generic;
using System.Net;
using System.Text;
using System.Web.Script.Serialization;
using Wrox.Twitter.JsonWithJavaScriptSerializer.Converters;
using Wrox.Twitter.JsonWithJavaScriptSerializer.Objects;
using Wrox.Twitter.NUrl;

namespace Wrox.Twitter.CompressingResponseData
{
    class Program
    {
        private const string Username = "username";
        private const string Password = "password";

        static void Main()
        {
            // Make an API call returning a large result set
            const string url =
            "http://twitter.com/statuses/friends_timeline.json?count=200";

            var request = (HttpWebRequest) WebRequest.Create(url);

            // Add authorization to the request
            var auth =
                Convert.ToBase64String(
                    Encoding.UTF8.GetBytes(Username + ":" + Password));

            request.Headers["Authorization"] = "Basic " + auth;

            // Enable automatic GZIP compression in the .NET Framework
            request.AutomaticDecompression = DecompressionMethods.GZip;

            // Execute the call as normal using NUrl
            var response = request.ExecuteGet();

            // The incoming data is streamed back to text, so no
            // coding changes are required, however, the actual
            // response was sent and received as compressed data
            var statuses = DeserializeStatuses(response);
            foreach(var status in statuses)
```

```
        {
            Console.WriteLine(status.Text);
        }

        Console.ReadKey();
    }

    private static List<TwitterStatus> DeserializeStatuses(string json)
    {
        var serializer = new JavaScriptSerializer();
        serializer.RegisterConverters(new List<JavaScriptConverter>
                            {
                                new TwitterConverter()
                            });

        var statuses = serializer.Deserialize<List<TwitterStatus>>(json);
        return statuses;
    }
  }
}
```

If you trace the request and response with Wireshark, you can confirm that the message was handled correctly using GZIP, even though you saw no noticeable difference in your responses in code.

```
Hypertext Transfer Protocol
    GET /statuses/friends_timeline.json?count=200 HTTP/1.1
    Authorization: Basic aWRyYXRoZXJiZTpzbGVlcGluZw==
    Host: twitter.com
    Accept-Encoding: gzip
    Connection: Keep-Alive

Hypertext Transfer Protocol
    HTTP/1.1 200 OK
    Date: Thu, 18 Jun 2009 13:13:39 GMT
    Server: hi
    Last-Modified: Thu, 18 Jun 2009 13:13:39 GMT
    Status: 200 OK
    X-RateLimit-Limit: 20000
    ETag: "988995959e1f595ebfbb294fea3a1683"-gzip
    X-RateLimit-Remaining: 19997
    Pragma: no-cache
    Cache-Control: no-cache, no-store, must-revalidate, pre-check=0, post-check=0
    Content-Type: application/json; charset=utf-8
    X-RateLimit-Reset: 1245334340
    Expires: Tue, 31 Mar 1981 05:00:00 GMT
    X-Revision: 41ef8d1e7066cc15b23421715b696e066eb8aea5
    X-Transaction: 1245330819-87182-14977
    Set-Cookie: lang=en; path=/
    Set-Cookie: lang=en; path=/
    [truncated] Set-Cookie: _twitter_sess=BAh7CToJdXNlcmkDGn6qOgdpZCIlNDQwND...
```

```
Vary: Accept-Encoding
Content-Encoding: gzip
Content-Length: 40986
Connection: close

Content-encoded entity body (gzip): 40986 bytes -> 258413 bytes
Line-based text data: application/json
```

This small adjustment will have a positive effect on the traffic footprint of your application. In Table 7-2, the values of a typical request containing 200 statuses from a user's friends timeline are shown in each of the supported data formats, both uncompressed and compressed. From the table's results you will discover that JSON is a more compact format when you need the full host of data elements, while RSS is the leanest format of all, though it returns only address links and the most basic information for your application.

Table 7-2: Payload Sizes of Friends Timeline Fetch (200 Results) by Format

Format	Uncompressed Size in Bytes	Compressed Size in Bytes
XML	383020	41375
JSON	258413	40986
RSS	96956	17313
Atom	171193	22781

With this information, it is easy to see that combining GZIP compression with RSS formats will yield the best performance in terms of bandwidth consumption for your Twitter applications. If you have a user cache in place, you can use RSS without requiring the contextual user information normally provided in a more expensive XML or JSON call.

Extending Twitter with Third-Party Applications

Twitter's power lies in its simplicity, which attracts developers who want to provide new features or combine existing features in novel ways to create more value for people who use the service. It's not surprising that as you imagine and execute your own exciting Twitter application story, a vibrant community of developers is doing the same thing, often providing their own APIs to allow you to extend your creations with features you won't have to reinvent. In this section you use a few popular third-party application APIs to include photo and trend features in your own Twitter services mash-up.

Third-Party Twitter Applications and Authorization

Although your own application may already use OAuth, following Twitter's recommendations, many third-party applications are still employing Basic authorization. This means that even though you are performing the due diligence of using the OAuth service to protect user credentials, this may impact your ability to integrate with other applications. This could compromise your user experience by then asking your users for their true credentials. Although most popular Twitter applications will eventually move to the OAuth standard, whether by request or due to the deprecation of Basic authorization, you need to account for this fact in your own application when deciding which services you wish to integrate.

Adding Photo Features with TwitPic, yFrog and Twitgoo

The concept of photos and tweeting as a great match is almost as old as the Twitter service itself. TwitPic is a service that allows you to send a raw image to a web service and have it returned as a compact URL, similar to URL shortening services but with the added ability to use the TwitPic API to fetch the thumbnail or just the full image. This is opposed to the standard URL that directs you to a landing page on the site itself with links to other photos posted by the same Twitter user. Because TwitPic's integration with Twitter is so deep (you must log in to TwitPic with your Twitter credentials), application developers are able to use TwitPic's API to build integrated photo features into their own Twitter applications. TweetDeck, for example, lets you view images posted using the TwitPic service directly in the client itself, without the user having to leave to visit another page to see the photo posted in the link. Another service, yFrog, powered by digital imaging veterans ImageShack, has emerged as an alternative to the TwitPic service, and its API is markedly similar to TwitPic, allowing you to consume either service with the same effort. Building on the example code demonstrated in the previous section "Uploading Files with Multi-Part Form Posts," the next code snippet shows posting a photo to either yFrog or TwitPic, and receiving back the URL to share with users on Twitter or another service.

```
using System;
using System.IO;
using System.Net;
using System.Text;
using Wrox.Twitter.NUrl;

namespace Wrox.Twitter.ThirdPartyApplications
{
    internal class Program
    {
        private const string Username = "username";
        private const string Password = "password";

        private static void Main()
        {
            // Use TwitPic, yFrog, or Twitgoo's identical API POST method
            //var url = "http://twitpic.com/api/upload";
```

```
            //var url = "http://twitgoo.com/api/upload";
            var url = "http://yfrog.com/api/upload";

            // This third party service requires Twitter credentials
            byte[] imageData;
            var multiPartRequest = BuildMultiPartImagePost(url,
                                                    "coffee-cup.jpg",
                                                    out imageData);

            var response = multiPartRequest.ExecutePost(imageData);

            Console.WriteLine(response);
            Console.ReadKey();
        }

        protected static HttpWebRequest BuildMultiPartImagePost
            (string url, string path, out byte[] bytes)
        {
            var boundary = Guid.NewGuid().ToString();
            var request = (HttpWebRequest) WebRequest.Create(url);

            request.AllowWriteStreamBuffering = true;
            request.ContentType =
                string.Format("multipart/form-data; boundary={0}", boundary);
            request.Method = "POST";

            var contents = BuildMultiPartFormRequestParameters(boundary, path);
            var payload = contents.ToString();

            // Twitter requires that images are posted as raw binary data
            bytes = Encoding.GetEncoding("iso-8859-1").GetBytes(payload);
            request.ContentLength = bytes.Length;
            return request;
        }

        protected static StringBuilder BuildMultiPartFormRequestParameters(
            string boundary, string path)
        {
            // Build a header and footer to separate form parts
            var header = string.Format("--{0}", boundary);
            var footer = string.Format("--{0}--", boundary);
            var contents = new StringBuilder();

            // Add the file payload
            AppendFileData(contents, path, header, "image/jpeg");

            // Add the user credentials as post fields
            AppendPostField(contents, "username", Username, header);
            AppendPostField(contents, "password", Password, header);

            // Add the multi-part footer
            contents.AppendLine(footer);
            return contents;
        }
```

```
private static void AppendPostField(StringBuilder contents,
                                     string name,
                                     string value,
                                     string header)
{
    // Separate each parameter with a boundary header
    contents.AppendLine(header);

    contents.AppendLine(
        string.Format("Content-Disposition: form-data; name=\"{0}\"",
                       name));
    contents.AppendLine();
    contents.AppendLine(value);
}

private static void AppendFileData(StringBuilder contents,
                                    string path,
                                    string header,
                                    string contentType)
{
    // Separate each parameter with a boundary header
    contents.AppendLine(header);

    // Load the entire image into a buffer
    var fileBytes = File.ReadAllBytes(path);

    // Prepare the file header
    const string fileMask =
        "Content-Disposition: file; name=\"{0}\"; filename=\"{1}\"";
    var fileHeader = String.Format(fileMask, "media", "photo");
    var fileData =
        Encoding.GetEncoding("iso-8859-1").GetString(fileBytes, 0,
                                                     fileBytes.Length);

    // Append the file header and its content in the multi-part form
    contents.AppendLine(fileHeader);
    contents.AppendLine(string.Format("Content-Type: {0}", contentType));
    contents.AppendLine();
    contents.AppendLine(fileData);
}
    }
}
```

In contrast with the original multi-part forms example, ImageShack, yFrog, and Twitgoo require you to pass the user's credentials with the request as HTTP POST parameters. These extra parameters are passed into the multi-part form body separated by the boundary header.

Stay on Top of Trends with TwitScoop

Although Twitter provides its own trending topics API, another web application, TwitScoop, provides a simple API to receive its own estimation of popular topics in the Twitter API. The following example demonstrates usage of this API to obtain trending results. TwitScoop provides a dedicated URL for your own application that, when accessed with a HTTP GET request, returns both a representation of recent trends as a tag cloud as well as regular trending information. You need to sign up with TwitScoop directly to get a URL assigned.

```
GET: http://www.twitscoop.com/your-custom-url.xml
<?xml version="1.0" encoding="UTF-8" ?>
<cloud type="array">
   <tag>
     <name>6pm</name>
     <url>http://www.twitscoop.com/search?6pm</url>
     <size>1</size>
   </tag>
   <tag>
     <name>doors</name>
     <url>http://www.twitscoop.com/search?doors</url>
     <size>1</size>
   </tag>
   <tag>
     <name>erase</name>
     <url>http://www.twitscoop.com/search?erase</url>
     <size>2</size>
   </tag>
   <tag>
     <name>family</name>
     <url>http://www.twitscoop.com/search?family</url>
     <size>1.5</size>
   </tag>
   <tag>
     <name>father</name>
     <url>http://www.twitscoop.com/search?father</url>
     <size>1</size>
   </tag>
   <tag>
     <name>florida</name>
     <url>http://www.twitscoop.com/search?florida</url>
     <size>2.5</size>
   </tag>
   <tag>
     <name>forgotten</name>
     <url>http://www.twitscoop.com/search?forgotten</url>
     <size>1</size>
   </tag>
   <tag>
     <name>fried</name>
     <url>http://www.twitscoop.com/search?fried</url>
     <size>1.5</size>
   </tag>
   <tag>
     <name>garage</name>
     <url>http://www.twitscoop.com/search?garage</url>
     <size>1</size>
   </tag>
   <tag>
     <name>goodmorning</name>
     <url>http://www.twitscoop.com/search?goodmorning</url>
```

```
      <size>1.5</size>
   </tag>
<trend>
   <name>attacking provided proxy</name>
   <detected>2 hours ago</detected>
   <url>http://www.twitscoop.com/search?attacking+provided+proxy</url>
</trend>
<trend>
   <name>masterchef</name>
   <detected>3 hours ago</detected>
   <url>http://www.twitscoop.com/search?masterchef</url>
</trend>
<trend>
   <name>poh</name>
   <detected>3 hours ago</detected>
   <url>http://www.twitscoop.com/search?poh</url>
</trend>
<trend>
   <name>yourghettowhen</name>
   <detected>5 hours ago</detected>
   <url>http://www.twitscoop.com/search?yourghettowhen</url>
</trend>
<trend>
   <name>ghetto</name>
   <detected>5 hours ago</detected>
   <url>http://www.twitscoop.com/search?ghetto</url>
</trend>
</cloud>
```

If your application makes heavy use of trending concepts to provide your applications' core functionality, researching several trending services, or perhaps building your own trend analytics using a higher rated Twitter Streaming API account would offer the most benefit for your project. Keep in mind that you need to send the TwitScoop developers an email before being granted access to the dedicated API URL.

Twitter Application Directories

Photos and trends are certainly not the end of innovation as far as third-party Twitter applications are concerned; there is a rapidly growing ecosystem of applications, with uses and APIs too numerous to list here, though the widespread adoption of RESTful principles means you can consume most of these external APIs using the knowledge you already possess. To help you find applications that may provide enhanced functionality for your work over and above what you intend to develop yourself, this list shows a number of popular Twitter application directories that can act as sources of inspiration or collaboration:

❑   http://twapps.com/

❑   http://twtbase.com/

❑   http://twitdom.com/

❑   http://twitter.pbworks.com/Apps

❑   http://bustatweet.com/

❑   http://twapplications.net/

Unit Testing Twitter

Developing against the Twitter API or any real-time web service is a volatile affair, by the very nature of the data you are attempting to capture and harness. Even when your Internet connectivity is fast and assured, you are likely to run into inconsistencies or errors during service outages or other reasons, not to mention how quickly progress on your RESTful service projects grinds to a halt when you board an airplane or otherwise lose your Internet connection. In this section you pick up some tips for real-time software development at 30,000 feet so you can build your Twitter applications before you need to, or are prevented from, connecting to the Twitter API directly.

Mocking RESTful Services

To mock any interaction with the web, it's necessary to stand in between the HTTP request that is sent from the framework and substitute that call for a simulated response. Because REST is based on addressability, one avenue to take is to generate a lookup of URL to a representative response that is always returned when the URL is referenced in a mocked request. Another approach could be to randomize the output to any URL, provided the mocked responses all shared the same output format and element structure, as in the case of the Twitter API where multiple entities such as statuses, users, and direct messages are explicitly represented. The following code examples set up mock HttpWebRequest and HttpWebResponse classes to perform the output substitution for you, as well as demonstrate a way to pre-populate the API addresses with mocked results. This makes it possible to develop code that calls the API directly and substitute for the proxy only when necessary. The first example outlines the mock request and defines explicit conversion operators to allow pre-existing code to transfer between mock and true objects.

```
using System;
using System.Net;

namespace Wrox.Twitter.MockingRequests
{
    public class MockHttpWebRequest : WebRequest
    {
        public Uri Origin { get; private set; }

        public string Response { get; set; }

        public MockHttpWebRequest(Uri origin)
        {
            Origin = origin;
        }

        public override WebResponse GetResponse()
        {
            var response = new MockWebResponse(Origin, Response);
            return response;
        }

        public override Uri RequestUri
        {
            get
```

```
        {
            return Origin;
        }
    }

    public static explicit operator MockHttpWebRequest (HttpWebRequest request)
    {
        return new MockHttpWebRequest(request.RequestUri);
    }

    public static explicit operator HttpWebRequest(MockHttpWebRequest request)
    {
        return (HttpWebRequest)Create(request.Origin);
    }

    public static MockHttpWebRequest FromWebRequest(WebRequest request)
    {
        return new MockHttpWebRequest(request.RequestUri);
    }
    }
}
```

The MockHttpWebResponse class implements the GetResponseStream event, creating a stream from the pre-defined response content set up in the matched request, which is shown in the next code listing:

```
using System;
using System.IO;
using System.Net;
using System.Text;

namespace Wrox.Twitter.MockingRequests
{
    public class MockWebResponse : WebResponse
    {
        private readonly Uri _origin;
        public string Content { get; private set; }

        public override Uri ResponseUri
        {
            get
            {
                return _origin;
            }
        }

        public MockWebResponse(Uri origin, string content)
        {
            _origin = origin;
            Content = content;
        }

        public override Stream GetResponseStream()
```

```
        {
            var data = Encoding.ASCII.GetBytes(Content);
            var ms = new MemoryStream(data);

            return ms;
        }

        public static explicit operator MockWebResponse(HttpWebResponse response)
        {
            var result = "";
            try
            {
                using (var sr = new StreamReader(response.GetResponseStream()))
                {
                    result = sr.ReadToEnd();
                }
            }
            catch (WebException ex)
            {
                if(ex.Response != null && ex.Response is HttpWebResponse)
                {
                    using(var sr = new StreamReader(ex.Response.GetResponseStream()))
                    {
                        result = sr.ReadToEnd();
                    }
                }
            }

            return new MockWebResponse(response.ResponseUri, result);
        }
    }
}
```

You can define the request and response classes as you would normally, and even use NUrl to initiate the request programmatically. When the request is executed, however, the mocked response content is returned rather than an attempt to access web resources. Approaching mocking in this way allows you to avoid having to rewrite much of your code when moving from mocked output to live data. The usage of the mocking pattern is shown in the next program, which shows that your mocking responses can operate in the same context as previous examples with very little difference in programming.

```
using System;
using System.Collections.Generic;
using System.Net;
using System.Web.Script.Serialization;
using Wrox.Twitter.JsonWithJavaScriptSerializer.Converters;
using Wrox.Twitter.JsonWithJavaScriptSerializer.Objects;
using Wrox.Twitter.NUrl;

namespace Wrox.Twitter.MockingRequests
{
    class Program
```

```
    {
        static void Main()
        {
            const string url = "http://twitter.com/statuses/friends.json";

            // Create a new request you intend to mock
            var request = (HttpWebRequest)WebRequest.Create(url);
            var mockRequest  = (MockHttpWebRequest)request;

            // Define the desired response
            mockRequest.Response = DataGeneration.CreateUsers(DataFormat.Json,100);

            // Send the request in the usual way, using NUrl;
            // this allows you to replace the mock request with a
            // real request at a later time without significant
            // code changes
            var response = mockRequest.Get();

            // You can deserialize as normal and work with classes
            var users = DeserializeUsers(response);
            foreach(var user in users)
            {
                Console.WriteLine(user.ScreenName);
            }

            Console.WriteLine("Press any key to end the example.");
            Console.ReadKey();
        }

        private static List<TwitterUser> DeserializeUsers(string json)
        {
            var serializer = new JavaScriptSerializer();
            serializer.RegisterConverters(new List<JavaScriptConverter>
                                          {
                                              new TwitterConverter()
                                          });

            var users = serializer.Deserialize<List<TwitterUser>>(json);
            return users;
        }
    }
}
```

The final piece of the mocking story is the ability to simplify the creation of usable mock data with the DataGeneration utility class, considering that the mocked response is a simple string. In the next section you'll employ a basic method of simulating user data by randomly generating appropriately formatted content using data templates.

Generating Data

Because the approach outlined here for mocking REST requests relies on pre-fabricated outputs, and because it is generally not good coverage if all API methods in your tests produce identical or stale-seeming results, you can help randomize REST outputs with the use of data generation utility classes.

What these classes do is allow you to randomly generate mock data so that the output is novel enough for you to test different scenarios. You could take this much further, of course, mapping the API's query parameters to the number and quality of the mock responses, such as when testing pagination methods, but the following set of examples demonstrating data generation tools for your mocking efforts is a good first step to developing Twitter applications without relying on a live API.

Mocking Text

A classic approach to generating dummy text for typesetting and web layouts, this code example produces a randomized list of *Lorem Ipsum* words, taken from an ancient Latin text authored by Cicero in 45 B.C. You can use the LoremIpsum class to generate Twitter statuses, user names, and bio data.

```
using System;
using System.Text;

namespace Wrox.Twitter.MockingRequests
{
    public static class LoremIpsum
    {
        private static readonly string[] _words = new[]
        {
            // See the downloaded code examples for a full word list
            "sed", "ut", "perspiciatis", "unde" ...
        };

        public static string Get(int count)
        {
            var sb = new StringBuilder();
            var random = new Random();

            for (var i = 0; i < count; i++)
            {
                var index = random.Next(_words.Length);
                var word = _words[index];
                sb.Append(word);
                if(i < count - 1)
                {
                    sb.Append(" ");
                }
            }

            return sb.ToString();
        }

        public static string Fill(int length)
        {
            var mandatory = new[] {"lorem", "ipsum", "dolor", "sit", "amet"};
            var sb = new StringBuilder();
            var random = new Random();

            if(length <= 1)
            {
                return "";
            }
```

```
            var count = 0;
            while(sb.Length < length && length - sb.Length > 1)
            {
                if(count <= 4)
                {
                    sb.Append(mandatory[count])
                        .Append(" ");
                }
                else
                {
                    var index = random.Next(_words.Length);
                    var word = _words[index];

                    var proposed = sb.Length + word.Length;
                    if (proposed <= length)
                    {
                        sb.Append(word);
                        if (sb.Length < length && length - sb.Length > 2)
                        {
                            sb.Append(" ");
                        }
                    }
                }
                count++;
            }

            return sb.ToString();
        }
    }
}
```

Because you need to cover multiple REST data formats depending on your application's needs, you can encapsulate the various formats into a DataTemplate class.

```
namespace Wrox.Twitter.MockingRequests
{
    public enum DataFormat
    {
        Xml,
        Json,
        Rss,
        Atom
    }

    public class DataTemplate
    {
        public DataFormat Format { get; private set; }
        public string Template { get; private set; }

        private const string JsonUser =
            @"{""favourites_count"":{0},
                ""description"":""{1}"",
                ""utc_offset"":-18000,
                ""profile_link_color"":""{2}"",
```

```
        ""statuses_count"":{3},
        ""following"":false,
        ""profile_background_tile"":"""",
        ""profile_sidebar_fill_color"":""{4}"",
        ""followers_count"":{5},
        ""profile_background_image_url"": """",
        ""url"":""http://wrox.com"",
        ""name"":""{6}"",
        ""time_zone"":""Eastern Time (US & Canada)"",
        ""friends_count"":{7},
        ""profile_sidebar_border_color"":""{8}"",
        ""protected"":false,
        ""status"":{9},
        ""profile_image_url"":"""",
        ""created_at"":""{10}"",
        ""notifications"":false,
        ""profile_background_color"":""{11}"",
        ""screen_name"":""{12}"",
        ""location"":""Mocks"",
        ""id"":{13},
        ""profile_text_color"":""{14}""}";

    public static DataTemplate JsonUserDataTemplate
    {
        get
        {
            return new DataTemplate()
                {
                    Template = JsonUser,
                    Format = DataFormat.Json
                };
        }
    }

        // Other formats elided...
    }
}
```

The next example provides a `DataGeneration` class with convenience methods to generate users, statuses, and direct messages. The user generation method is illustrated, with randomly generated values corresponding to format string parameters of the data templates defined in the previous example. A random color generator is used to create the user's profile colors and is converted to a string representation with an extension method. It is important that mocked responses reflect the same data that would come from a live request, especially when you are developing applications that use data binding or make assumptions about the underlying model.

```
using System;
using System.Collections.Generic;
using System.Drawing;
using System.Text;
using Wrox.Twitter.Objects;

namespace Wrox.Twitter.MockingRequests
```

```
{
    public static class DataGeneration
    {
        private static readonly Random _random = new Random();

        public static string CreateUsers(DataFormat format, int count)
        {
            var ids = new List<int>();
            var sb = new StringBuilder();

            for (var i = 0; i < count; i++)
            {
                var favoritesCount = _random.Next(500);
                var description = LoremIpsum.Fill(160);
                var profileLinkColor = CreateColor();
                var statusesCount = _random.Next(500);
                var profileSidebarFillColor = CreateColor();
                var followersCount = _random.Next(500);
                var name = LoremIpsum.Get(2);
                var friendsCount = _random.Next(500);
                var profileSidebarBorderColor = CreateColor();
                var status = CreateStatus(format, 1);
                var createdAt = DateTime.Now.ToString(TwitterExtensions.
RestDateFormat);
                var profileBackgroundColor = CreateColor();
                var screenName = LoremIpsum.Get(1);
                var profileTextColor = CreateColor();

                int id = 0;
                while (!ids.Contains(id) && id > 0)
                {
                    id = _random.Next();
                }
                ids.Add(id);

                DataTemplate template = null;
                switch (format)
                {
                    case DataFormat.Json:
                        template = DataTemplate.JsonUserDataTemplate;
                        break;
                }

                var user = String.Format(template,
                                        favoritesCount,
                                        description,
                                        profileLinkColor,
                                        statusesCount,
                                        profileSidebarFillColor,
                                        followersCount,
                                        name,
                                        friendsCount,
                                        profileSidebarBorderColor,
                                        status,
```

```
                                    createdAt,
                                    profileBackgroundColor,
                                    screenName,
                                    id,
                                    profileTextColor);

            sb.Append(user);
        }

        return sb.ToString();
    }

    public static string CreateStatuses(DataFormat format, int count)
    {
        // Details elided...
    }

    public static string CreateDirectMessages(DataFormat format, int count)
    {
        // Details elided...
    }

    public static string CreateColor()
    {
        var alpha = _random.Next(256);
        var red = _random.Next(256);
        var green = _random.Next(256);
        var blue = _random.Next(256);

        var color = Color.FromArgb(alpha, red, green, blue);
        return color.ToHexString();
    }
    }
}
```

Mocking is a powerful concept for opening development scenarios that don't require Internet connectivity or within an iterative development process where your user experience is developed prior to working directly with its underlying, connected services.

Summary

In this chapter a wide array of suggestions, caveats, and workarounds for key development tasks when working on Twitter applications was covered. Some highlights of these demonstrations include the following:

- ❏ Caching photos, users, and status data, and aging those caches gracefully.

- ❏ Setting up multi-part HTTP POST calls and sending photo data to Twitter's account API methods.

- ❏ Dealing with the challenges rate limiting imposes on responsive applications when working with large user bases or users with a large number of followers.

❑   Integrating third-party applications into your own work.

❑   Creating mock requests for testing application behavior when offline.

In the upcoming chapter, the concept of consuming REST APIs using the traditional polling approach is evaluated, where you request data and process incoming responses, whether or not the results are relevant or timely. You will evaluate the concept and implementation of push-based architectures using .NET, other services, and Twitter's latest API offering, so that you might only receive new data to process when it is actually available, rather than continuously polling or holding your own application hostage to cautious API consumption to avoid breaking rate limitations.

8

Data Push vs. Pull

Pushing Data

Your application design changes greatly when the concept of pushing data is introduced as a possibility. Up to this point, even technologies such as RSS and Atom, which present the illusion of pushing data when implemented in reader applications, rely on polling. Pushing data involves proactively sending data to a waiting client only when it is available; the client does not participate in the process or send any messages to the server after a connection is established.

Advantages

A push-based service allows clients to operate mostly independent of the server responsible for its data, reducing the dependency on a centralized location for data storage. Polling for data, especially on publically accessible applications, creates the potential for wasted resources. This happens when bandwidth is used to unnecessarily and continuously request updates from a server when none are available. Although caching is typically used to reduce the overhead of data storage access, a server must still honor each request, even if it is redundant. Pushing data solves this problem, reducing the load on a server dramatically when it is solely responsible for when and to what extent it informs clients of newly available data.

Disadvantages

One drawback to a push service is server overhead when tracking the status of clients that are registered to receive updates. Streaming data requires open connections to every interested subscriber, or frequent hit testing to ensure clients are able to receive messages. Holding references for many clients (and having many clients is a problem you likely want to have as a Twitter application developer), such as extensive caching mechanisms, can reduce your server's operating memory. Also, because updates are sent to clients who listen indefinitely, there is no rigid transaction in place to confirm that messages are sent successfully — a message is received by a client, or it isn't, and a confirmation is potentially issued from the client back to the server, or it doesn't. Accounting for service instability is an additional complexity that pull-based systems are spared when it is easy to deduce whether a call fails or succeeds, such as when making calls to Twitter's REST endpoints.

Using WCF Duplex Services

The .NET Framework supports push-based services using the duplex features of WCF. A *duplex service,* by definition, is a service that supports the ability to send messages from either endpoint, such as a Silverlight client and an ASP.NET web application on an IIS Server. The additional capacity to send messages from the server to the client is what opens up push-based scenarios in WCF. You can use the standard capability of a polling service to send a message from a client to your server. This will register that client to receive push messages, and by leveraging the server-side duplex option, the clients will receive them indefinitely or until they opt out.

Defining Contracts

To set up a server to send push messages to waiting clients, choose the *Web Application Project* type in Visual Studio. The first step to defining a push service is to set up a WCF service contract on the server defining the messages a client can send or receive. Although a push service by definition sends messages one way — from server to client — you must track clients on the server to know which clients are logged in and where to address messages. The following code example defines a service to contract the client's available messages, which in this case is a minimal set of operations for notifying the server that it is ready to receive push data.

```
using System.ServiceModel;
using System.ServiceModel.Channels;

namespace Wrox.Twitter.PushServer
{
    [ServiceContract(Namespace = "Wrox.Twitter.PushServer",
                     CallbackContract = typeof (IPushClient))]
    public interface IPushService
    {
        [OperationContract(IsOneWay = true)]
        void SignIn(Message message);

        [OperationContract(IsOneWay = true)]
        void SignOut(Message message);
    }
}
```

The client's contract defines two one-way operations. These methods don't keep a channel open on the server waiting for a response, but rather assume that the messages will reach their destination — which should be accounted for when handling code. The namespace of the ServiceContract is a hard-coded literal string, which is an important requirement for push services because a client must refer to an operation on a server explicitly by namespace, contract, and operation name. The Message class is part of the System.ServiceModel library, and you'll also need to reference System.ServiceModel. PollingDuplex to enable data push in WCF. If you have Silverlight 2 and Silverlight 3 SDKs installed on the same machine, for these examples you can reference either version of this .NET library, though you will see both when attempting to *Add References* in Visual Studio. The IPushClient contract is not currently defined. As a callback contract it defines the messages the client itself will receive, which is the heart of a push service. The following code illustrates a representative contract for pushing data to a listening client, created:

```
using System.ServiceModel;
using System.ServiceModel.Channels;

namespace Wrox.Twitter.PushServer
{
    [ServiceContract]
    public interface IPushClient
    {
        [OperationContract(IsOneWay = true)]
        void ReceivedData(Message message);

        [OperationContract(IsOneWay = true)]
        void SignedIn(Message message);

        [OperationContract(IsOneWay = true)]
        void SignedOut(Message message);
    }
}
```

The operations available to the client are one-way, similar to the server's contract, and provide confirmation for the SignIn and SignOut methods of IPushService (which help a client know when a server is ready to handle requests). The ReceivedData operation defines the main payload that you're interested in and is pushed to the relevant client; a fully defined push service would typically have multiple Message operations that push different sets of data depending on the context.

Creating a Host and Factory

The next step to setting up a duplex service is to create a custom ServiceHost to consume your duplex-enabled service contracts. The next code example shows a simple PollingDuplexServiceHostFactory which instantiates a new PollingDuplexServiceHost with an existing configuration:

```
using System;
using System.ServiceModel;
using System.ServiceModel.Activation;

namespace Wrox.Twitter.PushServer
```

```
{
    public class PollingDuplexServiceHostFactory : ServiceHostFactoryBase
    {
        public override ServiceHostBase CreateServiceHost(
            string constructorString,
            Uri[] baseAddresses)
        {
            return new PollingDuplexServiceHost(baseAddresses);
        }
    }
}
```

With the factory defined, the creation method of a `PollingDuplexServiceHost` will create a new custom binding pointing to the `IPushService` contract, and configures SOAP-based messaging for messages passed between endpoints in either direction. This action is illustrated in the following code:

```
using System;
using System.ServiceModel;
using System.ServiceModel.Channels;
using System.Text;

namespace Wrox.Twitter.PushServer
{
    public class PollingDuplexServiceHost : ServiceHost
    {
        public PollingDuplexServiceHost(params Uri[] addresses)
        {
            InitializeDescription(typeof (PushService),
                            new UriSchemeKeyedCollection(addresses));
        }

        protected override void InitializeRuntime()
        {
            // Define the binding and set time-outs
            var bindingElement = new PollingDuplexBindingElement
                                {
                                    ServerPollTimeout = TimeSpan.FromSeconds(3),
                                    InactivityTimeout = TimeSpan.FromMinutes(1)
                                };

            // Add an endpoint for the given service contract
            AddServiceEndpoint(
                typeof (IPushService),
                new CustomBinding(
                    bindingElement,
                    new TextMessageEncodingBindingElement(
                        MessageVersion.Soap11,
                        Encoding.UTF8),
                    new HttpTransportBindingElement()),
                String.Empty);

            base.InitializeRuntime();
        }
    }
}
```

The `PollingDuplexServiceHost` specifies strict timeouts for communications with connected clients, which you should account for in your fault handling for services.

Silverlight 3 Improves Polling Duplex Support

Silverlight 2 requires some additional effort to create duplex services due to the absence of service referencing support mirroring existing proxy generation utilities for other services; Silverlight 3 promises improved support, and fortunately, setting up a duplex service in this way is compatible in Silverlight 3, so you can use it with either version of the Framework.

Configuring Services

You can now declare the use of your custom duplex hosting classes by adding the factory type to the standard WCF `.svc` markup file accompanying your new web service as shown in the following code snippet:

```
<%@ ServiceHost
    Language="C#"
    Debug="true"
    Factory="Wrox.Twitter.PushServer.PollingDuplexServiceHostFactory"
    Service="Wrox.Twitter.PushServer.PushService"
    CodeBehind="PushService.svc.cs"
%>
```

Similarly, the protracted WCF configuration that lives in `web.config` requires no specialized configuration other than what is required to correctly publish a service and its behavior. In the following code, the `PushService` is configured to use a behavior that publishes its metadata for discovery, but does not define a service contract — this is because you will set up the client explicitly to reference and consume the service. It is not a feature so much as a missing ability to generate proxies for duplex services in Silverlight 2.

```
<system.serviceModel>
<services>
    <service
        name="Wrox.Twitter.PushService"
        behaviorConfiguration="Wrox.Twitter.PushServiceBehavior">
    <endpoint
        address="mex"
        binding="mexHttpBinding"
        contract="IMetadataExchange"/>
    </service>
</services>
<behaviors>
    <serviceBehaviors>
        <behavior name="Wrox.Twitter.PushServiceBehavior">
            <serviceMetadata httpGetEnabled="true" />
```

```
              <serviceDebug includeExceptionDetailInFaults="false" />
          </behavior>
      </serviceBehaviors>
  </behaviors>
  </system.serviceModel>
```

You now have contracts defined, duplex factories declared, and WCF services properly configured to implement a duplex service.

Server Messaging

The implementation of IPushService will contain the majority of the service logic, as it is where messages designed to push to registered clients will execute. When a client sends the SignIn message, the server will respond first by adding the client to an in-memory collection to track their availability for push messages, and then by starting a background process to poll for data from Twitter and push it to clients. The methods to respond to clients signing in and out are detailed, and illustrated by the next code example. The push service class contains several hard-coded strings to track the explicit service contract names to use when invoking the callback contract designed for client use.

```csharp
using System;
using System.Collections.Generic;
using System.ServiceModel;
using System.ServiceModel.Channels;
using System.Threading;
using Wrox.Twitter.NUrl;

namespace Wrox.Twitter.PushServer
{
    public class PushService : IPushService
    {
        private static readonly IDictionary<IPushClient, string> _clients =
            new Dictionary<IPushClient, string>();

        private const string Namespace = "Wrox.Twitter.PushServer/";
        private const string InterfaceDeclaringCallback = "IPushService/";

        // Namespace/InterfaceDeclaringCallback/Method
        private const string ReceivedDataAction =
            Namespace + InterfaceDeclaringCallback + "ReceivedData";
        private const string SignedInAction =
            Namespace + InterfaceDeclaringCallback + "SignedIn";
        private const string SignedOutAction =
            Namespace + InterfaceDeclaringCallback + "SignedOut";

        public void SignIn(Message message)
        {
            var client = OperationContext
                .Current.GetCallbackChannel<IPushClient>();

            var username = message.GetBody<string>();
            lock (this)
            {
                if (_clients.ContainsKey(client))
```

```
            {
                // Already signed in
                return;
            }

            // Prepare a message for the client including the action
            // and name of the user for confirmation
            var data = string.Format("{0}#{1}",
                                    SignedInAction,
                                    username);

            // Add the user to memory
            _clients.Add(client, username);

            // Send the callback contract SignIn action to the client
            CallClient(client,
                        data,
                        SignedInAction, (c, m) => c.SignedIn(m));
        }
    }

    public void SignOut(Message message)
    {
        // Release the client usern
        var client = OperationContext
            .Current.GetCallbackChannel<IPushClient>();
        var username = message.GetBody<string>();

        lock (this)
        {
            if (!_clients.ContainsKey(client))
            {
                // Already signed out
                return;
            }

            // Prepare a message for the client including the action
            // and name f the user for confirmation
            var data = string.Format("{0}#{1}", SignedOutAction, username);

            // Remove the client from memory
            _clients.Remove(client);

            // Send the callback contract SignedOut action to the client
            CallClient(client,
                        data,
                        SignedInAction,
                        (c, m) => c.SignedOut(m));
        }
    }

    // Use this method to send a message to a single client
    private static void CallClient(IPushClient client,
                                    string data,
                                    string action,
                                    Action<IPushClient, Message> operation)
```

```
        {
            var message = Message.CreateMessage(MessageVersion.Soap11,
                                          action,
                                          data);
            operation.Invoke(client, message);
        }
    }
}
```

The process is fairly methodical — a client proxy is saved in memory during sign in and discarded during sign out, a callback channel is opened for each message destined for the client, and SOAP messages are created and sent through the channel proxy when prepared. The naming of each callback contract is carefully added to each outgoing operation, as it must match the client-side implementation and naming scheme exactly. The method to push data follows the same pattern, except it will push its message to every client that is currently signed in; you can sign on to the duplex service with multiple web browser instances and see the same data returned in each. The code to push Twitter data to waiting clients is shown in the following listing, where the previously defined methods and variables are hidden from view.

```
using System;
using System.Collections.Generic;
using System.ServiceModel;
using System.ServiceModel.Channels;
using System.Threading;
using Wrox.Twitter.NUrl;

namespace Wrox.Twitter.PushServer
{
    public class PushService : IPushService
    {
        private static void PushData()
        {
            while (true)
            {
                // Grab some representative data from Twitter and
                // send it to all waiting clients
                var updates =
                    "http://twitter.com/statuses/public_timeline.json".Get();

                // Prepare a message with context for the results
                var data = string.Format("{0}#{1}", ReceivedDataAction, updates);

                // Send the callback contract ReceivedData action to all clients
                CallClients(data, ReceivedDataAction,
                            (c, m) => c.ReceivedData(m));

                // Wait for five seconds
                Thread.Sleep(5000);
            }
        }
```

```csharp
// Use this method to send a message to all listening clients
private static void CallClients(string data,
                                string action,
                                Action<IPushClient, Message> operation)
{
    var message = Message.CreateMessage(MessageVersion.Soap11,
                                        action,
                                        data);
    lock (_clients)
    {
        var keys = _clients.Keys;
        foreach (var key in keys)
        {
            operation.Invoke(key, message);
        }
    }
}
}
}
```

Client Consumption

To build a client to consume server messages and send a few of its own, add a new *Silverlight Application* to your solution. The client-side code to listen in on the messages the server is pushing starts with ensuring that a `crossdomainpolicy.xml` file exists in your existing server-side web application for Silverlight to reach the server. As a reminder, the content of this important file is listed here:

```xml
<?xml version="1.0" encoding="utf-8"?>
<access-policy>
  <cross-domain-access>
    <policy>
      <allow-from http-request-headers="*">
        <domain uri="*"/>
      </allow-from>
      <grant-to>
        <resource path="/" include-subpaths="true"/>
      </grant-to>
    </policy>
  </cross-domain-access>
</access-policy>
```

The messages that the server creates for delivery are delimited by the # character in the previous examples, due to the fact that a SOAP message might only carry a string value, with no indication at runtime of which client, or what method, was invoked to produce it. To work around this limitation, the name of the user who owns the message that is sent with the service us pre-pended to the beginning of the message body, , separating the author and the message by a # symbol. On the client side, you can split the incoming back into the `Action` that produced it, and the `Response` data you need. The following code illustrates the `EventArgs` classes that represent the events raised when a request to the server is made, or a message is received. This makes handling push data in your application possible as you are able to add handlers and process the inbound push.

```csharp
using System;

namespace Wrox.Twitter.PushClient
{
    public class DuplexRequestEventArgs : EventArgs
    {
        public string Message { get; private set; }

        public DuplexRequestEventArgs(string message)
        {
            Message = message;
        }
    }
}

using System;

namespace Wrox.Twitter.PushClient
{
    public class DuplexResponseEventArgs : EventArgs
    {
        public string Response { get; private set; }
        public string Action { get; private set; }

        public DuplexResponseEventArgs(string message, string action)
        {
            Response = message;
            Action = action;
        }
    }
}
```

The ChannelManager contains several methods and is meant to abstract away some of the complexities of sending and listening for messages on an open WCF channel. The first set of ChannelManager functions provides the SignIn and SignOut actions which correspond to the available callback contract operations. In addition, each action from the server or the contract is defined carefully to ensure the values match on the server.

```csharp
using System;
using System.ServiceModel.Channels;

namespace Wrox.Twitter.PushClient
{
    public partial class ChannelManager
    {
        // Remember to ensure this namespace matches the server-side contract
        private const string NamespaceCallback =
            "Wrox.Twitter.PushServer/IPushService/";

        // Incoming Messages From Server
        public const string StatusesAction = NamespaceCallback +
            "ReceivedStatuses";
        public const string SignedInAction = NamespaceCallback + "SignedIn";
        public const string SignedOutAction = NamespaceCallback + "SignedOut";
```

```
                // Outgoing Messages To Server
                private const string SignInAction = NamespaceCallback + "SignIn";
                private const string SignOutAction = NamespaceCallback + "SignOut";

                private static void SignIn(IOutputChannel channel)
                {
                    PerformAction(channel, SignInAction);
                }

                private static void SignOut(IOutputChannel channel)
                {
                    PerformAction(channel, SignOutAction);
                    _isClosing = true;
                }

                private static void PerformAction(IOutputChannel channel, string action)
                {
                    var message = Message.CreateMessage
                        (channel.GetProperty<MessageVersion>(), action, _screenName);

                    var sendCallback = new AsyncCallback(OnSend);

                    // Send the message on the prepared channel
                    SendMessage(channel, message, sendCallback);

                    // Tell the UI that a new action message was delivered
                    OnMessageSent(new DuplexRequestEventArgs(action));
                }
            }
        }
```

The next part of ChannelManager creation is the manager and tracking the UI thread so that control updates due to incoming data are correctly marshalled. Because the message passing logic runs asynchronously, the UI's SynchronizationContext is passed in the constructor to track it while the code instantiates a factory to open a channel. The SignIn and SignOut methods are convenience methods to make it easy to call them directly from the ChannelManager class without knowledge of what's required to open a WCF channel. The code for these aspects of ChannelManager is listed here:

```
using System;
using System.ServiceModel;
using System.ServiceModel.Channels;
using System.Threading;
using Push.Client.Extensions;

namespace Wrox.Twitter.PushClient
{
    public partial class ChannelManager
    {
        private const string ServiceUri = "http://localhost:9595/PushService.svc";

        private static PollingDuplexHttpBinding _binding;
        private static IDuplexSessionChannel _channel;
        private static string _screenName;
        private static SynchronizationContext _ui;
```

```csharp
        public static event EventHandler<DuplexRequestEventArgs> RequestSent;
        public static void OnMessageSent(DuplexRequestEventArgs args)
        {
            if (RequestSent != null)
            {
                RequestSent(null, args);
            }
        }

        public static event EventHandler<DuplexResponseEventArgs> ResponseReceived;
        public static void OnResponseReceived(DuplexResponseEventArgs args)
        {
            if (ResponseReceived != null)
            {
                ResponseReceived(null, args);
            }
        }

        public ChannelManager(SynchronizationContext ui)
        {
            _ui = ui;
            _binding = new PollingDuplexHttpBinding
                    {
                        InactivityTimeout = TimeSpan.FromMinutes(1),
                        MaxReceivedMessageSize = 10.Megabytes(),
                    };
        }

        public void SignIn(string screenName)
        {
            if (_isClosed)
            {
                _screenName = screenName;
                var openCallback = new AsyncCallback(OnOpenCompleteFactory);
                OpenFactory(_binding, openCallback);
            }

            SignIn(_channel);
            Listen(_channel);
        }

        public void SignOut()
        {
            if(_channel != null)
            {
                SignOut(_channel);
            }
        }
    }
}
```

The Megabytes extension method used in the previous code listing is a convenient way to express file or memory sizes explicitly. The code to make use of this utility method is in the following snippet.

```
public static class FileExtensions
{
    public static long Megabytes(this int value)
    {
        // Number of megabytes * 1024 kilobytes in a megabyte
        // * 1024 bytes in a kilobyte = total bytes
        return value * 1024 * 1024;
    }
}
```

The next aspect of ChannelManager deals with the asynchronous construction and execution of WCF channels through the duplex factory, handling their state, and sending messages. This is infrastructure code, and you can learn more about how it fits together with your specific logic by visiting MSDN at http://msdn.microsoft.com/en-us/library/cc645027(VS.95).aspx for a thorough explanation of the underlying WCF architecture. Beyond the task of channel creation, the important methods here are Listen and Heard, which process incoming messages, handle faults, and parse messages into usable data before raising events for your application UI to respond to.

```
using System;
using System.ServiceModel;
using System.ServiceModel.Channels;
using System.Windows;

namespace Wrox.Twitter.PushClient
{
    public partial class ChannelManager
    {
        private static bool _isClosing;
        private static bool _isClosed = true;

        #region http://msdn.microsoft.com/en-us/library/cc645027(VS.95).aspx
        private static void OpenFactory(Binding binding, AsyncCallback callback)
        {
            var factory = binding
                .BuildChannelFactory<IDuplexSessionChannel>
                    (new BindingParameterCollection());

            var factoryOpenResult = factory.BeginOpen(callback, factory);
            if (factoryOpenResult.CompletedSynchronously)
            {
                CompleteOpenFactory(factoryOpenResult);
            }
        }

        private static void OpenChannel(ICommunicationObject channel,
                                        AsyncCallback callback)
        {
            var channelOpenResult = channel.BeginOpen(callback, channel);
            if (channelOpenResult.CompletedSynchronously)
            {
                CompleteOpenChannel(channelOpenResult);
            }
        }
```

```
    }

    private static void OnOpenCompleteFactory(IAsyncResult result)
    {
        if (result.CompletedSynchronously)
        {
            return;
        }

        CompleteOpenFactory(result);
    }

    private static void CompleteOpenFactory(IAsyncResult result)
    {
        var factory = (IChannelFactory<IDuplexSessionChannel>)result.
        AsyncState;
        factory.EndOpen(result);

        var openCallback = new AsyncCallback(OnOpenCompleteChannel);
        _channel = factory.CreateChannel(new EndpointAddress(ServiceUri));

        OpenChannel(_channel, openCallback);
    }

    private static void OnOpenCompleteChannel(IAsyncResult result)
    {
        if (result.CompletedSynchronously)
        {
            return;
        }

        CompleteOpenChannel(result);
    }

    private static void CompleteOpenChannel(IAsyncResult result)
    {
        var channel = (IDuplexSessionChannel)result.AsyncState;
        channel.EndOpen(result);
        _isClosed = false;
    }

    private static void OnCloseChannel(IAsyncResult result)
    {
        if (result.CompletedSynchronously)
        {
            return;
        }

        CompleteCloseChannel(result);
    }

    private static void CompleteCloseChannel(IAsyncResult result)
    {
        var channel = (IDuplexSessionChannel)result.AsyncState;
        channel.EndClose(result);
```

```
            _channel = null;
    }

    private static void CloseChannel(IAsyncResult result,
                                     ICommunicationObject channel)
    {
        var resultFactory = channel
            .BeginClose
                (new AsyncCallback(OnCloseChannel), channel);

        if (resultFactory.CompletedSynchronously)
        {
            CompleteCloseChannel(result);
        }
    }

    private static void OnReceiveComplete(IAsyncResult result)
    {
        if (result.CompletedSynchronously)
        {
            return;
        }

        Heard(result);
    }

    private static void SendMessage(IOutputChannel channel,
                                    Message message,
                                    AsyncCallback callback)
    {
        var resultChannel = channel.BeginSend(message, callback, channel);
        if (resultChannel.CompletedSynchronously)
        {
            CompleteOnSend(resultChannel);
        }
    }

    private static void OnSend(IAsyncResult result)
    {
        if (result.CompletedSynchronously)
        {
            return;
        }

        CompleteOnSend(result);
    }

    private static void CompleteOnSend(IAsyncResult result)
    {
        var channel = (IDuplexSessionChannel)result.AsyncState;
        channel.EndSend(result);
    }
```

```csharp
#endregion

private static void Listen(IInputChannel channel)
{
    var result = channel.BeginReceive
        (new AsyncCallback(OnReceiveComplete), channel);

    if (result.CompletedSynchronously)
    {
        Heard(result);
    }
}

private static void Heard(IAsyncResult result)
{
    var channel = (IDuplexSessionChannel)result.AsyncState;

    try
    {
        var receivedMessage = channel.EndReceive(result);
        if (receivedMessage == null)
        {
            CloseChannel(result, channel);
            MessageBox.Show("Server prematurely closed the session");
        }
        else
        {
            // Because the SOAP message is a single string and does not
            // contain any context, a separator was used on the server to
            // help determine which user / client was involved.
            var message = receivedMessage.GetBody<string>();
            var separator = message.IndexOf("#");
            var action = message.Substring(0, separator++);

            var response = message.Substring(separator);
            var args = new DuplexResponseEventArgs(response, action);
            OnResponseReceived(args);

            if(_isClosing)
            {
                CloseChannel(result, channel);
                _isClosed = true;
                _isClosing = false;
            }
            else
            {
                Listen(_channel);
            }
        }
    }
    catch (TimeoutException)
    {
        _ui.Post(s =>
            MessageBox.Show("Service call timed out. Please retry."), null);
    }
```

```
        catch (CommunicationException)
        {
            _ui.Post(s =>
                MessageBox.Show("Unknown communications exception occured."), null);
        }
      }
    }
  }
```

WCF provides a flexible way to push messages from your own server to waiting clients. This is a good introduction to what is required to structure your Twitter applications so that they listen for incoming data rather than frequently polling to check for a change. This is not a push service in the true sense; your server is polling Twitter as it always has, but is simply delivering the data through a different vehicle. To take another step toward push services, you can enlist the help of other services to remove the necessity to poll Twitter itself before redistributing the results.

Using Gnip

While WCF allows you to push data to waiting clients, Twitter data is still consumed by polling the REST API. This is a suitable architecture for many applications, but not a true push service in the sense of receiving a broadcast directly from a publisher such as Twitter. In July 2008, Gnip launched and billed itself as a service designed to "make data portability suck less." Acting as an intermediary layer between multiple social services such as Twitter, Digg, Flickr, Delicious, StumbleUpon, and Tumblr, Gnip is designed to provide a way to receive updates from publishers as a push, or notify your application when polling will result in fresh content. Figure 8-1, from the Gnip API documentation at `http://docs.google.com/Doc?id=dpw6zj9_0fdcnttgd#current_activities`, shows the overall architecture of the Gnip service.

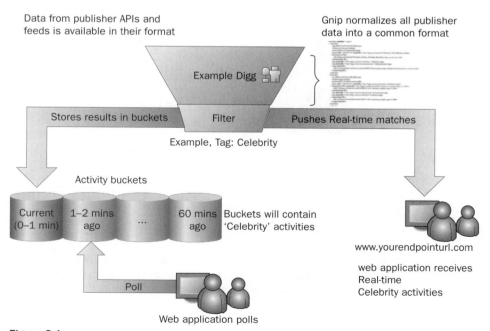

Figure 8-1

Gnip's .NET Convenience Library

The Gnip developers provide a .NET library meant to help with some of the REST principles and underlying object model of Gnip, made available at `http://github.com/gnip/gnip-dotnet`. The Gnip client library also requires a reference to the popular *log4net* project sponsored by Apache and available at `http://logging.apache.org/log4net/`, though the library includes a version of this dependency you can include in your projects. You already have a REST abstraction tool in NUrl, but the Gnip library provides support for the common Gnip-specific tasks of filter creation and activity and notification polling. You can also borrow the data classes from the library, shown in Figure 8-2, to speed up your understanding and use of the service and ease the work of object discovery and deserialization. Keep in mind that the Gnip library for .NET is not as fault-tolerant as NUrl (it will, for example, throw a `WebException` when it encounters any non-200 status, which is in line with what you discovered about working with REST in .NET in Handling Exceptions in Chapter 1. You might also want to make a few changes, or memorize the API itself for use with NUrl in more advanced scenarios.

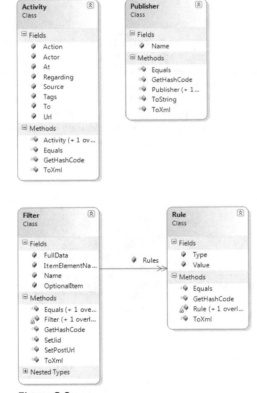

Figure 8-2

The underpinnings of Gnip as a push service are activities and notifications; activities are normalized information about a web publisher's updates, and are constrained by the filters containing rules that you created for your account. Figure 8-3 illustrates the `GnipConnection` and its available library methods, and other supporting classes.

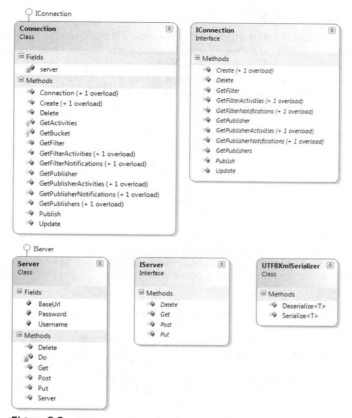

Figure 8-3

After you have established what publishers want to receive or pull updates from, and what rules are in place to filter that data, you can interact with the API based on your desired approach — whether that's polling activity buckets for new content, or opening an endpoint to receive pushed notifications.

Authenticating a Gnip Account

Gnip, as with Twitter, requires user account credentials which are passed in the HttpWebRequest with Basic authorization. The Connection class lets you pass these in to the constructor for reuse on multiple methods, shown here:

```
using Gnip.Client;

private const string GnipUsername = "username";
private const string GnipPassword = "password";

// Create a new client configuration
Config config = new Config(GnipUsername, GnipPassword);

// Make a new connection to Gnip using the convenience library
GnipConnection connection = new GnipConnection(config);
```

Setting Up Publisher Filters and Rules

Because Gnip normalizes data from multiple social streams, it's necessary to make a distinction for the publisher you care about, in this case Twitter, and its constraints. Twitter uses the notifications concept of Gnip, rather than the activities, as its primary feature is short notification messages rather than more involved activities such as those you might find on a community forum site like Digg. The next code example demonstrates creating a new filter for Twitter, consisting of a single rule: you're only interested in getting notified when @ev, the founder of Twitter, posts a new tweet.

```
using System;
using Gnip;
using Gnip.Client.Resource;

private const string GnipUsername = "username";
private const string GnipPassword = "password";
private const string FilterName = "founder";

// Create a new client configuration
var config = new Config(GnipUsername, GnipPassword);
// Make a new connection to Gnip using the convenience library
var connection = new GnipConnection(config);

// Get Twitter as a publisher
var twitter = connection.GetPublisher(PublisherType.Gnip, "twitter");

// Create a filter with partial data (full data is not allowed for Twitter)
var filter = new Filter(FilterName ) { IsFullData = false };

// Create a rule to govern the data returned by the filter
filter.Rules.Add(new Rule(RuleType.Actor, "ev"));

// Set up the new filter for Twitter on your Gnip account
connection.Create(twitter, filter);
```

Polling Activities

With a filter established, it is possible to poll Gnip for new notifications. Polling for activities or notifications occurs on *buckets* of data that are sliced into one-minute intervals; if you don't provide the library the DateTime instance representing a specific minute, the current minute is used with any data present at the time of the call. The following code example shows polling for up-to-the-minute notifications on the filter established in the previous snippet:

```
using System;
using System.Text;
using Gnip.Client;
using Gnip.Client.Resource;

// Poll for notifications matching the filter you created
var activities = connection.GetActivities(twitter, FilterName);

// Do something with your new activity data
var sb = new StringBuilder();
```

```
foreach(var activity in activities)
{
    sb.AppendLine(activity.Url);
}
```

Pushing Activities

Setting up a data push is extremely simple: just provide a string representing the publically accessible HTTP POST endpoint that Gnip can use to send your filter's updates, as shown here:

```
using System;
using Gnip.Client;
using Gnip.Client.Resource;
private const string GnipUsername = "username";
private const string GnipPassword = "password";
private const string FilterName = "founder";

// Create a new client configuration
var config = new Config(GnipUsername, GnipPassword);
// Make a new connection to Gnip using the convenience library
var connection = new GnipConnection(config);

// Get Twitter as a publisher
var twitter = connection.GetPublisher(PublisherType.Gnip, "twitter");

// Create a filter with partial data (full data is not allowed for Twitter)
var filter = new Filter(FilterName, "false");

// Create a rule to govern the data returned by the filter
filter.Rules.Add(new Rule(RuleType.Actor, "ev"));

// This would map to your own, publically available site
const string endpoint = "http://yoursite.com/api/examples/push";

// Add the HTTP POST endpoint for push delivery
filter.PostUrl = endpoint;

// Set up the new filter for Twitter on your Gnip account
connection.Create(twitter, FilterName);
```

Although declaring the REST endpoint to use for updates is simple, you need to create one in .NET and host it on online before you can take advantage of push features.

Using `WebHttpBinding` *for REST Services*

Gnip allows you to push or pull after you have a valid filter to work with. To activate push features, you need to provide an endpoint URL for the service to notify you when new data matching your publisher and filter configuration is available. Although you could open a web service in a number of ways in .NET, using WCF or simple web services, this is a good opportunity to learn how to build your own REST API rather than viewing the REST model exclusively as services for consumption. WCF in .NET 3.5 provides a powerful, declarative approach to create any form of REST endpoint, such as the necessary receiver for push data via HTTP POST. You can create a new *Web Application* project in Visual Studio to set up a new REST-enabled set of services. The first step to creating REST service methods is to define a

WCF ServiceContract, with OperationContracts for each method you intend to expose. Although these methods will eventually form a REST address, for now you can think of them just in terms of pure action methods: PollForData, SetupPushService, and ReceivedData, respectively. The following code demonstrates a plain WCF service contract prior to enabling REST support:

```
using System.ServiceModel;

namespace Wrox.Twitter.GnipReceiver
{
    [ServiceContract]
    public interface IRestApi
    {
        [OperationContract]
        string PollForData();

        [OperationContract]
        void SetUpPushEndpoint();

        [OperationContract]
        void ReceiveData(string data);
    }
}
```

To introduce REST in this contract, the WebGet and WebInvoke attributes are provided for further declaration; WebGet is exclusively used to map your standard service to HTTP GET requests, while WebInvoke supports the remaining POST, PUT, and DELETE method verbs. The next code listing shows the same WCF contract, this time with REST support defined:

```
using System.ServiceModel;
using System.ServiceModel.Web;

namespace Wrox.Twitter.GnipReceiver
{
    [ServiceContract]
    public interface IRestApi
    {
        [OperationContract]
        [WebGet(
            BodyStyle = WebMessageBodyStyle.Bare,
            RequestFormat = WebMessageFormat.Xml,
            ResponseFormat = WebMessageFormat.Xml,
            UriTemplate = "api/examples/get")]
        string PollForData();

        [OperationContract]
        [WebGet(
            BodyStyle = WebMessageBodyStyle.Bare,
            RequestFormat = WebMessageFormat.Xml,
            ResponseFormat = WebMessageFormat.Xml,
            UriTemplate = "api/examples/setup")]
        void SetUpPushEndpoint();

        [OperationContract]
        [WebInvoke(
            Method="POST",
```

```
        BodyStyle = WebMessageBodyStyle.Bare,
        RequestFormat = WebMessageFormat.Xml,
        ResponseFormat = WebMessageFormat.Xml,
        UriTemplate = "api/examples/push")]
    void ReceiveData(string data);
}
}
```

You'll notice a few things about the use of WebGet and WebInvoke, specifically the definition of body styles, request and response formats, and a declared instance of the UriTemplate class. The WebMessageBodyStyle enumeration lets you specify if any messages passed to or from the service call are wrapped in a message envelope, or transmitted as is; normally, because REST services are clean and work with recognized micro-formats, you'll set this value to Bare to avoid any extra overhead for consumers of your service. WebMessageFormat has values for both XML and JSON, which allows you to abstract much of the complexity of converting entities to XML or JSON. In fact, all you need to do is declare the desired types when passing in a custom object that declares DataContract and DataMethod properties to work with those types with your REST service at runtime. For this example, you only need to consider XML, as this is what Gnip supports. The UriTemplate is the most interesting of the web programming model attributes; using it, you can shape your REST endpoints. In the last example, the UriTemplates mapped standard service methods to api/examples/get, api/examples/setup, and api/examples/push, respectively. UriTemplates can also take parameters, mapping the names of the parameters in your method signature to the same names in the template delimited by set brackets. Although out of scope for this discussion, this is how you would map a service call taking several parameters to a clean RESTful HTTP GET service.

```
using System.ServiceModel;
using System.ServiceModel.Web;

namespace Wrox.Twitter.GnipReceiver
{
    [ServiceContract]
    public interface IRestApi
    {
        // This method would create clean URLs using only one operation, i.e.
        // /televisions/widescreen/12 or /travel/cruises/15
        [OperationContract]
        [WebInvoke(
            Method="GET",
            BodyStyle = WebMessageBodyStyle.Bare,
            RequestFormat = WebMessageFormat.Json,
            ResponseFormat = WebMessageFormat.Json,
            UriTemplate = "{category}/{product}/{id}")]
        void HackableUrl(string category, string product, int id);
    }
}
```

With a contract defined, WCF requires configuration to enable the web programming model and discover your new REST methods. The WCF configuration is mostly identical to any service, with a few key distinctions. First, ASP.NET compatibility mode is enabled to ensure WCF knows that requests should participate in the ASP.NET pipeline, i.e., any modules, handlers, and processing applies to the rest of your web application should apply to any services as well. Next, WebHttpBinding is used in place of other options such as BasicHttpBinding or a CustomBinding. And finally, new web behavior is defined with the `webHttp` attribute to declare that the web programming model is used to invoke services. These three configuration highlights are illustrated in the following code:

```
<system.serviceModel>
    <!-- Let WCF know that these services should travel through the ASP.NET pipeline -->
    <serviceHostingEnvironment aspNetCompatibilityEnabled="true" />
    <services>
        <service
            behaviorConfiguration="Wrox.Twitter.GnipReceiver.RestApiBehavior"
            name="GnipReceiver.RestApi">
            <endpoint address=""
        behaviorConfiguration="WebBehavior"
        binding="webHttpBinding"
        contract="Wrox.Twitter.GnipReceiver.IRestApi">
                <identity>
                    <dns value="localhost"/>
                </identity>
            </endpoint>
    <endpoint
        address="mex"
        binding="mexHttpBinding"
        contract="IMetadataExchange"/>
        </service>
    </services>
    <behaviors>
        <serviceBehaviors>
            <behavior name="Wrox.Twitter.GnipReceiver.RestApiBehavior">
                <serviceMetadata httpGetEnabled="true"/>
                <serviceDebug includeExceptionDetailInFaults="false"/>
            </behavior>
        </serviceBehaviors>
        <endpointBehaviors>
            <behavior name="WebBehavior">
                <!-- Enable the web programming model (REST) -->
                <webHttp/>
            </behavior>
        </endpointBehaviors>
    </behaviors>
</system.serviceModel>
```

With the configuration in place, you can implement the services themselves. The next code example combines the Gnip library methods with the service contract to create REST services for polling new data from Gnip, setting up a push endpoint, and finally, receiving data in the same format as they arrive through a poll, but through an HTTP POST-enabled endpoint.

```
using System;
using System.ServiceModel;
using System.ServiceModel.Activation;
using System.Text;
using Gnip.Client;
using Gnip.Client.Resource;
```

```
namespace Wrox.Twitter.GnipReceiver
{
    // You need to invoke the ASP.NET pipeline for this service
    [AspNetCompatibilityRequirements(
        RequirementsMode = AspNetCompatibilityRequirementsMode.Allowed)]

    // Assist serfvice performance by keeping a singleton and
    // allowing concurrent connections to it
    [ServiceBehavior(
        InstanceContextMode = InstanceContextMode.Single,
        ConcurrencyMode = ConcurrencyMode.Multiple)]
    public class RestApi : IRestApi
    {
        private const string GnipUsername = "daniel.crenna@gmail.com";
        private const string GnipPassword = "UGLY143d";

        private Config _config;
        private Publisher _twitter;

        #region IRestApi Members

        public string PollForData()
        {
            // Create a new configuration with your Gnip credentials
            var _config = new Config(GnipUsername, GnipPassword);

            // Make a new connection to Gnip using the convenience library
            var connection = new GnipConnection(_config);

            // Get Twitter as a publisher
            _twitter = connection.GetPublisher(PublisherType.Gnip, "twitter");

            // Look for an existing filter on your account
            var filter = connection.GetFilter(_twitter, "tweetsharp");
            if (filter == null)
            {
                // Create the filter to receive Tweets
                CreateNewFilter(connection, "tweetsharp", null);
            }

            // Poll for notifications matching the filter you created
            var notifications = connection.GetActivities(_twitter, filter);

            // Do something with your new activity data
            var sb = new StringBuilder();
            foreach (Activity activity in notifications.Items)
            {
                sb.AppendLine(activity.Url);
            }

            return sb.ToString();
        }

        public void SetUpPushEndpoint()
```

```
        {
            // Make a new connection to Gnip using the convenience library
            var connection = new GnipConnection(_config);

            // Look for an existing push filter on your account
            Filter filter = connection.GetFilter(_twitter, "push");
            if (filter == null)
            {
                // This would map to your own, publically available site
                const string endpoint = "http://yoursite.com/api/examples/push";

                // Create a filter that pushes updates to your URL
                CreateNewFilter(connection, "push", endpoint);
            }
        }

        public void ReceiveData(string data)
        {
            // This is where you would handle incoming data from Gnip,
            // deserialize it for your application, etc.
            Console.WriteLine(data);
        }

        #endregion

        private void CreateNewFilter(GnipConnection connection,
                                     string filterName,
                                     string url)
        {
            // Create a filter with partial data
            // (full Gnip data is not allowed for Twitter)
            var filter = new Filter(filterName) { IsFullData = false };

            // Create a rule to govern the data returned by the filter;
            // in this case you are asking for notifications for specific users
            filter.Rules.Add(new Rule(RuleType.Actor, "tweetsharp"));
            filter.Rules.Add(new Rule(RuleType.Actor, "dimebrain"));
            filter.Rules.Add(new Rule(RuleType.Actor, "jdiller"));
            filter.Rules.Add(new Rule(RuleType.Actor, "jakcharlton"));

            // Set up an endpoint for this filter
            if (!String.IsNullOrEmpty(url))
            {
                filter.PostUrl = url;
            }

            // Set up the new filter for Twitter on your Gnip account
            connection.Create(_twitter, filter);
        }
    }
}
```

When you call one of the methods you've mapped to a URL endpoint, you'll notice that the complete endpoint includes the full service name, in this case `RestApi.svc`. In other words, to call the `PollForData` method on your REST service you'd need to point NUrl to `http://yourdomain.com/RestApi.svc/api/examples/get`. This is a step removed from the clean URLs you can find elsewhere on the web, and it is possible to remove the service reference from your REST address with a little URL rewriting. In the following code example, an `IHttpModule` is constructed to look for the API method call, and if it is written in the desired format, it is mapped to the full service method URL. With this module installed in your `web.config`, you can write clean REST calls, and the previous URL example would appear as `http://yourdomain.com/api/examples/get` but map to the `RestApi` service.

```csharp
using System.Web;

namespace Wrox.Twitter.GnipReceiver
{
    public class RewriteModule : IHttpModule
    {
        private const string Identity = "api/";

        #region IHttpModule Members

        public void Dispose() {}

        public void Init(HttpApplication app)
        {
            // Inspect every new request for the full service path
            app.BeginRequest += ((sender, args) =>
            {
                var context = app.Context;

                var path =
                    app.Request.
                        AppRelativeCurrentExecutionFilePath
                        .ToLower();

                // The path is not an API call or is
pointing to the
                // true service address already
                if (!path.Contains(Identity) ||
                    path.Contains("RestApi.svc"))
                {
                    return;
                }

                // Send the friendly API URL to the true
service URL
                context.RewritePath("~/RestApi.svc",
                                    path,
                                    app.Request.Url.Query,
                                    false);
            });
        }

        #endregion
    }
}
```

You now have a means to participate in real push updates through the help of the Gnip service and its library, and you might even have new ideas about how to blend Twitter data with other established or emerging publishers to enhance your application's features and appeal. The next possibility for push scenarios is through receiving updates directly from Twitter; thanks to a recent decision, Twitter's own streaming capabilities are slowly making their way into the API!

Using the Twitter Streaming API

Some form of a true push service of Twitter updates has existed for a select number of consumers for a long time. Twitter has recently engaged with the developer community to alpha test a limited, publically available form of the service through a new *Streaming API*. Similar to the existing APIs, streaming is implemented as a REST service supporting XML or JSON formats and the HTTP GET method. The key difference is that the HTTP connection established during the call is kept alive, while a continuous stream of status updates is fed through it, one line at a time. Using the API, you could forego both polling in the background of WCF push service, and consuming a third-party aggregated push service such as Gnip, in favor of direct consumption from Twitter. You can find out more details and keep tabs on updates to this early service by visiting http://apiwiki.twitter.com/Streaming-API-Documentation.

Public Stream Methods

The status stream methods provide streaming for public timeline statuses, acting as a *firehose* for the entire raw Twitter message service itself.

Relative Method URLs:

```
http://stream.twitter.com/firehose.{format}
http://stream.twitter.com/gardenhose.{format}
http://stream.twitter.com/spritzer.{format}
```

HTTP Methods: GET
REST Formats: XML, JSON
Optional Parameters: delimited (all), count (firehose only)
Data Representation: A continuous stream of Twitter status objects.

Example

```
GET: http://twitter.com/statuses/spritzer.json
```

Special Considerations: Both *firehose* and *gardenhose* options are special, private service levels you must arrange with Twitter; all three methods provide tiered levels of quality in terms of the fidelity and frequency of status updates. The delimited query parameter allows you to specify the length of delimitation between each status, to aid in parsing results. By default, each status is output to the stream followed by a new line; if a stream is interrupted or waiting for updates, additional new lines will reach the stream as a form of keep-alive service. The count property applies to the firehose option and allows you to stream a backlog of updates prior to reconnecting with the live stream, which is helpful in case of service interruption. Specifying a negative value up to150,000 instructs the stream to only fetch backlogged statuses, closing the stream when finished. By specifying a positive value up to 150,000 through the specified backlog it will then transition to the live stream when finished.

User Stream Methods

In addition to the unfiltered stream of all incoming Twitter statuses, you can keep tabs on specific users, pushing those users' updates in real time while ignoring the majority of Twitter activity.

Relative Method URLs:

```
http://stream.twitter.com/birddog.{format}
http://stream.twitter.com/shadow.{format}
http://stream.twitter.com/follow.{format}
```

HTTP Methods: GET
REST Formats: XML, JSON
Optional Parameters: `count` (birddog and shadow only), `follow` (all)
Data Representation: A continuous stream of Twitter status objects.

Example

```
GET: http://stream.twitter.com/follow.json
```

Special Considerations: The private *birddog* and *shadow* options provide support for following 200,000 and 2,000 users per stream, respectively, while the public *follow* options tracks up to 200 users simultaneously. The count function works as previously described, helping to mitigate connectivity drops by working on past statuses relative to the current live stream.

Running a Twitter Stream

The following example demonstrates a functional Streaming API example, including deserialization of streamed data into Twitter data classes using the `JavaScriptSerializer` support you wrote in Chapter 3 Working with JSON Responses section. The example first creates a new `HttpWebRequest` designed to stay alive indefinitely, with some timeouts in place to help ensure the quality of the connection; the header is set directly to avoid a handshake as discussed in Chapter 1 Communicating with the Web and .NET. Thanks to .NET's well-architected HTTP communications, it is easy to open and maintain a stream of constant data pushed from Twitter.

```csharp
using System;
using System.Collections.Generic;
using System.IO;
using System.Net;
using System.Text;
using System.Web.Script.Serialization;
using Wrox.Twitter.JsonWithJavaScriptSerializer.Converters;
using Wrox.Twitter.JsonWithJavaScriptSerializer.Objects;

Stream stream = null;
try
{
    // ready the deserializer, as per Chapter 3
    var serializer = new JavaScriptSerializer();
    serializer.RegisterConverters(new List<JavaScriptConverter>
```

```
                            {
                                new TwitterConverter()
                            });

            const string url = "http://stream.twitter.com/spritzer.json";
            const string username = "username";
            const string password = "password";

            var pair = String.Concat(username, ":", password);
            var auth = Convert.ToBase64String(Encoding.UTF8.GetBytes(pair));

            var request = (HttpWebRequest) WebRequest.Create(url);
            request.Headers["Authorization"] = "Basic " + auth;
            request.KeepAlive = true;
            request.ReadWriteTimeout = 5000;
            request.Timeout = 5000;

            var response = request.GetResponse();
            using (stream = response.GetResponseStream())
            {
                using (var reader = new StreamReader(stream))
                {
                    string json;

                    // JSON statuses are output one line at a time
                    while ((json = reader.ReadLine()).Length > 0)
                    {
                        if (json.Equals(Environment.NewLine))
                        {
                            // A keep-alive was sent
                            Console.WriteLine("...");
                            continue;
                        }

                        // convert from JSON to a typed statuss
                        var status =
                            serializer.Deserialize<TwitterStatus>(json);
                        var message = String.Concat(status.User.ScreenName,
                                                    ":",
                                                    status.Text);

                        Console.WriteLine(message);
                    }

                    Console.WriteLine("Stream dried up.");
                }
            }
        }
        catch (Exception ex)
        {
            // It's better practice to handle expected exceptions explicitly
            Console.WriteLine(ex.Message);
        }
        finally
```

```
{
    // Make sure you're not holding on to a stream
    if (stream != null)
    {
        stream.Close();
    }

    Console.WriteLine("Press any key to end example");
    Console.ReadKey();
}
```

Because you know that JSON status response objects are output to the stream, the example uses the `StreamReader`'s `ReadLine` method to read an entire status at a time. If it encounters a new line character without any status, such as when the stream is acting in keep-alive mode, then no data is lost as the new line requires a few bytes to transmit. The `JavaScriptSerializer` goes to work after reading an entire line of JSON if the line wasn't simply a new line character, to deserialize that line into a true Twitter status object. Twitter recommends that this processing of raw string XML or JSON output occur in a dedicated process and separate from the stream (presumably because the time it takes to convert the data will result in dropped updates to avoid holding the up stream operation). For demonstration purposes, simple applications can occur in line with stream updates. Keep in mind that although the example is handling all faults by catching an `Exception` to remain sensitive to instability and properly dispose of any open streams in either case of success or failure (from an empty stream), this is not a good practice in production quality code.

If you run the resulting application, you will see a steady stream of Twitter statuses on the Console; this is a truly live broadcast of the Twitter service and opens many new possibilities for push-based architectures in your Twitter development endeavors.

Summary

In this chapter you tackled the concept of data push, the advantages and disadvantages of its use, and explored several approaches to building applications where your users receive data from the server proactively rather than making continuous requests. The following strategies were discussed in particular:

❑ You used the WCF Polling Duplex feature to define a push-based service, receiving messages in a Silverlight application that originated from an ASP.NET web application; behind the scenes, you polled Twitter for updates before pushing them to registered clients.

❑ You consumed Twitter push data from the Gnip service, a provider of push or pull data from multiple social web applications.

❑ You caught a glimpse of the new Twitter Streaming API, which provides true push-style status updates directly from Twitter, and used it to demonstrate the power of native push capability.

You've covered what you need to know about REST, Twitter's API, designing applications that work well with external services, and the architectural styles of push and pull employed by applications that consume micro-blogging services. Now that you have a solid foundation to rely on, the next chapter will introduce a new tool to your repertoire, TweetSharp, to handle the lower-level details of Twitter API communication. You can then focus just on the details about your particular, original idea that matters to you most.

## 9

Introduction to TweetSharp

"Tweetsharp makes it simple for a developer to get a program talking to the Twitter servers literally within a few minutes of clicking File-New Project by taking care of all of the low-level details and leveraging IntelliSense to guide the developer's hand."

Jason Diller, TweetSharp

Up until now you've used a handy utility class, NUrl, to make HTTP requests against the Twitter API. This is a functional approach and will help you build many simple applications, but as you layer those applications with growing complexity, and as the Twitter API continues to evolve, it is difficult to track every change and every nuance with utility code. Also, you will confront many common scenarios and feature requests across all your projects: shortening URLs, posting photos, and remaining mindful of API rate are common requests you'll see again and again. TweetSharp, an open source .NET library, allows you to compose queries for Twitter against the complete API, as well as handle authentication, caching, URL shortening, photo posting, and asynchronous operation all out of the box. When you start your next Twitter project, you only have to think about your idea; working with the Twitter API itself is handled for you, you just ask for what you want. In this chapter you learn how easy it is to get an application up and running with TweetSharp.

Hello, TweetSharp!

TweetSharp is licensed under the MIT license (http://www.opensource.org/licenses/mit-license.php), which means you are free to reference it and use it in your own Twitter applications without royalty. TweetSharp is designed in the spirit of a *fluent interface*, which means you create queries to send to Twitter on your behalf by expressing them in a chain of methods, each method building on the last. This style of programming is popular among many open source .NET projects, and helps ensure you are able to discover what you need to work with the library directly in Visual Studio.

What Is a Fluent Interface?

A common example of a fluent interface already in .NET is the `StringBuilder` class. Using `StringBuilder`, you can continuously call methods that return the same object, allowing you to chain methods together naturally, forming a kind of programmatic sentence that in English might sound similar to *do this, and then this, and then this*. While there are more characteristics than method chaining required in a textbook definition of a fluent interface, for the purposes of writing composable code, it is enough. Here is an example of using `StringBuilder` as a fluent interface:

```
var sb = new StringBuilder();

// Each method builds on the last in a chain
sb.Append("write this")
  .Append(" and then this ")
  .Insert(0, "First you should ")
  .AppendFormat("and do it on a {0}.",
                DateTime.Now.DayOfWeek);

Console.WriteLine(sb);
First you should write this and then this and do it on a Monday.
```

TweetSharp follows the same fluent interface pattern, and queries are evaluated and turned into web requests based on the chain of methods you provide. All TweetSharp queries begin with a call to `CreateRequest` on the `FluentTwitter` class. You can find this class in the main `Dimebrain.TweetSharp.Fluent` namespace, though you will discover two other namespaces in this chapter that provide their own features. The following TweetSharp query shows its nature as a fluent interface and provides the namespace declaration needed to start working with it. Remember that you need to reference the TweetSharp library in your Visual Studio Project. In addition, TweetSharp uses James Newton-King's JSON.NET open source project (hosted at `http://www.codeplex.com/json`), and provides this assembly as a dependency, though you do not need to reference or work with JSON.NET directly.

```
using Dimebrain.TweetSharp.Fluent;

// This is equivalent to
// http://twitter.com/statuses/public_timeline.xml
var query = FluentTwitter.CreateRequest()
    .Statuses().OnPublicTimeline();

var response = query.Request();
Console.WriteLine(response);
```

Core Feature Overview

In the previous example, you can spot that the methods used to send a public timeline request are very close to the actual Twitter API method address you would normally call with NUrl. TweetSharp's basic feature set is closely mapped to the API itself, and is *discoverable*. This means that as you express your intentions for the query, options will appear or disappear in Visual Studio's *Intellisense* support, depending on the query you're writing, removing the burden of trying to remember Twitter's API or consulting it online to make use of TweetSharp directly. In general, you have access to all Twitter API entities: `Accounts`, `Blocks`, `DirectMessages`, `Favorites`, `Friendship`, `Help`, `SocialGraph`, `Statuses`, and `Users` are all methods available on a new `FluentTwitter` query, and map directly to the equivalent API methods. You'll get an idea of how each of the main TweetSharp features works in this section with plenty of examples throughout this chapter.

.NET Framework Support

TweetSharp is written in .NET 3.5 SP1, but you may reference it in a .NET 2.0 project provided the .NET 3.5 assemblies are installed on the end user's machine. There are separate assemblies that target .NET Compact 3.5 and Silverlight 3.0 so that you may use it consistently across your Windows, web, and mobile applications.

Custom Client Configuration

Twitter applications are unique, and TweetSharp provides a way to identify them to Twitter using the `TwitterClientInfo` class. Although not officially used in any capacity, the development team at Twitter has identified some custom HTTP headers that may serve a future purpose — they identify your specific application. Table 9-1 outlines these custom headers and their respective properties on `TwitterClientInfo`. At this time, you cannot retrieve these values from requests directly from the Twitter API.

Table 9-1: Optional Twitter Request Headers

Header Name	TwitterClientInfo Property Name	Description
X-Twitter-Client	ClientName	Identifies the name of your unique application. When using search, this value is also set in the HTTP user agent header to identify the source of a search query.
X-Twitter-URL	ClientUrl	Provides a link to a page where users can go to find out more, or acquire your application.
X-Twitter-Version	ClientVersion	Displays your own application's build version, possibly useful for providing support.

Another feature of `TwitterClientInfo` is the ability to store the consumer key and consumer secret values that you retrieve when signing up a new OAuth account for your application. These consumer values are used to authenticate every call, and providing them in the `TwitterClientInfo` class means you can avoid having to declare them in each and every TweetSharp query you write. For Silverlight users, `TwitterClientInfo` also provides the `TransparentProxy` property; this property stores the client-side proxy that TweetSharp uses to make cross-domain calls, taking care of the details of working with Silverlight's browser security model and returning the correct results. In Chapter 10, example code is demonstrated to build a TweetSharp compatible client proxy for client-side queries. The following code shows a complete definition of a client using `TwitterClientInfo`:

```
var clientInfo = new TwitterClientInfo
{
    ClientName = "motto",
    ClientUrl = "http://getmotto.com",
    ClientVersion = "v1.0",
    ConsumerKey = "EQrjo7nYzrBoaVCeTsrOA",
    ConsumerSecret = "lvOqGKS20KdrPpZJfk92gGE3RF6u71VKI2TvvBoZc"
};
```

After the client information is set, there are a few ways this information is passed on to TweetSharp. First, the `CreateRequest` method provides an overload that takes a `TwitterClientInfo` instance. If you expect to develop on only one application identity, you can set client info globally with a static method. Both approaches are shown here:

```
// #1: Set the client info in the query creation method
var query = FluentTwitter.CreateRequest(clientInfo)
    .Statuses().OnPublicTimeline().AsJson();

// #2: Set the client info globally
FluentTwitter.SetClientInfo(clientInfo);

// All queries will use the clientInfo instance
var query = FluentTwitter.CreateRequest()
    .Statuses().OnPublicTimeline().AsJson();
```

If you do specify a consumer key and secret, they are used automatically when working with OAuth and the `AuthenticateWith` method which is covered later, otherwise you will need to provide them with every query. If your Twitter development is normally performed one application at a time, setting this information up-front and using the static setter method will ensure this set-up only needs to occur once — likely during the application's start-up cycle, to function correctly.

Identifying an Application by Source

There is some confusion surrounding how an application gets a qualified source link when appearing on Twitter's site or in the source element of an API call. The source link appears on the bottom of a status message and provides the name and link back to the URL of your application. In the past, Twitter provided a sign-up process that would grant you your own source value if your application met certain public criteria; you would then pass this on to the API method URL, or in to HTTP POST parameters, to identify the application when creating status updates or direct messages. Now, however, source identity is provided when you sign up for an OAuth account, demonstrated in Chapter 6; it is automatically tied to the consumer key and secret used to authorize the user's credentials. So, although `TwitterClientInfo` provides optional headers and allows you to store the consumer key and secret across multiple calls, these values do not map to Twitter's source definition and won't automatically appear on the site or in the API element data.

Representational Formats

Because Twitter's API supports XML, JSON, RSS, and Atom depending on the context, TweetSharp similarly provides methods meant for the end of your query expression that set the format: `AsXml`, `AsJson`, `AsRss`, and `AsAtom` respectively. If the Twitter API method you are intending to call does not support all these formats, only the formats that it will support are visible on your query and in Intellisense, simplifying the discovery of API features. If you just want to see what the API method call would look like before executing the request, you can call `AsUrl` at any time to obtain this information.

Query Format

To provide discoverability with Intellisense, TweetSharp requires you to structure your queries in a specific way. For example, after you call a format method such as `AsJson`, you cannot continue to compose your query, because supported formats are based on the query you wrote before calling the format method itself. After initialization, TweetSharp queries begin with a configuration phase, continue with a feature phase, and then conclude with the desired format. If no format is provided, the default XML format is used, or JSON is used where XML is not supported. The following code illustrates the three phases of a query:

```
// Initialization
var query = FluentTwitter.CreateRequest()
    // Configuration
    .Configuration.UseUrlShortening()
    .Configuration.UseGzipCompression()
    .AuthenticateAs("username", "password")
    // Feature
    .Statuses().Update("Check out #tweetsharp - http://tweetsharp.googlecode.com")
    // Format
    .AsJson();
```

When the query is defined, it is fully serializable, so it is possible to save it to disk for later use, and may be used to repeat requests where the defined behavior is expected.

Pagination

Where pagination is supported by the Twitter API, TweetSharp uses a consistent set of extension methods to use it. These methods are `Skip` and `Take`; each method takes an integer value representing the page to skip to, or the number of results to take, respectively. If you can't find `Skip` or `Take` in Intellisense while building your query, it means that the Twitter API does not support one or both of these methods for the query you have composed to that point.

Time Windows

Where Twitter uses the `since_id` and `max_id` elements to determine constraints on the recency of statuses returned in API calls, TweetSharp uses the `Since` and `Before` extension methods, both taking a number indicating the ID in question for the relevant query.

Authentication

TweetSharp supports Basic or OAuth authentication. To use Basic authentication, a form of direct impersonation, the `AuthenticateAs` method allows you to pass the query a username and password. If you are using OAuth and have an authenticated token and token secret, you can use these values and the `AuthenticateWith` method to proceed. The following example shows both authentication styles in a query requiring authorization:

```
// #1: Impersonate a user with their credentials (Basic Authentication)
var query = FluentTwitter.CreateRequest()
    .AuthenticateAs("username", "password")
    .Statuses().Update("Hello, Tweetsharp!")
    .AsJson();

// #2: Use an authenticated token to act on behalf of a user (OAuth)
var query = FluentTwitter.CreateRequest()
    .AuthenticateWith("consumerKey", "consumerSecret",
                      "token", "tokenSecret")
    .Statuses().Update("Hello, Tweetsharp!")
    .AsJson();
```

Operation Modes

It is possible to execute TweetSharp sequentially or asynchronously when targeting the .NET Framework on the desktop or .NET Compact Framework on mobile devices, while Silverlight offers support for asynchronous operation only, in line with how service execution is performed in that environment. With a query fully defined, you can call the `Request` method to send a sequential request that returns a string containing Twitter's response, or `RequestAsync` to send an asynchronous call that invokes a callback you provide when a response returns. The following example shows both styles of operation in action:

```
private static void OperationModes()
{
    // Create a query for reuse
    var query = FluentTwitter.CreateRequest()
        .Statuses().OnPublicTimeline();

    // #1: Retrieves the XML response from Twitter as a string
    var response = query.Request();
    Console.WriteLine(response);

    // #2: Sends the call asynchronously, and invokes the
    //     provided callback when Twitter returns a response
    query.CallbackTo(ProcessResponse);
    query.RequestAsync();
}

private static void ProcessResponse(object sender, WebQueryResponseEventArgs e)
{
    var response = e.Response;
    Console.WriteLine(response);
}
```

The signature of the `WebCallback` class that drives asynchronous operation is based on the event model already present in Window's Forms, ensuring a familiar environment. The `WebQueryResponseEventArgs` class contains a single property, `Response`, containing the same string result obtained when calling Twitter sequentially. You may also use an anonymous method to inline the desired action to take during a callback.

Data Class Conversion

One of the most useful features of TweetSharp is the ability to easily convert a response from Twitter into serializable, bindable data classes with a single method call, whether your response format is XML or JSON (but not RSS or Atom due to the sparse amount of data returned with those formats), and this feature exists in the `Dimebrain.Fluent.Model` namespace. To use data class conversion features, import the namespace as well as the `Dimebrain.Fluent.Extensions` namespace that provides the conversion extension methods. Now, after you have a string result from Twitter after executing a TweetSharp query, you can use one of the following extension methods to cast your result into the expected type or collection type, depending on the query you created: `AsStatus`, `AsStatuses`, `AsUser`, `AsUsers`, `AsDirectMessage`, and `AsDirectMessages`, respectively. If your query has the result that matches with the extension method you called, you will receive the appropriate class or collection, or `null`, to indicate there was a mismatch or perhaps an error returned from Twitter rather than a true result. The following example shows the use of data conversion to work with objects after a TweetSharp query executes:

```
// Get direct messages received since a given ID
var query = FluentTwitter.CreateRequest()
    .AuthenticateAs("username", "password")
    .DirectMessages().Sent().Since(123456789)
    .AsXml();

// Make the request to retrieve data
var response = query.Request();

// Cast the string response into classes
var messages = response.AsDirectMessages();

foreach(TwitterDirectMessage message in messages)
{
    // Work directly with objects, not data
    Console.WriteLine(message.RecipientScreenName);
    Console.WriteLine(message.Text);
}
```

Hello, Twitter!

Now that you know how TweetSharp is structured and how to obtain data using it after a query is defined, you can start working with it as a communications layer between your application and the Twitter API.

Fetching Timelines

The public, friend, and user timelines all return status elements scoped to their particular focus. The public timeline does not support paging, but the other timeline methods do. The following example shows valid queries for each timeline following their equivalent API call:

```
// http://twitter.com/statuses/public_timeline.json
var publicTimeline = FluentTwitter.CreateRequest()
    .Statuses().OnPublicTimeline()
    .AsJson();

// http://twitter.com/statuses/user_timeline.xml?screen_name=Dimebrain&count=50
var userTimeline = FluentTwitter.CreateRequest()
    .Statuses().OnUserTimeline().For("Dimebrain").Take(50)
    .AsXml();

// http://twitter.com/statuses/friends_timeline.json
var friendsTimeline = FluentTwitter.CreateRequest()
    .AuthenticateAs("username", "password")
    .Statuses().OnFriendsTimeline().Skip(2).Take(5)
    .AsJson();
```

It's worth noting that TweetSharp queries are not immune to the authentication requirements of Twitter's API. Because the second query defines a user whose timeline you're interested in, it does not require authentication as user timelines are public, though the last query does require authentication because it is tied directly to an authenticating user's identity (to retrieve only the status updates of friends).

Responses received when calling these methods may be deserialized into objects using the AsStatuses extension method. In Figure 9-1, TweetSharp's data model for statuses and users is illustrated, which shows that the underlying model is more sophisticated than the model classes you developed while working through Chapters 3 and 5.

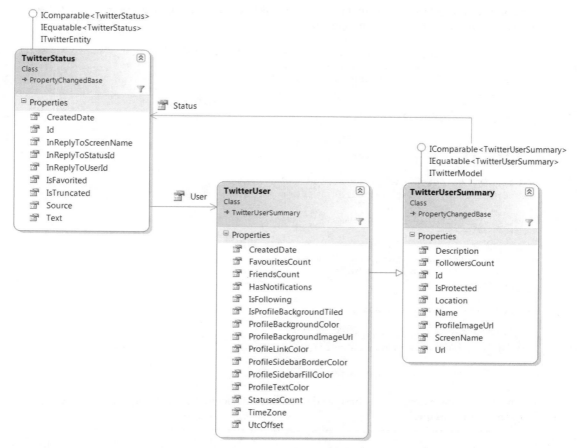

Figure 9-1

In particular, TweetSharp data classes implement IPropertyNotifyChanged to support data binding in WPF and Silverlight projects, and also implement the typed versions of IComparable and IEquatable, making it easy to avoid duplicates in visual collections or perform custom sorting. Because the collection-based extension methods such as AsStatuses and AsUsers return typed IEnumerable results, you are able to make use of the power of LINQ to further refine or manipulate results after they are received.

Obtaining User Profiles

A user's full account profile is returned with every status entity, and also through its own dedicated API call. To access user data in TweetSharp, you can use the User property of a TwitterStatus instance, or make a separate query to obtain a user's profile. Both methods are viable, as you may want to save on bandwidth and API calls by inspecting incoming statuses for user data rather than making separate requests. The next code example shows both approaches; the first approach retrieves a specific user's timeline and uses LINQ to select the first result from which to access the `User` property, while the second approach is a direct, unrated call for the same user.

```
// #1: The user object is brought along with any statuses
var query = FluentTwitter.CreateRequest()
    .Statuses().OnUserTimeline().For("wrox")
    .AsXml();

var response = query.Request();

// Use the AsStatuses conversion method
var statuses = response.AsStatuses();

// Use LINQ to fetch the first status and its user
TwitterUser user = statuses.First().User;

Console.WriteLine(user.ScreenName);

// #2: Retrieve a user object directly
var query = FluentTwitter.CreateRequest()
    .Users().ShowProfileFor("wrox")
    .AsJson();

var response = query.Request();

// Use the AsUser conversion method
TwitterUser user = response.AsUser();

Console.WriteLine(user.ScreenName);
```

You will notice that the extension method used to cast into object instances differs based on the expected results returned in each query.

Do You Need More Examples or Support?

TweetSharp has a growing community of developers who are using the library frequently to build their own Twitter applications. There are a number of resources you can turn to, to supplement these examples and get your support questions heard:

TweetSharp's Google Code Page and Wiki

(http://tweetsharp.googlecode.com)

TweetSharp's Google Group

(http://groups.google.com/group/tweetsharp)

TweetSharp's Web Site and Twitter Account

(http://tweetsharp.com and @tweetsharp)

Code Examples on Snipt

(http://snipt.org/box/tweetsharp)

In addition, plenty of people have posted blog articles with TweetSharp examples, which are just a search engine away.

Posting Statuses

TweetSharp handles the task of URL-escaping any messages you intend to post to Twitter, so you only need to provide the desired text in the query, illustrated in the next example:

```
var query = FluentTwitter.CreateRequest()
    .AuthenticateAs("username", "password")
    .Statuses().Update("Having fun with #tweetsharp")
    .AsJson();
```

In addition, Twitter provides a way to thread conversations; when replying to a specific status, the ID of that status is passed to the URL, and in TweetSharp you use the InReplyToStatus method to reference a status by ID or by instance, if you've already deserialized results into a status object. To use this method correctly with the Twitter API, you must mention the original status author's name somewhere in your message, otherwise your call to InReplyToStatus is ignored.

```
var query = FluentTwitter.CreateRequest()
    .AuthenticateAs("username", "password")
    .Statuses().Update("Thanks @for your message, I'll get back to you.")
    .InReplyToStatus(123456789)
    .AsXml();
```

Working with Direct Messages

The DirectMessages extension method in TweetSharp provides access to obtaining sent and received direct messages as well as issuing new ones to target users. You must use a form of authentication for each of these messages. The following code example shows the query structure for direct message manipulation in the default XML format:

```
using Dimebrain.TweetSharp.Fluent;

// Sending a new direct message
var query = FluentTwitter.CreateRequest()
    .AuthenticateAs("username", "password")
    .DirectMessages().Send("recipient", "What did you think?");

// Retrieving messages sent
var query = FluentTwitter.CreateRequest()
    .AuthenticateAs("username", "password")
    .DirectMessages().Sent();

// Retrieving messages received (100 results)
var query = FluentTwitter.CreateRequest()
    .AuthenticateAs("username", "password")
    .DirectMessages().Received().Take(100);

// Destroying an existing message
var query = FluentTwitter.CreateRequest()
    .AuthenticateAs("username", "password")
    .DirectMessages().Destroy(123456789);
```

Working with Friends and Followers

Twitter's friends and follower methods are strictly limited to 100 results per call, and TweetSharp must obey this restriction. In the next example, a query to retrieve the first page of 100 followers for the user `jdiller` is executed and deserialized into a collection of user objects and each follower's screen name is written to the screen.

```
using System;
using Dimebrain.TweetSharp.Extensions;
using Dimebrain.TweetSharp.Model;
using Dimebrain.TweetSharp.Fluent;

var query = FluentTwitter.CreateRequest()
    .AuthenticateAs("username", "password")
    .Users().GetFollowers().For("jdiller")
    .AsJson();

var response = query.Request();
var followers = response.AsUsers();

foreach(var follower in followers)
{
    Console.WriteLine(follower.ScreenName);
}
```

To retrieve every follower of a user with more than 100 followers requires paginations. Using TweetSharp's `Skip` extension method and some user profile information that tracks the number of followers a user has, you can write a simple looping routine that makes multiple calls to retrieve all users; the more followers or friends, the more API calls required to illustrate the entire user graph. This next example shows pagination at work to list all users an authenticated account follows. Remember that with very large lists of friends or followers, you could run out of API rate limit before completing this program.

```
using System;
using Dimebrain.TweetSharp.Extensions;
using Dimebrain.TweetSharp.Model;
using Dimebrain.TweetSharp.Fluent;

// Get the user's profile
var query = FluentTwitter.CreateRequest()
    .Users().ShowProfileFor("wrox")
    .AsXml();

var response = query.Request();
var user = response.AsUser();

// Calculate the number of pages using the
// user's number of friends
```

```
var count = user.FriendsCount;
var pages = Math.Ceiling(Convert.ToDouble(count)/100);


// 0 and 1 are the same page to Twitter,
// so start with 1 to avoid duplication
for(var i = 1; i <= pages; i++)
{
    query = FluentTwitter.CreateRequest()
        .AuthenticateAs("username", "password")
        .Users().GetFriends().For("wrox").Skip(i)
        .AsJson();

    response = query.Request();
    var friends = response.AsUsers();

    foreach (var friend in friends)
    {
        Console.WriteLine(friend.ScreenName);

    }
}
```

Working with Searches and Trends

Each Twitter Search API operator and parameter is treated as a first class method in TweetSharp, allowing you to compose your queries out of a series of smaller segments rather than as a long query string. This approach also helps properly URL-escape the outgoing request, and assists you when building advanced search forms within your own applications — as your user's selections are scriptable, serializable, and small changes can occur without tedious string comparison and matching. The next example illustrates a query using search operators and a parameter, obtaining the last five statuses that were written in the #tweetsharp channel and mentions the user @jdiller.

```
var query = FluentTwitter.CreateRequest()
    .Search().Query()
    .ContainingHashTag("#tweetsharp")
    .ReferencingUser("jdiller")
    .Take(5).AsJson();
```

In Table 9-2, a complete list of the search extension methods is illustrated, along with some extra definition. These methods map closely to the Search API itself, but you may want to see the complete picture. All extension methods are additive; when you use one, it is added to a chain of query text that is assembled when the request is made.

Table 9-2: TweetSharp Search Extension Methods

Method Name	Description
Containing	The basic query looks for text as it is written.
ContainingHashTag	Adds a clause that the results should also reference the specified hashtag channel.
ContainingLinks	Adds a clause that the results should also contain hyperlinks.
FromUser	Adds a clause that the results should originate from a specific user.
InLanguage	Filters search results to only those users whose identified profile language matches the provided two-character language ISO code.
NotContaining	Adds a clause that the results must not contain the text as written.
NotContainingHashTag	Adds a clause that the results should not come from a specified hashtag channel.
ReferencingUser	Adds a clause that the statuses should mention the given user.
Since	Adds a clause that the resulting statuses should occur after a given time or a given status ID; unlike the REST API, Search currently still supports a time-based Since operator.
SinceUntil	Adds a clause that the resulting statuses should occur only up to a specific time or status ID.
Skip and Take	Allows pagination with a search result; like the Search API, this cannot exceed a combined total of 1,500 results when a combination of Skip and Take is used; i.e. you cannot ask to skip to page 16 and take 100 results, as this is an implied total of 1,600 statuses.
ToUser	Adds a clause that the results should target a specified user.
Within / Of	This search result is used for location-based limiting. You must specify the number of miles to search within the Within method parameter, and follow that extension method call with the Of method, passing in the latitude and longitude of the location's center. If you want to use kilometers or yards rather than miles, you can call the Kilometers or Yards extension methods directly on the number value you pass into Within; i.e. Within(10.Kilometers()), otherwise the default of miles is used.
WithPositivity	Adds a clause that the results should contain positive author sentiment.
WithNeutrality	Adds a clause that the results should not contain any author sentiment.
WithNegativity	Adds a clause that the results should contain negative author sentiment (keep in mind that the presence of the :P emoticon is identified as negative sentiment by this operator).
WithQuestion	Adds a clause that the results should contain questions. In reality, this search operator is functionally equivalent to a plain search for the ? character.

Trending topics are retrieved with a simplified interface compared to the multitude of methods available for searches. Because Twitter's trending features allow you to find the most active search queries or hashtag channels by current, daily, and weekly trends, there are equivalent methods for each in TweetSharp. In the following code, trends are retrieved for the current, weekly, and daily time periods. The On or For extensions, which are equivalent, are used to define a starting date for daily or weekly trends, and ExcludeHashtags is an option available for filtering the trending topic list to avoid active hashtag channels and focus instead on raw searches.

```
using System;
using Dimebrain.TweetSharp.Extensions;
using Dimebrain.TweetSharp.Model;
using Dimebrain.TweetSharp.Fluent;

// Get the current trending topics
var query = FluentTwitter.CreateRequest()
    .Search().Trends().Current();

// Get daily trends from yesterday
var query = FluentTwitter.CreateRequest()
    .Search().Trends().Daily()
    .For(1.Day().Ago());

// Get weekly trends for three weeks ago,
// but don't factor hashtags into the result
var query = FluentTwitter.CreateRequest()
    .Search().Trends()
    .Weekly().For(3.Weeks().Ago())
    .ExcludeHashtags();

var response = query.Request();

// Convert results to trends data class
var weeklyTrends = response.AsTrends();

// Convert the last
var searchDate = weeklyTrends.SearchDate.FromUnixTime();
Console.WriteLine("Trends Searched On {0}", searchDate);

foreach(var trend in weeklyTrends.Trends)
{
    Console.WriteLine(trend.Name);
}
```

TweetSharp provides a custom data class for trending topics which you can leverage with the AsTrends extension method, which is called like other conversion methods on the string response received from Twitter. The TwitterSearchTrends class contains the date the search was performed, and an inner collection of TwitterSearchTrend instances that map the current trend, its query, and its relevant time. Because trending topics use UNIX time, you can also use the FromUnixTime extension method to convert long values into DateTime.

Using TweetSharp's Time Extension Helpers

When you are trying to describe `DateTime` values in TweetSharp or elsewhere, you can take advantage of TweetSharp's built-in extension methods that help you write human readable time values. For example, you can call the `Seconds`, `Minutes`, `Hours`, `Days`, `Weeks`, and `Months` method on any whole number to retrieve the `TimeSpan` corresponding to the time value, and then use the `Ago` or `FromNow` methods to relate the timespan to a tangible date in the past or future. This helps you write readable code, such as the following caching and trending examples:

```
// Caches the response to a query to retrieve a user profile
// for 12 hours before fetching directly from Twitter in subsequent
calls
var query = FluentTwitter.CreateRequest()
    .Configuration.CacheUntil(12.Hours().FromNow())
    .Users().ShowProfileFor("Dimebrain")
    .AsJson();

// Get daily trends from three days in the past
var query = FluentTwitter.CreateRequest()
    .Search().Trends()
    .Daily().For(3.Days().Ago());
```

Authenticating with OAuth

With TweetSharp, implementing OAuth authentication is a much less time-consuming process than the steps you took in Chapter 6 to implement your own OAuth library. TweetSharp has a built-in capacity to handle the OAuth workflow. Assuming you have configured TwitterClientInfo with your application's consumer key and secret, the first step in the workflow is to obtain an unauthorized request token. The next example shows how to obtain the request token in TweetSharp. When the response is received it is casted into an `OAuthToken` instance using the `AsToken` extension method. You may use this token instance in the future to exchange it for an access token after a user has authorized your application on Twitter's site.

```
using Dimebrain.TweetSharp;
using Dimebrain.TweetSharp.Extensions;
using Dimebrain.TweetSharp.Fluent;
using Dimebrain.TweetSharp.Model;

internal class Program
{
    private static void Main()
    {
        // Define a client configuration
        var clientInfo = new TwitterClientInfo
        {
            ClientName = "motto",
            ClientUrl = "http://getmotto.com",
            ClientVersion = "v1.0",
            ConsumerKey = "EQrjo7nYzrBoaVCeTsrOA",
```

```
        ConsumerSecret = "1vOqGKS20KdrPpZJfk92gGE3RF6u71VKI2TvvBoZc"
    };

    // Set client info globally
    FluentTwitter.CreateRequest(clientInfo);

    // Build a query to obtain a request token
    var query = FluentTwitter.CreateRequest()
        .Authentication.GetRequestToken();

    var request = query.Request();

    // Convert response into a token
    OAuthToken token = request.AsToken();
    Console.WriteLine(token.Token);
    Console.WriteLine(token.TokenSecret);

    Console.WriteLine();
    Console.WriteLine("Press any key to end example.");
    Console.ReadKey();
    }
}
```

The next step in the process predictably depends on whether you intend to authorize a desktop or web application. Desktop applications must send the user to a web browser, as you learned in Chapter 6; TweetSharp provides the `AuthorizeDesktop` method to perform that task automatically, or the `GetAuthorizationUrl` method to return only the necessary URL for you to perform the task yourself. In the following completed example, the request token is used to send a desktop user to Twitter's site for authorization. The call to `AuthorizeDesktop` executes a new browser process on the user's machine automatically; executing the query after that point will attempt to perform the same action as the `GetAccessToken` method, attempting to exchange the request token for the access token so that it is possible to authenticate future TweetSharp queries with the `AuthenticateWith` method.

```
using System;
using Dimebrain.TweetSharp;
using Dimebrain.TweetSharp.Extensions;
using Dimebrain.TweetSharp.Fluent;
using Dimebrain.TweetSharp.Model;

internal class Program
{
    private static void Main()
    {
        // Define a client configuration
        var clientInfo = new TwitterClientInfo
        {
            ClientName = "motto",
            ClientUrl = "http://getmotto.com",
            ClientVersion = "v1.0",
            ConsumerKey = "EQrjo7nYzrBoaVCeTsrOA",
            ConsumerSecret = "1vOqGKS20KdrPpZJfk92gGE3RF6u71VKI2TvvBoZc"
        };
```

```
            // Set client info globally
            FluentTwitter.CreateRequest(clientInfo);

            var query = FluentTwitter.CreateRequest()
                .Authentication.GetRequestToken();

            var response = query.Request();

            // Convert response into a token
            OAuthToken token = response.AsToken();
            Console.WriteLine(token.Token);
            Console.WriteLine(token.TokenSecret);

            // Obtain authorization (this method executes immediately)
            query = FluentTwitter.CreateRequest()
                .Authentication.AuthorizeDesktop(token.Token);

            // Authorization occurs elsewhere, in a browser
            Console.WriteLine("Press any key when application is authorized.");
            Console.ReadKey();

            // Executing the query will attempt to exchange for an
            // access token
            response = query.Request();
            token = response.AsToken();

            // This token is used to authenticate future calls
            Console.WriteLine(token.Token);
            Console.WriteLine(token.TokenSecret);
        }
    }
```

For web applications, you can redirect the user to the authorization URL yourself, and then use the GetAccessToken method to perform the exchange after Twitter calls back to your page with the authorized request token in the query string. These methods are shown in the next example:

```
using System;
using System.Configuration;
using System.Web.UI;
using Dimebrain.TweetSharp.Extensions;
using Dimebrain.TweetSharp.Fluent;
using Dimebrain.TweetSharp.Model;

protected void Page_Load(object sender, EventArgs e)
{
    // add these to web.config
    _consumerKey = ConfigurationManager.AppSettings["consumerKey"];
    _consumerSecret = ConfigurationManager.AppSettings["consumerSecret"];

    var requestToken = Request["oauth_token"];
    if (requestToken == null)
    {
```

```
        // A request token is required for the authorization URL
        var requestQuery = FluentTwitter.CreateRequest()
            .Authentication.GetRequestToken(requestToken.AsToken());

        var twitterResponse = requestQuery.Request();
        OAuthToken token = twitterResponse.AsToken();

        // You need to provide the callback URL via your application's
        // developer page on Twitter; this URL will receive the token
        // response in the query string required to perform the exchange
        var authorizeUrl = FluentTwitter.CreateRequest()
            .Authentication.GetAuthorizationUrl(token);

        // Send the user to the authorization page on Twitter
        Response.Redirect(authorizeUrl);
    }
    else
    {
        // This request is actually the callback from Twitter, so
        // exchange returned request token for access token
        var accessQuery = FluentTwitter.CreateRequest()
            .Authentication.GetAccessToken(_consumerKey, _consumerSecret);

        // Deserialize the token; you should persist this for
        // future use of TweetSharp for this user
        var twitterResponse = accessQuery.Request();
        OAuthToken token = response.AsToken();
    }
```

Assuming that the access token obtained from the previous code is valid and no service interruptions occurred, you can pass it in to any query using AuthenticateWith to provide the same API access as direct impersonation with Basic authentication, but without needing to know the user's real credentials. The following code shows how TweetSharp is used with the access token:

```
using System;
using Dimebrain.TweetSharp.Extensions;
using Dimebrain.TweetSharp.Model;
using Dimebrain.TweetSharp.Fluent;

// Remember to set the consumer key and secret
// or provided it in the method overloads
// for AuthenticateWith
var query = FluentTwitter.CreateRequest()
    .AuthenticateWith(access.Token, access.TokenSecret)
    .Users().GetFriends()
    .AsJson();

var response = query.Request();
var friends = response.AsUsers();
```

TweetSharp provides the methods necessary to work with OAuth in a quick and painless manner. Although you will know the work occurring behind the scenes to ensure your requests are properly signed, you only need to focus on your application's use of OAuth, and let TweetSharp manage the details for you.

Performance

TweetSharp provides much more than an Intellisense-powered wrapper for Twitter API calls or an abstraction of the OAuth workflow for authenticating users with the emerging standard for Twitter applications. TweetSharp also provides an additional layer of features useful for writing responsive applications that are mindful of bandwidth and user API constraints. In the next section you'll get an understanding of what's possible when writing applications that need to get the most out of Twitter.

Caching Queries

Depending on how your application is designed, you may need to provide a means for many concurrent users to request Twitter data from your application directly. This presents an opportunity for waste, either with public data, or data protected by user credentials, where the user controls when a polling operation occurred — such as when requests for data are triggered by a UI action. TweetSharp provides a caching layer accessible through the `Configuration` property; you can specify a sliding or absolute expiration on the cache, and requests that require user credentials are automatically cached for the specific user only, ensuring that data from other users is not consumed outside the intended audience. The following code demonstrates the use of caching in TweetSharp. When caching is enabled, the first request matching the URL will request directly from Twitter while subsequent calls within the expiration period are served from the cache, and no API call is made to Twitter.

```
using System;
using Dimebrain.TweetSharp.Fluent;

// #1: Absolute expiration, all subsequent calls
//     before the given time are served from cache
var query = FluentTwitter.CreateRequest()
    .Configuration.CacheUntil(10.Minutes().FromNow())
    .Statuses().OnPublicTimeline()
    .AsJson();

// #2: Sliding expiration, all subsequent calls
//     made while there has not been an inactivity period
//     of the allotted time are served from cache
query = FluentTwitter.CreateRequest()
    .Configuration.CacheForInactivityOf(10.Minutes())
    .Statuses().OnPublicTimeline()
    .AsJson();

// This request reaches Twitter
var response = query.Request();

// This request is served from the cache
response = query.Request();

// You can detect if a response was served from
// cache by checking the Response property of the query;
// if it was null, no API call was made
if(query.Response == null)
{
    // No API call was performed...
}
```

By default, the ASP.NET `Cache` class is used as the underlying caching mechanism behind TweetSharp, through the `IWebCache` interface that supports absolute and sliding expiration, but you may provide your own caching strategy by implementing either the `IWebCache` or `IClientCache` interfaces depicted in Figure 9-2.

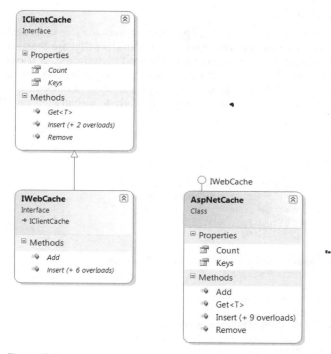

Figure 9-2

To use a custom cache provider, use the `CacheWith` method shown in the next code example:

```
using System;
using Dimebrain.TweetSharp.Core.Caching;
using Dimebrain.TweetSharp.Extensions;
using Dimebrain.TweetSharp.Fluent;

// Your custom cache must implement IClientCache
// or IWebCache, and should have an instantiation
// the MemcachedCache provided by Dimebrain.TweetSharp.Extras
// is used in this example
var cache = new MemcachedCache();

// Declare a custom cache for the query
var query = FluentTwitter.CreateRequest()
    .Configuration.CacheWith(cache)
    .Configuration.CacheUntil(10.Minutes().FromNow())
    .Statuses().OnPublicTimeline()
    .AsJson();
```

If you are using TweetSharp in a distributed cache environment, the `Dimebrain.TweetSharp.Extras` project available in the source code provides an example of implementing a TweetSharp caching scheme for *memcached*, a popular distributed caching technology, and the TweetSharp team will release support for Microsoft's Velocity caching in the near future.

Compressing Requests

In addition to caching requests, it is often helpful to compress the size of large API calls, as you learned in Chapter 7, to avoid incurring the cost of messages with sizes that are drastically reduced by GZIP compression. To enable GZIP compression, you only need to declare your use of it using the `Configuration` property. The following code shows how easy it is to enable compression. Keep in mind that this strategy is only useful for large message payloads, such as retrieving 100 results of friends or followers at a time through the API; otherwise you're likely to actually increase the size of the message rather than decrease it.

```
using System;
using Dimebrain.TweetSharp.Fluent;

// Write a query to retrieve the first 100 users
var query = FluentTwitter.CreateRequest()
    .AuthenticateAs("username", "password")
    .Users().GetFollowers()
    .AsJson();

// Wireshark reports this call was 115504 bytes
var response = query.Request();

// Enable GZIP compression on the same query
query = FluentTwitter.CreateRequest()
    .Configuration.UseGzipCompression()
    .AuthenticateAs("username", "password")
    .Users().GetFollowers()
    .AsJson();

// Wireshark reports this call was 24882 bytes
response = query.Request();
```

Asynchronous Operation

In many scenarios you may not want to halt the operation of your program while fetching data from Twitter, especially when working with a rich UI, where pausing to process data will always yield a poor user experience. For these situations, TweetSharp supports a simple asynchronous operation mode that allows you to provide a callback to invoke when a request returns, freeing up your time and your threads. The following example shows how to structure a TweetSharp query to use the `RequestAsync` method to send an API call on a separate thread. This time it uses an anonymous method rather than the complete event handler signature illustrated in the previous Core Feature Overview section. In the example, the asynchronous thread is blocked with a handle, simulating a sequential call, while in a real-world scenario you would create an event handler method similar to any .NET event.

```
using System;
using Dimebrain.TweetSharp.Extensions;
using Dimebrain.TweetSharp.Fluent;
```

```
// Create a new wait event to block the async call
var block = new AutoResetEvent(false);

// Create a query for asynchronous operation
var query = FluentTwitter.CreateRequest()
    .Statuses().OnPublicTimeline()
    .AsJson()
    .CallbackTo((s, e) =>
    {
        // Get the results from the returning response
        var statuses = e.Response.AsStatuses();

        // Signal that the thread completed
        block.Set();
    });

query.RequestAsync();

// Wait for asynchronous thread to complete
block.WaitOne();
```

Timed Tasks

Building on the asynchronous operation model is a feature that allows you to repeat calls automatically, which you may find useful for UI applications that refresh on set intervals. To take advantage of timed tasks, you must use the asynchronous operation and you can invoke the RepeatAfter and RepeatEvery extension methods; the former allows you to set up a finite number of repeat calls, while the latter provides a facility to continuously repeat the defined query. When a timed task is executing, you can access it programmatically to halt its operation through the TimedTasks collection on the FluentTwitter interface. The following example shows you what's required to define, execute, and halt a timed task:

```
using System;
// This namespace is necessary for referencing WebQueryResponseEventArgs
using Dimebrain.TweetSharp.Core.Web;
using Dimebrain.TweetSharp.Extensions;
using Dimebrain.TweetSharp.Fluent;

// #1: Repeat ten times, every 2 minutes
var query = FluentTwitter.CreateRequest()
    .AuthenticateAs("username", "password")
    .Statuses().Update("I'm still here!").AsXml()
    .RepeatAfter(2.Minutes(), 10);

// #2: Repeat a query indefinitely in 10 minute intervals
var query = FluentTwitter.CreateRequest()
    .Statuses().OnPublicTimeline().AsJson()
    .CallbackTo(ProcessResponse)
    .RepeatEvery(10.Minutes());

// Start a repetitive request normally
query.RequestAsync();
```

```
// Stop a repetitive request early
query.TimedTasks[0].Stop();

// Stop all timed tasks
query.TimedTasks.StopAll();

private static void ProcessResponse(object sender,
                                    WebQueryResponseEventArgs e)
{
    // Do work with the asynchronous results that return repeatedly...
}
```

Rate Throttling

Another asynchronous operation performance feature is the ability to queue queries until they are safe to execute without placing undue burden on, or maxing out, the rate limit of the authenticating account. TweetSharp will sort rate limited calls by priority, which you can override if desired, and internally estimate how many calls you are making against an account per hour. The first authenticated call is used to gauge the current state of the user or IP addresses API situation. The next example shows how to set up rate limiting for selected queries:

```
using System;
using Dimebrain.TweetSharp.Core.Web;
using Dimebrain.TweetSharp.Extensions;
using Dimebrain.TweetSharp.Fluent;

// #1: Use the default rate limiting algorithm
var query = FluentTwitter.CreateRequest()
    .Configuration.UseRateLimiting()
    .Statuses().OnFriendsTimeline()
    .CallbackTo(ProcessResponse)
    .RepeatEvery(5.Seconds());

// #2: Override the priority for this rate limited query
var query = FluentTwitter.CreateRequest()
    .Configuration.UseRateLimiting(ThreadPriority.Highest)
    .Statuses().OnPublicTimeline().AsJson()
    .CallbackTo(ProcessResponse)
    .RepeatEvery(10.Minutes());

private static void ProcessResponse(object sender,
                                    WebQueryResponseEventArgs e)
{
    // Do work with the asynchronous results...
}
```

Working with Rate Limits

The Twitter API provides two ways to determine the current rate limits of an account, and TweetSharp provides the same. The traditional method is to call the rate limit API method directly, while the more bandwidth-conscious approach involves inspecting the HTTP response headers for any rate-limiting information. TweetSharp harmonizes the latter approach by providing a RateLimitStatus property on the FluentTwitter query itself; whenever you make an authenticated call, check the property for the rate limit information you're looking for rather than making a separate call. You can still use the dedicated call, perhaps on a repeating asynchronous background thread, to update a UI with rate limit feedback if desired. This next code example shows how you would use either method of staying up to date with rate limits in TweetSharp:

```
using System;
using Dimebrain.TweetSharp.Core.Web;
using Dimebrain.TweetSharp.Extensions;
using Dimebrain.TweetSharp.Fluent;

// #1: Call the rate limit method directly
var query = FluentTwitter.CreateRequest()
    .AuthenticateAs("username", "password")
    .Account().GetRateLimitStatus().AsJson();

// Execute the request and cast the response
var response = query.Request();
var rateLimitStatus = response.AsRateLimitStatus();

Console.WriteLine("{0} / {1} remaining",
                  rateLimitStatus.RemainingHits,
                  rateLimitStatus.HourlyLimit);

// #2: Make a rate limited call and pick up the
//     rate information from the response
var query = FluentTwitter.CreateRequest()
    .AuthenticateAs("username", "password")
    .Users().GetFollowers().AsXml();

// Make the request; Twitter will return rate limit
// information in the response headers
var response = query.Request();

// Use the RateLimitStatus property of the last request
var rateLimitStatus = query.RateLimitStatus;

Console.WriteLine("{0} / {1} remaining",
                  rateLimitStatus.RemainingHits,
                  rateLimitStatus.HourlyLimit);
```

Handling Errors

TweetSharp isn't immune to the errors you can encounter when working with a real-time system such as Twitter. Fortunately you have a few options for gracefully handling errors received by TweetSharp and normally encountered when you attempt to deserialize a response into data classes. The following code example shows two ways you can handle errors when they occur, so that your application can respond predictably and recover, or retry requests.

```
using System;
using Dimebrain.TweetSharp.Core.Web;
using Dimebrain.TweetSharp.Extensions;
using Dimebrain.TweetSharp.Fluent;
```

```
// #1: Call the rate limit method directly
//      (the query is missing authentication)
var query = FluentTwitter.CreateRequest()
    .Statuses().OnUserTimeline()
    .AsJson();

// Make the request normally
var response = query.Request();

// #1: Check that the last response wasn't an error
if(query.HasError)
{
    // The response is an error so report on it
    var error = response.AsError();
    Console.WriteLine(error.ErrorMessage);
}
else
{
    // The response is valid, so proceed as normal
    var statuses = response.AsStatuses();
    foreach(var status in statuses)
    {
        Console.WriteLine(status.Text);
    }
}

// #2: Check a conversion attempt for null
var statuses2 = response.AsStatuses();
if(statuses2 == null)
{
    // The results could not be cast to the expected type
    var error = response.AsError();
    if(error != null)
    {
        // The response is an error, so report on it
        Console.WriteLine(error.ErrorMessage);
    }
    else
    {
        // You may have tried to cast to the wrong type
    }
}

private static void ProcessResponse(object sender,
                            WebQueryResponseEventArgs e)
{
    // Do work with the asynchronous results that return repeatedly...
}
```

With caching, compression, asynchronous operation, rate limiting, and error handling built in to the TweetSharp library, you have a lot of facility to ensure that Twitter applications built using it are responsive and informative in the face of the unpredictable.

Features

TweetSharp's capabilities are rounded out by some convenience features designed to speed up the development of Twitter applications and clients by implementing common requests directly in the library. These features are an emerging standard across most popular Twitter applications such as *TweetDeck*, *HootSuite*, and *Tweetie*. By leaning on TweetSharp to provide common functionality, you'll be able to tap into these features with minimal coding effort and know that the features are well-tested in plenty of community projects, both commercial- and community-based.

Relative Time

Relative time is a common pattern in today's social software that expresses discrete points in time in plain words, relative to the current time, i.e., *ten minutes ago*. You'll often want to express this user-friendly form of timekeeping in your Twitter application UI. To take advantage of relative time, you can use the `ToRelativeTime` extension method on an instance of `DateTime`. This extension method also provides an overload so that you can choose whether to express numbers in words or leave them as numbers, depending on your preference. The following code illustrates the complete use of this technique:

```
using System;
using Dimebrain.TweetSharp.Extensions;
using Dimebrain.TweetSharp.Fluent;

// fetch a user's profile
var query = FluentTwitter.CreateRequest()
    .Users().ShowProfileFor("Dimebrain")
    .AsJson();

var response = query.Request();
var status = response.AsUser().Status;

// Get the time of Dimebrain's last status
// expressed as relative time with numbers
var time = status.CreatedDate.ToRelativeTime();
Console.WriteLine(time);

// Display the same relative time using words
var timeWithWords = status.CreatedDate.ToRelativeTime(true);
Console.WriteLine(timeWithWords);
```

Shortening URLs

One popular phenomenon of micro-blogging culture is the use of URL shortening services to conserve space for links better used for messages. TweetSharp provides built-in support for several URL shortening services: *to.m8.to*, *tr.im*, *bit.ly*, *is.gd*, and *tinyurl*. When you activate URL shortening in TweetSharp, all the links in a Twitter status update are collected and sent to the appropriate service, and the resulting shortened URLs are used in place of the provided long form URLs. The result is a transparent and automatic shortening service that you don't need to think about. You may switch the provider service at any time, thus allowing you to provide multiple options to your own users, and any special considerations such as API keys and credentials for shortening services are handled with method overloads. This next code listing demonstrates how to enable URL shortening in TweetSharp:

```
using System;
using Dimebrain.TweetSharp.Extensions;
using Dimebrain.TweetSharp.Fluent;

// #1: Prepare a status update with a long URL;
//     It will get shortened with to.m8.to by default
var query = FluentTwitter.CreateRequest()
    .Configuration.UseUrlShortening()
    .AuthenticateAs("username", "password")
    .Statuses().Update("Check this out! http://tweetsharp.googlecode.com")
    .AsJson();

// #2: Use an alternate URL shortening service
var query = FluentTwitter.CreateRequest()
    .Configuration.UseUrlShortening(ShortenUrlServiceProvider.TinyUrl)
    .AuthenticateAs("username", "password")
    .Statuses().Update("Check this out! http://tweetsharp.googlecode.com")
    .AsJson();

// #3: Use an alternate URL shortening service requiring authentication
var query = FluentTwitter.CreateRequest()
    .Configuration.UseUrlShortening(ShortenUrlServiceProvider.Bitly,
                            "username",
                            "apiKey")
    .AuthenticateAs("username", "password")
    .Statuses().Update("Check this out! http://tweetsharp.googlecode.com")
    .AsJson();

// Send the request; shortening will occur first
var response = query.Request();

// Get the newly created status in the response
var status = response.AsStatus();

// Confirm that the URL was shortened properly
// "Check this out! http://m8.to/23X"
Console.WriteLine(status.Text);
```

Posting Photos

Many Twitter applications provide support for quickly posting photos along with your message via third-party image posting services. This is especially prevalent with mobile devices, where cameras are built in to the interface and offer one-click photo to Twitter integration. The two leading providers of Twitter photo sharing today are *TwitPic* and ImageShack's *yFrog* service, and both are supported in TweetSharp using a similar approach to URL shortening. To post a photo to accompany a status update or direct message, use the following code listing:

```
using System;
using Dimebrain.TweetSharp.Extensions;
using Dimebrain.TweetSharp.Fluent;
using Dimebrain.TweetSharp.Fluent.Services;
```

```
// #1: Post a photo with status update using TwitPic
var query = FluentTwitter.CreateRequest()
    .AuthenticateAs("username", "password")
    .Photos().PostPhoto("failwhale.jpg")
    .Statuses().Update("Awesome!")
    .AsJson();

var response = query.Request();
var status = response.AsStatus();

// Verify the created status has an image link
// i.e. "Awesome! - http://twitpic.com/6i9w4"
Console.WriteLine(status.Text);

// #2: Post a photo with a direct message using yFrog
query = FluentTwitter.CreateRequest()
    .AuthenticateAs("username", "password")
    .Photos().PostPhoto("failwhale.jpg", SendPhotoServiceProvider.YFrog)
    .DirectMessages().Send("recipient", "Awesome!")
    .AsJson();

response = query.Request();
var dm = response.AsDirectMessage();

// Verify the created direct message has an image link
// i.e. "Awesome! - http://yfrog.com/e0ehoj"
Console.WriteLine(dm.Text);
```

It's worth noting that both yFrog and TwitPic providers currently require Basic authentication, and have not embraced the OAuth model at the time of writing. If you want to build Twitter applications using OAuth, but still make use of these image posting services, you will need to either use TweetSharp's `ExternallyAuthenticateAs` method in place of `AuthenticateAs` to provide the user's true credentials to the service, or forego these services until they support OAuth; you might find it difficult convincing your userbase to use both, rather than one, of these authentication schemes.

Retweeting

With any community-based service, patterns and conventions begin to emerge. One of these conventions is the notion of *retweeting* others' messages to spread them across your network and otherwise promote your agreement or enthusiasm for the original message. Although retweeting is essentially appending the acronym RT to the beginning of someone else's message followed by his or her screen name, you can achieve this in TweetSharp without repetitive code by making use of the `Retweet` method — this is located on the `Statuses` extension method. This next example demonstrates retweeting an existing message:

```
using System;
using Dimebrain.TweetSharp.Extensions;
using Dimebrain.TweetSharp.Fluent;
using Dimebrain.TweetSharp.Model;

// Get a message to retweet, by ID
var query = FluentTwitter.CreateRequest()
    .Statuses().Show(1919679324)
    .AsXml();
```

```
var response = query.Request();
TwitterStatus status = response.AsStatus();

// #1: Retweet the message using the default 'RT' prefix
var query = FluentTwitter.CreateRequest()
    .AuthenticateAs("username", "password")
    .Statuses().Retweet(status)
    .AsJson();

// #2: Retweet the message using the Unicode "recycling" symbol
var query = FluentTwitter.CreateRequest()
    .AuthenticateAs("username", "password")
    .Statuses().Retweet(status, RetweetMode.SymbolPrefix)
    .AsJson();

// #2: Retweet the message using the 'via' suffix
var query = FluentTwitter.CreateRequest()
    .AuthenticateAs("username", "password")
    .Statuses().Retweet(status, RetweetMode.Suffix)
    .AsJson();

response = query.Request();
status = response.AsStatus();

// Confirm the retweet is properly formed
Console.WriteLine(status.Text);
```

Working with Proxies

Not every organization smiles on the use of social networking tools such as Twitter in the workplace, or, they may require routing traffic through special proxies as part of their IT infrastructure. You can support communication with proxies in TweetSharp through the Configuration property, either as proxies in the traditional routing sense, or transparent proxies that send requests to Twitter on your behalf, with only the URI domain changing but the API method path remaining intact. In the following example, TweetSharp is configured with both types of proxies. By default, if any proxy is defined in Internet Explorer, this proxy is used by TweetSharp; if you want to specifically avoid using a proxy in those situations, you can pass an empty string to the UseProxy method.

```
using System;
using Dimebrain.TweetSharp.Extensions;
using Dimebrain.TweetSharp.Fluent;
using Dimebrain.TweetSharp.Model;

// #1: Configure TweetSharp to use a standard proxy
var query = FluentTwitter.CreateRequest()
    .Configuration.UseProxy("http://myproxy.com")
    .AuthenticateAs("username", "password")
    .Statuses().OnUserTimeline()
    .AsJson();          .

// #2: Configure TweetSharp to use a transparent
//     proxy specifically for Twitter API calls;
//     http://twitter.com is replaced with the proxy
```

```
//     domain and path.
query = FluentTwitter.CreateRequest()
    .Configuration.UseTransparentProxy
    ("http://tweetsharp.cloudapp.net/proxy/")
    .AuthenticateAs("username", "password")
    .Statuses().OnUserTimeline()
    .AsJson();

var response = query.Request();
Console.WriteLine(response);
```

When working with transparent proxies in Silverlight you can refer to "Hosting a Twitter Proxy in the Cloud" in Chapter 10 of this book, which provides code and a detailed explanation of the use of transparent proxies on the client-side and the custom HTTP headers they require.

Unit Testing

One of the challenges of working with real-time, connected services such as Twitter is that you can't guarantee Internet connectivity for either yourself or the service you're consuming. When you need to develop applications in offline scenarios, progress grinds to a halt unless you have a way to simulate real responses.

Defining Mock Responses

TweetSharp gives you the capability to develop your Twitter applications even when offline using a mocking strategy. When you want to remove the simulated calls and work with live data, you can do so easily, without making drastic changes to the structure of your preceding query. Offline testing support in TweetSharp is provided by the Expect method, that takes an arbitrary graph of Twitter model objects as arguments, and returns those objects in a response *as if they came from Twitter itself*; this means that the data format matches Twitter's output faithfully, so that you can develop with confidence. The following code example shows how to use the Expect method to define the response you want returned from TweetSharp without making a network request:

```
using System;
using System.Linq;
using Dimebrain.TweetSharp.Extensions;
using Dimebrain.TweetSharp.Fluent;
using Dimebrain.TweetSharp.Model;

// Create a mock status for testing or development
var status = new TwitterStatus
                {
                    Id = 123456789,
                    Text = "This is a fake status",
                    CreatedDate = DateTime.Now
                };

// Create a query as normal, adding the Expect method
var query = FluentTwitter.CreateRequest()
    .AuthenticateAs("username", "password")
```

```
        .Statuses().OnUserTimeline()
        .AsJson()
        // Define the expectation
        // (any number and type of Twitter object)
        .Expect(status);

    // Execute the request normally; no call is made to Twitter
    var response = query.Request();
    var result = response.AsStatuses();

    // The mock status and the returned status are equal
    Console.WriteLine(status.Text);
    Console.WriteLine(result.First().Text);
```

When building a Twitter application offline, the Expect method is indispensable. However, when you want your application to communicate live, you can remove the Expect method and your query will function normally; if you want to keep the Expect invocation in your code but ignore it, you can use the Configuration property's DisableMocking method to continue to make requests against Twitter with minimal code changes.

Using Data Generation

Although mocking on its own is a useful feature, it is not always practical or desirable to create or load previously saved data to store for access using the Expect method. When you need more flexibility in your offline Twitter application development, TweetSharp provides data generation through the TwitterDataTools class. Using this class, you can generate mock objects that mimic the look and feel of real Twitter statuses with complete details, at which point you can pass the mock data directly into Expect or mix it with your own test data before doing so. The next code example shows how to use TwitterDataTools to create mocks to test a feature of an application:

```
    using System;
    using System.Linq;
    using Dimebrain.TweetSharp.Data;
    using Dimebrain.TweetSharp.Extensions;
    using Dimebrain.TweetSharp.Fluent;

    // Create a query that uses mock users
    var query = FluentTwitter.CreateRequest()
        .AuthenticateAs("username", "password")
        .Users().GetFollowers().AsJson()
        // Define the expectation using data tools
        .Expect(TwitterDataTools.GenerateUsers(100));

    var response = query.Request();
    var users = response.AsUsers();


    // Create a query that uses mock statuses
    var query = FluentTwitter.CreateRequest()
        .AuthenticateAs("username", "password")
        .Statuses().OnFriendsTimeline().AsJson()
```

```
        // Define the expectation using data tools
        .Expect(TwitterDataTools.GenerateStatuses(100));

var response = query.Request();
var statuses = response.AsStatuses();
```

Summary

TweetSharp is a great choice for cutting down the time it takes to learn the Twitter API to get productive to build new Twitter applications, but it also provides a convenience library around much of the skills and learning acquired in this book. Whether you decide to use TweetSharp, NUrl, or roll your own code to handle REST interaction with Twitter, you now have options. Another advantage to using TweetSharp is that it is an open source, MIT licensed project with a growing community. This means that you're likely to find help and, should you discover Twitter-related bugs or changes that could slow down your own development, can enjoy faster resolution of these issues as the community and TweetSharp's team respond to those changes proactively. In this chapter you learned how to leverage TweetSharp in the following ways:

❑   Mapping existing Twitter API methods to consistent fluent interface methods that are discoverable with Visual Studio Intellisense

❑   Converting Twitter's XML or JSON responses to data classes ready for serialization or data binding

❑   Using out of the box support to provide commonly requested third-party features such as URL shortening and posting photos

❑   Executing queries in sequential or asynchronous mode

❑   Leveraging built-in caching support and compression to save bandwidth when making calls to Twitter

❑   Responding to Twitter errors gracefully

❑   Testing new Twitter applications quickly using mocking to simulate real responses from the API without consuming bandwidth, or in situations where you're developing offline

In the next chapter, you will continue to use TweetSharp while building a Twitter application with Silverlight 3 and Windows Azure, showing that you can apply your knowledge of the TweetSharp library in the latest and greatest Microsoft technology projects.

10

Building a Cross-Platform Twitter Application

.NET is now a rich platform. You have the capability to build applications with consistent user experience and reusable code architectures that target Windows, as well as cross-platform options on the web and desktop. In this chapter, everything you've learned about application development with the Twitter API is put to use in a cross-platform, Twitter client application that you can run in a web browser or on a Windows or Mac desktop. Thanks to the power of Silverlight 3 and Windows Azure, both currently in Beta, you can build compelling Twitter applications on the cutting edge.

The Application: Twiticism.com

The application you'll build in this chapter is *Twiticism*, a simple real-time, cross-platform experience that lets users track the overall sentiment for a topic based on Search API queries. To build this application, you'll need to bring together all the skills, features, and considerations covered in earlier chapters. In addition, you'll learn how to build and deploy .NET applications on Microsoft's Azure services, enabling cloud-based hosted scenarios to help you ease the burden of deploying and scaling your own creations. You will engage with several technologies in this chapter:

- ❏ *Silverlight Tools for Visual Studio 2008 Beta 1*
- ❏ *Windows Azure Tools for Visual Studio 2008 CTP*
- ❏ *TweetSharp v1.0*

After completing this application, you will have a foundation of knowledge and skills needed to imagine, create, and deliver your own Twitter applications quickly and effectively.

Problem

Since the proliferation of blogs and other user-generated content, companies have invested heavily in efforts to help determine what people are saying about their products and services online, either to confirm positive advertising or development strategies, or attempt to correct poor experiences quickly — a disparaging comment on a popular site has a habit of reaching large numbers of people quickly, who may take the criticism at face value. Today, thanks to the real-time power of Twitter, the public opinion of products and services has escalated way beyond static user content and into a real-time, immediate pulse of information as it happens. Twitter's Search API provides a core set of features to help companies find positive and negative opinions about their service. Twiticism will allow a user to track products, services, or phrases and provide a visual cue to their overall impact, whether positive or negative, on Twitter. The application is simple, but you can extend it depending on your own experience and growth with Silverlight 3.

Design

Twiticism will utilize the time-saving features of TweetSharp to communicate with the Twitter API and schedule updates using timed tasks. Silverlight 3's powerful and simple offline support is used to allow application access across Windows and Mac computers to embrace cross-platform users. To help ensure the service is readily available and that scales are based on demand, the application will leverage multiple capabilities of Windows Azure services.

Why Windows Azure?

Windows Azure is a set of services that allow hosted web applications, storage, and even relational data to live in a data center or *cloud* hosted by Microsoft, logically separated from your own computing resources. This aspect of Azure is on par with any web site hosting service, where you prepare your application code to execute at an external location, and deploy that code to a production server. Where cloud services distinguish themselves are in how an application that runs on the cloud is designed to take advantage of automatic scaling. As the demand for resources from your application increases, the computing power necessary to meet those demands is similarly escalated to meet that demand, and is then scaled down during periods of low activity. The clear advantage to adopting an Azure-backed delivery model, aside from the ability to rely on a company such as Microsoft for high data availability, is the cost savings introduced when you only pay for the processing power you need. Rather than purchasing expensive server resources or hosted service levels that can handle your busiest times, you can sit idle during periods of low activity regardless of the cost. With Azure's focus on ease of deployment, it is an attractive choice to take advantage of cloud scaling for your application while still remaining within familiar surroundings both in Visual Studio and your choice of .NET development language.

> **Deploying Twiticism without Azure**
>
> Although the application is designed for hosting in the cloud, your needs may differ. The essential web and worker roles that encompass the core functionality of a cloud service application are easily ported to existing Silverlight or ASP.NET architectures thanks to the tight integration provided by Windows Azure Tools for Visual Studio. Much of what you will develop using cloud roles is structured similarly to familiar project types. You will need to replace Azure queues with another messaging construct such as *MSMQ* and WCF self-hosted services, in addition to restructuring your data access code to use SQL Server or another relational storage model. However, the power of Azure is worth consideration, especially for today's social web service applications. It is exercised here to help you get familiar with the latest technologies when building your own Twitter-based vision.

The Azure Cloud

Your use of Windows Azure for Twiticism covers two of the major feature areas the service offers: hosted services and storage services. Hosted services act as a logical server for your applications, while storage services provide web-accessible persisted state exposed through a REST API (the use of which you are now quite familiar). Interactions with your Azure services, including deployment, configuration, security, and metrics takes place through a web portal that is bound to you or your organization's Windows Live account. When Azure officially launches, payment for hosted services will occur through the same interface.

Azure Storage Services

Azure Storage Services, which includes the message queuing features that enabled scalable applications, is accessed through a REST API, similar to Twitter. In this case, you need to provide a different authentication scheme than either the Basic or OAuth implementations you are used to. Azure Storage Services uses a shared key scheme; your key is issued when you activate a new account and is displayed on the Azure portal page for your storage services project, as shown in Figure 10-1. The portal page will also have a secondary key in the event your primary key is compromised, as well as options to regenerate both.

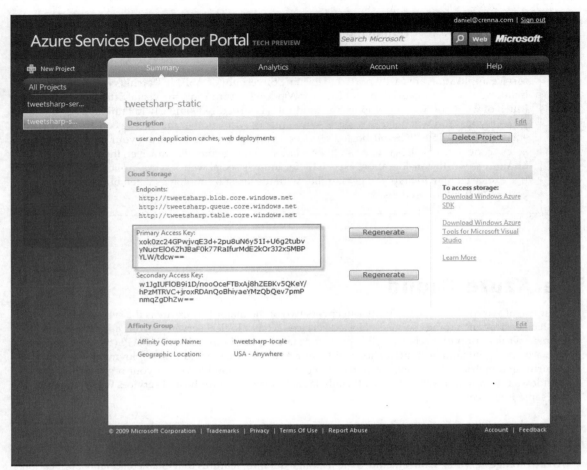

Figure 10-1

Because you have an understanding of how the web is programmed through REST services, you also now understand the essential communication elements of Azure's Storage API (you can read the full API documentation at `http://msdn.microsoft.com/en-us/library/dd179355.aspx`). Storage services are broken down into three distinct storage data types: *blobs* for static data such as music, photos, and videos; *queues* for passing messages between layers of your application; and *tables* for a scalable form of entity persistence. When you sign up for a storage account, all these types are available to you; Twiticism will make use of queues and tables.

Accessing each storage service type involves referencing each of their unique REST endpoints. In Table 10-1 a description of the endpoints is covered, depending on whether your application is targeting a deployed solution on Azure, or is still in development and using the provided *Azure Development Fabric*, which simulates the Azure experience locally. The fully qualified endpoint names are also provided on the storage services portal page illustrated previously.

Table 10-1: Azure Storage Services Endpoints

Storage Type	Azure Endpoint	Development Endpoint
Blobs (binary, static content)	`http://myaccount.blob.core` `.windows.net` **or** `https:// blob` `.core.windows.net`	`http://127.0.0.1:100000`
Queues (short messages for processing across application nodes)	`http://myaccount.queue` `.core.windows.net` **or** `https://` `queue.core.windows.net`	`http://127.0.0.1:100001`
Tables (nonrelational, attribute-based entity persistence)	`http://myaccount.table` `.core.windows.net` **or** `https://` `table.core.windows.net`	`http://127.0.0.1:100002`

Each respective storage endpoint is accessed either across boundaries using the fully qualified endpoint that includes the unique account name created at the time of service registration, or within your own Azure account using the SSL endpoints. The development endpoints always run on fixed ports. You can access these endpoints from any application, including those on the desktop, thanks to the RESTful service design. More commonly, and in Twiticism, communication with storage services occurs from an Azure Hosted Service.

Azure Hosted Services

The next major cloud-based component to Twiticism is the use of Azure Hosted Services to serve ASP. NET web application content, including the Silverlight binary deployment to the browser. When you install *Windows Azure Tools for Visual Studio*, developing hosted services feels similar to working with class ASP.NET web applications. The most significant difference working with Azure is how web applications are deployed; in Figure 10-2, a hosted service account is displayed on the portal page, showing the current state of both a production and staging environment.

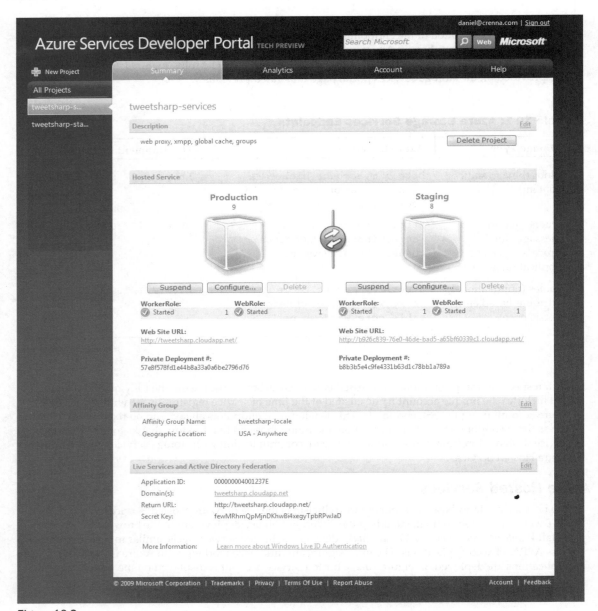

Figure 10-2

The URI to the production instance of a hosted service is fully qualified and based on the unique name provided during sign up, while the staging environment is assigned a Globally Unique Identifier (GUID). One of the benefits of Azure's URI assignment is that production and staging instances are swappable due to the underlying virtual IP address mapping; this means that after you have a tested deployment ready for prime time and it's running successfully on the staging instance, promoting it to production is effortless and nondestructive; if you discover a late-breaking flaw in the new version, you can swap the production and staging instances again without losing time or availability.

Creating an Azure Services Account

Gaining access to Azure services involves a sign-up process that is growing more widely available as development on the platform progresses, though it is possible that a waiting list will exist when you intend to sign up. To begin the process, visit `http://www.microsoft.com/azure/register.mspx`. Azure access is granted through Microsoft Connect Services when you sign up to participate in the Azure community. You will receive tokens to exchange for a limited number of instances of each Azure service type via email. Figure 10-3 shows the contact pages for the sign-up process as it exists today.

Figure 10-3

After you have received tokens, visiting the Azure portal will allow you to create new projects and define their name and description. It also provides the service locale to ensure Azure provisions computing power closest to the users you intend your application for, to help ensure a high quality of service.

The Things You Need for Programming Against Azure

Writing code that interacts with Azure services will always share the same account credentials which are used during request authentication or authorization, which is covered in the next section. Many of the forthcoming examples will draw these values from configuration files, but for your own preliminary work and testing, it is helpful to share a common base class that includes your Azure account name, secret key, and a format string to easily format REST calls against the Storage API based on the available endpoints for blob, table, and queue storage types. Remember to protect your account key whenever possible as it functions as your signature when managing your account. An example base class with this information is provided here:

```
namespace Twitticism
{
    public class AzureBase
    {
        // Replace this with your own Azure account
        protected const string AccountName =
            "twiticism";

        // Replace this with your assigned shared key
        // which is called the Primary Access Key on Azure's
        // portal page
        protected const string AccountSharedKey =
            "xok0zc24GPwjvqE3d+2pu8uN6y51I+U6" +
            "g2tubvyNucrElO6ZhJBaF0k77RaIfurM" +
            "dE2kOr3J2xSMBPYLW/tdcw==";

        // This is a format string mask for storage services endpoints,
        // {0} = Your Account Name
        // {1} = Storage Service Type (blob, queue, or table)
        // {2} = The RESTful resource you are accessing, plus any queries
        protected const string
            AzureStorageUrlBase= "http://{0}.{1}.core.windows.net/{2}";
    }
}
```

You can take a closer look at the REST API for storage services and how you can use your private key to authorize calls to get and create new data after the following things have been finished: you have created Azure services and know your storage service endpoints; and you have installed the Visual Studio tools necessary to abstract away the configuration differences between the ASP.NET application development intended for hardware and cloud-hosted deployment.

Shared Key Authentication

Azure uses a form of shared key encryption to ensure that only the intended user is developing against the hosted solution. Similar to OAuth, the shared key signature signing process involves a detailed list of steps to prepare a request for delivery. In summary, the following list describes the signature generation process:

❏ A signature base string is generated using the HTTP verb, ContentType and Content-MD5 header values if provided, Date or x-ms-Date header values, a normalized list of Azure-specific headers, and a normalized protected resource address.

❏ The signature base string is hashed using an HMAC-SHA1 cryptography provider.

❏ The outbound HttpWebRequest's authorization header is set to SharedKey encryption, associating your Azure service's account with the Base64 encoded hash value.

The following code provides an extension method to take an incoming HttpWebRequest and construct the authorization header used to send that request to your Azure REST service endpoints. The request's authorization header is set to conform to the Azure security steps previously outlined, using the current date and time to sign the request. It's important to note that Azure always expects and stores date information in the UTC format.

```
using System;
using System.Net;
using System.Security.Cryptography;
using System.Text;

namespace Twiticism.Shared
{
    public static class SharedKeyExtensions
    {
        private const string SignatureFormat
            = "{0}\n{1}\n{2}\n\nx-ms-date:{3}\n/{4}/{5}";

        public static void SignWithSharedKey(this HttpWebRequest request,
                                             string account,
                                             string action,
                                             string key)
        {
            SignWithSharedKey(request, account, action, null, key);
        }

        public static void SignWithSharedKey(this HttpWebRequest request,
                                             string account,
                                             string action,
                                             string md5,
                                             string key)
        {
            // Build a formatted date for the header
            // (uses RFC 1183 formatting)
            var date = DateTime.UtcNow.ToString("R");
            request.Headers.Add("x-ms-date", date);

            // Build the signature base from known elements
            var method = request.Method.ToUpperInvariant();
            var signatureBase = string.Format(SignatureFormat,
                                              method,
                                              md5 ?? "",
                                              request.ContentType,
                                              request.Headers["x-ms-date"],
```

```
                                          account,
                                          action);

        // Initialize the encryption provider and generate the hash
        var bytes = Encoding.UTF8.GetBytes(signatureBase);
        var crypt = new HMACSHA256(Convert.FromBase64String(key));
        var hash = Convert.ToBase64String(crypt.ComputeHash(bytes));

        // Sign the request
        var header = String.Format("SharedKey {0}:{1}", account, hash);

        // Set the request's authorization header
        request.Headers.Add("Authorization", header);
    }
  }
}
```

Further Reading in Azure

Although the basics of developing and deploying Azure applications is covered here, there are many more features and considerations to make when designing for the cloud. If you want to pick up where this chapter leaves off and take your Azure development to the next level, you can pick up Roger Jennings' *Cloud Computing with the Windows® Azure™ Platform* coming out soon by Wiley!

Designing Applications for the Cloud

An important consideration when building cloud-based applications is that scaling is not an automatic consequence of deployment; you must design your application so that multiple instances of your roles can work together seamlessly and in a disconnected manner. To achieve this, Azure provides the concept of roles, which are discrete task boundaries that can share state through Azure Storage Services and its REST API and other web-based data mechanisms; otherwise, these roles are logically separate, and your application's design should allow them to run independently of each other, either alone or alongside many instances which is often the case when an application is under heavy use.

Web Roles

A *web role* is basically equivalent to an ASP.NET web application running IIS. You can host ASP.NET applications, web services, or Silverlight applications in much the same way as you do today on standard hardware. You normally won't need to make any special considerations when developing ASP.NET features, other than logging and state management, which must come from outside the web role boundary, such as hosted storage, though you are certainly able to retrieve data from any web-enabled source; it is also possible to configure a form of local disk storage that you can use as temporary processing space.

Worker Roles

The worker role provides your application's parallel background services. A background process is particularly useful for cloud applications because these tasks can update hosted storage which is in turn consumed by web roles to serve updated content to users. Twitter applications are well served by a worker role because using one allows a convenient mechanism to host global user caching features discussed in Chapter 7 in the background, and make that data immediately available to hosted application web roles if desired.

Blobs

Earning their name through the classic data computing term Binary Large Objects (BLOB), blobs allow you to store static binary data up to 50GB per entity. Blobs can have public or private URI addresses, and may exist within a container to logically separate collections of blobs, similar to a typical file folder structure, though the blog container structure is flat as it is not possible to nest containers. One typical use of blobs is storing static content on your site; because the RESTful URI to your blob content typically doesn't change, it is highly cacheable on the user's browser, improving performance for them, and reducing bandwidth resources for you. Twitter uses this technique to store all user profile photos.

Queues

The glue that binds web and worker roles in a disconnected environment designed to scale is the ability to pass messages across boundaries. To accomplish this, Azure Storage Services provides the queue storage data type. An Azure queue is a time-sensitive collection of small messages that you can define and place in a queued data structure for background processing. Unfortunately, there is no way to guarantee that the messages that reach the queue will not contain duplicates, or will be in any specific order, such as the time of creation. Application designs will need to account for this possibility when dequeuing messages to process. Queue messages are limited to a scant 8kb; if you need to send larger messages to your application roles, you can send the URI to a blob in the message body instead, and make a separate call to retrieve the desired content.

Tables

Azure stores nonrelational, tabular data in Entity-Attribute-Value (EAV) format. This means that saved entities can exist in many representations depending on the format requested; there is no fixed table *schema* as you would find in a SQL Server table. An EAV table is more like a Dictionary class instance, relating attribute keys to their values. Because tables have no schema, they also have no concept of relationship, so it is impossible to join against other tables to locate specific content. This may not feel natural at first, but the use of EAV was a deliberate choice, as EAV design is highly scalable and performs well in the cloud, compared to relational table design. The REST API for Azure tables is implemented using *ADO.NET Data Services*, another Microsoft technology introduced in 2007 to provide the means to host existing data, whether that data is relational or nonrelational, behind RESTful services in a simple and secure manner. Because you can leverage existing .NET tools to consume ADO.NET Data Services directly, you can avoid mapping the more complex data representations used for Azure tables returned as XML, as you would map a Twitter entity representation, and focus only on creating simple objects that are converted to XML and back automatically.

SQL Server Data Services (SSDS) Offers Relational Data on Azure

Though Twiticism does not require a relational data structure, many data-rich applications do. SQL Server Data Services is an emerging Azure technology to provide a SQL-like experience in the cloud, and, as with Azure tables, is accessible through the ADO.NET Data Services API. For more information, you can visit `http://msdn` `.microsoft.com/en-us/sqlserver/dataservices/default.aspx`.

Debugging

Web and worker roles you create in Visual Studio behave as the Web Application and Console Application project types, respectively. This means you can choose the default start-up project in your solution and debug normally; this works well if you are testing roles using live Azure services on the web, but will not work if you haven't yet deployed your application. To mitigate this, you can also run the Azure project itself, which will create a specialized development environment to simulate a hosted cloud application; this environment is called the *Development Fabric*. In the fabric, all storage and hosted services are simulated, but provide a consistent experience for debugging. Figure 10-4 shows the Development Fabric in action, displaying the role initialization process for the Twiticism web role.

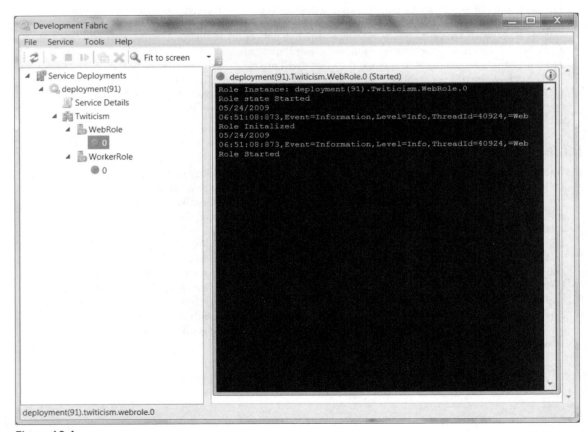

Figure 10-4

When Visual Studio starts a new debugging session for an Azure application, an instance of the Development Fabric will run in parallel, after ensuring a SQL Server database for local storage exists; if it does not exist, it will create one on the spot before running the development server, as shown in Figure 10-5.

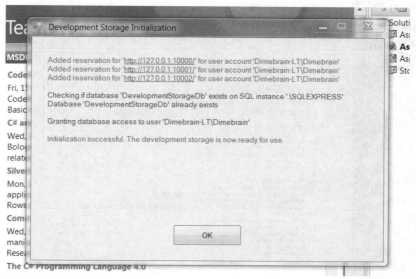

Figure 10-5

Logging

Logging is a cornerstone of development practice, and Azure provides a specialized class, `RoleManager`, for writing log messages at the alert, error, warning, information, and verbose log levels. The following short snippet demonstrates using this class to log a message when running in the fabric or in the cloud.

```
var message = "I don't think she can take much more of this, Captain!";
if (RoleManager.IsRoleManagerRunning)
{
    RoleManager.WriteToLog("Warning", message);
}
else
{
    Console.WriteLine(message);
}
```

Although the Development Fabric provides a direct console output view for messages logged using `RoleManager`, there is currently no automated way to obtain log messages after being registered. To retrieve a copy of the logs for a deployed Azure instance, use the *Configuration* button on your Azure services portal provided under the desired deployment, and select *Copy Logs* from the top of the configuration management page, as shown in Figure 10-6. This process will create a copy of the logs and store it as a blob within your Azure storage account. When this completes, you will need to interact with the blob API to retrieve the auto-generated log container and download the data.

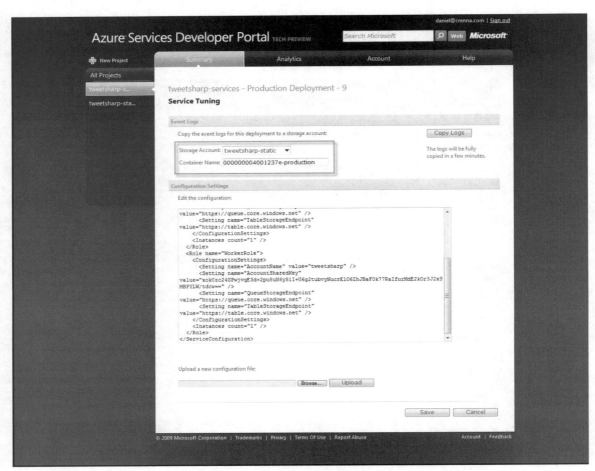

Figure 10-6

Run Visual Studio as an Administrator

The Azure Development Fabric requires elevated permissions to set up a simulated cloud environment for debugging your applications in Visual Studio. It is helpful to set up a shortcut on your desktop that automatically runs Visual Studio with administrator privileges to avoid forgetting and requiring a reboot of your development environment.

It's important to note that the development of Twiticism is directly against live Azure Storage Services. Azure also provides the Development Fabric, which is a locally scoped environment for building and testing Azure applications. The most important difference between the local fabric and a real Azure application is that a SQL Server database is created on the development host machine to stand in for

Azure storage; it is dangerous to assume that the genuine storage service will look or behave similar to this temporary replacement. However, because Azure will launch as a paid service, it is helpful to know how to run your application locally while still under development, to avoid incurring costs while developing, especially for bandwidth intensive applications that use storage regularly. Generally, switching from real Azure services to the Development Fabric is a painless process, only involving changes to your configuration file that maps the storage endpoints outlined earlier.

Creating a New Azure Application

To start a new Azure project, select the Cloud Service Project type and choose a new Web and Worker Cloud Service template, shown in Figure 10-7. The template will automatically set up a project tree that includes a web role and worker role, with the necessary configuration files to build out your services.

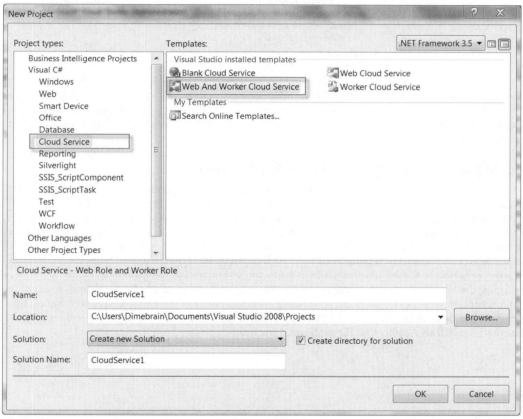

Figure 10-7

The project tree includes role management under the Roles folder, where you can add and remove new roles, as well as `ServiceDefinition.csdef` and `ServiceConfiguration.cscfg` files for setting up meta-data for your cloud environment. You can also publish your Azure application directly from the solution by choosing the root *Cloud Service Project*. The project tree for Twiticism is displayed in Figure 10-8.

Figure 10-8

From this point, development should feel familiar, and you can make good progress on your application ideas without considering Azure deployment details, until you need to start communicating across your roles to perform work. The next few sections will cover the Azure services that Twiticism will use to manage state.

Deploying and Promoting an Azure Application

After you have an application you are ready to see running in the cloud, Windows Azure Tools for Visual Studio provides an integrated experience for publishing your application in two files: the application package and a configuration file. To publish an Azure application, first select Publish from the Azure project's context menu that appears when you right-click the project itself. After the process completes, the folder containing your deployment files automatically opens in Windows, so you have a handy reference point for selecting your files. At this point, Windows will also launch your default browser, pointing to the Azure portal site. If you want to streamline the process even further, you can configure the Project Properties section of your Azure application to include the unique application ID that appears on your portal page for your hosted service, next to the unique URL; after you do this, the portal should open to the exact Azure project page you wish to deploy to. Figure 10-9 shows the Azure project page with an Application ID configured for this purpose.

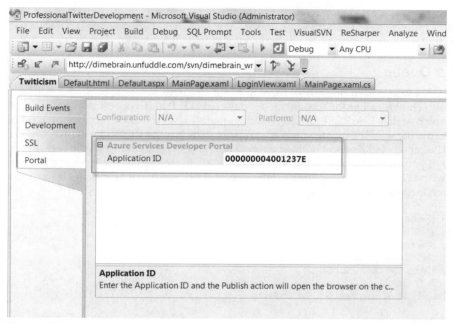

Figure 10-9

After the portal page opens, you will see two major deployment sections labelled *Production* and *Staging*, showing information about the state of each. Each Azure project supports these two independent environments to facilitate good development practice and to provide a way to quickly and easily transition from production code to updated staging code for both update and rollback scenarios. If an Azure instance is already running or initialized in the staging environment, you must delete it before publishing new code. Figure 10-2 showed the page that manages this process.

Production code must always come from the result of a promotion from staging to production, and existing production deployments are swapped when a new staging deployment is moved over an existing production deployment. To deploy new code to the staging environment, you simply select each of the available file input dialogs for the project deployment and configuration files, and upload both. After this is complete and Azure has successfully provisioned the environment, you can start the new code and test it, either through the full production URL, if applicable, or with a new GUID-based URL you can use privately while testing your new build in the staging environment.

Working with Azure Queues

An Azure queue is a collection of messages, with access controlled so that messages are either put into the queue or removed from the queue from processing in a first-in, first-out sequence; this is a core concept in computing, and is most like a line-up at a fast food restaurant, where *first come, first served*. This storage strategy allows multiple web and worker roles to both contribute messages to queues as well as process them, without requiring knowledge of the source of the message itself, which is essential in scalable architecture — a role does its job, whether there are no messages, or millions. Because messages must be destroyed to remove them from their place in the queue, Azure provides a visibility indicator that temporarily removes a message from sight for a configurable window of time while a role

355

is processing a message. When the role is finished with the message it must destroy it if the intent is not to have other similar roles perform work on the same message; if other factors prevent a successful operation, the message's invisibility will time out and will take it back to its original place in line.

Creating a Queue

The next code example demonstrates a method to create a new Azure queue under your account, using the base class shown earlier for account credentials. An HTTP PUT request is signed using the extension method shown earlier. The REST URI for creating queues is your hosted services queue endpoint, in addition to the name of the queue you wish to create, which is the RESTful resource you intend to address. The server will respond with an empty HTTP 201 (Created) message if queue creation is successful; if you attempt to create the same queue more than once, you will receive the same empty response with HTTP 204 (No Content), indicating that no additional processing occurred on the server because queue names must be unique.

```
using System;
using System.Net;
using System.Diagnostics;
using Twiticism.Shared;
using Wrox.Twitter.NUrl;

public class AzureQueue : AzureBase
{
    public void CreateQueue()
    {
        // Build an Azure endpoint URL with the queue action,
        // and ensure that the queue name is expressed in lower case
        const string createQueue = "myqueue";
        var url = string.Format(AzureStorageUrlBase,
                        AccountName,
                        "queue",
                        createQueue);

        // Create and sign a new request
        var request = (HttpWebRequest)WebRequest.Create(url);
        request.Method = "PUT";
        request.ContentLength = 0; // Provide an explicit length
        request.SignWithSharedKey(AccountName,
                        createQueue,
                        AccountSharedKey);

        // Use a modified version of NUrl to make the request
        var response = request.ExecutePut(new byte[]{});
        Console.WriteLine(response);

        // Ensure that Azure returned HTTP 201 (Created) if a queue was
        // created, or HTTP 204 (NoContent) if the queue already exists
        Assert.IsNotNull(NUrl.LastResponseStatusCode);

        Console.WriteLine("{0}:{1}", Convert.ToInt32(NUrl.LastResponseStatusCode),
            NUrl.LastResponseStatusDescription);

    ;
    }
}
```

Enhancing NUrl for Custom Authorization

In the preceding unit test example, NUrl was used in a new way to help test the HTTP status codes returned from Azure, as well as provide extension method exposure for the ExecutePut method, previously hidden in the NUrl implementation. Because you need to sign all Azure requests with a shared key, you can modify NUrl for this use.

Expose Execution Methods as Public Extension Methods, and Add Properties to Track The Previous Request'S Response

You can easily change the signatures of each private request execution call, switching them to public and adding this keyword to facilitate calling the static method directly on an instance of an HttpWebRequest similar to the ones you need to create to consume the Azure API. The following example shows this complete for the ExecutePut method:

```csharp
public static string ExecutePut(this WebRequest request, byte[]
content)
{
    Console.WriteLine("PUT: {0}", request.RequestUri);

    ClearLastResponse();

    try
    {
        using (var stream = request.GetRequestStream())
        {
            stream.Write(content, 0, content.Length);

            using (var response = request.GetResponse())
            {
                SetLastResponse(response);

                using (
                    var reader =
                        new StreamReader(response.
                            GetResponseStream()))
                {
                    var result = reader.ReadToEnd();
                    return result;
                }
            }
        }
    }
    catch (WebException ex)
    {
        return HandleWebException(ex);
    }
}

public static HttpStatusCode? LastResponseStatusCode
```

(continued)

```
{
    get; private set;
}

public static string LastResponseStatusDescription
{
    get; private set;
}

public static void ClearLastResponse()
{
    LastResponseStatusCode = null;
    LastResponseStatusDescription = null;
}

public static void SetLastResponse(WebResponse response)
{
    var httpResponse = (HttpWebResponse)response;
    LastResponseStatusCode = httpResponse.StatusCode;
    LastResponseStatusDescription = httpResponse.StatusDescription;
}
```

Deleting a Queue

Deleting a queue is identical to creating a queue, with the exception of the HTTP verb, which is in line with REST principles. To test delete operations, this example is a refactoring of the previous creation test, but uses an HTTP DELETE verb instead when building the request. Similarly, Azure will return HTTP 200 (OK) if the queue resource you specify is successfully removed and HTTP 203 (No Content) if the queue does not exist.

```
using System;
using System.Net;
using System.Diagnostics;
using Twiticism.Shared;
using Wrox.Twitter.NUrl;

public class AzureQueue : AzureBase
{
    private static HttpWebRequest TestRestWithAzureQueue(string httpMethod,
                                                         string queueName)
    {
        // Build an Azure endpoint URL with the queue action
        var url = string.Format(AzureStorageUrlBase,
                                AccountName,
                                "queue",
                                queueName);

        // Create and sign a new request
        var request = (HttpWebRequest) WebRequest.Create(url);
        request.Method = httpMethod.ToUpperInvariant();
```

```
        request.ContentLength = 0; // Provide an explicit length
        request.SignWithSharedKey(AccountName,
                                  queueName,
                                  AccountSharedKey);


        return request;
    }

    public void DeleteQueue()
    {
        var request = TestRestWithAzureQueue("DELETE", "myqueue");

        // Use a modified version of NUrl to make the request
        var response = request.ExecuteDelete();
        Console.WriteLine(response);

        Console.WriteLine("{0}:{1}",
                            Convert.ToInt32(NUrl.LastResponseStatusCode),
                            NUrl.LastResponseStatusDescription);

        // Ensure that Azure returned HTTP 204 (No Content) if a queue was
        // deleted or doesn't exist; no distinction is made here
        Debug.Assert(NUrl.LastResponseStatusCode != null);
        Debug.Assert(NUrl.LastResponseStatusCode == HttpStatusCode.OK ||
                    NUrl.LastResponseStatusCode ==
                    HttpStatusCode.NoContent);
    }
}
```

Listing All Queues on an Account

To round out your understanding of queues you can call a resource query to list all the queues that exist under your account credentials, which will return an XML representation of the results. The following code performs yet another REST call against your account's public queue endpoint, but this time using an HTTP GET verb and a query string containing a command to Azure to list queues.

```
using System;
using System.Net;
using System.Diagnostics;
using Twiticism.Shared;
using Wrox.Twitter.NUrl;

public class AzureQueue : AzureBase
{
    public void ListAllQueues()
    {
        // Build an Azure endpoint URL with the queue action
        const string listQueues = "?comp=list";
        var url = string.Format(AzureStorageUrlBase,
                                AccountName,
                                "queue",
                                listQueues);

        var request = (HttpWebRequest) WebRequest.Create(url);
```

```
        request.Method = "GET";
        request.ContentLength = 0;
        request.SignWithSharedKey(AccountName,
                                  listQueues,
                                  AccountSharedKey);

        var response = request.ExecuteGet();
        Console.WriteLine(response);
    }
}
```

The result of this REST call is an XML fragment containing the queues that exist, shown here:

```
GET: http://twiticism.queue.core.windows.net/?comp=list
<?xml version="1.0" encoding="utf-8"?>
<EnumerationResults
    AccountName="http://twiticism.queue.core.windows.net/">
    <Queues>
        <Queue>
            <QueueName>guc</QueueName>
            <Url>http://twiticism.queue.core.windows.net/guc</Url>
        </Queue>
        <Queue>
            <QueueName>myqueue</QueueName>
            <Url>http://twiticism.queue.core.windows.net/myqueue</Url>
        </Queue>
    </Queues>
    <NextMarker />
</EnumerationResults>
```

Working with Azure Tables

Azure tables use a similar API, but have different authentication needs. Although shared key encryption is still supported, the signature method is slightly different: no line is dedicated to the Date format, only x-ms-date is used, and the value of x-ms-date is written without the header name. To accommodate this additional format, you can modify the signature extension method code to function as a generic signing utility. In addition to this change, this is the first time you will post data to the Azure service, and the signature method provides a line dedicated to an MD5 hash value for a reason — when you send content, you can enhance the reliability of your service call by providing the MD5 hash equivalent in the request for the content you are sending. In the next code listing, overloaded methods are used to provide a way to switch from standard shared key signing to signing with Azure tables, as well as introduce the MD5 hashing feature for any requests that post content.

```
using System;
using System.Net;
using System.Security.Cryptography;
using System.Text;

namespace Twiticism.Shared
{
    public static class SharedKeyExtensions
```

```
{
    // This is the standard Shared Key signature
    private const string SignatureFormat
        = "{0}\n{1}\n{2}\n\nx-ms-date:{3}\n/{4}/{5}";

    // Tables uses an altered version of the shared key format
    private const string SignatureFormatForTables
        = "{0}\n{1}\n{2}\n{3}\n/{4}/{5}";

    public static void SignWithSharedKey(this HttpWebRequest request,
                                         string account,
                                         string action,
                                         string key)
    {
        // Sign a request with no content body
        SignWithSharedKey(request,
                          account,
                          action,
                          null,
                          key,
                          SignatureFormat);
    }

    public static void SignWithSharedKey(this HttpWebRequest request,
                                         string account,
                                         string action,
                                         string content,
                                         string key)
    {
        // Sign a request with content to post
        SignWithSharedKey(request,
                          account,
                          action,
                          content,
                          key,
                          SignatureFormat);
    }

    public static void SignWithSharedKeyForTables(
        this HttpWebRequest request,
        string account,
        string action,
        string content,
        string key)
    {
        // Sign a request with the tables signature format,
        // and content to post
        SignWithSharedKey(request,
                          account,
                          action,
                          content,
                          key,
                          SignatureFormatForTables);
    }
```

```
public static void SignWithSharedKey(this HttpWebRequest request,
                                     string account,
                                     string action,
                                     string content,
                                     string key,
                                     string format)
{
    // Build a formatted date for the header
    // (use RFC 1183 formatting)
    var date = DateTime.UtcNow.ToString("R");
    request.Headers.Add("x-ms-date", date);

    // Hash any content for reliability using MD5
    string md5 = null;
    if (!String.IsNullOrEmpty(content))
    {
        md5 = HashWith<MD5CryptoServiceProvider>(content);
        request.Headers.Add("Content-MD5", md5 ?? "");
    }

    // Build the signature base from known elements,
    // including the selected format string
    var method = request.Method.ToUpperInvariant();
    var signatureBase = string.Format(format,
                                      method,
                                      md5 ?? "",
                                      request.ContentType,
                                      date,
                                      account,
                                      action);

    // Generate a hash value for the signature
    var hash = HashWith<HMACSHA256>(signatureBase, key);

    // Sign the request
    var header = String.Format("SharedKey {0}:{1}", account, hash);

    // Set the request's authorization header
    request.Headers.Add("Authorization", header);
}

// A generic hashing method lets you specify the type
private static string HashWith<T>(string input)
    where T : HashAlgorithm
{
    return HashWith<T>(input, null);
}

private static string HashWith<T>(string input, string sharedKey)
    where T : HashAlgorithm
```

```
    {
        var inputData = Encoding.UTF8.GetBytes(input);
        var keyData = Convert.FromBase64String(sharedKey ?? "");

        // HMAC-SHA1 uses the shared key to sign
        HashAlgorithm algorithm = null;
        if (typeof (T).Name.Equals("HMACSHA256"))
        {
            algorithm = new HMACSHA256(keyData);
        }

        // MD5 does not need a key to sign
        if (typeof (T).Name.Equals("MD5CryptoServiceProvider"))
        {
            algorithm = new MD5CryptoServiceProvider();
        }

        if (algorithm == null)
        {
            return input;
        }

        var hash = algorithm.ComputeHash(inputData);
        return Convert.ToBase64String(hash);
    }
  }
}
```

Creating a Table

To create a table, you need to provide content for an HTTP POST request, as well as use the special authentication scheme previously provided. For complete API details you can visit http://msdn .microsoft.com/en-us/library/dd135729.aspx. By following that documentation you can pick out the XML format you need to send along with the call to request a new table creation, which is listed here:

```
<?xml version="1.0" encoding="utf-8" standalone="yes"?>
<entry
    xmlns:d="http://schemas.microsoft.com/ado/2007/08/dataservices"
    xmlns:m="http://schemas.microsoft.com/ado/2007/08/dataservices/metadata"
    xmlns="http://www.w3.org/2005/Atom">
    <title />
    <updated>2009-03-18T11:48:34.9840639-07:00</updated>
    <author>
      <name/>
    </author>
    <id/>
    <content type="application/xml">
      <m:properties>
        <d:TableName>mytable</d:TableName>
      </m:properties>
    </content>
</entry>
```

The first thing to notice about the prescribed format is the use of a specific date format for the updated element that functions as a timestamp whether the table was created or updated, and does not need to be the same time as the signed request that delivers it. The date format is a familiar one, as it's the Atom standard that is used when working with Atom data in Twitter. In fact, Azure tables use the Atom format for all interaction with tables. To create a table, pre-format the required Atom fragment with the desired table name and date and send it with an HTTP POST, which is demonstrated in the next code listing:

```
using System;
using System.Net;
using System.Text;
using Twiticism.Shared;
using Wrox.Twitter.NUrl;

public class AzureTables : AzureBase
{
    // 2009-05-19T19:37:30.0990000Z
    private const string AtomDateFormat =
        "yyyy-MM-ddTHH:mm:ss.fffffffZ";

    // A format string containing the table creation data
    private const string TableTemplate =
@"<?xml version=""1.0"" encoding=""utf-8""?>
<entry
xmlsn:d=""http://schemas.microsoft.com/ado/2007/08/dataservices""
xmlsn:m=""http://schemas.microsoft.com/ado/2007/08/dataservices/metadata""
xmlsn=""http://www.w3.org/2005/Atom"">
<title />
<updated>{0}</updated>
<author>
<name />
</author>
<id />
<content type=""application/xml"">
<m:properties>
  <d:TableName>{1}</d:TableName>
</m:properties>
</content>
</entry>";

    public void CreateTable()
    {
        const string tableName = "mytable";

        // Point to the Tables endpoint
        var url = string.Format(AzureStorageUrlBase,
                                AccountName,
                                "table",
                                "Tables");

        // Prepare table data to POST
        var date = DateTime.UtcNow;
        var content = string.Format(TableTemplate,
                                    date.ToString(AtomDateFormat),
```

```
                                             tableName);

            var data = Encoding.ASCII.GetBytes(content);

            // Build a new request (declare it as Atom format)
            var request = (HttpWebRequest) WebRequest.Create(url);
            request.Method = "POST";
            request.ContentType = "application/atom+xml";
            request.ContentLength = content.Length;

            // Prepare the request with table content to sign with MD5
            request.SignWithSharedKeyForTables(AccountName,
                                               "Tables",
                                               content,
                                               AccountSharedKey);

            // Send the request and output the result
            var response = request.ExecutePost(data);
            Console.WriteLine(response);
        }
    }
```

The response for a successful table creation is a link back to the table, including the URI query needed to reference that table in further calls to add and retrieve entities. The endpoint for this call also includes the `Tables` resource as part of the URI.

```
POST: http://tweetsharp.table.core.windows.net/Tables
<?xml version="1.0" encoding="utf-8" standalone="yes"?>
<entry xml:base="http://tweetsharp.table.core.windows.net/"
xmlns:d="http://schemas.microsoft.com/ado/2007/08/dataservices"
xmlns:m="http://schemas.microsoft.com/ado/2007/08/dataservices/metadata"
xmlns="http://www.w3.org/2005/Atom">
  <id>http://tweetsharp.table.core.windows.net/Tables('mytable')</id>
  <title type="text"></title>
  <updated>2009-05-24T18:33:01Z</updated>
  <author>
    <name />
  </author>
  <link rel="edit" title="Tables" href="Tables('mytable')" />
  <category term="tweetsharp.Tables"
scheme="http://schemas.microsoft.com/
ado/2007/08/dataservices/scheme" />
  <content type="application/xml">
    <m:properties>
      <d:TableName>mytable</d:TableName>
    </m:properties>
  </content>
</entry>
```

Introducing `StorageClient`

Up to this point you have worked directly with Azure's REST APIs to accomplish tasks, and it is important to recognize that this, as with working with the Twitter API, at its lowest level is how you work with any RESTful service. Having this knowledge is very useful when you work with any abstraction or tool that hides these details, such as TweetSharp, because you will be better able to diagnose issues or extend code to meet your needs. Also, REST is meant to be simple, and although the specific security requirements and feature surface of any API takes some learning, a lot of work is done for you when you have confidence working with REST directly. That said, the Windows Azure SDK provides an example library called `StorageClient` that you can use to hide the details of making REST calls. The `StorageClient` example code is located in its own folder within the compressed `samples` `.zip` file included where you installed the Windows Azure SDK. To use `StorageClient`, you must provide the same Azure account details used previously in a base class in your Azure application's configuration for the library code to pick up and use that information to sign requests. You must first define the settings you need in the `ServiceDefinition.csdef` file that accompanies a new Azure project. An example of the settings to define for both web and worker roles is listed next. At this stage you are only defining what settings your application should look for, not providing any values.

```xml
<?xml version="1.0" encoding="utf-8"?>
<ServiceDefinition
  name="Twiticism"
  xmlns="http://schemas.microsoft.com/ServiceHosting/2008/10/ServiceDefinition">
  <WebRole name="WebRole">
    <InputEndpoints>
      <InputEndpoint name="HttpIn" protocol="http" port="80" />
    </InputEndpoints>
    <ConfigurationSettings>
      <Setting name="AccountName"/>
      <Setting name="AccountSharedKey"/>
      <Setting name="BlobStorageEndpoint"/>
      <Setting name="QueueStorageEndpoint"/>
      <Setting name="TableStorageEndpoint"/>
    </ConfigurationSettings>
  </WebRole>
  <WorkerRole name="WorkerRole">
    <ConfigurationSettings>
      <Setting name="AccountName"/>
      <Setting name="AccountSharedKey"/>
      <Setting name="BlobStorageEndpoint"/>
      <Setting name="QueueStorageEndpoint"/>
      <Setting name="TableStorageEndpoint"/>
    </ConfigurationSettings>
  </WorkerRole>
</ServiceDefinition>
```

After you've defined the requisite settings, you can define them by name and value in the `ServiceConfiguration.cscfg` file that lives alongside the definition file in an Azure project. Notice that the endpoints are not defined by account name explicitly, but rather by their secure, root endpoint values.

```xml
<?xml version="1.0"?>
<ServiceConfiguration
    serviceName="Twiticism"
    xmlns="http://schemas.microsoft.com/ServiceHosting/2008/10/
ServiceConfiguration">
  <Role name="WebRole">
```

```
      <Instances count="1"/>
      <ConfigurationSettings>
        <Setting name="AccountName" value="twiticism"/>
        <Setting name="AccountSharedKey" value="..."/>
        <Setting name="QueueStorageEndpoint" value="https://queue.core.windows.net" />
        <Setting name="TableStorageEndpoint" value="https://table.core.windows.net" />
      </ConfigurationSettings>
    </Role>
    <Role name="WorkerRole">
      <Instances count="1"/>
      <ConfigurationSettings>
        <Setting name="AccountName" value="twiticism" />
        <Setting name="AccountSharedKey" value="..." />
        <Setting name="QueueStorageEndpoint" value="https://queue.core.windows.net" />
        <Setting name="TableStorageEndpoint" value="https://table.core.windows.net" />
        <Setting name="BlobStorageEndpoint" value="https://blob.core.windows.net" />
      </ConfigurationSettings>
    </Role>
  </ServiceConfiguration>
```

Working with Table Entities

Because REST services normally returned widely accepted micro-formats (such as XML, JSON, RSS, and Atom) to represent entities, you have a familiar problem of requiring a way to move quickly from the returned representation to .NET objects to perform work. As you can see in the following example output of Azure table results, parsing the values into a convenience class would require a lot of time and effort. Fortunately, this verbose XML data representation is not new to Azure; it is the same format used by ADO.NET Data Services and a set of client libraries for both Silverlight and ASP.NET exist to help convert XML results to data classes. The `StorageClient` SDK example builds on those ADO.NET Data Services offerings, adding the ability to sign requests. To create a new entity to store in an Azure table, you can start by defining a simple class similar to the one here, which is used later to store user data in a cache.

```csharp
using System;

namespace Twiticism.Shared.Model
{
    // This class represents an id -> screen_name mapping
    public class UserCacheEntry
    {
        public int Id { get; set; }
        public string ScreenName { get; set; }
        public DateTime Updated { get; set; }
    }
}
```

There's nothing exciting about this plain container class, but you need to perform a few tasks to enable it for storage. The first step is to inherit from the `TableStorageEntity` class. This class provides the two required keys that Azure tables use to track an entity across storage instances: the `RowKey` and `PartitionKey`. The `RowKey` functions similar to a relational database key, while the `PartitionKey` contains a reference to the particular slice of data the entity lives in, because storage can span multiple sites. For this demonstration you only need to set a single `PartitionKey`. The following code shows what your entity will look like after it's inherited from `TableStorageEntity`:

```
using System;
using Microsoft.Samples.ServiceHosting.StorageClient;

namespace Twiticism.Shared.Model
{
    // This class represents an id -> screen_name mapping
    public class UserCacheEntry : TableStorageEntity
    {
        private int _id;

        public int Id
        {
            get
            {
                return _id;
            }
            set
            {
                _id = value;
                RowKey = _id.ToString();
            }
        }

        public string ScreenName { get; set; }

        public DateTime Updated { get; set; }

        public UserCacheEntry()
        {
            // You could get this from an instance-level config
            PartitionKey = "users";
        }
    }
}
```

Your class doesn't look much different after the fact; it's inheriting from `TableStorageEntity`, a backing field keeping the `Id` and `RowKey` synchronized, and a constructor declaration to set the `PartitionKey` where the entity is stored. Now that your entity is primed for table storage, you need to create a new data context you can use to query, save, and delete instances. This is quite easy; create a new class that derives from `TableStorageDataServiceContext`, and create a property to build a new query instance.

```
using System.Data.Services.Client;
using Microsoft.Samples.ServiceHosting.StorageClient;

namespace Twiticism.Shared.Model
{
    public class TwiticismContext : TableStorageDataServiceContext
    {
        public DataServiceQuery<UserCacheEntry> UserCacheTable
        {
```

```
                        get
                        {
                            return CreateQuery<UserCacheEntry>("users");
                        }
                    }
                }
            }
```

With a context in place, you can adopt a style similar to LINQ to SQL to access a new
`TwiticismContext` to work with your table entities. You can further streamline this process by creating
a `UserCacheRepository` class that performs the work against the new `UserCacheTable` context.
The following listing shows repository methods to get, create, and update records. You'll notice that the
underlying ADO.NET Data Services `DataServiceContext` class that provides the persistence features
does not support all LINQ query operators. For a breakdown of which features are supported, you can
visit `http://msdn.microsoft.com/en-us/library/dd179445.aspx`.

```csharp
using System;
using System.Collections.Generic;
using System.Linq;
using Microsoft.ServiceHosting.ServiceRuntime;

namespace Twiticism.Shared.Model
{
    // Manages ADO.NET Data Service persistence against
    // The "users" Azure Table Storage collection.
    public class UserCacheRepository
    {
        private const string TableName = "users";

        // Get a single entity by ID
        public UserCacheEntry GetById(int id)
        {
            var db = new TwiticismContext();
            var entry = db.UserCacheTable
                // SingleOrDefault is not supported directly,
                // but you can use Where and query over
                // that result using LINQ extension methods
                .Where(u => u.Id == id)
                .SingleOrDefault();

            return entry;
        }

        // Get a list of entities matching the given IDs
        public IEnumerable<UserCacheEntry> GetByIds
            (IEnumerable<int> ids)
        {
            var db = new TwiticismContext();

            var entries = db.UserCacheTable
                .Where(u => ids.Contains(u.Id));

            foreach (var entry in entries)
```

```
            {
                if (entry != null)
                {
                    yield return entry;
                }
            }
        }

        // Get an entry by screen name
        public UserCacheEntry GetByScreenName(string screenName)
        {
            var db = new TwiticismContext();
            var entry = db.UserCacheTable
                .Where(u => u.ScreenName == screenName)
                .SingleOrDefault();
            return entry;
        }

        // Remove an entry
        public bool RemoveEntry(UserCacheEntry entry)
        {
            try
            {
                var db = new TwiticismContext();
                db.AttachTo(TableName, entry);
                db.DeleteObject(entry);
                db.SaveChanges();

                return true;
            }
            catch (Exception ex)
            {
                RoleManager.WriteToLog("Error", ex.Message);
                return false;
            }
        }

        // Update an existing entry
        public bool UpdateEntry(UserCacheEntry entry)
        {
            try
            {
                var db = new TwiticismContext();
                db.AttachTo(TableName, entry);
                db.UpdateObject(entry);

                return true;
            }
            catch (Exception ex)
```

```
        {
            RoleManager.WriteToLog("Error", ex.Message);
            return false;
        }
    }


    // Add a new entry
    public bool AddEntry(int id, string screenName)
    {
        try
        {
            var db = new TwiticismContext();
            var entry = new UserCacheEntry
                        {
                            Id = id,
                            ScreenName = screenName,
                            Updated = DateTime.UtcNow
                        };
            db.AddObject(TableName, entry);
            db.SaveChanges();

            return true;
        }
        catch (Exception ex)
        {
            RoleManager.WriteToLog("Error", ex.Message);
            return false;
        }
    }
}
}
```

Remember, you don't need to use the `StorageClient` sample code to access Azure tables, you can build your own tools using the ADO.NET Data Services client libraries by referencing `System.Data .Services.Client`, but it is a useful tool for getting started with Azure, and the majority of your application needs are covered with its use. You don't need to feel limited by its specific implementation; it's just REST services under the hood after all. In fact, MSDN recommends you don't use the `StorageClient` example for production quality applications, as it is not designed for performance or stability. You can continue to build from the authentication examples you already know to build your own implementation for storage access if your needs go beyond the basic demonstration of the `StorageClient` library.

Hosting a Twitter Proxy in the Cloud

As you are now well aware, Twitter does not provide a way to make cross-domain calls from a client-side application across the full spectrum of API calls. Because Twiticism is a Silverlight 3 application, it will need a way to make these calls through a proxy, while remaining hosted in the Azure cloud. Because web roles are similar to classic ASP.NET web applications, it is possible to host a Twitter proxy between the Silverlight client instance and the originating logical server in much the same way as you might with any web application scenario using WCF services. However, protracting services in this way requires you to define a method for each scenario your application has for consuming data from the Twitter API.

Instead, you can write an `HttpModule` that runs on your web role, and forwards all traffic intended for Twitter, returning the appropriate responses. Before starting, remember that Silverlight places the following security restrictions on your calls using `WebClient` or `HttpWebRequest`:

❏ If you are sending a GET call, you cannot provide *any* custom headers.

❏ If you are using POST, you can only send custom headers and a subset of existing request headers, but cannot, for example, set the authorization header directly.

❏ Any cross-domain call must first obtain approval from a cross-domain policy file at the endpoint.

Because of these restrictions, you cannot provide authentication information to Twitter's API directly. Instead, you can use pre-established custom headers to stand in for real HTTP headers, and set them accordingly when the module processes the incoming request. The headers that TweetSharp currently recognizes are covered in Table 10-2. You can always provide your own if you're writing a custom header, but these values will allow you to work with TweetSharp directly in Silverlight without requiring WCF services in between.

Table 10-2: Custom Twitter Proxy Values Supported by TweetSharp

Header	Description
X-Twitter-Auth	Use this value to provide Basic or OAuth authentication values.
X-Twitter-Method	Because custom headers are only allowed via a POST call, if you want to send a GET or DELETE to Twitter's API, you need to set it explicitly here.
X-Twitter-Accept	To support compression, set this value to include gzip, deflate, or both.
X-Twitter-Agent	This value provides the equivalent of UserAgent if you need to tell Twitter who you are, which is the case when you want to identify your application to the Search API.

The next listing will provide code to set up your proxy. The `HttpModule` intercepts every incoming request and inspects whether it is intended for the proxy endpoint, i.e., the URL ends with /proxy/. Next, all the appropriate headers are mapped to a new, server-generated `HttpWebRequest` that does not suffer Silverlight's limitations; any custom headers needed are found and preferred over the headers found on the request itself. Finally, NUrl is leveraged again to send the newly created request to Twitter, to process the response, and write that response out for the original caller to consume.

```
using System;
using System.Collections.Generic;
using System.Net;
using System.Web;
using Microsoft.ServiceHosting.ServiceRuntime;
using Wrox.Twitter.NUrl;

namespace Twiticism_WebRole.Proxy
```

```
{
    public class TwitterProxyModule : IHttpModule
    {
        // These headers are not standardized and
        // may change depending on the proxy you are using
        private const string ProxyAcceptHeader = "X-Twitter-Accept";
        private const string ProxyAgentHeader = "X-Twitter-Agent";
        private const string ProxyAuthorizationHeader = "X-Twitter-Auth";
        private const string ProxyMethodHeader = "X-Twitter-Method";

        // These URL authority slugs handle Twitter's branching API
        private const string TwitterAuthority = "http://twitter.com";
        private const string TwitterSearchAuthority =
            "http://search.twitter.com";

        // These are headers to avoid setting on the proxy call
        private static readonly ICollection<string>
            _ignoredHeaders
                = new[]
                    {
                        // restricted
                        "Connection",
                        "Keep-Alive",
                        "Accept",
                        "Host",
                        "User-Agent",
                        // set explicitly
                        "Content-Length",
                        "Content-Type",
                        "Accept-Encoding",
                        "Authorization",
                        // custom headers
                        ProxyMethodHeader,
                        ProxyAuthorizationHeader,
                        ProxyAcceptHeader,
                        ProxyAgentHeader
                    };

        #region IHttpModule Members

        public void Dispose() { }

        public void Init(HttpApplication context)
        {
            context.BeginRequest += ContextBeginRequest;
        }

        #endregion

        private static void ContextBeginRequest(object sender, EventArgs e)
```

```
{
    var context = (HttpApplication) sender;
    var request = context.Request;

    var path = request.Path.ToLowerInvariant();
    if (!path.StartsWith("/proxy/"))
    {
        // This is not a proxy request
        return;
    }

    // Check to see if this is a search query
    var authority = TwitterAuthority;
    if (path.Replace("/proxy/", "").StartsWith("search"))
    {
        authority = TwitterSearchAuthority;
    }

    var message =
        String.Format("Proxy request handled for {0} from {1}.",
                    request.Path,
                    request.UserHostAddress);

    if (RoleManager.IsRoleManagerRunning)
    {
        RoleManager.WriteToLog("Information", message);
    }
    else
    {
        Console.WriteLine(message);
    }

    // Build the Twitter destination URI and redirect
    var url =
        string.Concat(authority,
                    request.Url.AbsolutePath.Replace("/proxy/", "/"),
                    request.Url.Query,
                    request.Url.Fragment);

    string response;

    try
    {
        // Set stock properties for the proxied call
        var proxyRequest = (HttpWebRequest) WebRequest.Create(url);

        // Set the HTTP method, preferring a proxy header
        var methodOverride = request.Headers[ProxyMethodHeader];
        proxyRequest.Method = methodOverride != null
                                ? request.Headers[ProxyMethodHeader]
                                : request.HttpMethod;

        // Set the user agent, preferring a proxy header
```

```csharp
var userAgent = request.Headers[ProxyAgentHeader];
proxyRequest.UserAgent = userAgent != null
                            ? request.Headers[ProxyAgentHeader]
                            : request.UserAgent;

// Set compression support, preferring a proxy header
// Use compression if indicated
var acceptEncoding =
    request.Headers[ProxyAcceptHeader] ??
    request.Headers["Accept-Encoding"];

if (acceptEncoding != null)
{
    acceptEncoding = acceptEncoding.ToLower();
    if (acceptEncoding.Contains("gzip"))
    {
        proxyRequest.AutomaticDecompression =
            DecompressionMethods.GZip;
    }
    else if (acceptEncoding.Contains("deflate"))
    {
        proxyRequest.AutomaticDecompression =
            DecompressionMethods.Deflate;
    }
}

proxyRequest.ContentType = request.ContentType;
proxyRequest.ContentLength = request.ContentLength;
proxyRequest.Referer = request.UrlReferrer != null
                            ? request.UrlReferrer.ToString()
                            : null;
proxyRequest.KeepAlive = true;

// If the requester can't declare auth (Silverlight),
// pick it from a custom header; this overwrites and
// current authorization value
if (request.Headers[ProxyAuthorizationHeader] != null)
{
    proxyRequest.Headers["Authorization"]
        = request.Headers[ProxyAuthorizationHeader];
}

// Map remaining request headers
foreach (var header in request.Headers.Keys)
{
    var name = header.ToString();
    if (_ignoredHeaders.Contains(name))
    {
        continue;
    }

    var value = request.Headers[name];
    proxyRequest.Headers[name] = value;
}
```

```
                var stream = context.Request.InputStream;
                var content = new byte[context.Request.InputStream.Length];
                stream.Read(content, 0, (int) context.Request.InputStream.Length);

                response = RequestByProxy(proxyRequest, content);
            }
            catch (WebException ex)
            {
                response = ex.Message;
            }

            context.Response.ClearContent();
            context.Response.Write(response);
            context.Response.Flush();
            context.Response.End();
        }

        private static string RequestByProxy(WebRequest request, byte[] content)
        {
            switch (request.Method)
            {
                case "GET":
                    var get = request.ExecuteGet();
                    return get;
                case "POST":
                    var post = request.ExecutePost(content);
                    return post;
                default:
                    throw new NotImplementedException(
                        "Only GET and POST are supported.");
            }
        }
    }
}
```

The final step is to configure your web role to use the module by adding it to `web.config`. Here is an example of the values used for the Twiticism web role:

```
<system.web>
    <httpModules>
        <add name="ScriptModule"
            type="System.Web.Handlers.ScriptModule,
                System.Web.Extensions,
                Version=3.5.0.0,
                Culture=neutral,
                PublicKeyToken=31BF3856AD364E35"/>
        <!-- Proxy module processes all incoming requests -->
        <add name="TwitterProxyModule"
            type="Twiticism_WebRole.Proxy.TwitterProxyModule,
                Twiticism_WebRole,
                Version=1.0.0.0,
                Culture=neutral"/>
    </httpModules>
</system.web>
```

You now have a TweetSharp-compatible proxy running that you can use for all your Silverlight requests to Twitter. To use it, just structure any request intended for `http://twitter.com`, and send it to `http://myaccount.cloudapp.net` instead, where *myaccount* is the name of your Azure account running the web role hosting the proxy. Here is an example for using the proxy with TweetSharp:

```
var proxy = "http://myaccount.cloudapp.net";

var twitter = FluentTwitter.CreateRequest()
    .Configuration.UseTransparentProxy(proxy)
    .AuthenticateAs(Username, Password)
    .Statuses().Update("testing")
    .CallbackTo((s, e) => { ... });

twitter.RequestAsync();
```

Running a Global User Cache in the Cloud

In Chapter 7 you learned the value of storing your own user cache to effectively work with accounts with large numbers of friends and followers without reducing the user's experience due to the volume of API calls required to fill in the user graph. Twiticism could potentially leverage a global user cache built using TweetSharp and run as an Azure worker role to keep a large set of user mappings available close to the application, without having to use a user's limited API limit trying to track information about the user's followers and friends. Although Twiticism doesn't require this information, it still sends an Azure queue message for each new user it encounters to keep the global user cache process working to assemble the information. Building a reliable user cache involves considering a few key points:

❏ You should use a white-listed account or IP address when making calls to fetch users. Although the API method to fetch a user's details doesn't require authorization, it is still limited, which means you will quickly use up the default 100 API calls per hour granted to anonymous IP.

You can inspect the last response received for headers providing the current number of remaining hits, or make a second call to `/account/rate_limit_status` to obtain your response values.

❏ If you run out of API hits, make sure your caching code will wait for an API hit refresh rather than relentlessly repeating calls, which is a waste of yours and Twitter's valuable resources.

❏ Users do not normally change their screen name, so you do not have to constantly update their cache values; in this example, user data is stored for up to one day, at which point revisiting the user will result in an update to their entry.

The global user cache background process checks the Azure queue called *guc* for any messages, which only contain the screen name of a newly discovered user. This user becomes the root point for all caching operations. Twitter's social graphing API methods are then used to collect a list of all IDs for the user's followers and friends. Each ID received is checked against the current cache, and if a record for the ID doesn't exist or is older than a day, that user's details are fetched from Twitter and placed into the cache. After this process is complete for a user, the message passed into the queue is deleted, and the application goes to sleep for 10 seconds. When it wakes up, it will check the queue again, retrieving as many messages as it can (the maximum number of messages per queue request is currently 32). This design means you can feed the caching process users from any source, such as followers of your application or users from the public timeline. Over time, the cache will grow to cover most users, and your applications can check this source first for screen name data, falling back to the API only when a user isn't found. Of course, you can cache much more than the ID and screen name of a user, as in this example, including the entire user representation, if desired. Here is the complete code listing covering the global user caching worker role.

```csharp
using System;
using System.Collections.Generic;
using System.Linq;
using System.Threading;
using Dimebrain.TweetSharp.Extensions;
using Dimebrain.TweetSharp.Fluent;
using Dimebrain.TweetSharp.Model;
using Microsoft.Samples.ServiceHosting.StorageClient;
using Microsoft.ServiceHosting.ServiceRuntime;
using Twiticism.Shared.Model;

namespace Twiticism_WorkerRole
{
    public class WorkerRole : RoleEntryPoint
    {
        // These are the credentials of the white-listed account
        // used for collecting user data; you can also have your
        // IP address white-listed
        private const string TwitterPassword = "Password";
        private const string TwitterUsername = "Username";

        private static MessageQueue _queue;
        private static UserCacheRepository _repository;

        public override void Start()
        {
            RoleManager.WriteToLog("Information",
                             "Twiticism background processing started.");

            try
            {
                // Start the user caching process
                RunGlobalUserCache();
            }
            catch (Exception ex)
            {
                // It's a jungle out there, log any unexpected behavior
                // so you can account for it and refactor your code
                RoleManager.WriteToLog("Error", ex.StackTrace);
            }
        }

        private static void RunGlobalUserCache()
        {
            // Ensure the queue and table exist before caching
            ResolveQueue();
            ResolveTable();

            // Create a new instance of a repository to handle
            // saving and retrieving entries in the cache
```

```
    _repository = new UserCacheRepository();

    // Ensure the credentials used are valid; if not,
    // don't waste bandwidth on a doomed process
    var query = FluentTwitter.CreateRequest()
        .Accounts().VerifyCredentials();

    var response = query.Request();
    if (response.AsError() != null)
    {
        // Credentials are invalid
        RoleManager.WriteToLog("Error", "Invalid credentials.");
    }

    while (true)
    {
        // Check the queue for messages to process,
        // retrieving as many messages as possible;
        var messages = GetMessages(_queue);

        foreach (var message in messages)
        {
            // The message is the root screen name to cache
            var screenName = message.ContentAsString();

            // Log the message receipt
            var log = string.Format("Caching data for {0}.", screenName);
            RoleManager.WriteToLog("Information", log);

            try
            {
                // Update the cache with all user followers
                CacheFollowers(screenName);

                // Update the cache with all user friends
                CacheFriends(screenName);

                // Discard the message so it isn't processed again
                _queue.DeleteMessage(message);
            }
            catch (Exception ex)
            {
                // Log the error
                RoleManager.WriteToLog("Error", ex.StackTrace);

                // Ignore this message until it can be
                // processed correctly
                continue;
            }
        }

        // Wait ten seconds between executions
        Thread.Sleep(10000);
    }
}
```

```
        private static void CacheFollowers(string screenName)
        {
            // Obtain the social graph list of follower IDs
            // for the user in the message
            var query = FluentTwitter.CreateRequest()
                .Configuration.UseGzipCompression()
                .AuthenticateAs(TwitterUsername, TwitterPassword)
                .SocialGraph().Ids()
                .ForFollowersOf(screenName)
                .AsJson();

            // Make the request to Twitter
            MakeCacheQuery(query);
        }

        private static void CacheFriends(string screenName)
        {
            // Obtain the social graph list of follower IDs
            // for the user in the message
            var query = FluentTwitter.CreateRequest()
                .Configuration.UseGzipCompression()
                .AuthenticateAs(TwitterUsername, TwitterPassword)
                .SocialGraph().Ids()
                .ForFriendsOf(screenName)
                .AsJson();

            // Make the request to Twitter
            MakeCacheQuery(query);
        }

        private static void MakeCacheQuery(ITwitterLeafNode socialGraph)
        {
            var response = socialGraph.Request();

            // Avoid processing the queued message if
            // Twitter didn't respond correctly
            if (response.AsError() != null)
            {
                // Wait out any API limits on this IP address
                WaitForApiRateRefresh(socialGraph);
                return;
            }

            // Find any uncached users and fetch them
            UpdateCache(response);
        }

        private static void WaitForApiRateRefresh(ITwitterNode query)
        {
            // Get the rate limit status data from the
            // returned API call
            var limit = query.RateLimitStatus;
            if (limit == null)
```

```
        {
            return;
        }

        if (limit.RemainingHits >= 1)
        {
            return;
        }

        // Wait for the prescribed time
        var span = DateTime.UtcNow.Subtract(limit.ResetTime);
        var waitingPeriod =
            Convert.ToInt32(
                span.Duration().TotalMilliseconds);

        Thread.Sleep(waitingPeriod);
    }

    private static void UpdateCache(string response)
    {
        // Twitter returns a large collection of user IDs
        // for every friend or follower, depending on the call
        foreach (var id in response.As<List<int>>())
        {
            var entry = _repository.GetById(id);
            if (entry == null)
            {
                // Create a new entry
                var user = FetchUser(id);
                if (user != null)
                {
                    _repository.AddEntry(user.Id, user.ScreenName);
                }
            }
            else
            {
                // If the cache is older than a day,
                // update the entry
                if (entry.Updated.Subtract(DateTime.UtcNow)
                        .Days >= 1)
                {
                    var user = FetchUser(id);
                    entry.ScreenName = user.ScreenName;
                    entry.Updated = DateTime.UtcNow;

                    _repository.UpdateEntry(entry);
                }
            }
        }
    }

    private static List<Message> GetMessages(MessageQueue queue)
```

```
    {
        var messages = new List<Message>(0);
        var waitingMessages = queue.GetMessages(32);
        if (waitingMessages != null &&
            waitingMessages.Count() > 0)
        {
            // The message fetch can return null
            messages.AddRange(waitingMessages);
        }
        return messages;
    }

    private static TwitterUser FetchUser(int id)
    {
        try
        {
            // Fetch the user profile data for caching
            var query = FluentTwitter.CreateRequest()
                .AuthenticateAs(TwitterUsername, TwitterPassword)
                .Users().ShowProfileFor(id)
                .AsJson();

            // Make the request to Twitter
            var response = query.Request();

            // Skipping this entry if Twitter
            // didn't respond correctly
            if (response.AsError() != null)
            {
                return null;
            }

            // Create a new cache entry
            var user = response.AsUser();
            return user;
        }
        catch (Exception)
        {
            // Ignore any errors; it's not important
            // if this user is missed this time around
            return null;
        }
    }

    private static void ResolveQueue()
    {
        var queueInfo = StorageAccountInfo.
            GetDefaultQueueStorageAccountFromConfiguration();

        // Create the queue; if it already exists, nothing will happen
        var storage = QueueStorage.Create(queueInfo);
        _queue = storage.GetQueue("guc");
        _queue.CreateQueue();
    }
```

```
private static void ResolveTable()
{
    var tableInfo = StorageAccountInfo.
        GetDefaultTableStorageAccountFromConfiguration();
    var table = TableStorage.Create(tableInfo);

    // You can't create the same table safely, so check
    // for existence first before attempting to recreate it
    if (!table.DoesTableExist("users"))
    {
        table.CreateTable("users");
    }
}

public override RoleStatus GetHealthStatus()
{
    return RoleStatus.Healthy;
}
```

One of the primary constraints of the Twitter API is filled thanks to this background process, and Azure's worker role infrastructure allows you to deploy a simple and scalable console application in the cloud for any processing requirement. You may have ideas for your own background tasks that save to Azure storage and provide new capabilities for your application.

ASP.NET Membership in the Cloud

Up to this point, Twiticism hasn't had the need to manage more state than a queue of messages and a simple table to enable a global user cache. However, managing more complex state and user account credentials is a core component of any web application that needs to provide personalized data for users. It is possible to use Azure with the classic ASP.NET Membership Provider to provide user management capability, and is made possible through Azure's table storage mechanism covered earlier. Because Silverlight 3 is used as the presentation technology, you first need to set up a WCF service to manage interaction with any ASP.NET Membership provider on the server side, whether it's using table storage or SQL Server. This is a simple service, providing two methods for logging in and creating a new user, respectively. The WCF service definition is listed next, showing the service host mark-up and service contract interface. Each of these definitions should exist in a separate file, the service markup in an .svc file, and the accompanying code in a .cs file, respectively.

```
<%@ ServiceHost
    Debug="true"
    Service="Twiticism_WebRole.Services.MembershipService"
    Language="C#"
    CodeBehind="MembershipService.svc.cs" %>

using System.ServiceModel;
using System.Web.Security;

namespace Twiticism_WebRole.Services
```

```
    {
        [ServiceContract(Namespace = "http://twiticism.com/membership")]
        public interface IMembershipService
        {
            [OperationContract]
            bool Login(string username, string password);

            [OperationContract]
            MembershipCreateStatus SignUp(string username, string password, string
email);
        }
    }
```

The service implementation uses standard ASP.NET provider classes; you wouldn't know this service code was destined for the cloud otherwise. Because you're using a Silverlight application, you need to declare the AspNetCompatibilityRequirementsAttribute on the service implementation to ensure the service itself takes part in the ASP.NET pipeline. Because WCF services can run in multiple hosts including self-hosting Windows applications, it does not support ASP.NET features by default. The full implementation for the membership service is listed here:

```
using System.ServiceModel.Activation;
using System.Web.Security;

namespace Twiticism_WebRole.Services
{
    [AspNetCompatibilityRequirements
        (RequirementsMode = AspNetCompatibilityRequirementsMode.Allowed)]
    public class MembershipService : IMembershipService
    {
        #region IMembershipService Members

        public bool Login(string username, string password)
        {
            if (Membership.ValidateUser(username, password))
            {
                FormsAuthentication.SetAuthCookie(username, false);
                return true;
            }
            return false;
        }

        public MembershipCreateStatus SignUp(string username,
                                             string password,
                                             string email)
        {
            MembershipCreateStatus status;
            Membership.CreateUser(username,
                          password,
                          email,
                          null,
                          null,
                          true,
                          out status);
```

```
                return status;
        }

        #endregion
    }
}
```

With the service filled out, it's time to hook up Azure table storage as the backend Membership Provider storage. Fortunately the Azure SDK samples include an AspNetProviders project that brings this functionality to your application. To enable it, the default membership configuration is replaced in web.config for the table storage version, which you can get by referencing the AspNetProviders binary provided by the SDK. The following listing shows the relevant service and provider sections of Twiticism's membership feature:

```
<system.web>
    <authentication mode="Forms"/>
    <anonymousIdentification enabled="false" />

    <membership defaultProvider="TableStorageMembershipProvider"
                userIsOnlineTimeWindow="20" >
      <providers>
        <clear/>
        <!-- Use the Azure SDK TableStorageMembershipProvider -->
        <add name="TableStorageMembershipProvider"
             type="Microsoft.Samples.ServiceHosting.
                   AspProviders.TableStorageMembershipProvider"
             description="Twiticism Membership"
             applicationName="Twiticism"
             enablePasswordRetrieval="false"
             enablePasswordReset="true"
             requiresQuestionAndAnswer="false"
             minRequiredPasswordLength="1"
             minRequiredNonalphanumericCharacters="0"
             requiresUniqueEmail="true"
             passwordFormat="Hashed"
             />
      </providers>
    </membership>
</system.web>
<system.serviceModel>
    <behaviors>
        <serviceBehaviors>
        <!-- Define the Membership Service Behavior -->
        <behavior name="Twiticism_WebRole.Services.MembershipServiceBehavior">
         <serviceMetadata httpGetEnabled="true" />
         <serviceDebug includeExceptionDetailInFaults="true" />
          <serviceCredentials>
            <userNameAuthentication
              userNamePasswordValidationMode="MembershipProvider"
              membershipProviderName="TableStorageMembershipProvider" />
          </serviceCredentials>
        </behavior>
        </serviceBehaviors>
    </behaviors>
```

```
<!-- Enable WCF support for the ASP.NET pipeline and its features -->
<serviceHostingEnvironment aspNetCompatibilityEnabled="true" />
<services>
 <service
    behaviorConfiguration="Twiticism_WebRole.Services.MembershipServiceBehavior"
    name="Twiticism_WebRole.Services.MembershipService">
    <endpoint address=""
              binding="basicHttpBinding"
              contract="Twiticism_WebRole.Services.IMembershipService">
      <identity>
        <dns value="localhost" />
      </identity>
    </endpoint>
    <endpoint
        address="mex"
        binding="mexHttpBinding"
        contract="IMetadataExchange" />
  </service>
  </services>
</system.serviceModel>
```

With these components in place you can set up ASP.NET Membership in your Silverlight applications, using Azure tables as the backend data store. Figure 10-10 shows Twiticism's sign-up page powered by ASP.NET Membership and WCF services.

Figure 10-10

To call the WCF service that enables membership, you add a *Service Reference* in your Silverlight application to the MembershipService created previously. In the code-behind for the sign-up button, the service client is instantiated and used to make a service call to create a new user. If the returned value for the MembershipCreateState is valid, the new user is logged in and his or her username is stored for reference. The following code shows the logic behind the SignUpView, a Silverlight UserControl containing the presentation and logic for that page. An event is raised when the service call successfully returns a newly created user; otherwise, and based on the returned value, an extension method is used to pop up a browser window letting the user know there was a problem with the sign-up process.

```csharp
using System.Windows;
using Twiticism_Application.MembershipProxy;

namespace Twiticism_Application.Views
{
    public partial class SignUpView
    {
        public SignUpView()
        {
            InitializeComponent();
        }

        private void btnSignUp_Click(object sender, RoutedEventArgs e)
        {
            // A little client-side validation to ensure passwords match
            if (!txtPassword.Password.Equals(txtConfirmPassword.Password))
            {
                "Your password and its confirmation must match.".Alert();
            }

            var username = txtUsername.Text;
            var password = txtPassword.Password;
            var email = txtEmail.Text;

            // Create a new proxy client instance to make a call
            var client = new MembershipServiceClient();
            client.SignUpCompleted += client_SignUpCompleted;
            client.SignUpAsync(username, password, email);
        }

        private void client_SignUpCompleted(object sender,
                                    SignUpCompletedEventArgs e)
        {
            var status = e.Result;
            switch (status)
            {
                case MembershipCreateStatus.DuplicateEmail:
                case MembershipCreateStatus.DuplicateUserName:
                    ApplicationMessages.UserAlreadyExists.Alert();
                    break;
                case MembershipCreateStatus.InvalidEmail:
                case MembershipCreateStatus.InvalidPassword:
                case MembershipCreateStatus.InvalidUserName:
                    ApplicationMessages.InvalidCredentials.Alert();
                    break;
                case MembershipCreateStatus.ProviderError:
                    ApplicationMessages.ServiceError.Alert();
                    break;
                case MembershipCreateStatus.Success:
                    App.CurrentUser = txtUsername.Text;
```

```
                        ApplicationEvents.OnLoginSuccessful(this);
                        break;
                }
        }

        private void HyperlinkButton_Click(object sender, RoutedEventArgs e)
        {
            ApplicationEvents.OnLoginClicked(this);
        }
    }
}
```

Although Silverlight is not the focus of this chapter or book, it is an excellent choice for developing rich client applications and provides a programming model that is very similar to current Windows development. Because of its cross-platform support, it is an attractive choice if you want to build a Twitter application that reaches the broadest possible audience while providing powerful features; if you were intent on building a Windows application in WPF, you may find that Silverlight 3 provides enough of a user experience to warrant making the switch, which opens up your project to a Mac user base in addition to Windows. You can look at the code for the Twiticism application in more detail in the code download for this book, which will help demonstrate a basic and functional Silverlight UI that will help form a starting point for your own work. When you are creating a new Silverlight 3 application in your Visual Studio Solution, you should set your Azure Web Role as the default web application location to host it, which is the default option if a Cloud Services Application already exists in your solution.

Silverlight Application Highlights

A few pieces of the Twiticism application on the Silverlight side stand out. If you have decided to leverage Silverlight's presentation capability and cross-platform support to build your Twitter application, these components may help you jumpstart that effort.

Building a Twitter Image Handler

One of the challenges of working with Silverlight on the web is that, due to its compact size and characteristics as a .NET subset, it does not provide every capability of the .NET Framework. One in particular you'll run into quickly is that it can only support displaying JPEG and PNG image formats. Normally, this is not a problem when you can control your site's content, but when *mashing up* various social services, and in this case Twitter in particular, you could run into application errors trying to display images in different formats. According to the API, Twitter supports JPEG and PNG, but also GIF and BMP image formats for a user's profile image. This means that a large percentage of users' images will create application exceptions when loaded into a Silverlight Image control! To help get around this situation, you can adopt a strategy similar to the Twitter proxy you created to support client-side, cross-domain calls to the service; an image handler can run on your web role or ASP.NET server application hosting your Silverlight content, and process image URLs passed to it, passing back a normalized image format that Silverlight can display. Because converting images dynamically and sending the content back is a relatively expensive process, it might be helpful for you to employ the reasoning found in Chapter 7 to cache those images within your Silverlight application's local storage after this work is performed the first time, even though caching is applied in-memory by default for images loaded into an `Image` control whose URLs do not change. The following handler code will provide this image conversion service:

```
using System.Collections.Generic;
using System.Web;

namespace Twiticism_WebRole.Proxy
{
    public class TwitterImageHandler : IHttpHandler
    {
        // To help with errors, you can provide Twitter's default image
        // instead, which is in a format Silverlight already supports natively
        private const string TwitterDefaultImage =
            "http://static.twitter.com/images/default_profile_bigger.png";

        // Disallow using the proxy for anything but
        // recognized Twitter URLs
        private static readonly ICollection<string>
            _recognizedSources = new List<string>
                                     {
                                         "http://static.twitter.com",
                                         "http://s3.amazonaws.com"
                                     };

        #region IHttpHandler Members

        public bool IsReusable
        {
            get { return true; }
        }

        public void ProcessRequest(HttpContext context)
        {
            // Look for the URL to process in the query string
            var request = context.Request;
            var url = request.QueryString["url"];

            if (url == null)
            {
                // No URL request found
                return;
            }

            // Ensure the purpose of the handler request is for Twitter
            var isValidSource = false;
            foreach (var source in _recognizedSources)
            {
                isValidSource |= url.StartsWith(source);
            }
            if (!isValidSource)
            {
                return;
            }
```

```
                    // Sometimes an image cannot be found, even when
                    // referred properly, or due to an error or timeout;
                    // in those cases you can return the Twitter default
                    // to avoid client-side exceptions
                    var image = url.GetImage() ?? TwitterDefaultImage.GetImage();

                    // Normalize all image types to PNG format
                    var bytes = image.ToPngBytes();
                    context.Response.BinaryWrite(bytes);
                    context.Response.End();
                }

            #endregion
        }
    }
```

A few image extensions are used in the handler code to increase its readability. What remains is the logic to convert data loaded from a URL into a .NET Image instance, so it can be saved as a different format using .NET's robust image manipulation capability. It's worth noting that the System.Drawing namespace that's used to convert the images isn't officially supported by ASP.NET, though many developers have employed it in this fashion successfully. The following code provides helpful utilities for loading and converting images:

```
using System;
using System.Drawing;
using System.Drawing.Imaging;
using System.IO;
using System.Net;

namespace Twiticism_WebRole.Proxy
{
    public static class ImageExtensions
    {
        public static byte[] ToJpegBytes(this Image image)
        {
            if (image == null)
            {
                return null;
            }
            using (var ms = new MemoryStream())
            {
                image.Save(ms, ImageFormat.Jpeg);
                return ms.ToArray();
            }
        }

        public static byte[] ToPngBytes(this Image image)
        {
            if (image == null)
            {
                return null;
            }
```

```
            using (var ms = new MemoryStream())
            {
                image.Save(ms, ImageFormat.Png);
                return ms.ToArray();
            }
        }

        public static Image ToImage(this byte[] bytes)
        {
            using (var ms = new MemoryStream(bytes))
            {
                var image = Image.FromStream(ms);
                return image;
            }
        }

        public static Image GetImage(this string url)
        {
            Image image;
            try
            {
                var request = (HttpWebRequest) WebRequest.Create(url);
                var response = (HttpWebResponse) request.GetResponse();

                var stream = response.GetResponseStream();
                image = Image.FromStream(stream);
            }
            catch (Exception)
            {
                image = null;
            }
            return image;
        }
    }
}
```

Configuring the handler in `web.config` is straightforward and shown here. Notice that GET is the only supported HTTP verb, because fetching an image through a URL rarely needs more information than the image address itself.

```
<httpHandlers>
<!-- Image handler cleans Twitter images for Silverlight consumption -->
<add verb="GET"
     path="images"
     type="Twiticism_WebRole.Proxy.TwitterImageHandler" />
</httpHandlers>
```

Now, when your Silverlight application needs to load a Twitter profile or background image, it can use the new, substitute URL that points to your image handler, and know that it will receive a Silverlight-compatible PNG image in return. The next code highlight uses this handler to prepare search results for presentation.

Building a Twitter Search Poller

The heart of the Twiticism application is the concept of being able to routinely mine Twitter for positive, neutral, and negative comments about a particular topic or query. To achieve this, a polling mechanism is used to make asynchronous calls to Twitter that process each of the three possible sentiments for a query, and update a visual collection of tweets in response. TweetSharp has support for Silverlight, so creating queries against the Twitter API from request code directly inside Silverlight application only requires that a transparent proxy is available that recognizes TweetSharp's custom headers. The code to build such a proxy was revealed earlier in this chapter. There are a couple of points to consider when reviewing the next code listing, which manages three asynchronous calls to Twitter on a timer, refreshing every 20 seconds:

❑   As each result returns independently it is compared for duplicates in the current view, and then the data collection is re-sorted based on the time of the tweet so that the most recent tweets are always displayed at the top of the ListBox control displayed on the page.

❑   An ObservableCollection in Silverlight is a specialized collection class that notifies other objects when items inside its collection are added, removed, or updated. This is helpful to avoid repetitive data binding code, but comes with a price; actions performed on the collection are not thread-safe and must occur on the main UI thread. In this special case, sorting is required for incoming tweets from the API, and so a custom SortableObservableCollection is required.

❑   A SynchronizationContext is referenced in this code, and is in actuality the main UI thread. By referencing the main thread using SychronizationContext, actions that must execute on this thread can be queued up using the Post method. This is similar to Windows Forms application development that must use the Invoke method to marshal UI logic back to the main thread to avoid cross-thread exceptions.

Here is the code to manage the core logic of Twiticism, using TweetSharp to perform three independent calls to the Search API and dynamically loading those results into a collection bound to the UI:

```
using System.Threading;
using System.Windows.Browser;
using System.Windows.Controls;
using System.Windows.Threading;
using Dimebrain.TweetSharp.Core.Web;
using Dimebrain.TweetSharp.Extensions;
using Dimebrain.TweetSharp.Fluent;
using Dimebrain.TweetSharp.Model;

namespace Twiticism_Application.Twitter
{
    public class TweetPoller
    {
        // This is the location of your Azure hosted solution,
        // appending a path the HTTP module recognizes
        private const string TwitterProxyUrl =
            "http://twiticism.cloudapp.net/proxy/";


        // This is the location of your Azure hosted solution,
        // appending a path to an image handler proxy
```

```
private const string TwitterImageHandler =
    "http://twiticism.cloudapp.net/images.axd?url=";


// A collection of fetched tweets, used for comparison and sorting
private static readonly SortableObservableCollection<Tweet> _tweets =
    new SortableObservableCollection<Tweet>();

private static SynchronizationContext _context;
private static ListBox _listBox;

private static long? _sinceId;
private static DispatcherTimer _timer;

public static int Score { get; set; }

public static SynchronizationContext Context
{
    get { return _context; }
    set
    {
        _context = value;
        DataBind();
    }
}

public static ListBox Container
{
    get { return _listBox; }
    set
    {
        _listBox = value;
        DataBind();
    }
}

private static void DataBind()
{
    if (Context != null && Container != null)
    {
        Context.Post(s => Container.ItemsSource = _tweets, null);
    }
}

public static void Start(string query)
{
    Score = 0;
    _sinceId = null;

    _timer = new DispatcherTimer {Interval = 20.Seconds()};
    _timer.Tick += delegate
```

```
                            {
                                // Send three async calls to get the specified
                                // query; positive, negative, and neutral comments
                                var positive = CreateSearchQuery(query);
                                positive.WithPositivity()
                                    .CallbackTo(ProcessPositiveStatuses)
                                    .RequestAsync();

                                var neutral = CreateSearchQuery(query);
                                neutral.WithNeutrality()
                                    .CallbackTo(ProcessNeutralStatuses)
                                    .RequestAsync();

                                var negative = CreateSearchQuery(query);
                                negative.WithNegativity()
                                    .CallbackTo(ProcessNegativeStatuses)
                                    .RequestAsync();
                            };

        _timer.Start();
    }

    private static ITwitterSearchQuery CreateSearchQuery(string query)
    {
        var search = FluentTwitter.CreateRequest()
            .Configuration.UseGzipCompression()
            .Configuration.UseTransparentProxy(TwitterProxyUrl)
            // Search for the given query
            .Search().Query().Containing(query)
            // Get the maximum one-page result
            .Take(100);

        // Only get the most recent statuses
        if (_sinceId.HasValue)
        {
            search.Since(_sinceId.Value);
        }
        return search;
    }

    public static void Stop()
    {
        _timer.Stop();
        Context.Post(s => _tweets.Clear(), null);
    }

    private static void ProcessPositiveStatuses(object sender,
                                                WebQueryResponseEventArgs e)
    {
```

```csharp
    var result = e.Response.AsSearchResult();

    // Convert the incoming response into statuses
    ProcessStatuses(result, UserSentiment.Positive);
}

private static void ProcessNeutralStatuses(object sender,
                                        WebQueryResponseEventArgs e)
{
    var result = GetSearchResult(e);

    // Convert the incoming response into statuses
    ProcessStatuses(result, UserSentiment.Neutral);
}

private static void ProcessNegativeStatuses(object sender,
                                        WebQueryResponseEventArgs e)
{
    var result = GetSearchResult(e);

    // Convert the incoming response into statuses
    ProcessStatuses(result, UserSentiment.Negative);
}

private static void CreateNewTweet(TwitterSearchStatus status,
                                UserSentiment sentiment)
{
    // Silverlight can't process certain image types, and since
    // it's impossible to know for sure what format it's arriving as,
    // to avoid client-side exceptions use a pre-processing image
    // handler to ensure all images are in a valid format
    var url = status.ProfileImageUrl;
    var image = string.Concat(TwitterImageHandler, url);
    var tweet = new Tweet
                {
                    Id = status.Id,
                    CreatedDate = status.CreatedDate,
                    ImageUrl = image,
                    Text = HttpUtility.HtmlDecode(status.Text),
                    Sentiment = sentiment
                };

    // Do this on the UI thread, because the owner collection
    // isn't thread-safe
    Context.Post(s =>
                {
                    // Make sure you don't add duplicates to the view
                    if (_tweets.Contains(tweet))
                    {
```

```
                                    // Change sentiment, which can happen when
                                    // moving from neutral to +ve or -ve
                                    var index = _tweets.IndexOf(tweet);
                                    _tweets[index].Sentiment = tweet.Sentiment;
                                    return;
                                }

                                // Add the counted tweet
                                _tweets.Add(tweet);
                            },
                        null);
    }

    private static void ProcessStatuses(TwitterSearchResult result,
                                        UserSentiment sentiment)
    {
        if (result == null)
        {
            // Twitter likely returned an error,
            // so ignore this result
            return;
        }

        // Blend these results with those already in the view
        foreach (var status in result.Statuses)
        {
            CreateNewTweet(status, sentiment);
        }

        // Re-sort the list visually (the binding will pick up changes)
        Context.Post(s =>
                        {
                            CalculateScore();

                            _tweets.Sort(
                                (x, y) =>
                                y.CreatedDate.CompareTo(x.CreatedDate)
                                );
                        },
                    null);
    }

    private static void CalculateScore()
    {
        Score = 0;
        foreach (var tweet in _tweets)
        {
            // Adjust the overall sentiment score
            switch (tweet.Sentiment)
            {
```

```
                    case UserSentiment.Positive:
                        Score++;
                        break;
                    case UserSentiment.Negative:
                        Score--;
                        break;
                }
            }
        }

        private static TwitterSearchResult GetSearchResult(
            WebQueryResponseEventArgs e)
        {
            var result = e.Response.AsSearchResult();
            if (result != null)
            {
                // Track the most recent status so future polls
                // only look for new results
                _sinceId = result.MaxId;
            }
            return result;
        }
    }
}
```

The supporting `SortableObservableCollection` class is listed in the next example while the `UserSentiment` enumeration is defined with the values `Positive`, `Neutral`, and `Negative`.

```
using System;
using System.Collections.Generic;
using System.Collections.ObjectModel;
using System.ComponentModel;

namespace Twiticism_Application
{
    // A simple sub-class that lets you provide a lambda sorting
    // mechanism to an ObservableCollection. The advantage here is
    // that when you sort the collection, bindings will update
    // automatically.
    public class SortableObservableCollection<T> :
        ObservableCollection<T>
    {
        public void Sort(Comparison<T> comparison)
        {
            var sorted = new List<T>(this);
            sorted.Sort(comparison);

            ClearItems();
            foreach(var item in sorted)
            {
                Add(item);
            }
        }
    }
}
```

Finally, the Tweet class, which implements equality operators in order to exist in a collection that requires sorting and comparison, is shown in the following code.

```
using System;

namespace Twiticism_Application.Twitter
{
    public class Tweet
    {
        // This is here to protect against duplicates
        public long Id { get; set; }

        public string ImageUrl { get; set; }
        public string Text { get; set; }
        public UserSentiment Sentiment { get; set; }

        // This is here for sorting
        public DateTime CreatedDate { get; set; }

        public bool Equals(Tweet other)
        {
            if (ReferenceEquals(null, other)) return false;
            if (ReferenceEquals(this, other)) return true;

            return other.Id == Id;
        }

        public override bool Equals(object obj)
        {
            if (ReferenceEquals(null, obj)) return false;
            if (ReferenceEquals(this, obj)) return true;
            return obj.GetType() == typeof (Tweet) && Equals((Tweet) obj);
        }

        public override int GetHashCode()
        {
            return Id.GetHashCode();
        }
    }
}
```

Going Cross-Platform

Silverlight 3 makes it easy to run your Silverlight applications on the desktop of Windows or Mac computers. When you create a new Silverlight application, the AppManifest.xml file in the Project Properties folder contains application-specific settings as well as a commented section of XML related specifically to out-of-browser support. You only need to uncomment the relevant lines and provide a few details about your application to enable out-of-browser support. Here is the AppManifest.xml file for Twiticism:

```
<Deployment xmlns="http://schemas.microsoft.com/client/2007/deployment"
        xmlns:x="http://schemas.microsoft.com/winfx/2006/xaml">
```

```
<Deployment.Parts>
</Deployment.Parts>

<!-- Uncomment the markup and update the fields below
    to make your application offline enabled -->
<Deployment.ApplicationIdentity>
    <ApplicationIdentity
        ShortName="Twiticism"
        Title="Twiticism">
        <ApplicationIdentity.Blurb>
          Professional Twitter Development
        </ApplicationIdentity.Blurb>
    </ApplicationIdentity>
</Deployment.ApplicationIdentity>
</Deployment>
```

To install an out-of-browser Silverlight 3 application, you can right-click the application surface in a browser and choose the option from the configuration context menu. In Figure 10-11, Twiticism is running as a standalone application on Windows Vista.

Figure 10-11

When you update your application, similar to how caching works in a web browser, the new version is automatically downloaded when a user runs the desktop variant of your application, so no further setup is required on your part to publish important updates.

Summary

You've made it! A lot of information and newly acquired skills have come together in a functional Twitter application that uses a broad range of .NET features, both nascent and mature. In this chapter it all came together, and you went through the process of gaining understanding in the following areas:

❑   Planning the design of a Twitter application with a practical purpose, using several .NET technologies.

❑   Using TweetSharp to accelerate development of Twitter API features, using its fluent queries and asynchronous tasks to simplify your application's Twitter communication on both the client and the server.

❑   Working with Azure Storage Services to communicate across scalable web roles using queues, and store and manage simple state using tables.

❑   Building a global user cache and Twitter proxy designed for cloud operation, as well as an image handler for ensuring compatible image data in Silverlight applications that use Twitter image data.

❑   Using Silverlight 3 to create a client-side application that uses ASP.NET Membership features on Azure; combines multiple results returning asynchronously in real-time, and can run on the desktop of both Windows and Mac computers.

Your next steps will see you imagining, designing, building, and deploying your own unique Twitter applications on the latest technologies provided by the .NET Framework. As the web continues to expand and evolve, many new services will emerge to give you even more inspiration for useful software projects that bring people together and solve real problems. Twitter is a phenomenon that has shown that real-time communication with technologically savvy people around the globe is a new standard for communication and a powerful search paradigm all on its own. Now that you can speak the language of today's web, and have a solid base of skills to build professional-quality Twitter applications, and a practical approach to building REST libraries for any service, I sincerely wish you success with your own development endeavors.

Index